More Than Night

MORE THAN NIGHT

FILM NOIR IN ITS CONTEXTS

James Naremore

Updated and Expanded Edition

University of California Press

University of California Press, one of the most
distinguished university presses in the United States,
enriches lives around the world by advancing
scholarship in the humanities, social sciences,
and natural sciences. Its activities are supported
by the UC Press Foundation and by philanthropic
contributions from individuals and institutions.
For more information, visit www.ucpress.edu.

University of California Press
Oakland, California

© 1998, 2008 by The Regents of the University
of California

ISBN: 978-0-520-25402-2 (pbk. : alk. paper)

The Library of Congress has cataloged an earlier
edition of this book as follows:

Library of Congress Cataloging-in-Publication Data

Naremore, James.
    More than night : Film noir in its contexts /
James Naremore.
        p.   cm.
    Includes bibliographical references and index.
    ISBN: 0-520-21294-0 (pbk. : alk. paper)
    1. Film noir—History and criticism.   I. Title.

PN1995.9.F54N37   1998
791.43'655—dc21   97-33090

Manufactured in the United States of America

25 24 23 22 21 20
10 9 8 7 6 5

For Darlene, who made it possible;
for Alex and Patrick, who may someday read it;
and in memory of Bernard Benstock,
mentor and friend,
who knew *Double Indemnity* by heart.

The streets were dark with something more than night.

RAYMOND CHANDLER,
"The Simple Art of Murder," 1944

CONTENTS

ILLUSTRATIONS

PREFACE TO THE 2008 EDITION

More Than Night was an unusually pleasurable book to write, and when I looked back at it after almost ten years in order to prepare a new edition, I was surprised at how little I wanted to change. I might have enjoyed writing at greater length about a larger number of films, but the scope of the book necessarily limited the opportunity to discuss many of my favorite pictures in detail. I chose instead to view noir from a series of seven broad vantage points, and in the process I pushed against the normal boundaries of the term, insisting that it can't be neatly defined, that it isn't exclusively American, and that the discourse surrounding it is largely a postmodern development. I continue to believe that this is the best way to understand film noir, but I must admit that in a few cases my approach required me to concentrate on the margins rather than the center of the noir category. I should perhaps emphasize that even though I've questioned the assumptions behind many earlier writings, I agree with all previous commentators that the beating heart of film noir can be located in Hollywood during the 1940s and 1950s. This was a period when the industry regularly turned out modest, relatively unsung thrillers, often produced according to formula and released without fanfare, that were nearly always worth seeing. Even today, some of the lesser known films of the type—to mention only two, Roy William Neill's *Black Angel* (1946) and John Berry's *Tension* (1949)— remain deeply satisfying exercises in style and storytelling. Such films are the truest kind of noir, and fortunately we have access to increasing numbers of them on cable TV and DVD. I've listed a good many of their titles in the pages that follow.

This new edition of *More Than Night* involves no radical changes in the original text but enables me to correct several factual errors that have been pointed out by friends and reviewers. It also enables me to write a new chapter in which I expand on some basic issues, review some recent literature, and discuss examples of film noir from the first decade of the twenty-first century. For advice and help with this task I owe special thanks to Jonathan Rosenbaum and to several other individuals: Dudley Andrew, Barbara Klinger, Veronica Pravadelli, Robert Rehak, Francois Thomas, and, as always, Darlene J. Sadlier. At the University of California Press, I thank Joe Abbott, Lindsie Bear, Mari Coates, Mary Francis, and Caroline Knapp. I've also benefited from a generation of undergraduate and graduate students at Indiana University and the University of Chicago, who gave me the pleasure of introducing them to famous examples of film noir and made numerous smart observations about the films. I'm particularly grateful to these students for confirming my instinctive feeling that noir continues to be a vital and relevant subject of study.

ACKNOWLEDGMENTS

My work on this project was assisted by fellowships from the John Simon Guggenheim Foundation, the Center for Advanced Study in the Visual Arts at the National Gallery of Art, and the Office for Research and the Graduate School at Indiana University. Portions of the text, in somewhat different form, were originally published in *Film Comment, Film Quarterly,* and *Iris: A Journal of Theory on Image and Sound.* I am grateful to the editors of those journals—Richard T. Jameson, Ann Martin, Janice Morgan, and Dudley Andrew—for their encouragement and wise suggestions. Several libraries also provided assistance. I am particularly indebted to Sam Gill and the staff at the Margaret Herrick Library of the Motion Picture Academy of Arts and Sciences and to the various professionals at the University of California, Los Angeles, Special Collections Department, the Library of Congress, the Museum of Modern Art Stills Archive, and the Lilly Library.

Five individuals were of special help, and I list them here in alphabetical order. Leo Braudy assured me from the beginning that I was on the right track and took me on a memorable tour of noir locales in Los Angeles. Dana Polan supported my proposal with his characteristic enthusiasm and generosity and offered many important suggestions for improving the final manuscript. Eric Rentschler wrote a careful and intelligent report on my first draft, helping me to see parts of it more clearly. Jonathan Rosenbaum was both my culture hero and my friend, reading parts of the work in progress and giving me the benefit of his astute critical perceptions and inexhaustible knowledge. Robert Stam praised my work throughout and was continually willing to write letters of recommendation.

Among my colleagues at Indiana University, Patrick Brantlinger and Barbara Klinger were strong intellectual influences, and I hope they will recognize how much I owe them. A number of people offered information or encouraged me through conversation and letters—especially Christopher Anderson, David Anfam, Eva Cherniavsky, John Dyson, Jonathan Elmer, Tom Foster, Terry Hartnett, Joan Hawkins, D. K. Holm, Cimberli Kearns, Michael Morgan, Justus John Nieland, Mark Rappaport, Robert Ray, Teller, François Thomas, Alan Trachtenberg, and Peter Wollen.

I was unusually fortunate in having Edward Dimendberg as my editor at the University of California Press. Ed has written a great deal about film noir and will soon publish a book on the topic. I have never had an editor who was so informed and perceptive about my particular subject matter. Throughout, I was amazed by his broad knowledge of twentieth-century culture, his willingness to supply bibliographic information, and his close attention to details. He is certainly not responsible for my errors or misjudgments, but I would not have done as well without him. I am also indebted at the Press to Carolyn Hill and Scott Norton, who saw the book through production.

Finally, as always, I owe thanks to Darlene J. Sadlier, who gave me moral support, companionship, and intelligent criticism, and who endured the whole process with remarkable grace—in part, no doubt, because she likes film noir as much as I do.

This Is Where I Came In

When I was "at the cinema age" (it should be recognized
that this age exists in life—and that it passes) I
never began by consulting the amusement pages to
find out what film might chance to be the best, nor
did I find out the time the film was to begin.
ANDRÉ BRETON, "As in a Wood," 1951

For most people, the term *film noir* conjures up a series of generic, stylistic, or fashionable traits from certain Hollywood pictures of the 1940s
and 1950s. There are, for example, noir characters and stories (drifters
attracted to beautiful women, private eyes hired by femmes fatales, criminal gangs attempting to pull off heists); noir plot structures (flashbacks,
subjective narration); noir sets (urban diners, shabby offices, swank nightclubs); noir decorations (venetian blinds, neon lights, "modern" art); noir
costumes (snap-brim hats, trenchcoats, shoulder pads); and noir accessories (cigarettes, cocktails, snub-nosed revolvers). There are also noir
performances, often associated with the "radio voices" of actors like Alan
Ladd and Dick Powell; noir musical styles, consisting not only of or-
chestral scores by Max Steiner, Bernard Herrmann, and David Raksin,
but also of mournful jazz tunes, the essence of which have been captured
on two retro albums made in the late 1980s and early 1990s by the Charlie Haden Quartet; and noir language, derived mainly from the hard-
boiled speech in Dashiell Hammett and Raymond Chandler. ("Is there
any way to win?" Jane Greer asks Robert Mitchum in *Out of the Past.*
"There's a way to lose more slowly," he replies.) To the informed tourist,

there are even real places, especially in Los Angeles, that seem bathed in the aura of noir: the Alto Nido residence hotel at Franklin and Ivar, just up the street from where Nathanael West wrote *Day of the Locust;* the Bradbury Building, featured in several movies and later chosen as the site of a P.E.N. ceremony honoring Billy Wilder; and most of all, the Glendale train station at night, looking much more colorful and charming than in *Double Indemnity,* where it was blacked out by wartime restrictions on lights.

These signs of film noir have influenced countless Hollywood directors of the poststudio era, who often recycle them or use them as a lexicon for parody and pastiche. Meanwhile, in the literature on movies, a slightly more complicated discourse on noir has grown steadily over the past three decades. Numerous books and essays have been written on the topic, usually analyzing thrillers or crime pictures of the 1940s and 1950s in terms of their cynical treatment of the American Dream, their complicated play with gender and sexuality, and their foregrounding of cinematic style. We might say, in fact, that film noir has become one of the dominant intellectual categories of the late twentieth century, operating across the entire cultural arena of art, popular memory, and criticism.

In the following book, I do not deny the importance or relevance of our culture's pervasive ideas about "noirness," but I treat the central term as a kind of mythology, problematizing it by placing the films, the memories, and the critical literature in a series of historical frames or contexts. One of the most important of these contexts, about which I say rather little in the book proper, is undoubtedly my own personal history, and I should perhaps acknowledge that determinant here at the beginning, before proceeding with my critical and scholarly concerns. The best place to start is in the mid to late 1950s, shortly before and during my adolescence, when the movies were still a relatively cheap form of entertainment. Television had not yet come to every household (my father purchased our first set around 1955), and most neighborhoods had second-run or rerelease theaters where the films changed every few days. At such places, moviegoing involved a feeling of circularity and flow; one often entered in the middle of a feature and then stayed to see the short subjects, the previews, and the opening one had missed. Even in the first-run venues at the heart of the city, it was not unusual to watch the show in a nonlinear or flashback style. Hence the popular expression, "This is where I came in."

I always liked the pictures about urban adventure. As a child at the Saturday matinees, I preferred The Bowery Boys or Boston Blackie to

Roy Rogers. At the most visceral level, I was less a connoisseur of city movies than a lover of the air-conditioned darkness and quicksilver imagery of the theaters themselves, which offered temporary release from the humid southern towns where I lived. In my early adolescence, I often assumed a semifetal position, knees against the seat in front of me, absorbed not so much in the stories as in the photography, performance, and sound. What I remember best are the fetishized details—Lizabeth Scott's unreal blondness and husky voice in *Dark City,* or Edmond O'Brien's rumpled suit as he runs desperately down the crowded street in *D.O.A.*

Later in the decade, after I began to acquire an artistic interest in movies, my imagination was fired by black-and-white photography and melodramatic danger. This was the age of Elvis and Cinemascope, but I was stunned by *Killer's Kiss,* a cheap thriller about which I had heard nothing. (I can recall exiting the theater and searching the poster outside to find that the name of the director was Stanley Kubrick.) I especially liked such films when they offered nonconformist philosophical or social criticism and when their endings seemed a bit less than happy. Among my favorites were the rereleases of *Detective Story* (a police procedural about a violent cop who learns that his wife once had an abortion), *The Asphalt Jungle* (a blow-by-blow account of an attempted robbery, in which the criminals are the most sympathetic characters), and *Ruthless* (a rise-to-success narrative that depicts the hero as a heel). I was equally affected by first-run showings of *The Wrong Man* (a true story about an innocent man accused of a crime), *End as a Man* (a frightening portrait of a charismatic young sadist in a southern military school), *Sweet Smell of Success* (a dark satire about an influential Broadway columnist and a sleazy press agent), and *Attack!* (an antiwar movie in which most of the officers are either insane or corrupt). For similar reasons, I was delighted by the blending of menace and iconoclasm in a couple of escapist pictures about romance and suspense: *His Kind of Woman* and *Strangers on a Train.* During those years, I bought a paperback reprint of Raymond Chandler's *Simple Art of Murder* and virtually memorized the tough-guy cadences of the title essay. I also saw part of an Orson Welles picture for the first time—the grotesquely sinister opening sequence of *Journey into Fear,* which I glimpsed late at night on a snowy television set.

How intriguing to discover, long afterward, that I had been living through the last decade of historical film noir. I say "historical" because the basic term can refer both to the present-day cinema and to an extinct genre. The temporal distinction seems important, and yet it is also simplistic or misleading. Most contemporary writing and filmmaking associated with noir provokes a mourning and melancholy for the past, made all the more poignant because the objects being mourned are still with us on TV. To use a specifically Freudian language (which many of the old films themselves seem to elicit), our contemporary fascination with noir may entail a sort of *Nachträglichkeit,* or a method of dealing with the present by imagining a primal scene. The memories I have just recorded are no exception; they are influenced by things that happened afterward, and they omit many features of the complex popular culture I once experienced.

The term *film noir* was barely known in America when I went through what André Breton calls "the cinema age." But it was not completely unknown. In a recent anthology of writings on the subject, Alain Silver and James Ursini have published a 1956 photograph of director Robert Aldrich, standing on the set of *Attack!* and holding a copy of Raymond Borde and Étienne Chaumeton's *Panorama du film noir américain.* Perhaps Aldrich was trying to tell us something about his work—or perhaps he was merely acknowledging the fact that Borde and Chaumeton greatly admired his previous picture, *Kiss Me Deadly.* At any rate, during the years before the classic Hollywood studios were completely reorganized, before a wave of innovative European cinema began to enter the American market, and before I myself had ever heard of film noir, several pictures that today's critics often describe as noir cohered in my own mind and helped to give me a sense of movies as an art.

More than Night pays these and other movies like them an indirect tribute, offering a wide-ranging and synoptic discussion of American film noir between 1941 and the present. My topic is large, and in covering such an extensive time period I inevitably fail to mention some important titles. For example, I decided to keep influential directors such as Alfred Hitchcock and Orson Welles, about whom I have written elsewhere, slightly at the margins of my study—this despite the fact that the burning "R" at the end of *Rebecca* and the burning "Rosebud" at the end of *Citizen Kane* echo one another, and despite the fact that both films are crucial to the way we think about Hollywood in the 1940s. I nevertheless discuss European and British pictures that influenced Hollywood, and I pay a good deal of attention to the French intellectual context in which the idea of noir was first articulated. I also nominate neglected titles as films noirs, or at least question their absence in previous writings, and I explore the noir elements of the other media in some detail.

In order to do justice to the paradoxes of history, I shuttle back and forth in time. The reader will find that my early chapters have more to do with classic Hollywood and that my later ones are increasingly concerned with the present day. Even so, the book is not strictly chronological, and (somewhat like the old Hollywood moguls) I do not expect that everyone will consume what I have produced in linear fashion. I can only suggest that those who want to understand my general assumptions should go directly to the first chapter, which is my true introduction and touches upon most of my themes. In chapter 1, I contend that film noir has no essential characteristics and that it is not a specifically American form. I also try to confirm the truth of a recent observation by J. P. Telotte, who says that all arguments about the nature of noir have "as much to do with criticism itself, especially with the varying ways that we define film genres," as they do with our putative objects of study.[1] Telotte's point was reinforced for me shortly after the first draft of my chapter was written, when I saw Quentin Tarantino's *Pulp Fiction.* At the beginning of that movie, two gangsters talk about the difference between cheeseburgers in Paris and cheeseburgers in the United States. One of them notes that "Cheese Royale" sounds better than "Big Mac." Along similar lines, I would suggest that because "film noir" sounds better than a good many American terms that might be used, it has affected the way we view certain mass-produced items.

Like almost every other critic, I begin by calling attention to the fact that film noir is an unusually baggy concept, elaborated largely after the fact of the films themselves. I suspect, however, that the often-expressed critical concern over the term's meaning and utility may arise out of a misunderstanding of how generic or historical concepts are formed. The logic of genre construction has not been my primary interest, but it may help to note in passing that much can be learned about such matters from cognitive scientist George Lakoff's *Women, Fire, and Dangerous Things* (1987), which sounds rather like a film noir. (Interestingly, the 1932 adaptation of *The Maltese Falcon* was called *Dangerous Female,* and the working title for the Billy Wilder–Raymond Chandler adaptation of *Double Indemnity* was *Incendiary Blonde.*) Lakoff is a powerful critic of the Aristotelian notion that categories are made up of items with common properties—a notion also rejected by empirical research and by such diverse theorists as Ludwig Wittgenstein, J. R. Austin, and Jacques Derrida. Virtually all contemporary language philosophers agree that people do not form concepts by placing similar things together. Instead, they create networks of relationship, using metaphor, metonymy, and forms of imaginative association that develop over time. As a result, every important term in art criticism indicates something like the "family tree" that British critic Raymond Durgnat once used to describe film noir.

Cognitive science prefers to avoid Durgnat's organic imagery; it argues that categories form complex radial structures, with vague boundaries and a core of influential members at the center. But neither tree diagrams nor radial structures are employed by most film historians, who operate within the realm of what Lakoff calls "objective semantics" and hope to classify movies according to their necessary and sufficient characteristics. Perhaps the very word *genre*, with its etymological links to biology and birth, promotes a kind of essentialism; but even when writers about film noir claim to be speaking of something other than a genre, they keep trying to list its definitive traits. To avoid troubling anomalies, they sometimes argue that the noir form is "transgeneric." The problem here is that such an argument also applies to the ostensibly stable genres: there are western musicals (*Oklahoma*), western melodramas (*Duel in the Sun*), western science-fiction pictures (*Westworld*), and western noirs (*Pursued*). The fact is, every movie is transgeneric or polyvalent. Neither the film industry nor the audience follows structuralist rules, and movie conventions have always blended together in mongrelized ways. By the same token, every important category is shaped by what Lakoff describes as a "chaining" technique that develops historically and socially. Certain items along the chain will be connected in different ways and will be utterly unlike others. (*Clash by Night* has nothing specific in common with *Laura*, even though both movies have been called noir.) Thus, no matter what modifier we attach to a category, we can never establish clear boundaries and uniform traits. Nor can we have a "right" definition —only a series of more or less interesting uses.

As will be seen, my own approach has less to do with cognitive theory than with cultural and social history. It may seem odd, however, that after questioning most of the usual generalizations about film noir in my first chapter, I go on to use the term in a familiar way and to employ a more or less conventional historiography. I would explain the apparent contradiction by pointing out that *film noir* functions rather like big words such as *romantic* or *classic*. An ideological concept with a history all its own, it can be used to describe a period, a movement, and a recurrent style. Like all critical terminology, it tends to be reductive, and it sometimes works on behalf of unstated agendas. For these reasons, and because its meaning changes over time, it ought to be examined as a discursive construct. It nevertheless has heuristic value, mobilizing specific themes that are worth further consideration.

The subsequent chapters of my book explore these themes, but I often qualify or challenge what is normally said about them. In chapter 2, I consider the literary basis of dark thrillers in the early 1940s, arguing that our typical view of pulp fiction is oversimplified and that the "original" films noirs can be explained in terms of a tense, contradictory assimilation of high modernism into the American culture industry as a whole. Chapter 3 deals with the related problem of noir's so-called resistance to Hollywood norms. Although I claim that film noir as a whole has no essential politics, in this chapter I concentrate on a specific set of noirlike movies from the years immediately after World War II and show how a political movement or cultural formation within Hollywood struggled against censorship and political repression by using dark thrillers for critical ends.

The remaining parts of the book are increasingly devoted to the relationship between historical film noir and the present-day cinema. In chapter 4, I discuss the economic determinants of Hollywood movies and the widespread critical tendency to canonize certain types of B pictures. I argue that many classics of so-called low-budget film noir were actually intermediate-level productions, designed to cross over into respectable areas of the market during a period when the B movie itself was dying off. I nevertheless try to illustrate the charms of specific B movies and to show how a tradition of low-budget crime melodrama carries over into made-for-TV films and video-store "erotic thrillers."

Chapter 5 deals with motion-picture style, but I do not attempt to discuss this theme in a comprehensive way. Such a task would probably be impossible; as I indicate early in the chapter, there has never been a single noir style—only a complicated series of unrelated motifs and practices. Even so, noir is commonly identified with certain visual and narrative traits. I am interested in the way several of these traits have been used to support an ongoing tradition of neo-noir, and I have analyzed the problem under two of its aspects: first, the historical shift from an industry dominated by black and white to an industry dominated by color; and second, the increasing role played by parody, pastiche, and fashion in the development of a self-consciously postmodern genre.

In chapter 6, I discuss the central metaphor of darkness in the term *film noir*, arguing that one of its many implications is racial. As many critics have remarked, the classic films noirs are preoccupied with eroticism and decadence, often showing encounters between straight white males and homosexuals or sexually independent women; but many of these films also involve encounters with racial "others." In order to call attention to the racial theme, I offer a brief history of the ways in which films noirs have depicted Asian Americans, Latin Americans, and African Americans. Much of the chapter consists of little more than a survey, but it ends by giving special attention to recent pictures directed by African Americans, on the grounds that black social-protest literature has always had an important connection with noir.

My seventh and final chapter is also a survey, but it has an even broader scope and a more loosely discursive organization. Here I discuss noir in the largest possible context, showing how our conception of the term is shaped not only by films and critical writing, but also by all the media that constitute the information age. This chapter concludes by offering a map of the contemporary theatrical marketplace and calling attention to the different market niches that film noir tends to fill. Its major purpose, however, is to indicate how pervasive and adaptable the idea of noir has become and to provide examples of how noir affects things other than movies.

Perhaps an alternate subtitle for the project might have been "Seven Ways of Looking at American Film Noir," because each of my chapters takes up a slightly different viewpoint. In each case, I try to achieve comprehensiveness; yet the individual chapters could have been elaborated into separate books, and I have no illusions that they are the last word on the issues they discuss. At least I have been able to include historical data that cannot be found elsewhere, and I offer new interpretations of several familiar films. I hope that my indebtedness to other writers will be evident and that I have opened paths for subsequent critics to explore. Certainly there will be more writing on the topic. As we shall discover almost immediately, film noir is both a thing of the past, extending to a time before I came in, and a symptom of the media-obsessed present. It began in Europe, but it has now become a persistent feature of American culture and will remain so into the future.

The History of an Idea

Only that which has no history is definable.
FRIEDRICH NIETZSCHE, *On the Genealogy of Morals*, 1887

The past is not dead. It isn't even past.
WILLIAM FAULKNER, *The Sound and the Fury*, 1929

It has always been easier to recognize a film noir than to define the term. One can imagine a large video store where examples of such films would be shelved somewhere between gothic horror and dystopian science fiction: in the center would be *Double Indemnity*, and at either extreme *Cat People* and *Invasion of the Body Snatchers*. But this arrangement would leave out important titles. There is in fact no completely satisfactory way to organize the category; and despite scores of books and essays that have been written about it, nobody is sure whether the films in question constitute a period, a genre, a cycle, a style, or simply a "phenomenon."[1]

Whatever noir "is," the standard histories say that it originated in America, emerging out of a synthesis of hard-boiled fiction and German expressionism. The term is also associated with certain visual and narrative traits, including low-key photography, images of wet city streets, pop-Freudian characterizations, and romantic fascination with femmes fatales. Some commentators localize these traits in the period between 1941 and 1958, whereas others contend that noir began much earlier and never went away.[2] One of the most comprehensive (but far from complete) references, Alain Silver and Elizabeth Ward's *Film Noir: An Encyclopedic Reference to the American Style* (revised edition, 1992) begins in 1927 and ends in the present, listing over five hundred motion pictures of various stylistic and generic descriptions.[3]

Encyclopedic surveys of the Silver and Ward type are educational and entertaining, but they also have a kinship with Jorge Luis Borges's fictional work of Chinese scholarship, *The Celestial Emporium of Benevolent Knowledge,* which contains a whimsical taxonomy of the animal kingdom: those belonging to the Emperor; mermaids; stray dogs; those painted with a fine camel's hair brush; those resembling flies from a distance; others; and so on. Unfortunately, nothing links together all the things described as noir—not the theme of crime, not a cinematographic technique, not even a resistance to Aristotelian narratives or happy endings. Little wonder that no writer has been able to find the category's necessary and sufficient characteristics and that many generalizations in the critical literature are open to question. If noir is American in origin, why does it have a French name? (The two Frenchmen who supposedly coined the term, writing separate essays in 1946, were referring to an international style.) More intriguingly, if the heyday of noir was 1941–1958, why did the term not enjoy widespread use until the 1970s? A plausible case could indeed be made that, far from dying out with the old studio system, noir is almost entirely a creation of postmodern culture—a belated reading of classic Hollywood that was popularized by cinéastes of the French New Wave, appropriated by reviewers, academics, and filmmakers, and then recycled on television.

At any rate, a term that was born in specialist periodicals and revival theaters has now become a major signifier of sleekly commodified artistic ambition. Almost 20 percent of the titles currently on the National Film Preservation List at the Library of Congress are associated with noir, as are most of the early volumes in the British Film Institute "Film Classics" series of monographs on famous movies. Meanwhile, "neo-noirs" are produced by Hollywood with increasing regularity and prominence. Consider the last three American winners of the Grand Prize at Cannes: *Wild at Heart* (1991), *Barton Fink* (1992), and *Pulp Fiction* (1994). Consider also such big-budget television productions as *Twin Peaks, Wild Palms* (marketed as "TV noir"), and *Fallen Angels.*

Some of these instances might be described as pastiche, but pastiche of what? The classical model is notoriously difficult to pin down, in part because it was named by critics rather than filmmakers, who did not speak of film noir until well after it was established as a feature of academic writing. Nowadays, the term is ubiquitous, appearing in reviews and promotions of many things besides movies. If we want to understand it, or to make sense of genres or art-historical categories in general, we need to recognize that film noir belongs to the history of ideas as much as to the history of cinema; in other words, it has less to do with a group of artifacts than with a discourse—a loose, evolving system of arguments and readings that helps to shape commercial strategies and aesthetic ideologies.

It seems odd that film theorists did not arrive at this conclusion long ago. After all, the Name of the Genre (or mood, or generic tendency, or whatever) functions in much the same way as the Name of the Author. In a well-known essay, French philosopher Michel Foucault argues that the "author function" is tied to the "institutional system that encompasses, determines, and articulates the universe of discourses."[4] The author, Foucault says, is chiefly a means of textual *classification,* allowing us to establish relations of "homogeneity, filiation, authentification of some texts by the use of others" (147). At bottom, these relations are "projections," governed by belief in "a point where contradictions are resolved, where incompatible elements are at last tied together or organized around a fundamental and originating contradiction" (151).

Could we not say exactly the same things about the "genre function"? And could we not ask of it many of the same questions that Foucault asks of authorship: "What are the modes of existence of this discourse?" "Where has it been used, how can it circulate, and who can appropriate it?" (160) In the case of film noir, one of the most amorphous categories in film history, these questions seem particularly apt. To answer them, this chapter examines the historical context of seminal writings about noir. Throughout, instead of looking for the essential features of a group of films, I try to explain a paradox: film noir is both an important cinematic legacy and an idea we have projected onto the past.

NOIR IS BORN: PARIS, 1946–1959

The end of World War II in Paris gave rise to what might be called a noir sensibility; but this sensibility was expressed through many things besides cinema, and if I had to choose a representative artist of the period, it would not be a filmmaker. Instead I would pick the somewhat Rimbaud-like personality Boris Vian, who was a friend of the ex-surrealist Raymond Queneau and the existentialist Jean-Paul Sartre. Vian wrote witty avant-garde novels, protoabsurdist plays, satiric columns for *Les temps modernes,* music criticism for *Jazz Hot,* and over five hundred Dylanesque protest songs (including "Le déserteur," which remains an anthem of French antiwar movements); meanwhile, he played trumpet and sang in Le Tabou and other Saint-Germain nightspots. During his lifetime, however, he was best known for a *roman noir* that did not bear his name.

In the summer of 1946, Vian was approached by an editor who wanted to create a list of murder novels that would rival the popular, black-covered *Série noire*, recently inaugurated at Gallimard. Within two weeks, Vian composed *J'irai cracher sur vos tombes* (I'll spit on your graves), which he published under the name "Vernon Sullivan," an identity he adopted on several occasions, claiming to have translated Sullivan's work "from the American."[5] An ultra-violent mixture of situations from William Faulkner's *Sanctuary* and Richard Wright's *Native Son,* the novel concerns a black man who passes for white in a southern town and exerts racial vengeance by dominating, raping, and murdering two white women. In a preface, Vian said that the book could never have been printed in the United States because it involved black violence against whites. But there were also problems in France, where *J'irai cracher* became the first novel to be prosecuted for obscenity since *Madame Bovary.* The case took a bizarre turn when a middle-aged Parisian salesman strangled his young mistress and committed suicide in a hotel room near the Gare Montparnasse, leaving an open copy of the book next to the murdered woman's body, one of its grisly passages underlined. Vian was briefly jailed and required to pay a fine, and for the rest of his life he suffered from notoriety and ill health. Although he remained active on the literary and cabaret scenes, he sometimes described himself as *"ex-écrivain, ex-trompettiste"* (ex-writer, ex–trumpet player). Then in the summer of 1959, he entered a Paris movie theater to watch a press screening of French director Michel Gast's adaptation of *J'irai cracher,* a project he disliked but had been unable to prevent. As he sat alone in the dark auditorium, his heart failed and he died.[6]

The themes and motifs of Vian's life and work—indigo moods, smoky jazz clubs, American fiction, and romantic isolation—resemble those in movies of his day, and his scandalous novel foregrounds two issues that seem relevant to film noir: sexual violence and racial blackness or otherness. Psychoanalytic feminism tells us something about the first issue (much feminist theory grows out of the study of American films noirs), although the discussion needs to be historicized and linked to changing patterns of censorship.[7] In regard to the second issue, we need to examine the metaphor of darkness. The discourse on noir grew out of a European male fascination with the instinctive (a fascination that was evi-

dent in most forms of high modernism), and many of the films admired
by the French involve white characters who cross borders to visit Latin
America, Chinatown, or the "wrong" parts of the city. When the idea of
noir was imported to America, this implication was somewhat obscured;
the term sounded more artistic in French, so it was seldom translated as
"black cinema."[8]

I say more about such matters in subsequent chapters; for now, however, the publication and eventual adaptation of *J'irai cracher* interest me
for historical reasons, because they coincide with what I shall call the
first (or historical) age of American film noir: the period between the postwar arrival of Hollywood movies in Paris and the beginnings of the
French New Wave. We can never know when the first film noir was made
(examples have been claimed as far back as D. W. Griffith's *Muscateers
of Pig Alley* [1912] and Louis Feuillade's *Fantomas* [1913]), but everyone agrees that the first *writings* on Hollywood noir appeared in French
film journals in August 1946—at exactly the moment when "Vernon Sullivan" was composing his novel. The term was used by analogy with the
Série noire, and it surfaced in discussions of five features made before,
during, and after the war, all of which had just been exhibited in suc-
cession on Paris movie screens: *The Maltese Falcon; Double Indemnity;
Laura; Murder, My Sweet;* and—somewhat surprisingly, in light of the
fact that it disappears from most subsequent writings—*The Lost Weekend.* Another picture released in Paris that summer, *The Woman in the
Window,* described by one French reviewer as a "bourgeois tragedy," was
later to become a noir classic.[9] The forthcoming Metro-Goldwyn-Mayer
production of *The Postman Always Rings Twice* was mentioned alongside the initial group of five, and *Citizen Kane,* which was also mentioned,
was placed in a class by itself. Critical discussion centered mainly on the
first four thrillers—which, even though they were not exactly alike (*The
Maltese Falcon* does not have a first-person narrator or flashbacks, and
Laura is not based on a hard-boiled novel), seemed to belong together.
These films would become the prototypical members of an emergent category, and they would have an unusual influence on French thinking for
over a decade.

In one sense the French invented the American film noir, and they did
so because local conditions predisposed them to view Hollywood in certain ways. As R. Barton Palmer observes, postwar France possessed a
sophisticated film culture, consisting of theaters, journals, and "cine-
clubs" where movies were treated as art rather than as commercial
entertainment.[10] Equally important, the decade after the liberation was

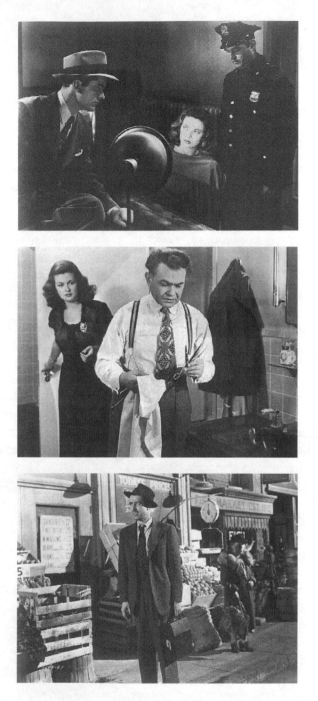

FIGURES 1–3. Which of these films was not
described as an American film noir by French writers
in the summer of 1946: *Laura* (1944), *The Woman
in the Window* (1944), or *The Lost Weekend* (1945)?
Answer on p. 13. (Museum of Modern Art Stills
Archive.)

characterized by a strong resurgence of Americanism among French directors and critics, many of whom sought to refashion their art cinema along the more "authentic" lines of Hollywood genre movies.[11] A *nouvelle vague* would eventually grow out of this dialectic between America and Europe, and the so-called film noir—which was visibly indebted to European modernism—became the most important category in French criticism.

The French were also predisposed to invent American noir because it evoked a golden age of their own cinema. They were quick to observe that the new Hollywood thrillers resembled such Popular Front films as *Pépé le Moko* (1936), *Hôtel du Nord* (1938), and *Le jour se lève* (1939)—a group of shadowy melodramas, set in an urban criminal milieu and featuring doomed protagonists who behaved with sangfroid under pressure.[12] The term *film noir* had in fact been employed by French writers of the late 1930s in discussions of these films. Film historian Charles O'Brien points out that in the years immediately before the war, the word *noir* often had pejorative connotations and was frequently used by the right-wing French press in their attacks on the "immorality and scandal" of left-wing culture.[13] *Noir* was nevertheless embraced as a descriptive adjective by several writers on the Left (particularly after the war), and the style favored by the Popular Front, whether it was called "noir" or not, constituted a respectable and quite recognizable type of filmmaking for most critics throughout the world. Thus, when *Double Indemnity* was released in the United States in 1944, a reviewer for *The Hollywood Reporter* noted that it was "more than a little reminiscent of the late lamented, excellent French technique." (To reassure moviegoers, he added, "This is not to say that it is 'arty'" [24 August 1944].)

French writers after the war might have recognized the equally significant contributions of other European nations to the evolution of the crime or espionage film. For example, they could have alluded to Alfred Hitchcock's British thrillers of the 1930s and—had they known it—to Carol Reed's *Night Train to Munich* (1940). These were the films with which American reviewers compared the 1941 version of *The Maltese Falcon;* in fact, when Billy Wilder completed *Double Indemnity,* he told the *Los Angeles Times* that he intended to "out-Hitchcock Hitchcock."[14] In 1946, however, the French not only ignored the British but also conspicuously avoided the Germans.[15] Instead, the two earliest essays on Hollywood film noir—Nino Frank's "Un nouveau genre 'policier': L'aventure criminelle," published in the socialist *L'écran français* in August 1946, and Jean-Pierre Chartier's "Les Américains aussi font des films 'noirs,'" published three months later in the more conservative *Revue du cinéma* (an ancestor of *Cahiers*)—treated the American pictures as if they were a new phenomenon with only a few Gallic predecessors.

For Nino Frank, it seemed that a young generation of Hollywood auteurs, led by John Huston, Billy Wilder, and Raymond Chandler, had rejected the sentimental humanism of "museum objects" like John Ford, Frank Capra, and William Wyler.[16] The new filmmakers specialized in the *policier* (police story), which, according to Frank, always deals with the "social fantastic" and the "dynamism of violent death" (8); unlike earlier practitioners, however, the Americans were more concerned with "criminal psychology" and were therefore making "criminal adventures" or *"films 'noirs'"* (14). Such films were convoluted, harsh, and misogynistic, but they made the characters in most movies seem like "puppets" (14). Moreover, they often employed a first-person narration and flashbacks that fragmented the story, producing a montage. Frank claimed that Sacha Guitry had been the first to use this technique, in *Le roman d'un tricheur* (1936), but he wondered whether or not Hollywood had outclassed Paris. Henceforth, the French would need to make "somber" films in which there was "more dynamism in an unmoving shot than in a majestic panorama" (14).

Jean-Pierre Chartier also treated the American films as a group, but he disliked their "pessimism and disgust toward humanity" and suggested that the puritanical Breen Office had deflected the characters' sexual motives into an "obsessive criminal fatality."[17] In some respects, his remarks were reminiscent of the conservative reactions to French noir during the *avant guerre*, except that the Americans seemed to him far more decadent than the French Popular Front had been. Although he admired the first-person narration in *Murder, My Sweet* (which reminded him of "the old avant-garde"), Chartier was troubled by the moral effect of the Hollywood series as a whole:

> One may speak of a French school of film noir, but *Le Quai des brumes* or *Hôtel du Nord* have at least accents of rebellion, a fleeting image of love that gives hope for a better world, . . . and if the characters are desperate, they rouse our pity or sympathy. Nothing of that here: these are monsters, criminals whose evils nothing can excuse, whose actions imply that the only source for the fatality of evil is in themselves. (70)

In the United States, most of these films had been nominated for Academy Awards and had attracted a good deal of public and critical attention. Reviewers had seen a vague connection between them, but no one tried to invent a new term.[18] *The New Yorker* described *Double Indemnity* as a "murder melodrama" (16 September 1944), and *The Los Angeles Times* called it an "intellectual exercise in crime" (10 October 1944). (*Times* critic Philip K. Scheuer, who admired the Wilder film, added a qualification: "I am sick of flash-back narration and I can't forgive it here.") *Newsweek* said that *Murder, My Sweet* was a "brass-knuckled thriller" (26 February 1945), and *The Hollywood Reporter* noted that Paramount was investing heavily in the "hard-boiled, kick-em-in-the-teeth murder cycle" (28 January 1946). The Americans also grouped the films in ways that now seem unusual: *The Los Angeles Times* compared *Double Indemnity* with the MGM adaptation of William Saroyan's *Human Comedy* (6 August 1944), and Manny Farber, writing in *The New Republic,* compared it with Preston Sturges's *Miracle of Morgan's Creek* (24 August 1944).

French writers, in contrast, were fascinated with the noir metaphor, and in subsequent discussions they elaborated the tensions between the two essays by Frank and Chartier. Over the next decade, as the category expanded and became the subject of retrospectives and catalogues raisonnés, French critics often followed Frank's line, praising noir for its dynamism, its cruelty, and its irrationality; but they also searched the dark Hollywood streets for what Chartier had called "accents of rebellion" against the "fatality of evil." Some of the reasons behind this potentially contradictory response were evident during a round-table discussion at *Cahiers du cinéma* in 1957, when André Bazin remarked in passing that in the French prewar cinema, "even if there wasn't exactly a genre there was a style, the realist *film noir.*" Bazin was nostalgic for a lost national identity, but he also recognized that noir had philosophical or ideological significance: French films of the type, he argued, were indebted to surrealism and might have been developed along the lines of literary existentialism.[19]

As Bazin's remarks suggest, French discussion of American film noir was conditioned by the prevailing and sometimes conflicting trends in Left Bank intellectual culture. The importance of existentialism to the period has long been recognized; what needs to be emphasized is that existentialism was intertwined with a residual surrealism, and surrealism was crucial for the reception of any art described as "noir." Gallimard's *Série noire* was conceived and edited by Marcel Duhamel, who assisted in the development of the "Exquisite Corpse" game in 1925, and who participated in the surrealist *researches* into sexuality during the early 1930s;[20] the Popular Front film noir, especially in such instances as *Quai des brumes,* was strongly associated with the surrealism of Jacques Prévert; the *Anthologie d'humour noir* (1940) was edited by André Breton himself; and critical discussion of American films noirs in the 1950s was conducted chiefly in surrealist journals. Indeed, Nino Frank's seminal essay, which emphasizes "criminal adventure" and the "dynamism of violent death," is replete with surrealist values.

From their beginnings in the years after World War I, the surrealists used cinema as an instrument for the destruction of bourgeois art and the desublimation of everyday life. Breton and his associates would pop briefly in and out of movie theaters and write lyrical essays about their experiences, developing what Louis Aragon called a "synthetic" or tangential criticism, which was designed to extract latent, chiefly libidinal meanings from single images or short sequences. This project was facilitated by movies with improbable, confusing, or incoherent narratives: the bad film, the crazy comedy, the horror film, and—especially in the post–World War II era—the Chandleresque detective film, which often lost control of its plot and became a series of hallucinatory adventures in the criminal underworld.[21]

The surrealists were "dreaming" cathected details from the cinematic mise-en-scène, but not just any detail caught their eye. They were profoundly attracted to the cinema of the "social fantastic," to stories of doomed erotic love, and to thrillers with Sadeian titles. Among their particular favorites were movies about gangsterism and murder, in part because such pictures depicted violent, antisocial behavior, and in part because they bestowed an aura of the marvelous upon urban decor. As Aragon wrote in 1918, American crime films "speak of daily life and manage to raise to a dramatic level a banknote on which our attention is riveted, a table with a revolver on it, a bottle that on occasion becomes a weapon, a handkerchief that reveals a crime, a typewriter that's the horizon of a desk."[22]

Aragon might well have been describing thrillers of the 1940s, which were perversely erotic, confined largely to interiors, photographed in a deep-focus style that seemed to reveal the secret life of things, and often derived from the literature of alcohol—a substance especially conducive of desire, enervation, euphoria, confusion, and nightmare. Not surprisingly, such films were admired and discussed in *L'Age du cinéma,* a surrealist publication of 1951, and in *Positif,* an influential journal that maintained strong connections with surrealism throughout the 1950s and the early 1960s. They were also given important study in a book that was profoundly surrealist in its ideological aims: Raymond Borde and Étienne Chaumeton's *Panorama du film noir américain* (1955), which has been described as a "benchmark" for all later work on the topic.[23]

Raymond Borde was a frequent contributor to *Positif* and the director of *Pierre Molinier* (1964), a surrealist film with offscreen commentary by André Breton. But we do not need to consult his or Chaumeton's vitae, since their intellectual heritage is apparent from the outset: the *Panorama* is introduced by Marcel Duhamel, who fondly recalls the years 1923–1926, when he and other members of the surrealist group, including Breton, Raymond Quenoau, Benjamin Peret, Jacques Prévert, and Yves Tanguy, watched American gangster films that were "curious, nonconformist, and as noir as one could desire."[24] As if this were not enough, Borde and Chaumeton choose a phrase from Lautréamont, the surrealist's favorite poet, as an epigraph: "The bloody channels through which one pushes logic to the breaking point."

Despite their obvious ideological purpose, Borde and Chaumeton often seem unclear or inconsistent. They initially describe film noir as a series, but at later points they also discuss it as a genre, a mood, and a zeitgeist. In the introduction, Duhamel claims that noir is as old as cinema and has never been healthier, whereas in the text, Borde and Chaumeton say that the American series began in 1941 and ended in the early 1950s. (A postscript to the 1988 paperback edition moves the end of noir forward to 1955 and then notes its "fascinating renaissance" in *Point Blank, Dirty Harry*, and *Badlands*.)[25] Throughout, an "objective" tone serves as a mask for the indulgence of a desire. Borde and Chaumeton have surprisingly little to say about visual style (the French were generally unimpressed by what Bazin later called "plastics," or expressionist imagery); in fact, they emphasize that the dark atmosphere of Hollywood crime movies is *"nothing in itself"* and ought not to be adopted for its own sake (180). Instead, they place great emphasis on the theme of death, and on "essential" affective qualities, which at one point they list in the form of five adjectives typical of surrealism: "oneiric, bizarre, erotic, ambivalent, and cruel" (3).[26] Sometimes one of these qualities is said to dominate: *The Shanghai Gesture* (which had prompted one of the surrealist experiments in "irrational expansion") is supposedly "oneiric," whereas *Gilda* is "erotic" (3). Sometimes, too, the traits are unevenly distributed, with the "noir aspect" manifesting itself in a tangential form that resembles Aragon's synthetic criticism: "*The Set Up* is a good documentary about boxing: it becomes film noir in the sequence where accounts are settled by a savage beating in a blind alley. *Rope* is a psychological film that can be linked to the noir series only because of its spellbinding sadism" (3).

But according to Borde and Chaumeton, there are also noir narratives and characters; and at this level film noir becomes a full-fledged outlaw genre, systematically reversing Hollywood's foundational myths. True films of the type, Borde and Chaumeton insist, not only take place "inside the criminal milieu," but also represent "the point of view of criminals" (7). Such films are "moral" in an approximately surrealist sense: instead of incorruptible legal agents, they give us shady private eyes, crooked police, murderous plainclothes detectives, or lying district attorneys. Often they depict the gentry as corrupt, and whenever they deal with gangsters, they replace the "grand primitives" of earlier gangster movies like *Scarface* with angelic killers or neurotics (7).

It follows that the ideal noir hero is the opposite of John Wayne. Psychologically, he is passive, masochistic, morbidly curious; physically, he is "often mature, almost old, not very handsome. Humphrey Bogart is the type" (10). By the same logic, the noir heroine is no Doris Day. Borde and Chaumeton never allude to the Marquis de Sade's Julliette, one of the most famous sexual terrorists in French literature, but the character they describe resembles her in every respect save the fact that she is "fatal even to herself" (10).[27] Beautiful, adept with firearms, and "probably frigid," this new woman contributes to a distinctive noir eroticism, "which is usually no more than the eroticization of violence" (10).[28] Her best representative on the screen, Borde and Chaumeton argue, is Gloria Grahame, who, even though she was seldom cast as a femme fatale, always suggested "cold calculation and sensuality" (125).

Above all, Borde and Chaumeton are intrigued by the way film noir has "renovated the theme of violence" (10). One of the major accomplishments of the series, they observe, is to replace the melodramatic combat of arms between hero and villain (the swordplay at the climax of a swashbuckler, the gun duel at the end of a western, and so on) with a richly elaborated "ceremony of killing." Death in such films usually takes the form of a professional execution (a locus classicus is *The Killers,* a 1946 adaptation of Ernest Hemingway) or a sadistic ritual: in *The High Wall,* a publisher of religious books murders an elevator repairman by hooking an umbrella under the stool on which the man is standing, sending him plummeting down an empty shaft; in *Kiss of Death,* a demented gangster laughs as he shoves a little old lady in a wheelchair down a flight of stairs; in *Brute Force,* a fascistic prison guard tortures inmates with an elaborate, stylized brutality; and in *Border Incident,* an undercover policeman is slowly run over by a tractor and a field plow while his helpless confederate stands by and watches.

"In this incoherent brutality," Borde and Chaumeton remark, "there is the feeling of a dream" (12). Indeed, the narratives themselves are often situated on the margins of dreams, as if to intensify the surrealist atmosphere of violent confusion, ambiguity, or disequilibrium that Borde and Chaumeton regard as the basis of noir. "All the components of noir style," they write, are designed to "disorient the spectator" by attacking certain conventions: "a logical action, an evident distinction between good and evil, well-defined characters with clear motives, scenes that are more spectacular than brutal, a heroine who is exquisitely feminine and a hero who is honest" (14). The "vocation" of film noir is to reverse these norms and thereby create a specific tension that results from the disruption of order and *"the disappearance of psychological bearings or guideposts"* (15).

But film noir was also a prisoner of conventions. Borde and Chaumeton contend that in the 1940s, films about crime and gangs possessed a bizarre quality reminiscent of the surrealists or Kafka; by the 1950s, however, the implicit social criticism in thrillers was smothered by banal plot devices, and the "exploitation of incoherence" was becoming predictable (180). Even the original pictures were beginning to look dated: at a revival of *Murder, My Sweet* presented by the Cine-Club of Toulouse in 1953, people laughed whenever Philip Marlowe lost consciousness and disappeared into a black pool, and in the discussion afterward the picture was treated as a "parody of horror" (181).

From the perspective of the mid 1950s, it appeared that noir was dying. Borde and Chaumeton attribute this "decadence" to the exhaustion of a formula and to the rise of neorealist social-problem pictures. To these factors, we might add several economic and political determinants: in response to television and the growing leisure industry, Hollywood was turning to Cinemascope, color, and biblical epics; at the same time, many of the key writers and directors of the previous decade had been blacklisted by the major studios. As if to signal the end of a cycle, urban thrillers were increasingly produced for the lower end of the market. Hence, the two pictures of the 1950s that the *Panorama* singles out as truly disorienting were both filmed on relatively low budgets, without stars. The first is Joseph H. Lewis's *Gun Crazy* (1950), the story of a murderous heterosexual couple of "exemplary beauty" (9), which allows the woman to wear pants and act as the aggressive partner. Borde and Chaumeton regard *Gun Crazy* as a profound and unselfconscious expression of the surrealist credo; in their words, it is "one of the rarest contemporary illustrations of *L'AMOUR FOU* (in every sense of that term)," and it deserves to be called "a sort of *L'Age d'Or* of the American film noir" (118).

Next in importance is the Robert Aldrich adaptation of Mickey Spillane's *Kiss Me Deadly* (1955), which Borde and Chaumeton discuss in their 1988 postscript. Like *The Maltese Falcon,* this film involves a private eye and the search for a mysterious object; nevertheless, Borde and Chaumeton describe it as the "despairing opposite" of the picture that inaugurated the noir series: "From the eve of war to the society of consumption, the tone has changed. A savage lyricism throws us into a world in complete decomposition, ruled by debauchery and brutality; to the intrigues of these wild beasts and specters, Aldrich provides the most radical of solutions: nuclear apocalypse" (277).

Nowadays, both *Kiss Me Deadly* and *Gun Crazy* sometimes provoke the same unwanted laughter that greeted *Murder, My Sweet* in 1953. Even so, Borde and Chaumeton's achievement in discussing these and other films is remarkable. Without complete access to American culture, they identify scores of interesting movies that might have been forgotten, and they create an entire category that functions normatively. Here as in many later writings, *noir* is not merely a descriptive term, but a name for a critical tendency within the popular cinema—an antigenre that reveals the dark side of savage capitalism. For Borde and Chaumeton, the essence of noirness lies in a feeling of discontinuity, an intermingling of social realism and oneiricism, an anarcho-leftist critique of bourgeois ideology, and an eroticized treatment of violence. Above all, noir produces a psychological and moral disorientation, an inversion of capitalist and puritan values, as if it were pushing the American system toward revolutionary destruction. We might debate about whether such qualities are in fact essential to the Hollywood thriller (if any quality can be essential), but there is no question that they are fundamental to surrealist art.

Via the *Panorama* and similar writings, surrealism might be said to have provided an organizing metaphor and an aesthetic rationale for the film noir. Perhaps it also fostered the tendency of later critics to read individual pictures slightly against the grain, emphasizing tone or mood rather than narrative closure—a technique frequently used to bestow cult value on mass art. But as I have already indicated, French discussion of noir was also affected by existentialist literature and philosophy, which placed emphasis on different matters. Existentialism was despairingly humanist rather than perversely anarchic; thus if the surrealists saw the postwar American thriller as a theater of cruelty, the existentialists saw it as a protoabsurdist novel. For critics who were influenced by existentialism, film noir was attractive because it depicted a world of obsessive return, dark corners, or *huis-clos*. It often employed settings like the foggy seaside diner on the road between San Francisco and Los Angeles in *Fallen Angel,* where Dana Andrews gets off a bus and seems unable to leave. ("I'm waiting for something to happen," he tells Alice Fay. "Nothing's going to happen," she responds.) Or it was like the dark highway in *Detour,* where Tom Neal keeps thumbing a ride, trying to avoid his brutal destiny.

In the years before and after the war, when the French themselves were entrapped by history, several of the most important themes of existential philosophy were elaborated through readings of Dashiell Hammett, Chandler, and James M. Cain, who were often bracketed with Wright, Hemingway, John Dos Passos, and Faulkner. The French actually "discovered" some of these novelists, just as they later discovered the Hollywood auteurs. (In 1946, even Faulkner was a relatively neglected figure in the United States, where much of his income came from movies like *The Big Sleep* and from a story he had published in *Ellery Queen's Mystery Magazine;* meanwhile, Jean-Paul Sartre described him as a "god.") The interest of Parisian intellectuals in a certain kind of American literature became so intense that the British author Rebecca West teased Cain, "You were a fool not to be born a Frenchman. The highbrows would have put you in with Gide and Mauriac if you had taken this simple precaution."[29]

There was truth in West's observation. The French liked their Americans exotic, violent, and romantic.[30] They wrote a great deal about southern gothicism and tough-guy modernism, and they usually ignored anything that did not offer what André Gide called "a foretaste of Hell." Gide himself declared that Hammett's *Red Harvest* was "the last word in atrocity, cynicism, and horror";[31] André Malraux described Faulkner's *Sanctuary* as "the intrusion of Greek tragedy into the thriller"; and Albert Camus confessed that he had been inspired to write *The Stranger* after reading Cain's *Postman Always Rings Twice.*

This passion for literary toughness has an interesting relation to the social and political climate after the war. In the United States, the postwar decade was the period of Korea, the red scare, and the return to a consumer economy; in France, it was the period of colonial rebellion and parliamentary confusion leading up to the Charles de Gaulle government. Authors in both countries who had once been Marxist, such as John Dos Passos and André Malraux, completely reversed themselves; others, such as Dashiell Hammett, were imprisoned or blacklisted. The Western Left had been in disarray since the Nazi-Soviet pact, and the situation in France was complicated by the fact that the country had recently emerged from

what the French themselves described as *les années noires*—a time of occupation, torture, compromise, and collaboration. Faced with a choice
between capitalism and Stalinism, many French artists tried to achieve
"freedom" through individualized styles of resistance. For them, prewar
American novels offered a model—especially novels depicting a violent,
corrupt world in which ambiguous personal action is the only redemptive gesture. In *Qu'est-ce que la littérature?* (1947), Sartre wrote, "As for
the Americans, it was not their cruelty or pessimism which moved us.
We recognized in them men who had been swamped, lost in too large a
continent, as we were in history, and who tried, without traditions, with
the means available, to render their stupor and forlornness in the midst
of incomprehensible events."[32]

That same year, Sartre claimed that modern life had become "fantastic," made up of a "labyrinth of hallways, doors, and stairways that lead
nowhere, innumerable signposts that dot routes and signify nothing."[33]
Recalling the fear of Nazi torture recently experienced by French citi-
zens, he advocated a literature of "extreme situations" that would be
narrated ambiguously, without "all-knowing witnesses" (154–55). The
novel, he insisted, must shift from "Newtonian mechanics to generalized
relativity"; it should be peopled with "minds that [are] half lucid and
half overcast, some of which we might consider with more sympathy than
others, but none of which [should] have a privileged point of view" (155).

Sartre was particularly impressed by Faulkner's experiments with
multiple-perspective narration in *The Sound and the Fury* (1929), but he
also praised the way Americans used a free-indirect style. In 1938, he had
argued that John Dos Passos was the greatest contemporary novelist; as
proof, he quoted a passage from *USA* describing a fistfight in a Paris café:
"Joe laid out a couple of frogs and was backing off towards the door,
when he saw in the mirror that a big guy in a blouse was bringing down
a bottle on his head with both hands. He tried to swing around but he
didn't have time. The bottle crashed his skull and he was out." Here was
pure existential consciousness, divested of authorial comment, observing
itself in a mirror and registering the action like a camera-obscura, as if
René Descartes and Henri Bergson were the "couple of frogs" laid out
on the cafe floor. Here, too, though Sartre did not say so, was the familiar voice of American pulp fiction. Sartre believed that this voice amounted
to "a technical revolution in the art of telling a story," and for over a decade
he and other French novelists tried to emulate its effects, aiming for what
Roland Barthes later described as a zero-degree style.[34]

Unlike the surrealists, who made the movies essential to their project, the existentialists were literary and rather dubious about Hollywood. Nevertheless, given the intellectual fashion Sartre helped to establish, it is not surprising that many of the younger French cinéastes embraced American thrillers with special fervor. These pictures were often based on the novels of respected authors; they were sometimes narrated from multiple points of view; and they offered a labyrinthine, enclosed mise-en-scène peopled with alienated characters. Thus in 1955 Eric Rohmer observed, "Our immediate predilection tends to be for faces marked with the brand of vice and the neon lights of bars rather than the ones which glow with wholesome sentiments and prairie air."[35]

Rohmer and several of his colleagues at *Cahiers du cinéma* belonged to a generation that imbibed its existentialism and phenomenology from André Bazin, who was a more conservative and in some ways more consistent writer than Sartre.[36] In *Qu'est-ce que la littérature?* Sartre struggled to reconcile modernist narration with political engagement; Bazin could avoid the problem, because his essays, posthumously collected in *Qu'est-ce que le cinéma?* (1958–1962), were couched in terms of moral dilemmas or the problem of death. Like most of the French, Bazin was interested in modern American fiction, and he often used a Sartrean vocabulary ("freedom," "fate," "authenticity," and so on). In fact, many of the basic tenets of his theoretical writing resemble Sartre's arguments about literature, minus any traces of Marxism. On the grounds of "realism," for example, Sartre wanted to do away with both omniscient narration and temporal ellipsis; modern narratives, he argued, should resemble *Ulysses,* employing multiple perspectives and detailed renditions of a day, an hour, or even a minute (158). For his part, Bazin argued that cinema should provide relatively passive observation rather than intrusive commentary and should make greater use of long takes or *temps morts,* such as the coffee-making sequence in De Sica's *Umberto D.* In place of Sartre's neutral or ambiguous literary narrators, however, Bazin valorized the camera, which he regarded as a phenomenology machine that could preserve ambiguous reality without the tendentious intervention of a human hand.[37]

Bazin's style of existentialism is everywhere apparent in his 1957 eulogy for Humphrey Bogart, written only two years before Bazin's own death. According to Bazin, Bogart was important because "the *raison d'être* of his existence was in some sense to survive," and because the alcoholic lines visible on his face revealed "the corpse on reprieve within each of us" (Hillier, 98). Jean Gabin, the star of prewar French films noirs, seemed romantic by comparison; Bogart was a man "*defined by* fate," and because he was associated with "the *noir* crime film whose ambiguous hero he was to epitomize," he became the quintessential "actor/myth of the postwar period" (Hillier, 99). Bazin argued that Bogart's portrayal of Sam Spade was equivalent to the almost simultaneous release of *Citizen Kane:* "It must be the case," he wrote, "that there is some secret harmony in the coincidence of these events: the end of the prewar period, the arrival of a certain novelistic style of cinematographic *écriture,* and, through Bogart, the triumph of interiorization and ambiguity" (Hillier, 100).

The "ambiguity" of which Bazin speaks is quite different from the disorientation or inversion of norms valued by the surrealists. It has more to do with ethical complexity and with the cinema's ability to capture what Bazin elsewhere calls the "structure of reality" in all its phenomenological uncertainty. Likewise, Bazin's "interiorization" has little to do with the Freudian subconscious. It suggests instead a radical isolation or individuality that forces the subject to create identity out of existential choice. Bazin apparently believed that the "secret harmony" linking Bogart and Orson Welles was a cultural by-product of what French literary critic Claude-Edmonde Magny (in a book heavily influenced by Sartre) called "the age of the American novel."[38] On a more general level, however, the themes of isolation, uncertainty, and ambiguity must have exerted a strong appeal to anyone who was wary of collective politics and inclined to treat social issues in terms of personal ethics.

During this period, younger critics at *Cahiers du cinéma* began to project Bazin's ideas onto Hollywood, sometimes treating the film noir as if it were an existential allegory of the white male condition. The favored existential hero, however, was not Bogart but Nicholas Ray, who had directed *They Live by Night, In a Lonely Place,* and *On Dangerous Ground.* François Truffaut wrote that the essential theme of Ray's films was "moral solitude," and Jacques Rivette argued that Ray was concerned with "the interior demon of violence, which seems linked to man and his solitude."[39] At this juncture, the terms *film noir* and *auteur* began to work in tandem, expressing the same values from different angles. (It is no accident that the two terms would enter the English language at the same moment.) Film noir was a collective style operating within and against the Hollywood system; and the auteur was an individual stylist who achieved freedom over the studio through existential choice. But the auteur was more important than the genre. Unlike Borde and Chaumeton, who used the names of directors only as a convention of French scholarship, the *Cahiers* group always subordinated general forms to personal visions. In other words, France was not far from the *nouvelle vague*.

To see what the future had in store, we need only consider Claude Chabrol's 1955 *Cahiers* essay "The Evolution of the Thriller," which pays special attention to *Kiss Me Deadly*. Like Borde and Chaumeton, Chabrol regarded this picture as a watershed, although he believed its significance had less to do with the end of a genre than with the creation of a cinema of authors. By the mid 1950s, Chabrol argued, the literary sources of film noir had "dried up," and the plots and mise-en-scènes were clichéd. There was no question of renewing the form, but it had become a "wonderful pretext": "[*Kiss Me Deadly*] has chosen to create itself out of the worst material to be found, the most deplorable, the most nauseous product of a genre in a state of putrefaction: a Mickey Spillane story. Robert Aldrich and A. I. Bezzerides have taken this threadbare and lackluster fabric and woven it into rich patterns of the most enigmatic arabesques."[40]

Clearly, an art cinema based on transformation of "the worst material" was about to appear. In 1959, Jean-Luc Godard's *Breathless* was released, and Truffaut's *Shoot the Piano Player* soon followed. Both films were fusions of Bazinian neorealism and surrealist disjunctions; both were littered with references to Bogart, *Gun Crazy, On Dangerous Ground,* and so on; and both made film noir available as a "pretext" for directors who wanted to assert their personalities. Also in 1959, Boris Vian died in a Paris movie theater. The first age of film noir had ended.

DARKNESS EVERYWHERE

The discourse on American film noir was initiated by two generations of Parisian intellectuals, most of whom declared the form extinct soon after they invented it. Many of the films they discussed had been directed by European émigrés (mainly Germans), who used tough, Hemingwayesque dialogue and American production values to bestow a kind of glamour upon the dark emotional moods favored by Continental artists of the postwar decade. For the French especially, an American star like Bogart epitomized these moods. Bogart's persona was tough, introspective, emotionally repressed, and fond of whiskey and cigarettes; within certain limits, he suggested a liberal intellectual, and he was sometimes cast in the role of a writer or director. Hence the Bogart thriller became a mirror in which European cinéastes could see their own faces.

Significantly, the French began to lose interest in noir at about the time their own art cinema became internationally successful. But the vogue for realistic, atmospheric novels and films about criminal violence had never been confined to France, and it never disappeared. In Argentina, for example, a craze for hard-boiled fiction lasted from 1946 until 1960, and a large critical literature grew up around Spanish-language translations of Hammett, Chandler, and David Goodis. Many authors in Western Europe and Latin America worked in the tough-guy vein (Argentina's Rodolfo J. Walsh began writing noir political fiction in the 1960s), and filmmakers in several countries made pictures that resembled dark Hollywood thrillers. Meanwhile, crime in the city, which is one of America's favorite themes, continued to be exploited by politicians, journalists, and artists of every kind. Thus when French critical terminology crossed to Britain and America, it exerted considerable influence and acquired new interpreters. Eventually, as old movies became increasingly available on television or in retrospectives, a European image of America was internalized by the Americans themselves. By the 1990s, noir had acquired the aura of art and had evolved into what Dennis Hopper describes as "every director's favorite genre."[41]

In the Anglo-Saxon world, the idea of noir was nourished at first by the growth of film cults and college film societies. (I myself saw many of the classic 1940s films for the first time at the University of Wisconsin in the late 1960s.) As J. Hoberman and Jonathan Rosenbaum have shown, informal institutions similar to the French cine-clubs began to proliferate in New York during the late 1950s—especially in the East Village, where revival theaters featuring noir classics rubbed shoulders with storefront exhibitions of the newly emerging American underground cinema. At the Charles Theater on Avenue B "Edgar G. Ulmer (director of cheap B movies like *The Naked Dawn* and *Murder Is My Beat*) was celebrated along with the Marx Brothers; and Orson Welles's *Touch of Evil* was touted as a masterpiece superior to *Citizen Kane*."[42] In 1964, *Time* magazine drew national attention to the annual Humphrey Bogart Festival at the Brattle Theater in Cambridge, Massachusetts. Not unlike Belmondo in *Breathless,* a generation of Harvard undergraduates were imitating Bogey, quoting lines from his major films and shouting "More! More! More!" in time with the slugs he pumped into Edward G. Robinson at the climax of *Key Largo*. Such behavior, Hoberman and Rosenbaum wryly observe, was perhaps reinforced by those students "who had spent their junior year abroad" (28–30).[43]

The interest in noir was also stimulated by alternative critics and journalists. In Britain, one of the most influential writers of this kind was
Raymond Durgnat, who played a key role in adapting surrealist taste to
the youth-oriented, pop-art environment of the 1960s. Durgnat's many
publications of a surrealist bent include books or monographs on Josef
von Sternberg, Luis Buñuel, and Hitchcock; on the crazy comics; and on
the history of eroticism in the cinema. He is also the author of "Paint It
Black: The Family Tree of Film Noir" (1970), published originally in London (the title alludes to a Rolling Stones song of the period) and reprinted
in a shorter version in New York four years later. During the 1960s and
early 1970s, much of Durgnat's writing appeared in *Films and Filming*,
a fairly large-circulation review filled with grainy, black-and-white stills
of half-clothed movie stars in vaguely lurid, often sadomasochistic poses.
(These stills have something in common with the illustrations in Borde
and Chaumeton's *Panorama*, but they also feature cheesecake and beef-
cake material from a more hedonistic, sexually liberated era.) At the same
time, Durgnat coedited and contributed extensively to *Motion*, a short-
lived film journal that published special issues on the French New Wave
and on "Violence and Sadism in the Cinema."

Motion's issue number 6 (autumn 1963) provides a good indication
of the relatively avant-garde politics of the journal as a whole. Among
Durgnat's contributions is "Standing Up for Jesus," a satiric invective
against the Arnoldian, Leavisite, and "Hoggartite" attitudes of *Sight and
Sound*, the nation's most prestigious film magazine. According to
Durgnat, the typical university-educated Englishman never speaks "a
good word for Jerry Lewis, Bugs Bunny, 'Mad,' 'Galaxy,' Humph, The-
lonious Monk, Bootsie and Snudge, singers like Eartha Kitt, Edith Piaf,
Cleo Lane, songs like 'September in the Rain' or 'Tell Laura I Love Her'"
(26). In an attempt to rectify this situation, *Motion* offers a "symposium"
on B-movie epics and Italian peplum, featuring Richard Whitehall on
Flash Gordon and Durgnat himself on Hercules; an eight-page *"cinémateque imaginaire"* entitled "The Gentle Art of Titillation," composed
entirely of campy, black-and-white pinups suggesting various forms of
Hollywood fetishism, transvestitism, and sadism; a brief gloss on the pinups, entitled "La femme est magique!" (a line spoken by Aznavour in
Shoot the Piano Player); an essay by Ian Johnson on *Night of the Hunter*,
describing the film as a "childhood dream"; and a free-associative "ram-
ble" by Barrie Pattison, intended to illustrate "the irrationality of films
and memories of films." On page 59 are several letters to the editor re-

sponding to an earlier special number on sex and violence. Among the letters is this communication:

> Dear Sirs,
>
> Congratulations on your violence issue, the best, most comprehensive treatment of the theme I, for one, have seen. . . . A special bravo for Ian [Johnson's] article on the fascinating *Peeping Tom* . . . and to both of you for having the guts to reprint in English Joubert's piece on the Japanese cathartic cinema.
>
> In the Dassin piece, which seems to me to overrate that gentleman's recent productions, I was amazed to see no mention of *Night and the City,* which besides being his most accomplished film, is the one in which violence is the most successfully integrated into the fabric of the film through an extraordinary animal symbolism. . . .
>
> Then, too, I was surprised to find so little attention paid to the two American directors who seem to me to display the most consistent preoccupation with the erotic implications of violence. I refer to Sam Fuller and Kubrick. The latter, in fact, who is obviously more self-conscious than the former, strikes me as the most kinky director around, with the possible exception of Buñuel. I am thinking especially of the scene in *Killer's Kiss* in which the monstrous dance-hall proprietor tries to get his girl hot by making her watch the handsome boxer-hero get his brains bashed out on TV.
>
> NOEL BURCH
> 75 Blvd Montparnasse, Paris 6

At the time, Noel Burch was an avant-garde filmmaker living in Paris. (One of his early pictures was *Noviciat,* an overtly masochistic fantasy that casts Annette Michelson in the role of a dominatrix.) Within a decade, he would become known as the author of *Theory of Film Practice* (1973, originally published in *Cahiers du cinéma* in 1969), one of the most widely discussed books in the history of academic film studies. On the surface, Burch's book is an exercise in structural or "serial" formalism; notice, however, that it contains a chapter entitled "Structures of Aggression," in which he comments on the "dialectic of prohibition and transgression explored by Georges Bataille" and on the "poetic" uses of a "tension that arises when taboos are violated."[44] Although Burch never uses the term *film noir*, his work provides evidence that a surrealist or noirlike attitude toward "cathartic" violence persisted in vanguard film theory well into the 1970s.

Where film noir in particular is concerned, Durgnat was the writer who most forcefully transmitted surrealist values into an English-language context. The American version of his well-known essay on noir's "family tree" is accompanied by a chart that amounts to a sort of irrational expansion of the noir metaphor, exploring its various "branches." The chart is faux-scientific, filled with arbitrary subcategories and word-play (such as "Dept. of Post-Korean Paranoia," "Gay Blades and Straight Razors," "Le Film Blanc," "Gumshoedammerung"); it lists individual films under more than one rubric; and, alongside the usual noir classics, it includes such titles as *Jezebel, Monsieur Verdoux, The Picture of Do-rian Gray, Portrait of Jennie, Cronaca di une Amore, Confessions of a Nazi Spy, The Treasure of the Sierra Madre* ("John Huston's Great Film Noir"), *The Blue Angel, King Kong, Shadows, The Man with a Golden Arm,* and *2001.*

Like Borde and Chaumeton, Durgnat identifies noir with gangsters, cops, criminal adventure, love on the run, bourgeois murder, fatal pas-sion, sexual pathology, and so on. But unlike most of the French, he in-sists that noir has no historical limits; its essential "motif[s] and tone[s]," he argues, are "perennial, drawing on the unconscious superego's sense of crime and punishment."[45] Despite the confusions of this terminology (unconscious superego?), Durgnat obviously believes that noir has Freudian causes that transcend period, genre, and even politics. He is quite good at showing how noir can be appropriated in Hollywood by both Republican and Democratic directors, and he claims that the nar-ratives associated with the term are as old as *Oedipus Rex;* they can take fascist, Marxist, or liberal forms, and their attitude toward crime "is as often nihilistic, cynical, or stoic as it is reformatory" (6). This argument not only collapses distinctions between high art and Hollywood, but also obliterates every other historical or generic boundary. Ultimately, noir drifts like a fog across the whole of western culture, threatening to dis-solve any trace of identity and difference.

In contrast, most of the new generation of writers in the United States treated film noir nostalgically, as a phenomenon linked to classic Holly-wood in the 1940s. They were strongly influenced by the auteurist phase of *Cahiers du cinéma,* and in the years before videocassette recorders were invented, they gained much of their viewing experience through New York's underground network of "film buffs." In *Love and Other Infec-tious Diseases* (1989), Molly Haskell's vivid and moving account of her marriage to Andrew Sarris, we find a useful description of the amateur collectors and archivists of the 1960s, most of whom exhibited movies in offices, apartments, and lecture halls:

> These were the sort of people you never see or read about, people the media has passed over because in our high-profile success-oriented world they are invisible, "losers." As a group, they were almost entirely male—probably

because voyeurism is essentially a male activity, as is complete surrender to
fantasy. . . .

Yet Andrew, though resembling them in some outward aspects, wasn't quite
one of them. For one thing, he was more interested in good movies than in
obscure ones. Once there was a choice between seeing Hitchcock's *Shadow
of a Doubt* and a rural B picture called *The Girl of the Limberlost,* and Andrew's was the only hand raised in favor of the former. . . . Andrew was
archival in his attempt to see everything, constantly promoting the cause of
film preservation, but he was continually refining his tastes, whereas a good
many of the buffs collected information quantitatively.[46]

Sarris was, of course, the most important American exponent of the
French *politique des auteurs.* Through his classroom lectures, books, and
weekly columns in *The Village Voice,* he challenged prevailing ideas about
Hollywood and offered a refreshing alternative to established film criticism. Classical in his tastes but committed to the belief that style is the
expression of personality, he seldom wrote directly about genres or collective styles; even so, he helped to establish a canon of great Hollywood
directors, several of whom were associated with what was increasingly
being described as film noir.

Manny Farber, whose work I discuss in a later chapter, was an equally
important writer on Hollywood thrillers and pop auteurs during this period, but Farber's approach was quite different from Sarris's. In *Negative Space* (1971), a brilliant collection of essays from the 1950s and
1960s, Farber never uses the term *film noir*, and his reviews from the
1940s are less enthusiastic about such pictures as *The Maltese Falcon* and
Double Indemnity than one might expect. His influential essay "Underground Films" is nevertheless a classic example of avant-garde appreciation of lowbrow culture, demonstrating the affinity between the most
hip and the least respected domains of art. Here and elsewhere, Farber's
attitude toward genre movies is in striking contrast with that of a cold-
war liberal like Robert Warshow, and his commentaries on the tough-
guy films of Howard Hawks, Anthony Mann, John Farrow, and Samuel
Fuller did much to encourage a taste for pulp among American cinéastes.

Against this intellectual background—which was strengthened by the
box-office success of European art films, by changes in censorship and
Hollywood production methods, and by teaching at such institutions as
New York University and Columbia—a kind of American new wave began to appear. Self-conscious auteurs such as Peter Bogdanovich, Martin Scorsese, and Brian DePalma were influenced by French criticism of
the 1950s, and all of their early, low-budget films were somewhat noirish

in tone. The figure who most shaped American ideas about noir, however, was Paul Schrader, a young screenwriter and soon-to-be director whose "Notes on *Film Noir*," written for a Los Angeles museum retrospective and published in 1972 in the New York–based *Film Comment* (a journal that has always been especially interested in noir), became the best-known statement on the topic in the English language.

Near the beginning of the "Notes," Schrader acknowledges his indebtedness to Borde and Chaumeton, and to a great extent the first part of his essay merely outlines their historical argument. Like the authors of the *Panorama,* he thinks of film noir chiefly as a series or cycle (usually he calls it a "period"): *The Maltese Falcon* begins it, *Kiss Me Deadly* provides its definitive or conclusive masterpiece, and *Touch of Evil* serves as its "epitaph."[47] But to this chronological scheme, Schrader adds Raymond Durgnat's idea that noir is also a collection of transhistorical motifs, tones, or moods; as a result, he oscillates between discussion of a dead period and discussion of a specific noir style that might be revived by contemporary filmmakers.

Unlike the writers he cites, Schrader is not particularly surrealist in his preoccupations. Instead, he is strongly attracted to existentialist themes, and he puts great emphasis on German expressionism. Partly for this reason, he writes skillfully and at length about visual style (from the vantage point of 1972, it was much easier to see that thrillers of the 1940s and 1950s *had* a style). He also adds certain new-critical arguments that were familiar to readers of Sarris. For example, he repeatedly insists that art is more important than sociology, and he shows how cinematic tradition nourishes individual talents; thus he nominates photographer John Alton to a pantheon, and he claims (correctly) that "film noir was good for practically every director's career" (62).

An even more crucial aspect of "Notes on *Film Noir*" derives from something it never mentions: the Vietnam War, which functions as a structuring absence. In his third paragraph, for instance, Schrader calls attention to *Easy Rider* (1969) and *Medium Cool* (1969), two films that were popularly associated with the counterculture and the antiwar movement. Both pictures, he argues, are "naive and romantic" in comparison with noir classics such as *Kiss Me Deadly* and *Kiss Tomorrow Goodbye*. He also predicts that "as the current political mood hardens, . . . [t]he Forties may be to the Seventies what the Thirties were to the Sixties" (53).

In *The Great War and Modern Memory* (1977), Paul Fussell has observed that writers always struggle to depict a new war by borrowing motifs from the previous one. Something akin to this process can be seen in Schrader's essay, although in 1972 the Vietnam conflict had been on television for years, its imagery flowing together with the assassinations of the Kennedys and Martin Luther King, the military occupation of college campuses, the shootings at Kent State, the riots at the 1968 Democratic convention, the burning of Watts, and countless other scenes of domestic and international violence. Given such a context, *Kiss Me Deadly* may not seem "naive and romantic," but neither does it seem especially shocking. By the same token, Schrader's essay is less interested in finding motifs adequate to the present than in withdrawing into a mood of despair and bitter disengagement. His major theme is the "creative funk" that supposedly followed in the wake of victory over economic depression and fascism. He places great emphasis on an atmosphere of Germanic determinism and irony—a pervasive gloom that hints at some irredeemable evil and meanwhile exposes "the underside of the American character" (53). Ultimately, he praises noir less because it constitutes a social protest than because it looks stylish, cynical, and pessimistic; its chief value, he says, lies in the fact that in the period between 1941 and 1958, "Hollywood lighting grew darker, characters more corrupt, themes more fatalistic, and the tone more hopeless" (53). Perhaps nothing is more indicative of his attitude (and that of many Americans in his generation) than his description of what he calls "the overriding noir theme." According to Schrader, noir expresses "a passion for the past and present, but also a fear of the future. Noir heroes dread to look ahead, but instead try to survive by the day, and if unsuccessful at that, they retreat into the past. Thus film noir's techniques emphasize loss, nostalgia, lack of clear priorities, and insecurity, then submerge these doubts into mannerism and style" (58).

Not surprisingly, Schrader was to explore these themes and tendencies in his films—especially in his script for Martin Scorsese's *Taxi Driver* (1976), which did as much as any critical essay to make noir seem relevant to the period. Treating Vietnam and presidential assassination as mere epiphenomena, this film concentrates on violence, perversion, and decay as seen through the eyes of a cabdriver in the midnight streets of New York. The film's antihero, Travis Bickle, is a returning Vietnam vet, analogous to all those returning World War II soldiers in Hollywood thrillers of the 1940s. (Schrader would use the same theme again in his script for *Rolling Thunder* in 1977.) The major irony, however, turns on the fact that Bickle is also a sexually repressed paranoid (in some ways like Hitchcock's Norman Bates) and the only character who possesses a moral vision. For various social and psychological reasons, Bickle is a

FIGURE 4. The psychotic
veteran in *Taxi Driver* (1976).
(Museum of Modern Art Stills
Archive.)

seething cauldron of inarticulate rage; even so, his noirlike offscreen narration is highly poetic, and Robert DeNiro's introspective, ascetic performance makes him seem like a Bressonian saint. This irony is reinforced
by the film's extraordinarily bloody climax, because the characters who
receive Bickle's "protection" and chaste love—a child prostitute and a
WASP princess who works in a political campaign—are little more than
projections of his disturbed sexuality.

On one level, *Taxi Driver* can be understood as what Robert Ray calls
a "left cycle" response to the popular success of *Dirty Harry* (1971), *Billy
Jack* (1971), and *Death Wish* (1974)—all of which were melodramatic,
right-wing movies about urban vigilantes, clearly inspired by the political turbulence of the Vietnam years. At another level, however, as both
Ray and Robin Wood observe, the film is ideologically contradictory or
incoherent. The Calvinist Schrader and the Catholic Scorsese have created a deeply conservative picture about original sin and the absolute
evil of modernity. Their treatment of sex, for example, has relatively little
in common with French surrealism and a good deal in common with such
modernist literary works as T. S. Eliot's *Waste Land* and Graham
Greene's *Brighton Rock,* which I discuss in the next chapter. Like most
of the high modernists (as distinct from the political avant-garde), they
use images of the nocturnal city to suggest a Dostoyevskian nightmare

FIGURE 5.
A postmodern image
of film noir.

of the soul. Also like the modernists, they store up what Eliot called "fragments" of artistic tradition to stave off spiritual despair.[48] Hence *Taxi Driver* is laden with new-wave allusions to other movies or directors, including not only thrillers of the 1940s (strongly evoked in the music score, which was Bernard Herrmann's last), but also Robert Bresson's *Pickpocket,* Ford's *Searchers,* and Godard's *Two or Three Things I Know about Her.*

Seen in retrospect, *Taxi Driver* belongs in company with several major Hollywood productions of the decade—including *The Long Goodbye* (1973), *Chinatown* (1974), and *Body Heat* (1981)—which were made with a nostalgic idea of film noir in mind. However, despite its allusiveness and almost scholarly self-awareness, it is neither a period movie nor a pastiche. Instead, chiefly because of Scorsese, it transforms what Schrader regards as the definitive motifs of film noir into a kind of neo-expressionism that is ideally suited to color and wide screens. Perhaps

FIGURE 6.
Noir as fashion.

more important, together with Schrader's own essay, it helps to encourage the notion that film noir is essentially apolitical, characterized by pessimism and existential anguish.[49]

In effect, film noir did not become a true Hollywood genre until the Vietnam years, when productions such as *Taxi Driver* appeared with some regularity. Whether classic noir ever existed, by 1974 a great many people believed in it, and American movie critics were regularly exploring its implications.[50] Some of the best directors of thrillers from the 1950s returned to such films and adapted them to new styles of production—see, for example, Don Siegel's *Charley Varrick* (1973) and Robert Aldrich's *Hustle* (1975). At this point, *noir* had fully entered the English language, and it formed a rich discursive category that the entertainment industry could expand and adapt in countless ways.

Any proper history of noir in America therefore needs to address or at least acknowledge many things besides Hollywood in the 1940s and

1950s—among them, the vast changes in the economics and censorship of movies since the end of World War II; the "New Hollywood" of the 1970s; the rise of academic film theory; and the increasing dissolution of boundaries between high, vernacular, and commercial art. Today, the "original" films noirs still circulate, and the literary forms with which they are associated still flourish. Noir in the late twentieth century spreads across virtually every national boundary and every form of communication, including museum retrospectives, college courses, parodies, remakes, summertime blockbusters, mass-market paperbacks, experimental literature and painting, made-for-TV films (as we shall see, there is a significant B-movie industry known in the trade as "cable noir"), and soft-core "erotic thrillers" that go directly to video stores.

Why has noir become so important? The answer is beyond the scope of a chapter, but it seems obvious that the idea has been useful to the movie industry, providing artistic cachet and spectacular opportunities for both the Hollywood auteurs of the 1970s and the sex-and-violence specialists of the 1980s. The more interesting question is whether a category developed by critics to influence what Borde and Chaumeton called "the occidental and American public of the 1950s" can function in the same way for us. If we could ask the original French commentators what American film noir represented, they might agree that it was a kind of modernism in the popular cinema: it used unorthodox narration; it resisted sentiment and censorship; it reveled in the "social fantastic"; it demonstrated the ambiguity of human motives; and it made commodity culture seem like a wasteland. Later European art directors (including not only Godard and Truffaut but also Alain Resnais, Michaelangelo Antonioni, Bernardo Bertolucci, Wim Wenders, and Rainer Fassbinder) saw noir as a dying form that could be transmogrified; it could retain its psychological and social edge, but it could also be treated at a distance, in the interests of a critical and self-reflexive analysis of contemporary life.

Today, when the media are pervasive and the counterculture hardly exists, film noir represents something far more complicated. Good and bad examples are created in every mode of production, but Hollywood usually reconstructs its old pictures, borrowing the allusive techniques of 1960s art films to make audiences feel sophisticated.[51] This strategy also extends beyond Hollywood, as two examples illustrate. First is the cover of a presskit for *A Dama do Cine Shanghai* (The lady from the Shanghai cinema, 1987) by Brazilian director Guilherme de Almeida Prado, in which the star image of Rita Hayworth is used in a nostalgic, somewhat campy way to suggest a movie about movies (figure 5). Second is a page from the fashion section of the *New York Times Magazine* of May 23, 1993, showing a model dressed in a "film noir" (figure 6). The caption tells us, "Something filmy, see-through and black is this summer's No. 1 sensation. It will be seen on the street, the beach, the ballroom and maybe even the board room."

Obviously, a concept that was generated ex post facto has become part of a worldwide mass memory; a dream image of bygone glamour, it represses as much history as it recalls, usually in the service of cinephilia and commodification. Not every recent instance of film noir (even Prado's work) can be explained in this way. Nevertheless, as Fredric Jameson and others have argued, the term plays a central role in the vocabulary of ludic, commercialized postmodernism.[32] Consequently, depending on how it is used, it can describe a dead period, a nostalgia for something that never quite existed, or perhaps even a vital tradition. One thing is clear: the last film noir is no easier to name than the first. A fully historicized account of the category needs to range across the twentieth-century imagination, engaging in an unusually comprehensive analysis.

MODERNISM AND
BLOOD MELODRAMA

Three Case Studies

After an art-historical category has been named and its key members identified, critics usually try to explain its causes or genealogy. This is the
task undertaken in the second chapter of Raymond Borde and Étienne
Chaumeton's *Panorama du film noir américain,* in which the authors discuss six major "sources" of American film noir. Three of the sources are
sociological: a new realism about violence in the wake of World War II,
a rise in the American crime rate, and a widespread institutionalization
and popularization of psychoanalysis. The rest are artistic: the hard-
boiled crime novel, the European cinema, and certain Hollywood genres of the 1930s—especially horror films at Universal, gangster movies
at Warner, and classic detective pictures at Fox.

Somewhat surprisingly, Borde and Chaumeton argue that European
cinema was a "feeble" influence and that American noir should be understood chiefly within the "Hollywood professional context." Even so,
the genres they mention (such as the 1930s horror picture) were sometimes indebted to European émigrés, and the artistic ideology they describe clearly belongs to an older, cosmopolitan tradition. At one point,
they argue that noir made gangsters more psychologically complex and
sympathetic, horror more quotidian, and detective fiction less rational.
Leaving aside the references to popular formulas, these are more or less
the values of modernist literature since the beginning of the century.

Here we need to keep in mind that virtually all of the initial cycle of
American films noirs were adapted from critically admired novels. We

also need to remember that the Parisian critics who invented the idea of American film noir in the late 1940s were writing at a time when their city was attempting a return or a repetition of its cultural role in the 1920s and 1930s. Existentialism was replacing surrealism as the dominant philosophy, but Paris was once again a staging ground for revolutionary artistic movements, a capital of jazz, and a cheap haven for foreign writers. The initial discourse on Hollywood's dark cinema therefore coincides with one of the last important moments in the history of international modernism. Sometimes the connection between the Parisian cinéphiles and the older generation of high modernists was quite specific. For example, Nino Frank, who is usually credited with the first application of the term *film noir* to American thrillers, was a close friend of James Joyce during the 1930s and helped Joyce translate "Anna Livia Plurabelle" into Italian; according to Joyce's biographer, Richard Ellmann, Frank often took Joyce to the movies.

This does not mean that the French imagined everything they saw at the cinema. If Paris was a center of modernism, so, in a more qualified sense, was Los Angeles, which provided a temporary home for central European exiles from the war and for major American writers such as William Faulkner. A great many films of the 1940s were clearly indebted to modernist art, and sometimes the indebtedness went beyond mere technique. During the period in question, however, it makes just as much sense to argue that certain directors, writers, and photographers were trying to invest melodramatic formulas with a degree of artistic significance. By 1945, modernism had assumed an overriding importance, supplementing the older canon, shaping most artistic practices, and determining critical interpretation of the past and the present. It was quite simply the most respected art among the educated classes—the kind that was regarded as more authentic, more important as a commentary on modern experience, and more relevant to the intellectual concerns of the day. It was also becoming institutionalized and fully absorbed into what Max Horkheimer and Theodor Adorno called "the culture industry." Thus in a 1944 commentary on James Hadley Chase's best-selling noir novel, *No Orchards for Miss Blandish*, George Orwell grumbled, "Freud and Machiavelli have reached the outer suburbs."[1]

If modernism did not directly cause the film noir, it at least determined the way certain movies were conceived and appreciated. There was, in fact, something inherently noirlike in the established tradition of modern art. To make this point clear, let me offer a few commonplace generalizations about high modernism—bearing in mind that, like film noir, modernism is an idea constructed ex post facto by critics, and that it refers to a great many artists of different styles, sexes, nationalities, religious persuasions, and political inclinations. (One of the first appearances of the term in English is in a 1927 poetry anthology by Robert Graves and Laura Riding, but it did not gain widespread use until the 1960s.) I shall draw most of my examples from English and American literature, in part because noir has always had strong literary associations, and in part because I am leading up to a discussion of several English-language writers who worked for the movies.

First of all, modernism was an older, more wide-reaching manifestation of the same dialectic between Europe and America (or between vanguard art and mass culture) that produced the discourse on film noir itself. A metropolitan development largely associated with white male artists, it was fully established in New York, Chicago, and the major European capitals by 1914, slightly before World War I shattered the confidence of the previous century's established institutions. Because it was generated during the second industrial revolution, it was frequently about things such as metro stations, rail travel, cinemas, jazz, and the spaces of urban modernity. But modernism had a complex, ambivalent relation to the dominant economy. After World War I, as economic power shifted westward, and as Hollywood began to dominate the world's imagination, the leading modern writers grew increasingly conflicted in their attitude toward the United States, which seemed both a dynamic force of change and a threat to civilized Europe. This ambivalence was especially apparent in Weimar Germany, where a complex discourse on Americanism persisted throughout the 1920s; its larger history, however, can be traced back to nineteenth-century artists such as Charles Baudelaire, whose paradoxical aestheticism was developed in direct response to bourgeois capitalism and the rise of urban mass culture.[2]

In some of its most elite manifestations (such as the writings of T. S. Eliot), modernism was critical not merely of America but of modernity altogether—including Enlightenment rationalism, industrial technology, and liberal or social democracy.[3] In formal terms, it was often detached, aestheticized, and self-reflexive, and at its extremes it led to what Spanish philosopher José Ortega y Gasset called a "dehumanization." The most radical modernist painting emphasized the surface of the canvas rather than the thing depicted; and the most radical modernist writing, beginning with Stéphane Mallarmé, subverted what Roland Barthes would later term "readerly" values. The modernist devaluation of content, however, was usually more advertised than practiced. One of the obvious aims of the new art was to create scandal and thereby challenge dominant values at the levels of both the signifier and the signified. Vanguard art in the 1920s was not merely a matter of paintings that problematized vision or novels in which nothing seemed to happen; it was also an assault on bourgeois Europe's ideals of sexuality, family, and religion, and on provincial America's fundamentalism and Babbittry.

Even before the censorship scandals over *Madame Bovary, Ulysses,* and *The Rainbow,* European literature was preoccupied with individual subjectivity—a topic that led naturally to explorations of sex and the "primitive" unconscious. Prior to World War I, in the work of British and American authors such as Henry James, Joseph Conrad, and Ford Maddox Ford (all of whom were indebted to Gustave Flaubert), impressionistic narration and the control of point of view became the hallmarks of modern literary art. Additional support for "deep" narrative techniques, involving stream of consciousness and nonlinear plot, was ultimately found in Friedrich Nietzsche, Henri Bergson, and Sigmund Freud. Sometimes these techniques were used to reveal savagery or death instinct—a killer inside us, living below the surface of rational life.[4] Furthermore, the new novel mounted an implicit critique of industrial modernity's sense of progressive or nonrepeatable time. As David Lodge puts it, one of the chief characteristics of modernist fiction is that it "eschews the straight chronological ordering of its material, and the use of a reliable, omniscient and intrusive narrator. It employs, instead, either a single, limited point of view or multiple viewpoints, all more or less limited and fallible; and it tends toward a complex or fluid handling of time, involving much cross-reference back and forward across the temporal span of the action."[5]

The modernist concern with subjectivity and depth psychology was given a further impetus by social modernity and the emancipation of women, which brought new subjectivities into being. However, the relationship between modernism and the new woman was troubled, particularly in the case of the male moderns, who offered a liberating honesty about sex while at the same time mounting a gendered opposition to establishment culture. A locus classicus is the climactic scene of Conrad's *Heart of Darkness* (often described as the urtext of British modernism), in which Marlow finds it impossible to tell the truth to Kurtz's sheltered fiancée, "the Intended." At about this time in London, T. E. Hulme and Ezra Pound were attempting to replace the flowery rhetoric of late-Victorian poetry with "hard" and "clear" imagery. Attacks on the supposedly genteel, ladylike taste of the middle class were intensified in the years after World War I, when all forms of writing, from verse to journalism, became more plainspoken and "masculine." For those writers who had experienced combat, beautiful images and poetic diction seemed almost obscene: a horse should be called a horse, not a "steed" or a "charger," and a good novelist or newspaper editor should approach language in much the same way as Pound approached poetry, ruthlessly cutting excess verbiage and euphemisms.[6] The time was ripe for movements such as the German *Neue Sachlichkeit,* for the iconoclastic criticism of H. L. Mencken, and for tough-guy stylists such as Louis-Ferdinand Céline and Ernest Hemingway.

But if the old sensibility was characterized as feminine, so were the more threatening aspects of the modern society—at least in the hands of many male artists. As Andreas Huyssen points out in *After the Great Divide* (1986), one important characteristic of high modernism was its growing hostility toward mass culture, which it often personified in the form of a woman. (Here it should be noted that the modernists did not dislike popular art; what they increasingly criticized was a commodified, mass-produced, supposedly "feminine" culture that took the form of slick-paper magazines, Books-of-the-Month, and big-budget productions from Broadway and Hollywood.) At this level, the masochistic eroticism of the aesthetes and decadents at the end of the nineteenth century sometimes joined forces with an almost sexual ambivalence toward industrial progress, which was associated with erotic females who threaten men. Consider Franz Kafka's *Trial,* in which a nightmare bureaucracy is connected with lascivious and enigmatic women; consider also the German art cinema of the 1920s, especially *Metropolis* and *Pandora's Box,* in which a beautiful robot and a sexy flapper evoke fears of creeping Americanization. In English literature, a loosely related example is T. S. Eliot's *Waste Land*—one of the most influential poems of the early twentieth century, in which a free-floating male sexual anxiety blends with dystopian horror.[7]

The themes I have been discussing tended to converge on representations of the Dark City, a literary topos inherited from the nineteenth century, which became more significant than ever. William Blake's London had been the blighted, "mind-forged" creation of industrial rationality; Baudelaire's Paris had been the perversely seductive playground of a flaneur; oppressive and pleasurable, alienating and free, the Dark City possessed many contradictory meanings, all of which were carried over into the modernist era. In the twentieth century, however, the streets at night were transformed into the privileged mise-en-scène of the masculine unconscious (most notably in the Nighttown episode of *Ulysses,* in which a notorious harlot turns men into swine). For some modernist artists, the nocturnal city also began to resemble an American-style metropolis—a spreading empire of mechanization and kitsch that endangered the urbanity of old Europe.

A great deal more could be said about high modernism, but these observations should indicate the degree to which early examples of the so-called film noir tend to reproduce themes and formal devices associated with landmarks of early-twentieth-century art. Like modernism, Hollywood thrillers of the 1940s are characterized by urban landscapes, subjective narration, nonlinear plots, hard-boiled poetry, and misogynistic eroticism; also like modernism, they are somewhat "anti-American," or at least ambivalent about modernity and progress.[8] By the same token, critical discourse on these films usually consists of little more than a restatement of familiar modernist themes.

The affinity between noir and modernism is hardly surprising. In the decades between the two world wars, modernist art increasingly influenced melodramatic literature and movies, if only because most writers and artists with serious aspirations now worked for the culture industry. When this influence reached a saturation point in the late 1930s and early 1940s, it inevitably made traditional formulas (especially the crime film) seem more "artful": narratives and camera angles were organized along more complex and subjective lines; characters were depicted in shades of gray or in psychoanalytic terms; urban women became increasingly eroticized and dangerous; endings seemed less unproblematically happy; and violence appeared more pathological.

The qualified transformation of thrillers was aided by Hollywood's appropriation of talent and ideas from Europe, where intellectuals had more power than in the United States, and where a less rationalized, more elite media culture produced the Weimar silent film, the French film noir, and the Gaumont-British pictures of Alfred Hitchcock. The European art cinema was unable to compete with Hollywood on its own ground, but it strongly influenced many American directors and genres. The Weimar Germans (led by Fritz Lang) specialized in gothic horror, criminal psychology, and sinister conspiracies; the French (including René Clair, Marcel Carné, and Jacques Prévert) produced realist pictures about working-class crime; Hitchcock (assisted by such figures as Michael Balcon, Charles Bennett, and Ivor Montagu) concentrated on international intrigue. What united the three types of cinematic modernism was an interest in popular stories about violence and sexual love, or in what Graham Greene once called "blood melodrama."[9]

A similar development can be seen in the world of Anglo-American literature, where the major forms of "bloody" popular fiction, including the detective story, the spy thriller, and the gothic romance, were "made new" in the 1920s and 1930s. These forms had long been of interest to vanguard artistic intellectuals; in fact, shortly after the turn of the century, crime and paranoid conspiracy fiction strongly appealed to the leading psychological novelists in Britain and America. Henry James, for example, experimented with both the ghost story and the spy novel, and Joseph Conrad, who specialized in ironic tales of "secret sharers" and imperialist adventurers, once told a French colleague that society itself was nothing more than a criminal conspiracy: "Crime is a necessary condition for all types of organizations. Society is essentially criminal—or it would not exist."[10] By the 1930s, Wyndham Lewis was complaining that the entire social imaginary resembled a *Kriminalroman*.

Authors like Conrad and James, however, did not seem to be writing for the same public as Agatha Christie and Dorothy Sayers. (James described "The Turn of the Screw" as "an *amusette* to catch those not easily caught . . . the jaded, the disillusioned, the fastidious.")[11] In the English language during the first three decades of the century, crime novels were usually conservative, supporting the prewar culture that modernism regarded as bankrupt. The Christie-style detective story, one of the most successful creations of modern publishing, seemed especially retrograde when viewed from a modernist perspective and was sometimes criticized for appealing to a genteel audience of females and academics.[12] Two symptomatic developments of modernity enabled a countertradition to emerge: first was the rapid growth in the 1920s of sensationalized American pulp fiction addressed chiefly to working-class men; second was the development in the late 1920s and 1930s of literary novels about crime, published in hardback and supported by middle-class book clubs. In these venues, a second-generation modernism interacted with mass culture and eventually made its way into the respectable realms of New York publishing, Broadway theater, and Hollywood.

In one sense, the movies had always been interested in the new wave of crime writers; of the four American thrillers initially described as noir by the French, two were remakes. Unlike their predecessors, however, all four of the 1940s pictures were A-budget productions, bearing the marks of literary sophistication, attracting favorable commentary from urban reviewers, and competing for Academy Awards.[13] Likewise, Hollywood was never unaware of vanguard European cinema. The most obvious sign of "artistic-ness" in America during the interwar years was a slightly UFA-esque or expressionist style, which gained favor soon after the New York premiere of *The Cabinet of Dr. Caligari* in 1920.[14] Hence the most critically respected film produced in Hollywood prior to 1941 was F. W. Murnau's *Sunrise,* and the most respected film after 1941 was Orson Welles's *Citizen Kane.* What seemed different about *Kane* was its synthesis of cinematic and literary modernism: it showed the influence of expressionism, surrealism, and Soviet montage, but at the same time it reminded critics of *Heart of Darkness, The Great Gatsby,* and the *USA* trilogy. (On top of everything, it made use of an irreverent, somewhat wisecracking dialogue that was associated with Herman Mankiewicz, Ben Hecht, Charles MacArthur, and the "newspaper wits" who had worshipped H. L. Mencken.)

Welles was only the most spectacular manifestation of a growing acceptance of modernist values throughout the culture. Eric Hobsbawm observes that before 1914, the philistine public jeered at postimpressionism, Igor Stravinsky, and the Armory Show; afterward, that same public usually fell silent before artistic "declarations of independence from a discredited pre-war world."[15] Such art, Hobsbawm remarks, was not necessarily what most people actually enjoyed; it nevertheless managed to coexist with "the classic and the fashionable," becoming "proof of a serious interest in cultural matters" (181). Meanwhile, from the late 1920s until the 1940s, under the shadow of depression, fascist dictators, and European war, many artists turned to socialism and were increasingly attracted to popular forms and realist narratives (a trend encouraged by the Popular Front, which is discussed more fully in the next chapter). Given this tendency, plus the culture industry's appetite for talent, traces of modernism were increasingly absorbed into everyday life.

In the process of becoming normalized, modern art inevitably lost some of its critical edge. Its early manifestations were shocking and willfully difficult, resisting the marketplace and often treating the audience as what Baudelaire and Eliot called a "*hypocrite lecteur.*" By midcentury, nearly all the modernist leopards were safely ensconced in the temple, and serious art was expected to create an atmosphere of toughness, darkness, and alienation.[16] There is a sense, however, in which modernism and mass culture had never been quite so far apart as we imagine. Fredric Jameson, who defines modernist art in terms of its resistance to the culture industry, notes that there were also "profound structural relations" between modernism and the new economy.[17] A text like *Heart of Darkness,* for example, is both an experimental narrative and an adventure story derived from the "sensation" literature of the mid-Victorian period; as Jameson has remarked, Conrad's work in general reveals "the emergence not merely of what will be contemporary modernism . . . but also, still tangibly juxtaposed with it, what will variously be called popular culture or mass culture, the commercialized discourse of what, in late capitalism, is often described as media society."[18]

The contradiction Jameson observes is especially apparent in the Hollywood film noir, which is both a type of modernism and a type of commercial melodrama. I refer not only to the *melos* of the Hollywood style, but also—more importantly—to the "moral occult" of tales in which the forces of good battle violently against the forces of evil. Especially in Hollywood, melodrama is a conservative or sentimental form associated with stalwart heroes, unscrupulous villains, vivid action, and last-minute rescues. Certain attributes of modernism (its links to high culture, its formal and moral complexity, its disdain for classical narrative, its frankness about sex, and its increasingly critical stance toward America) threatened this kind of film and were never totally absorbed into the mainstream. High modernism and Hollywood "blood melodrama" nevertheless formed a symbiotic relationship that generated an intriguing artistic tension.

By way of illustrating this phenomenon, let me now turn to three case studies that provide evidence of a link between modernism and mass culture on the grounds of noir narrative. The first involves Dashiell Hammett, who is widely recognized as the founder of the hard-boiled detective novel; the second deals with Graham Greene, who, according to Borde and Chaumeton, "played a role in the birth of film noir (*This Gun for Hire*), in the acclimatization of noir in England (*Brighton Rock*), and in its international development (*The Third Man*)" (18); and the third centers on the Billy Wilder–Raymond Chandler adaptation of James M. Cain's *Double Indemnity,* which is arguably the definitive film noir of the 1940s. Each of the writers I discuss brought an intense awareness of modernist literature to the making of criminal adventures, and each gained money and fame from the Hollywood studios. Taken together, their work demonstrates how a certain kind of "art thriller" could be critical of the institutions that supported it; but at the same time, their careers reveal that the movie studios needed to lighten or ameliorate the darkness of modernism and mute its intensity.

BELIEVING IN NOTHING

The earliest and most radical of the popular modernists was Dashiell Hammett, a working-class author who began his career in the pulps and soon crossed over to the prestigious firm of Alfred A. Knopf. During his most productive years, Hammett managed to reconcile some of the deepest contradictions in his culture: he was an ex–Pinkerton detective who looked like an aristocrat, and a writer of pulp mysteries who was treated as an authority on language by none other than Gertrude Stein. The most important innovator of popular detective fiction since Edgar Allan Poe, he was also at various points an advertising man, a Hollywood hack, a drinking partner of William Faulkner, a writer for a comic strip, and a committed Marxist.[19]

Hammett's early stories and novels were published by a factory of cheap, all-fiction periodicals that provided melodramatic fantasy to an audience of millions in the days before paperbacks and television. Historian Lee Server remarks that in their heyday—chiefly the 1920s and 1930s—the pulps were "held accountable to few standards of logic, believability, or 'good taste.'"[20] Whenever they exhausted the possibilities of standard characters or genres (science fiction, western, spy, South Seas adventure, or modern romance), they spawned new formulas and strange hybrids (sword-and-sorcery, "weird menace," gangster, superhero, or masked avenger). The detective story was among the most popular of the pulp commodities, and it came in every variety: "spicy" detective, cowboy detective, occult detective, and so on. Like all the other genres, it was packaged behind lurid, brightly hued covers depicting half-dressed women and men frozen in violent tableaux.

Pulp authors were paid so little that they usually specialized in a kind of automatic writing. By contrast, Hammett was a painstaking craftsman, and he became a fairly well paid star. Together with fellow *Black Mask* writer Carroll John Daly, he seems to have "invented" the tough detective sometime around 1923, in clear reaction against the amateur, puzzle-solving sleuths descended from Poe and Sir Arthur Conan Doyle. In keeping with the general atmosphere of *Black Mask,* his early stories and novels have as much speed as a Keystone Cops movie and more dead bodies than an Elizabethan tragedy. Sometimes the hero's toughness is exaggerated to the point of burlesque: at one point in *Red Harvest* (1929), the Continental Op spends all night drinking gin with a blond floozy, takes a cold bath, and has a fight with a killer, whom he overpowers and hauls to the police; he then takes another cold bath and has a fight with *two* killers, knocking one out and beating the other to the draw; soon afterward, having been grazed on the wrist by a stray bullet, and without even the benefit of another cold bath, he captures an escaped convict and solves a murder mystery that has baffled the local police for years.

But Hammett also had high literary aspirations and serious political convictions. *Red Harvest* vividly describes corruption in the Wild West during a period of murderous labor struggles, White House scandals, and Prohibition-style gangsterism; never overtly tendentious, it is nonetheless a deadpan exposé of union busting and police violence, filled with cataclysmic bloodshed and raw exploitation of the weak by the strong. Its title is a pun, referring not only to gory violence but also to the potential rise of the Communist International. Equally important, its protagonist—the fat, fortyish, but incredibly tough Continental Op—is quite different from the hypermasculine figures on pulp covers, and from the sort of hero that *Black Mask* editor Joseph T. "Cap" Shaw seems to have imagined for his readers. Shaw was a man of action who clearly had a great deal to do with the birth of hard-boiled fiction; in his editorial statements, however, he sounded like a disciple of Teddy Roosevelt. The ideal consumer of *Black Mask*, he wrote, "is vigorous-minded, hard, in a square man's hardness; hating unfairness, trickery, injustice, cowardly underhandedness; standing for a square deal and a fair show in little or big things . . . ; not squeamish or prudish, but clean, admiring the good in man and woman; not sentimental in a gushing sort of way, but valuing true emotion . . . and always pulling for the right guy to come out on top."[21] In contrast, Hammett's Op is a faceless employee of a factory (more like an actual reader or writer of the pulps), and the violence he experiences makes him feel "blood simple." At one point, he thinks he might even have stabbed a woman while he was drunk or drugged.

Throughout the novel, Hammett reveals a sophisticated awareness of current literary trends. From the first sentence ("I first heard Personville called Poisonville by a red-haired mucker named Hickey Dewey in the Big Ship in Butte"), it is clear that he is making art out of the vernacular. All of his later protagonists would speak in this unorthodox style, and they bring a new voice to the detective story. It isn't quite the voice of Reason, as with Dupin or Holmes, because it has less to do with solving puzzles than with exposing falsehood or naïveté; nor is it quite the voice of Metaphysics or Morality, as with Father Brown, because Hammett is skeptical of absolutes and his heroes are not virtuous. It sounds more like the voice of Male Experience, addressing seductive women or mendacious crooks after a period of knowing silence. When an aging capitalist in *Red Harvest* tells the Op that he wants a "man" to "clean this pigsty of a Poisonville for me, and to smoke out the rats, little and big," the Op replies, "What's the use of getting poetic about it? If you've got a fairly honest piece of work to be done in my line, and you want to pay a decent price, maybe I'll take it on." When Brigid O'Shaunnessy in *The Maltese Falcon* tells Sam Spade that he can't turn her over to the police because he loves her, he comments, "But I don't know what that amounts to. Does anyone ever? . . . Maybe next month I won't. . . . Then I'll think I played the sap." Such a voice can't be taken in by abstract appeals to morality or even love, and while it usually situates itself on the side of the Law, it is too honest to give the usual reasons for being there. As Ned Beaumont says in *The Glass Key,* "I don't believe in anything."[22]

Interestingly, Hammett was a writer of verse as well as detective stories, and before turning to pulp fiction he published a story and an essay in H. L. Mencken's *Smart Set,* the most sophisticated "little magazine" in America, which also featured work by James Joyce and the leading modernist authors. Although Hammett's politics were always leftish, in some ways he was exactly the kind of writer Mencken admired: he reacted against the vaguely "feminine" tone of 1890s aestheticism by introducing a profound skepticism into realist narrative, and he stripped literary language of what Pound and others called "rhetoric." The only difference between Hammett and the high modernists was that he applied an emerging sensibility to popular adventure stories, attacking bourgeois culture from "below" rather than from above.

Actually, neither Hammett nor pulp fiction was quite so low on the cultural scale as historians usually suggest. *Black Mask* had been founded by Mencken and George Nathan in 1920 as a way of supporting *The Smart Set,* and it was a more respected journal than Mencken himself allowed (even Woodrow Wilson was a subscriber). *Red Harvest* appeared there in installments, at a time when "Cap" Shaw was trying to boost the literary reputations of his writers by having them experiment with longer forms. Hammett immediately submitted the manuscript of his novel to the Alfred A. Knopf company, where Mencken and Nathan were valued authors, and in an accompanying letter he pointed out his former connection with *The Smart Set.* The manuscript was read by Blanche Knopf, one of the most astute editors of the period, who was the leader of a modernist literary salon in New York. Knopf immediately recognized Hammett's talent, but she thought that "so many killings on a page . . . make the reader doubt the story."[23] Hammett obligingly dropped two dynamitings and a tommy-gun attack, and in response to Knopf's query about his future plans, wrote that he had hopes of "adapting the stream-of-consciousness method, conveniently modified, to a detective story." He also remarked, "I'm one of the few—if there are any more—people moderately literate who take the detective story seriously. . . . Some day somebody's going to make 'literature' of it (Ford's *The Good Soldier* wouldn't have needed much altering to have been a detective story), and I'm selfish enough to have my hopes" (quoted in Johnson, 72).

Blanche and Alfred Knopf were the publishers of several important American novelists, including William Faulkner and Willa Cather; together with Mencken, they were also key figures in the transmission of European literary modernism to the United States. Over the next two decades, they gave their imprimatur to hard-boiled writing, developing the careers of Hammett, James M. Cain, and Raymond Chandler and eventually piquing the interest of the movie studios. By this means, Hammett joined the main current of American literature; he never wrote the stream-of-consciousness novel he planned, but within a year of submitting *Red Harvest*, he told Blanche Knopf that he had borrowed part of the plot from Henry James's *Wings of the Dove* to complete *The Maltese Falcon* (1930), the book that firmly established his reputation as a serious author.

From the beginning, *Falcon* was admired by intellectuals, who observed that the crime was messy, the chase circuitous, and the solution to the murder less important than the depiction of a criminal milieu. To slightly revise a question asked by Edmund Wilson (one of Hammett's supporters and America's leading critic of literary modernism), Who cares who killed Miles Archer? Spade's famous speech to Brigid at the end of the novel mocks the idea of a just solution to murder, just as the Falcon itself mocks the idea of ownership or private property. Born of a "Holy War" that, as Gutman says, "was largely a matter of loot," the Falcon is little more than an embellished form of raw capital, and it belongs to "whoever can get hold of it." The novel's final irony is that the rara avis turns out to be just as counterfeit as the characters. A phallic signifier, it provides a motive for the frantic activity of the novel; but when the paint is peeled away, all that remains is a lead shape, an empty object of exchange. Both the enigma of the murder and the search for the treasure are rendered absurd. The world, as Spade explains to Brigid in his parable about the Flitcraft case, is founded on a void.

The vaguely existential philosophy that Spade is often said to represent, and the fantasy he satisfies, is at the core of what Leslie Fiedler identifies as the "American romance": a stoic masculine individualism, living by its wits and avoiding social, economic, and sexual entanglements. This sort of romance is sometimes misogynistic and homophobic, and because of its hostility toward bourgeois marriage, it often results in latently homosexual narratives about male bonding. We find such qualities everywhere in Hammett, but what makes him slightly unusual is that he subverts the classic formulas of the romantic quest, undermining the phallic stoicism of his detectives. Spade is an unusually ruthless hero, more disturbing than any of his movie incarnations; he moves with ease through an underworld composed almost entirely of women and bohemian homosexuals, so that even his masculinity seems ambiguous; and in the end, he behaves more like a survivor in the jungle than like an agent of justice.

This nihilism and pervasive feeling of moral and sexual ambiguity becomes even more evident in Hammett's next novel, *The Glass Key* (1931), which Diane Johnson has described as a complex treatment of "male friendship, male loyalty, and male betrayal" (87). The plot is set in motion by a Freudian murder: a state senator kills his son—with a walking stick, no less. Later, the senator's daughter, Janet Henry, tells the gambler-detective Ned Beaumont about one of her dreams, in which a glass key opens a door to chaos and then shatters. The dream foreshadows Ned Beaumont's discovery of a "key" to the murder and at the same time comments on the novel's many symbolic castrations. At one point, Beaumont coolly seduces a newspaper publisher's wife, driving the publisher to suicide; and in the last chapter, he takes Janet Henry away from his closest friend, political boss Paul Madvig. In the extended, sadomasochistic torture scenes of chapter 4, in which the thug Jeff keeps calling Beaumont "sweetheart," the phallic anxiety threatens to become literal: "'I got something to try.' He scooped Ned Beaumont's legs and tumbled them on the bed. He leaned over Ned Beaumont, his hands busy on Beaumont's body" (86).

The Glass Key could be described as Hammett's novel of the Dark City, his version of *The Waste Land*. He was reading Eliot at the time he wrote the novel, and Lillian Hellman claimed that when she first met him in 1930, they spent hours talking about the poet. He even names one of the streets in his corrupt, fictional city "upper Thames Street" (*The Waste Land,* line 260), and he makes Ned Beaumont a somewhat dandified figure who feels an Eliot-like cultural nostalgia: Beaumont's rooms are decorated "in the old manner, high of ceiling and wide of window," and when Janet Henry first sees them she remarks, "I didn't think there could be any of these left in a city as horribly up to date as ours has become" (141).

The indirect link with high modernism is further reinforced by a neutral, camera-eye narrative technique. Here as in all his other fiction, Hammett dispenses with both "interior" psychological views and nineteenth-century omniscience; as a result, he gives the reader no comfortable position from which to make judgments. The crooked politicians, the sadistic gangsters, the naive females, the cruelly detached gambler-protagonist—all these are familiar pop-cultural stereotypes, but they are presented without any character who, like Chandler's Marlowe, acts as a spokesperson for liberal humanism. Although *The Glass Key* has all the adventure and suspenseful action of a melodrama, and much of the social detail of a muckraking naturalist novel, it deprives us of the usual melodramatic sermons, sentiments, or philosophical conclusions. What, finally, are we to think of Beaumont and Madvig? How are we to condemn the city without feeling like the "respectable element" whom Beaumont mocks? There is no answer to these questions, because, like nearly all of Hammett's novels, *The Glass Key* ultimately deals with what Stephen Marcus calls the "ethical unintelligibility of the world."[24] Thus when Ned Beaumont reveals the identity of the villain, we do not feel that the story has been brought to a neat closure. At best, something criminal has been exposed in society's basic institutions; the villain's crime is merely a symptom of a deeper, systemic problem that seems beyond the power of individuals to solve.

Hammett's last novel, the comic *The Thin Man* (1934), is a partial exception to these rules. It was inspired by his relationship with Lillian Hellman and is the closest he came to a conventional, puzzle-style detective story or a romance about marriage. The setting is glamorous, the protagonist is a sophisticated amateur detective (more precisely, a retired private eye married to a Park Avenue heiress), and the mystery is solved when all the suspects are rounded up in the penultimate chapter. Even so, Nick and Nora Charles occasionally seem like members of Hemingway's lost generation:

> We went into the living room for a drink. Some more people came in. Harrison Quinn left the sofa where he had been sitting with Margot Innes and said: "Now ping-pong." Asta jumped up and punched me in the belly with her front feet. I shut off the radio and poured a cocktail. The man whose name I had not caught was saying: "Comes the revolution and we'll all be lined up against the wall—first thing." He seemed to think it was a good idea.[25]

The comedy here is darkly absurd, and Nick Charles is clearly using liquor as an anesthetic. Much as he and Nora like one another, he is a potential doppelgänger of Jorgenson, the gigolo who has married Mimi Wynant, and the only time he stops drinking is when he becomes interested in solving a murder. With only a slight turn of the screw, *The Thin*

Man could have been as disturbing as any of Hammett's previous writings. The chief metaphor of the novel is cannibalism; moreover, as usual, Hammett ends on an ironic note, reminding us that nothing has fundamentally changed and casting doubt on the detective's solution. In the final chapter, Nick explains everything to Nora, who is no adoring Watson. "This is just a theory, isn't it?" she asks. Nick says he is only trying to describe what is probable, and reaches for another drink. Nora complains, "It's all pretty unsatisfactory" (180).

These were Hammett's last published words as a novelist, and it may be significant that he gave them to a woman. He had already begun selling his hard-boiled thrillers to Hollywood, but his career as a scriptwriter was brief and undistinguished. Soon after achieving literary fame, he began to drink heavily, doing odd jobs at various studios and behaving as if, in the words of Nunnally Johnson, "he had no expectation of being alive much beyond Thursday" (quoted in Johnson, 124). Meanwhile, his work was altered or adjusted to suit the studios' proven formulas. In July 1930, for example, David O. Selznick wrote to B. P. Schulberg, the chief executive at Paramount, recommending that Hammett be put under contract because he had recently "created quite a stir in literary circles by his creation of two books for Knopf, *The Maltese Falcon* and *Red Harvest*." Selznick announced that Hammett possessed "more originality than Van Dine," and might do "something new and startlingly original for us"; in the same breath, however, he offered the profoundly unoriginal suggestion that Hammett ought to be put to work on a "police story" for Paramount star George Bancroft, who had scored a great success in Josef von Sternberg's 1927 gangster movie, *Underworld*.[26] Hammett was immediately offered a short-term contract with Paramount and was paid an extra five thousand dollars for writing a story called "After School," which became *City Streets* (1931). Scripted by Oliver H. P. Garrett and directed by Rouben Mamoulian, this highly sentimental melodrama was filmed in a symbolic, aestheticized, rather Sternbergian manner that clearly shows the influence of *Underworld;* it has brilliant visual "touches," but as Andrew Sarris remarks of the Sternberg film, its gangster protagonists (including Gary Cooper and Sylvia Sydney) have about as much connection to waking reality or to the hard-boiled tradition as the motorcyclists in Cocteau's *Orphée*.[27]

That same year, Warner Brothers began its famous series of realistic gangster pictures, and alongside *Little Caesar* it produced a relatively faithful adaptation of *The Maltese Falcon,* starring Ricardo Cortez and Bebe Daniels. Because this version was shot in Warner's fast-paced, low-

budgeted, proletarian style, it sometimes feels more like pulp fiction than
Hammett's original. Scriptwriter Brown Holmes preserved most of the
novel's action and dialogue but none of its subtlety; at the end of the picture, we learn that Wilmer has killed off both Caspar Gutman and "Joe"
Cairo and that Sam Spade has been rewarded with a political appointment as special investigator for the district attorney's office. Ricardo
Cortez makes Spade seem like a ruthless opportunist, but it is difficult
to say whether this effect is intended. The acting and direction are quite
broad, and with the possible exception of Dwight Frye as Wilmer, none
of the characters seem as decadent or perverse as the ones in the novel.
Even Spade's womanizing is treated as little more than an opportunity
for some cheerfully randy, pre-Code cheesecake.

In contrast, *The Thin Man,* Hammett's least characteristic novel,
proved to be a gold mine. The 1934 MGM adaptation, scripted by Albert Hackett and Francis Goodrich, was turned into a sort of screwball
detective story, which made good use of William Powell and Myrna Loy.
Powell had played an elegant sleuth before, but he and Loy together created a refreshingly modern and risqué couple, offering Depression-era
audiences an amusing fantasy of wealth, sexiness, and irresponsibility
within marriage. *The Thin Man* was one of the top ten moneymakers of
1934, and it spawned five sequels between 1935 and 1947 (not counting a radio series of the 1930s, a TV series of the 1950s, a made-for-TV
movie in 1977, and a Broadway musical in 1991). In each successive picture, Powell and Loy became increasingly domesticated. Their last effort, *The Song of the Thin Man,* was made in what is usually regarded
as the peak year of American film noir: it features Gloria Grahame, it
takes place in the world of New York jazz clubs, and one of its characters suffers from an "obsessive guilt complex"; nevertheless, it feels like
a cross between an MGM musical and a TV sitcom (all the more so because young Dean Stockwell plays Nick Jr.).

The Thin Man led to a brief cycle of what *The New York Times* described as "hilarious homicide" pictures (15 June 1935), and the film
created a virtual subgenre of married-couple detective stories. Thus, although the first version of *The Maltese Falcon* had not been a hit, there
was now a resurgence of interest in Hammett. In response, Warner's remade *Falcon* in 1935 as a "hilarious homicide" movie entitled *Satan Met
a Lady,* with Bette Davis as a wicked woman named Valerie Purvis and
Warren William as a private eye named Ted Shane. The script was once
again written by Brown Holmes, but this time the settings were plush
and the action was spread across a broad landscape. Unfortunately, *Sa-*

tan Met a Lady is an almost painfully bad movie. Warren William bears a slight physical resemblance to Hammett, but he behaves like a fading and boorish Shakespearean actor in the mold of John Barrymore. Bette Davis is overweight and visibly uninterested in the proceedings, perhaps because the script is so absurd. Caspar Gutman becomes "Madame Barabas" (Alison Skipworth); Joel Cairo becomes "the tall Englishman" (Arthur Treacher); and the Falcon itself is transformed into "Roland's Trumpet," a medieval hunting horn stuffed with diamonds. Director William Dieterle attempts to create a farcical tone, but most of his efforts are shrill and clumsy. One of the few redeeming elements is the dumb-blond performance of young Marie Wilson (later to become famous in radio's *My Friend Irma*) as Shayne's secretary.

Also in 1935, Paramount filmed *The Glass Key,* a project it had considered as early as 1931 but had dropped because of Hays Office objections to any movie depicting corruption among "municipal and state office holders."[28] The revised version, starring George Raft and Edward Arnold, was reminiscent of the Warner gangster cycle, but it avoided censorship problems by making "Ed" Beaumont a professional bodyguard rather than a gambler and by portraying Paul Madvig as a man who no longer has associations with the mob. Beaumont's seduction of the newspaper editor's wife was omitted altogether, and his beating at the hands of Jeff was depicted offscreen. (The Production Code Administration [PCA] demanded that Jeff's reference to Beaumont as a "massacrist" be dropped, and the studio complied.) The resulting picture was a competent if unoriginal thriller that became one of the top box-office hits of the 1936–1937 season.

At this point, Hammett's reputation as a literary artist was well established. (*Falcon* was translated into French in the mid 1930s, and it soon developed an international following. It was also issued in a Modern Library edition in 1934.) Ironically, however, with the possible exception of *The Thin Man,* Hollywood had never made a film based on his work that was true to the spirit of what he had written or worthy of critical attention. Five more years would pass before John Huston, a scriptwriter who began his career by publishing Hemingwayesque stories in Mencken's *American Mercury,* chose a Hammett novel for his directorial debut at Warner Brothers. His 1941 version of *The Maltese Falcon* is widely regarded as the most faithful screen adaptation of Hammett, but it is also an innovative film that transforms its source, bestowing upon it an aura of modernist cinema that American reviewers immediately associated with Hitchcock and prewar France.

FIGURES 7–9. Three early films based on Dashiell Hammett: Gary Cooper and Sylvia Sydney in *City Streets* (1931), Ricardo Cortez and Beebe Daniels in *The Maltese Falcon* (1931), and Warren William and Marie Wilson in *Satan Met a Lady* (1935). (Museum of Modern Art Stills Archive.)

Huston's screenplay involved little more than an intelligent editing of the novel, which is mostly dialogue anyway. He telescoped scenes, cut minor characters (including Caspar Gutman's daughter), and made slight changes to get past the censors. And yet, even though the words are mainly Hammett's, the film has a style of its own. Part of this effect is the result of the brilliantly cosmopolitan and slightly campy ensemble of players, who are somewhat different from the characters in the novel. Humphrey Bogart is the physical opposite of the "blond satan" described by Hammett, and Sydney Greenstreet is a less flabby and bombastic Gutman. Peter Lorre is not so effeminate or bejeweled as the original Joel Cairo; and although Elisha Cook Jr. has the right stature for the "boy" Wilmer, he seems always to have had the pinched face of an old man. Most unusual of all is Mary Astor, who has a lovely but rather matronly face and build, and who conveys an upper-class sophistication that is almost entirely lacking in Hammett. The scenes between her and Bogart have a humor and intelligence that runs beneath the surface of the words, so that lines Hammett wrote flatly and seriously gain a new life. When Astor tosses her head back on a couch, gazes up at the ceiling, and gives a description of Floyd Thursby ("He never went to sleep without covering the floor around his bed with crumpled newspaper so nobody could come silently into his room"), her manner is so outrageous and chic that she makes Bogart smile. She knows that he knows that she's putting on an act. As Spade would say, now she's *really* dangerous.

The photography and mise-en-scène of Huston's film also create a slightly different impression from the novel. Hammett's art is minimalist, but Huston is an expressive storyteller who likes to make statements through his images. This version of *Falcon* has the same art director (Robert Hass) as the original Warner adaptation, and the same photographer (Arthur Edeson) as *Satan Met a Lady;* nevertheless, it has a much more artfully stylized and vaguely symbolic look than either of its predecessors. Everything in the film is designed to emphasize a vivid contrast between the "masculine" ethos of Spade and the "femininity" of the villains; meanwhile, the latest developments in film stock and camera technology heighten the fetishistic qualities of the settings. Edeson (who had also photographed *Frankenstein* at Universal) adopts a *Kane*-like technique, employing a 21 mm lens to give depth and resolution to his shots. His camera is repeatedly positioned at a low level, which brings ceilings into view and creates a dynamic, foreboding sense of space. In similar fashion, his many sharp, low-angle close-ups provide a grotesque comedy: Lorre brushes the tip of his fancy walking stick across his lips; Cook's psychotic eyes brim with tears; and Greenstreet's sinister face appears just above his vast belly.

In the leading role, Humphrey Bogart establishes Spade as one of the cinema's enduring icons, but he also gives the character more psychological "depth" than Hammett had done. Sullen, brooding, and edgy, he seems obsessed with Brigid. When he kisses her for the first time, his face is twisted with anguish, and when he announces that he is turning her over to the police, he looks almost desperate. Huston reinforces this effect through his editing and rewriting of Spade's famous concluding speech to Brigid, which omits certain of Hammett's harshest lines, such as "Suppose I do [love you]? What of it? Maybe next month I won't." Here as elsewhere, the film is less skeptical, more passionate and psychologically intense than the original story. (Adolph Deutsch's rich, sinister music score contributes to the effect; by contrast, the 1932 film version has almost no music.) Significantly, Huston deletes Spade's parable about the Flitcraft case, in part because he is less interested in the philosophical implications of the quest for the black bird than in the greed, treachery, and occasional loyalty of the various characters. The focus at the end is on Gutman's resilience as he taps a bowler hat on his head and gaily wanders off to find the real falcon; on Spade's repressed hostility as he calls the police; and on Brigid's fear as she descends in an elevator cage. This version of *Falcon* is an allegorical drama about the psychodynamics of masculinity, involving what James Agee called "a romanticism about danger."[29] The falcon, like the film itself, becomes "the stuff that dreams are made of" (a line Huston contributed), and the search for it is invested with oneiric intensity.

But if this adaptation of *The Maltese Falcon* is romantic, it is also strikingly witty, especially at the level of performance. Again and again, the players create their best effects from calculated understatement, employing a swift, oblique, somewhat arch style of acting. Notice, for example, the way Bogart tosses off a joke about third-degree methods when the police break into his apartment and find Lorre and Astor locked in a struggle; and notice a long shot toward the end of the film, when Lorre stands in the background, barely noticeable at the corner of the frame, withdrawing an unlit cigarette from his mouth, his great frog eyes staring with pity, his hand reaching down to pat Elisha Cook on the shoulder. Against this clever indirection, and somehow enhancing it, is the mannerism of the camera technique. Ultimately, the film is just stylized enough to represent the private-eye story as a male myth rather than a slice of life, and Huston's wit is just sly enough to humanize the action without destroying its power as melodrama.

FIGURE 10. The original promotion for John Huston's *Maltese Falcon* (1941) bears little relation to the actual film. In this poster, the studio capitalized on Humphrey Bogart's earlier appearances as a gangster in *The Petrified Forest* (1936) and *High Sierra* (1941), and on Hammett's reputation as the author of a popular "screwball" murder mystery, *The Thin Man* (1934). (Museum of Modern Art Stills Archive.)

The success of the 1941 version of *The Maltese Falcon* inspired Paramount to remake *The Glass Key* in 1942. This adaptation was scripted by pulp writer Jonathan Latimer, one of Hammett's imitators, and was designed as a vehicle for Alan Ladd, who had achieved great success that same year in Paramount's *This Gun for Hire.*[30] It features low-key photographic effects by Theodore Sparkuhl, and it restores a good deal of the sexually perverse material that the first adaptation omitted. Ned Beaumont's seduction of the newspaper editor's wife (Margaret Hayes) is cruel and titillating, and even more remarkable are Beaumont's repeated beatings at the hands of Jeff (William Bendix), which are the most disturbingly violent scenes in any Hollywood picture of World War II. Despite *The Glass Key*'s occasional challenges to the Production Code, it concludes in sentimental fashion: Paul Madvig (Brian Donlevy) recognizes that Beaumont and Janet Henry (Veronica Lake) are two kids who "have got it bad for each other," and he cheerfully gives his blessing to their impending marriage.

In writing the novels upon which *The Thin Man* and *The Maltese Falcon* were based, Hammett was indirectly responsible for two of the most important film cycles of the classic studio era. He was in fact an unusually "movielike" author, who possessed an ear for American speech and a sense of the texture of modern life—including the tunes people sang, the clothes and hairstyles they wore, the furnishings in their rooms, and the way they posed in magazine photographs. As John Huston recognized, Hammett's novels were already virtual scripts, containing little more than objective descriptions and exchanges of pungent dialogue.[31] And yet Hammett had a contempt for Hollywood, and Huston was the only director who gave his work cinematic distinction. In the 1940s and for a long time afterward, an accurate rendition of this popular but in some ways radically skeptical novelist would have been politically controversial, morally challenging, and perhaps excessively artful in the eyes of the major studios.

Sympathy for the Devil

Soon after Hammett modernized the American detective story, Graham Greene and his contemporaries (including Hitchcock and Eric Ambler) performed a similar transformation of British crime and spy fiction. The transformation is remarked upon in Greene's *Ministry of Fear* (1943), when the hero experiences a tormented dream in which he speaks to his mother about an older England: "People write about it as if it still went on; lady novelists describe it over and over in books of the month, but it's not there any more."[32] Greene's dismissal of "lady novelists" is consistent with the fact that most of the women in his thrillers are either passive or benighted consumers of mass culture. Yet his air of toughness and less-deceived realism is disingenuous, because his own success derived from books of the month.

The Oxford-educated son of a middle-class family, Greene began his career as an undistinguished and rather old-fashioned poet and then attempted historical fiction and biography with mixed success. His first major opportunity came in the early 1930s, when his publisher, the Heinemann company, pressured him for a novel that could be sold to the movies and at the same time offered as a selection of the British Book Society. This last organization had been founded in 1928 by best-selling authors Arnold Bennett and Hugh Walpole, A. R. Frere-Reeves of Heinemann, and a number of writers who knew Greene personally; it had over ten thousand subscribers who were offered a monthly volume, and it could guarantee a large sale for any author. Greene responded with *Stambol Train,* a novel about international intrigue that was chosen as the Society's "Main Selection" and, in 1934, turned into a Hollywood movie entitled *Orient Express,* starring Heather Angel. (*Variety* described the production as "another of those *Grand Hotel* on wheels ideas" [6 March 1934], and Greene later wrote that the only things Hollywood preserved from his novel were the parts that were "cheap and banal enough to suit the cheap banal film" [quoted in Sherry, 1:590].)

Greene had long since become a convert to Catholicism and socialism, and during his university years he developed an intense admiration for the writings of Conrad, James, Ford, Pound, and Eliot.[33] He was happy to take money from the Book Society and Hollywood, but he was uneasy about popularity; thus one of the characters he invented for *Stambol Train* is a rather nasty parody of J. B. Priestly, a sentimental, quasi-Dickensian novelist who was Heinemann's perennial bestseller. To make his uneasiness even more clear, Greene labeled this book and all his subsequent thrillers "entertainments," marking them off from his more ambitious writings about religion and politics. He was nevertheless fascinated by exotic settings and physical danger, and he had a gift for mystery and suspense. While working on *Stambol Train,* he reread *Heart of Darkness,* noting in his diary that it was possible to "write finely" within the conventions of an adventure story (quoted in Sherry, 1:421). The trick was to invert certain conventions, at the same time offering sensational action that would provoke anxieties appropriate to the Depression.

Since childhood, Greene had been enamored of the popular spy novels of John Buchan, whom he praised for writing about "adventure in familiar surroundings happening to unadventurous men."[34] By the 1930s, however, Buchan's patriotic stories of World War I seemed badly out of date. His heroes were square-jawed Tory gentlemen, rugged South African landowners, and North American tycoons who believed in the natural superiority of the British race; his settings were pastoral, infused with a Wordsworthian love of the Scottish countryside; his religion and morality were derived from *Pilgrim's Progress;* and his plots were virtually devoid of sex. In writing his own thrillers, Greene preserved Buchan's skillful plotting and sense of violence breaking through polite British civilization, but he took a different approach to almost everything else. His protagonists were psychologically twisted criminals or drab socialist intellectuals, hunted down by the forces of what one of them calls "an old world . . . full of injustice and muddle"; his settings were thoroughly urban, rendered through a vivid, imagistic prose; his narration made use of internal monologues and complex shifts in point of view; and his endings were darkly ironic, pervaded by a sense of Kafkaesque guilt. He was quite good at exploring the ambiguous borderland between the individual subject and the authoritarian state, and he often played upon the intertwined public and private implications of "spying," hinting at his characters' deep-seated sexual motives. Perhaps most important, he created a feeling of dread by observing the seedy details of ordinary life—as when he wrote that the protagonist of *The Ministry of Fear* "was often ill, his teeth were bad and he suffered from an inefficient dentist" (21).

All of Greene's entertainments took place in what reviewers and critics described as "Greeneland"—a world of dingy rooming houses, canned fish, drooping aspidistras, and doomed characters. "The sordid sends Greene into lyrical flights," one commentator remarks, but it is difficult to say whether the mise-en-scène of the novels is intended to evoke a *nostalgie de la boue,* a disgust at genteel poverty, or an Orwellian fear of dropping out of the middle class.[35] The atmosphere frequently resembles T. S. Eliot in his brooding, overtly anti-Semitic period. In *A Gun for Sale* (1936), for example, the protagonist visits an abortionist named Doctor Yogel to have surgery performed on a harelip. Yogel works out of a dimly lit office on a back street; his fingernails are dirty, he smells of brandy, and he sweats as he approaches with a scalpel. Trembling and squinting in the bad light, he mutters, "I'm used to it . . . I have a good eye."[36]

Greene's anti-Semitism in the 1930s is implicit, but it is nonetheless systemic (a trait he also shares with Buchan). His least sympathetic characters include a Jewish arms manufacturer who arranges the murder of a socialist War Minister, a Jewish gangster with "raisin eyes" who controls the underworld in Brighton, and a Jewish aristocrat who runs a supermodern resort called the Lido. He seems to associate Jewishness not only with a dark racial otherness but also, more specifically, with modernity and American-style capitalism—and in this regard he is remarkably like Eliot, to whom he frequently alludes.[37] "Greeneland" could in fact be understood as what Michael Shelden calls "a province of the Waste Land" (99), or as a conscious imitation of Eliot's poetry in the period between 1912 and 1922. Borrowing heavily from nineteenth-century French literature, Eliot wrote about an "unreal city" made up of cheap hotels, half-deserted streets, rat-infested canals, newspapers in vacant lots, lonely typists in empty rooms, snippets of banal conversation, and random scraps of pop tunes. Greene imported all these details into his thrillers, bringing with them many of Eliot's religious, racial, and cultural ideas. As a result, he gave melodrama a metaphysical aura and a complex ideological effect. In political terms, he was a radical leftist, outraged by social injustice; but in religious and cultural terms, he was a radical conservative, appalled by the loss of "organic" society and by the rise of kitschy resorts or modern housing developments such as the one in *A Gun for Sale,* where the architecture is fake Tudor and the main street is called Shakespeare Avenue. As one of his characters remarks, the modern world represents "something worse than the meanness of poverty, the meanness of spirit" (44).

But the fallen world of "Greeneland" also resembled a certain kind of movie. In his student days Greene had been the film critic for *Oxford Outlook* (his brother Hugh was the first president of the Oxford film society), and for several years he was an avid reader of *Close Up,* a high-modernist film journal whose contributors included H. D. and other important literary figures. From the beginning of his career he nourished an ambition to write for motion pictures, and from 1935 until 1940 he contributed a regular column of film reviews to *The Spectator* and *Night and Day* (the latter a British version of *The New Yorker*). These reviews were clearly related to his aims as a novelist, as we can see from his descriptions of the scenes or images he admires; his attitude toward popular melodrama, however, was qualified or critical, foreshadowing the noirlike cinema he would help to create in the years after the war.

Like nearly all the latter-day modernists, Greene was dismayed by

American modernity, which was epitomized in the Hollywood film fac-
tories. In the opening lines of his first review for *The Spectator,* he de-
cries "the bright slick streamlined civilization . . . whose popular art is
on the level of *The Bride of Frankenstein.*" James Whale's film, he argues, was "set in motion by a vast machinery of actors, sound systems
and trick shots and yes-men; presently, I have no doubt, it will be color-
shot and televised; later in the Brave New World to become a smelly"
(5).[38] Two years later, reviewing Whale's *Road Back,* he was even more
savage:

> [What the film] really emphasizes is the eternal adolescence of the American
> mind, to which literature means the poetry of Longfellow and morality means
> keeping Mother's Day and looking after the kid sister's purity. One came
> daunted out of the cinema and there, strolling up the Haymarket, dressed in
> blue uniforms with little forage-caps and medals clinking, were the American
> Legionnaires, arm in arm with women dressed just the same—all guide-books,
> glasses, and military salutes: caps marked Santa Anna and Minnesota: hair—
> what there was of it grey, but with the same adolescent features, plump,
> smug, sentimental, ready for the easy tear and the hearty laugh and the fra-
> ternity yell. What use in pretending that with these allies it was ever possible
> to fight for civilization? For Mother's Day, yes, for anti-vivisection and hu-
> manitarianism, the pet dog and the home fire, for the co-ed college and the
> campus. Civilization would shock them: eyes on the guide-book for safety,
> they pass it quickly as if it were a nude in a national collection. (172–73)

Greene repeatedly complained about the mixture of sentiment and
chrome plated sleekness in Hollywood. He was opposed to sound, color,
and every new technical development in film—although in later years,
watching "Monsieur Godard," he admitted to a nostalgia for the "dead
thirties" and for "Cecil B. DeMille and his Crusaders" (4). He admired
Capra's *Mr. Smith Goes to Washington* and especially Lang's *Fury,* but
the ordinary run of genre movies rarely provoked his interest. Ironically,
his first review for *The Spectator* contains a passing reference to the 1934
Paramount adaptation of Hammett's *Glass Key,* which he describes as
"unimaginatively gangster." He was more attracted to a few scenes in
Goldwyn's *Dead End,* in which Humphrey Bogart conveyed a "ruthless
sentimentalist who has melodramatized himself from the start," and in
which director William Wyler supplied a proper background of "beetle-
ridden staircases and mud and mist" (181). He also praised the RKO
adaptation of Maxwell Anderson's *Winterset,* a verse drama about
crime in the city; he especially liked "the whole wintry scene in the drench-
ing sleet under the sooty arches," which reminded him of "the Jacobeans
at their most bloody and exact" (143).

Aside from documentaries like *Night Mail,* Greene also had little regard for British films. He even criticized Hitchcock, whom he described as talented but Hollywoodish, more interested in spectacle and visual gags than in realism or dramatic values. He repeatedly complained of "how inexcusably [Hitchcock] spoilt *The Thirty-Nine Steps*" (1–2), and he gave only qualified praise to *Sabotage,* Hitchcock's adaptation of Conrad's *Secret Agent.* The "dark drab passionate" qualities of this story, he argued, could "never find a place in the popular cinema," except perhaps in the hands of a French director like Jacques Feyder (123).

It was the French whom Greene admired above all. The most enthusiastic review he ever wrote was for *Pépé le Moko* (released in London in 1937), which seemed "a whole continent away from the usual studio banalities":

> Perhaps there have been pictures as exciting on the "thriller" level as this before (though it would be hard to equal the shooting of Regis, the informer, with its comic horror: the little fat eunuch sweating and squealing in the corner between the aspidistra and the mechanical piano, the clash and clatter of the potted music as his dying friend is helped across the room to finish him at point-blank range, friends steadying the revolver on its mark), but I cannot remember one which has succeeded so admirably in raising the thriller to a poetic level. *Winterset* seems a little jejune and obvious and literary beside it. *Fury,* perhaps, is its equal, but in *Fury* Fritz Lang was not allowed to follow his subject to the right, the grim conclusion. *His* hero couldn't burn; but Pepe cuts his throat with a penknife in his handcuffed hands outside the dock gates as the steamer leaves for France. The theme of no freedom anywhere is not lost in a happy ending. (145)

These are precisely the effects Greene was trying to achieve as a novelist, and he found them everywhere in French cinema. When he saw *Hôtel du Nord,* he admired "the tuft of cotton-wool in the young man's ear which seems to speak of a whole timid and untidy life" (230). In Julian Duvivier's *Carnet de bal,* he discovered a series of admirably sordid effects: "the seedy doctor at Marseille so used to furtive visitors and illegal operations that he doesn't wait for questions before he lights the spirit flame: the dreadful cataracted eye: the ingrained dirt upon his hands: the shrewish wife picked up in God knows what low music-hall railing behind bead curtains: the continuous shriek and grind of wench and crane" (184).

Again and again, Greene praised the French for their "realistic" and "poetic" qualities. (Had he known of a movement called "poetic realism," he would surely have embraced it.)[39] Their best films contained values he had admired since 1928, when he wrote his first article on movies for the London *Times*—an article that clearly shows his fascination with an ironic mixture of romance, perversity, and quotidian horror, communicated through realistic black-and-white photography. "The object of film," he asserts, "should be the translation of thought back into images. America has made the mistake of translating it into action." (Another way of making this point would be to say that Hollywood valued plot over mood, or "content" over "form.") Repeatedly he cites a moment from his favorite silent picture, *Greed*, to illustrate the imagistic "passion" that film has at its disposal: "The scene was a rainy day at a seaside 'resort.' The lovers were shown only as two backs, receding down a long breakwater, on each side a leaden sea and a lashing rain, which failed to disturb their complete self-absorption" (quoted in Sherry, 1:414).

The French often conveyed this sort of poeticized fatalism, but equally important where Greene was concerned, they made innovative use of crime stories. The Popular Front developed a left-wing, modestly budgeted art cinema, grounded in local color and dealing with murder and romance; this strategy was a challenge to Hollywood, and it seemed to offer possibilities for the British industry. Greene recognized that film was a mass medium, and he believed that highly charged poetic imagery should rise out of popular narrative. He insisted that "if you excite your audience first, you can put over what you will of horror, suffering, truth" (quoted in Sherry, 1:597). The logical formula for such effects, he observed, was "blood melodrama." The problem in England was that "there never has been a school of popular English blood. We have been damned from the start by middle-class virtues, by gentlemen cracksmen and stolen plans and Mr. Wu's." The solution was "to go further back than this, dive below the polite level, to something nearer to common life." If the British could only develop "the scream of cars in flight, all the old excitements at their simplest and most sure-fire, then we can begin—secretly, with low cunning—to develop our poetic drama. . . . Our characters can develop from the level of *The Spanish Tragedy* toward a subtler, more thoughtful level" (quoted in Sherry, 1:597).

In America, Dashiell Hammett had already achieved a mixture of artistry and raw, bloody excitement—especially in *Red Harvest,* one of the few Hammett novels that classic Hollywood never adapted.[40] Greene, however, was much more attracted to the native English tradition of revenge tragedy. Once again he was following the lead of Eliot, who had a fondness for the sort of imagery one might find in a horror movie, and whose critical writings of the 1920s and 1930s stimulated a revaluation of such perversely violent Jacobean dramatists as John Webster and John Ford. Indeed the mutually reinforcing influence of Eliot, Jacobean revenge tragedy, and the prewar French cinema explains virtually all of Greene's writing in this period. *A Gun for Sale,* for instance, is a revenge narrative set in an urban wasteland, featuring not only a memorably violent and "cinematic" opening chapter, but also a religious motif. (A hired killer becomes a scapegoat and an ironic Christ figure.)

The same nexus of interests becomes even more evident in *Brighton Rock* (1938), Greene's strangest, most serious, and certainly most noir thriller, which in its English edition was not classified as an entertainment. The plot of this unusual novel involves a gang war in the English coastal resort of Brighton: a small-time journalist named Hale indirectly helps a Jewish crime lord to kill off a rival mobster named Kite. In retaliation, Hale is kidnapped and sadistically murdered by Pinkie Brown, a boyish, baby-faced killer who regards Kite as his surrogate father. A barmaid named Ida Arnold, who enjoyed casual sex with Hale on the day of his death, becomes a sort of detective or agent of vengeance. With Ida's assistance, the police corner Pinkie—but not before he seduces and marries an innocent working girl named Rose in order to prevent her from revealing evidence that might incriminate him. In a scene reminiscent of countless gangster movies, the young psychopath attempts to evade capture and dies a spectacular death, leaving the pregnant Rose behind to face a grim future.

Brighton Rock's events may seem generic, but its mood is reminiscent of pictures such as *Hôtel du Nord,* its epigraph comes from *The Witch of Edmunton,* and its themes are indebted to Eliot's commentary on the poetry of Charles Baudelaire. The last of these sources was particularly important. In a famous essay, Eliot argues that Baudelaire was an instinctively religious artist who believed in original sin, not in "natural" sex or the "Right and Wrong" of secular humanism. The Frenchman's greatest achievement as a poet, Eliot claims, lay in his recognition that "what distinguishes the relations of man and woman from the copulation of beasts is the knowledge of Good and Evil."[41] Such a man might choose Satanism and be forever damned, but at least he was no wishy-washy liberal; according to Eliot, "in a world of electoral reforms, plebiscites, sex reform, and dress reform, [damnation] is an immediate form of salvation—of salvation from the ennui of modern life, because it . . . gives some significance to living" (181).

Eliot's argument had a demonstrable effect on Greene, who turned

Pinkie Brown into a working-class Baudelaire.[42] At the same time, Greene made use of a technique he had learned from Henry James: the manipulation of the reader by shifting the point of view from one center of consciousness to another. *Brighton Rock* begins with Hale, the murder victim; then it moves to Ida, a bosomy, fun-loving woman of the people, who sets out after the killer because, as she tells us, "I believe in right and wrong."[43] As the plot develops, however, Ida begins to resemble one of those Americans Greene had seen walking down Haymarket, who stood for "humanitarianism, the pet dog and the home fire." In effect, she is an allegorical figure, representing Woman as Modernity and Mass Culture. Not surprisingly, she gets her values from Hollywood melodrama: "she cried in cinemas at *David Copperfield,*" Greene tells us; "easy pathos touched her friendly and popular heart" (41).[44] The "Boy" Pinkie, in contrast, is a Satanist who enjoys slicing people with razors and provoking the wrath of God each time he commits a murder. Through his eyes, the Americanized culture of Brighton takes on a surreal quality. During one of his conversations with Rose, a seaside orchestra can be heard in the background: "Suddenly at the stale romantic tune the orchestra was playing—'lovely to look at, beautiful to hold, and heaven itself'—a little venom of anger and hatred came out on the Boy's lips" (66).

Given the choice between Ida's sentimental humanitarianism and Pinkie's twisted Catholicism, Greene has more sympathy for the young killer. He is also intrigued by the sadomasochistic relation between Pinkie and Rose, which differs strikingly from the casual, earthy lovemaking enjoyed by Ida. In the second half of the novel, Greene exploits this perverse bonding for all it is worth, emphasizing the spiritual conflict for souls rather than the secular battle for lives. Pinkie believes in the possibility of salvation and is fascinated with priests, but he also has a disgust of sex and a need to push Rose into eternal damnation. When he catches a glimpse of her thigh, Greene tells us that "a prick of sexual desire disturbed him like a sickness" (130). Near the end of the novel, Kite appears to him in a dream—bleeding from the mouth, offering a razor, and murmuring "Such tits." Like Prince Hamlet, Pinkie believes that his dead father is asking for revenge, but he has a better plan than straightforward murder: he gives the devoutly Catholic Rose a revolver and tempts her with a mutual suicide pact that he has no intention of joining. "All you need do is pull on this," he says. "It isn't hard. Put it in your ear—that'll hold it steady" (349).

Fortunately, the police arrive in the nick of time. Pinkie dies a horrible death, smashing a bottle of vitriol in his face and plunging over a cliff. In a final twist, however, Greene denies his readers even a religious consolation. Disturbed because Pinkie died without asking forgiveness for his sins, Rose visits St. John's church in Brighton, where a priest alludes to the conservative Catholic Charles Péguy and tells her of the "appalling . . . strangeness of the mercy of God": "If [Pinkie] loved you, surely, that shows there was some good" (357). When we last see Rose, she is returning to her room to listen to a recording Pinkie made for her on Brighton Pier. She does not know (but we do) that the message on the record is "God damn you, you little bitch, why can't you go back home forever and let me be?" This conclusion raises the stakes of melodrama and then, in the fashion of the darkest Jacobean revenge dramas, it knocks out all the props. Notice, too, how it reverses the situation at the end of *Heart of Darkness,* where Marlow refuses to tell the upper-class "Intended" that Kurtz's last words were "The horror, the horror!" In *Brighton Rock,* a working-class woman is about to learn the full truth about the man she has married, from his own lips. Greene's closing sentence tells us that "she walked rapidly in the thin June sunlight towards the worst horror of all" (358).

In 1938, there was little chance that such a novel could be turned into a movie; but in 1947, with the war ended, with noirlike cinema in vogue, and with Greene established as a successful author who had provided material for Hollywood, *Brighton Rock* became a West End play and then a British film. The theatrical version, written by Terence Rattigan, omitted the novel's shocking conclusion, but Greene was determined that the film would not do the same.

Before discussing Greene's motion-picture adaptation of *Brighton Rock,* however, something needs to be said about Hollywood's uses of his work during and immediately after the war, when he achieved international celebrity. At first Greene was a problem for the studios, because he was a best-selling author who subverted popular conventions. Classic Hollywood's method of dealing with him is perhaps best illustrated by *This Gun for Hire* (1942), one of the earliest and most commercially successful adaptations of his crime fiction. Paramount had acquired rights to *A Gun for Sale* before it was published in 1936, but the studio did not develop a script until 1941—after the Warner remake of *The Maltese Falcon,* after the Hawthornden Prize for British literature had been awarded to Greene's *Power and the Glory,* and after the war had made overt criticism of fascism acceptable.[45] Under the credits to the completed film, the studio exhibited a leather-bound copy of the novel, as if to cap-

italize on Greene's literary prestige. Yet the narrative we see on the screen
is quite different from the one Greene had written. The novel tells the
story of a hired killer named Raven (an obvious allusion to Poe), who
assassinates a socialist war minister in prewar England. Raven's employers hope to turn a profit in the munitions industry, but when they
double-cross the killer by paying him in stolen banknotes, he exacts
vengeance; in the end, he becomes an unwitting agent of social justice
and a scapegoat who meets violent death at the hands of the law. (He is
reluctantly betrayed by an attractive working-class woman whom he has
begun to trust.) The Paramount screenplay, credited to Albert Maltz and
W. R. Burnett (the author of *Little Caesar*), moves the locale to America and smoothes over most of Greene's ironies—all in the interest of
wartime propaganda. In the fashion of many other crime films of the early
1940s (such as *All Through the Night,* a Bogart gangster picture made
at Warner in the same year), it converts the villains into Nazi fifth-colum-
nists and the protagonist into a victim of Depression-era social injustice
who becomes a champion of democracy. It also changes the hero's looks:
the novel's Raven suffers from a harelip, but the film's Raven, played by
Alan Ladd, is a strikingly attractive young man whose only imperfection
is a slightly deformed left wrist.[46] In fact, *This Gun for Hire* turned Ladd
and Veronica Lake into the sexiest commodities in Hollywood; a pair of
diminutive and sullenly pretty blonds, they seem an almost incestuous
couple, and the dark, Germanic setting provides a foil to their California-
style beauty.

Despite these and other changes, Paramount did not make a bad film.
The studio divested the novel of its anti-Semitic elements and some of its
heavy symbolism, and it added a photographic expressionism that has
its own particular merits. When *This Gun for Hire* reached Paris in 1946,
it was received as a key work in a developing noir "series." Borde and
Chaumeton ranked it among three seminal pictures: *The Maltese Falcon*
provided film noir with its criminal psychology; *The Shanghai Gesture*
created a distinctive noir eroticism; and *This Gun for Hire* established
both a new character type (the "angelic killer") and the convention of a
surreal chase through an urban landscape (45). The opening sequence
of the Greene adaptation was singled out for special praise: from a low
angle, we see Alan Ladd sitting on a bed in a sleazy boardinghouse, loading a gun while honky-tonk music drifts through a window; he rises, puts
on a hat and coat, and gently feeds milk to a stray cat; a housemaid enters, wearing lipstick and a low-cut blouse, as if she has just stepped off
the cover of a pulp magazine; she tries to chase away the cat, and Ladd

slaps her in the face. Here as elsewhere, Ladd's behavior is deadpan, enigmatic, and graceful; he seems quite unlike Greene's Raven, but also unlike any Hollywood hero or villain of the previous decade. Borde and Chaumeton quote two lines from Baudelaire that "seem to have been written for him": *"Je te frapperai sans colère / Et sans haine, comme un boucher"* (46; "I will strike you down without anger / And without hatred, like a butcher"). The allusion is in some ways appropriate—not because Ladd resembles a butcher, but because he conveys the impression of a coolly lethal dandy.

The same mixture of glamour and moral unease can be seen in Paramount's 1945 adaptation of *The Ministry of Fear,* an enjoyably paranoid "wrong man" thriller that, in comparison with Greene, looks rather glossy and Hitchcockian.[47] Ironically, the Hollywood film that best evokes "Greeneland" is the 1945 Warner production of *The Confidential Agent,* which derives from a novel that Greene regarded as one of his worst. (He wrote the book at breakneck speed, devising a parodic happy ending in which the improbably matched hero and heroine sail off to do battle against fascism.) In the film, Charles Boyer plays a former concert pianist who travels to 1930s England on a secret mission for the Spanish Republicans. (By the end of the war, it was perfectly safe to make anti-Franco movies.) Boyer's costar, Lauren Bacall, fresh from *To Have and Have Not,* plays the alcoholic daughter of a British industrialist. "Don't be melodramatic," she says at one point, "I can't stand melodrama." Boyer shrugs and replies, "Well, sometimes it just happens that way." And indeed the picture sometimes makes Boyer's attitude plausible. The settings are drab, the hero's ostensible allies are no more trustworthy than his enemies, and all of the actors look realistically downtrodden. George Coulouris is especially effective in the role of a Mosley-style xenophobe who has an artificial hand. Boyer, whom Greene admired for his ability to "wear worry like a habit on his forehead" (quoted in Sherry 2:16), is repeatedly subjected to sadomasochistic humiliations—as when a thug beats him up under the lights of a car while Bacall and Coulouris stand on the roadside and watch. However, the most skillfully photographed and exciting scene in the film is almost Dickensian: Boyer's only friend, a shabby but sexy young housemaid (Wanda Hendrix), is pushed from a window by two grotesque villains (Katina Paxinou and Peter Lorre). When Boyer learns of the crime, he seizes a gun and sets out for vengeance. "I've been beaten and robbed," he announces, "but that girl was murdered! And for this, someone is going to pay!"

All this changed after the war, when Greene briefly became an auteur in the British industry and was given a measure of control over the final product. The 1947 adaptation of *Brighton Rock,* produced by the Boulting brothers and scripted by Greene and Terence Rattigan, makes an interesting contrast to the Hollywood features I have been describing and is the picture that comes closest to the values Greene espoused in his prewar novels and criticism. Like many other crime films of the period, *Brighton Rock* mixes location photography with expressionistic studio sets, but its costuming and interiors resemble the 1930s French cinema or the Warner gangster cycle. It is in fact a kind of historical film, chiefly because the city of Brighton feared that Greene's depressing story might discourage tourism. To calm local officials, the producers garbed the characters in prewar costume and introduced a "crawl" explaining that contemporary Brighton had become a safe and happy playground. *Brighton Rock* is flawed by this gesture—also by John Boulting's uneven direction and by Hermione Baddeley's rather brassy portrayal of Ida Arnold. Because the immediate source for the screenplay was Rattigan's theatrical adaptation, the picture never achieves the subjective intensity of Greene's novel or of *The Fallen Idol* (1948), the noirish and highly Jamesian murder story Greene made immediately afterward with Carol Reed. And yet, it contains an effective performance by Richard Attenborough as Pinkie Brown—a disturbingly androgynous character whose moods alternate between Napoleonic swagger and infantile terror. It also depicts Greene's version of the Waste Land quite accurately: sunny but rather tacky images of Brighton beach are set off against sinister views of the pier at night, and the white interior of a modern luxury hotel is counterpointed with Pinkie's gangland slum, where the sound of squalling babies can be heard through open windows. Perhaps more important, *Brighton Rock* is the only film based on one of Greene's crime novels that emphasizes his paradoxical religious symbolism. As a result, it has one of the most unsettling conclusions of any thriller of the period.

The last scene of the picture begins with a dissolve from the black, rainswept waters of Brighton Pier, where Pinkie has fallen to his death, to a brightly lit room in a Catholic home for wayward women. Rose, accompanied by a nun, sits on the edge of a bed, wearing a shabby frock and holding a portable phonograph. "I ought to have gone with him!" she cries. "I don't want any absolution ever!" Cut to a close up of the lipsticked nun, who speaks rather sanctimoniously about the "appalling strangeness of the mercy of God," and who suggests that if Pinkie was capable of love he has some hope for salvation. "I'll show you!" Rose announces, and she puts her treasured record on the player. At this point, we have already seen Pinkie inside the recording booth, leaving a sadistic message: "What you want me to say is I love you. You little tramp! Why don't you go away forever and let me be?" We have also seen him unsuccessfully try to smash the record, which he realizes could be used as evidence against him in the event of Rose's death. Now we hear his voice again: "What you want me to say is I love you." Suddenly the record sticks: "I love you. I love you. I love you." As the words repeat themselves, a smiling Rose walks out of frame toward an open window, and the camera tracks forward to a cross on the wall, holding an image of the crucified Christ.

Greene later spoke about the film's conclusion as if it were a concession to the popular audience: "Anybody who wanted a happy ending would feel that they had had a happy ending" (quoted in Shelden, 345). But even if we assume that the record will always stick, the effect is anything but happy. The new version merely brings us a bit closer to the irony at the end of *Heart of Darkness,* where a woman is told a lie to protect her from the horrible truth. Perhaps for this reason, *Brighton Rock* was unsuccessful at the box office—especially in America, where it was eventually retitled *Young Scarface* and treated as a gangster movie. In the years before the liberalization of censorship codes and the development of a large distribution network for art films, it was viewed as a cross between an unfashionable genre picture and a respectable literary adaptation. *Variety* reported that *Brighton Rock* had been released at a moment when Hollywood was "frowning" on stories about gangsters and that it was likely to "meet with serious objections from America's Production Code Administration." To make matters worse, its Cockney accents would be confusing to American viewers, and its religious symbolism would probably "arouse the ire of Catholics." The only selling point for the project, *Variety* concluded, was that it was based on a "best seller" by Graham Greene (6 July 1947).

No such problems affected Greene's later and much more famous movie, *The Third Man* (1949), an international coproduction based on an original screenplay by Greene, which was financed in Hollywood style by Alexander Korda and David Selznick. In contrast with *Brighton Rock,* this film treats Greene's religious themes with a discreet irony: at one point Harry Lime tells his friend Holly Martins, "Of course I still *believe,* old man. . . . I'm not hurting anybody's *soul* by what I do." At the same time, it features a thrilling chase sequence by Carol Reed, a popular music score by Anton Karas, and a memorable star performance by

Orson Welles. It therefore fulfills Greene's long-standing desire to make an effective thriller that also functions as an art movie. On the second of these levels, *The Third Man* offers not only the neo-*Calagarisme* of Carol Reed's tilted camera, but also a quasi-documentary tour of Vienna, one of the cradles of both modernism and Hitlerian fascism, which has been reduced by the war to a kind of "Greeneland." Consider, too, the thematic and technical elements of Greene's screenplay. The protagonist and narrator of the story, Holly Martins, resembles both a Jamesian innocent and a Conradian secret sharer. Like Marlow in *Heart of Darkness*, Martins is an impetuous, sentimental romantic; also like Marlow, he searches out a villain who makes a delayed entrance, after being described by several people. Significantly, one of these narrators is a man named Kurtz, who, in a conversation with Martins, claims to have been Harry Lime's best friend —"after you, of course."

As everyone now knows, Orson Welles wanted to make his own film of *Heart of Darkness,* which he put aside shortly before making *Citizen Kane.* Here, merely by virtue of his charm, he transforms Harry Lime into the most dangerous of the "angelic" or Luciferian killers who populate Greene's fiction. His entrance is so impressive that it tends to make the audience forget exactly what crimes Lime is supposed to have committed (something involving black-market penicillin and dead babies).[48] What everyone recalls is a burst of zither music and a series of images that confirm Greene's 1928 argument about the "poetic" force of silent movies: a tall figure slipping into the shadowed doorway of a house (the home of the young Mozart); a cat licking a pair of black Oxfords; and a sudden, spotlighted view of Welles in a black hat and topcoat, the camera zooming toward him as he smiles like a ham actor who has been caught doing something naughty.

"Don't be melodramatic, old man," Harry Lime says to Holly Martins as they ride the giant Ferris wheel above Vienna. But of course Lime (whose name has an affinity with Greene) is the most melodramatic character in the film—a dashing, flamboyant outlaw, reminiscent of Fantomas or the Shadow. The naive Martins adores him, and because Martins is played by Joseph Cotten, we cannot help but be reminded of Jed Leland's relationship with Charles Foster Kane. The beautiful and masochistically romantic Anna (Alida Valli) pines for him, even after he turns her over to the Soviet authorities. For these two and for the audience, Lime provides a glamorous alternative to the social engineering in postwar Vienna, where the forces of modernity have divided a "smashed and broken" city into four zones, and where the charming old ring at the center

FIGURES 11–13. Three "angelic killers" in films based on Graham Greene: Alan Ladd in *This Gun for Hire* (1942), Richard Attenborough in *Brighton Rock* (1946), and Orson Welles in *The Third Man* (1949).

is patrolled by military units representing each of the occupying powers. The cold war has already begun, and daily life for the Viennese is constricted by rationing, checkpoints, identification papers, and worthless currency. Lime operates above and below this world—chiefly in the miraculously clean and undivided sewers, where the police wear white uniforms resembling those of a ski patrol. The most beautiful, dramatically lit scenes in the picture take place in his watery underground, and one of the most poignant sequences is the moment when he is trapped and killed there by a man who has always loved him.[49]

In this film, however, the seductions of melodrama are never offered without countervailing irony or deflation. Martins is an American "scribbler" who specializes in pulp westerns; he has experienced outlaws only in his imagination, and, like the movie audience, he gradually realizes that his attraction to Lime amounts to a complicity with evil. Lime, meanwhile, is revealed as a witty sociopath. During his ride on the Ferris wheel, he chews an antacid tablet and projects a fake cheerfulness, comparing himself to a modern-day bureaucrat: he, too, has a "five-year plan," the only difference being that he deals with "the suckers" instead of "the people" and with "dots" instead of statistics.

Eventually, Lime dies. But there is something almost sacrificial about the image of his fingers reaching through a manhole cover in the street,

FIGURE 14. Harry Lime, "crucified" in a sewer.

and about Martins's coup de grâce, which is administered offscreen. After Lime is gone, the film does nothing to assuage the sense of moral ambiguity he has created. Martins and Anna do not go off into the sunset,
as they do in Greene's novelized version of the story; instead, Carol Reed
shows Anna walking past Martins and ignoring him as he stands near
the Vienna graveyard where Lime is buried.[50] Unlike most characters in
a closing shot, Anna walks toward the camera and exits behind it, leaving Martins alone at the left of the screen among a line of barren trees.
A moment of dead time follows, with the zither music playing and the
unbalanced composition waiting to be filled. It is a remarkably artful and
wistful ending, simultaneously repudiating the pleasures of melodrama
and mourning their loss. In its last seconds, the film seems to wish for
Lime's return, if only because he is the most colorful and "alive" person
we have met.

    Such a delicate balancing act could only have been made possible by
the forces of cultural history. *The Third Man* is one of the best and most
representative films of a period when a certain kind of high art had fully
entered public consciousness and when European sobriety and American entertainment sometimes worked in tandem. Greene was conscious

of the formal dialectic required by the times, and in one of the earlier episodes of *The Third Man*, he comments upon it. Holly Martins is picked up by a mysterious cabdriver in front of the Sacher hotel and driven through the dark streets at high speed. "Have you got orders to kill me?" Martins shouts, but the driver ignores him, turning a corner and slamming on the brakes in front of an imposing building. The doors burst open, and the bewildered Martins finds himself at a Kafkaesque gathering of the "British Cultural Reeducation Service," where he is the guest of honor. He is introduced as "Mr. Holly Martins, from the other side," and a series of grotesque characters pepper him with questions: "Do you believe, Mr. Martins, in the stream of consciousness?" "Now Mr. James Joyce, where would you put him?" Hopelessly confused, Martins tells the disappointed group that his chief influence is Zane Grey.

In this scene, Greene is obviously satirizing middlebrow culture (how often he must have been asked the same questions), but he is also paying homage to the literature that shaped his career. The first book he read as a child was a potboiler called *Dixon Brett, Detective,* and his first act upon visiting Paris in the 1920s was to make his way to Sylvia Beach's bookshop, where he purchased a copy of *Ulysses.*[51] *The Third Man* brings these two literary extremes and two kinds of pleasure into melancholy union, and in the process it achieves a distensive or double-edged irony characteristic of Greene's thrillers in general: on the one hand, the emotional flourishes and intensities of melodrama are treated with modernist skepticism; but on the other hand, scenes of everyday life are haunted by a bloody and romantic passion.

THE DEATH CHAMBER

Historians have long known that Billy Wilder originally filmed a different ending to *Double Indemnity.* In the first version, insurance agent Walter Neff (Fred MacMurray) was put to death in a California gas chamber. Wilder once told an interviewer that Neff's death was among "two of the best scenes I've ever shot in my whole life" (the other being the original opening to *Sunset Boulevard*); it was, however, a controversial way to end the film, and he eventually dropped it because he felt that an execution was "unnecessary."[52]

Perhaps Wilder was correct to make this choice. Few would deny that *Double Indemnity* is a definitive film noir and one of the most influential movies in Hollywood history. Then again, Wilder may have cut something important because of pressure from both the studio and the Breen

Office, which insisted that the gas chamber sequence was "unduly grue-
some."[53] Unfortunately, critics have never really debated the issue; they
usually take the director's statements at face value, arguing that a protracted depiction of death by gas would have been unnecessary and in-
appropriately grim.

In what follows, I propose a contrary view, based in part on the closing pages of Wilder's and Raymond Chandler's script, and in part on the
internal evidence of the film itself. Walter Neff's death in the gas chamber (which was not suggested by the James M. Cain novella) is a logical
outgrowth of several important motifs in *Double Indemnity,* and it reveals the full implication of those motifs. Without it, claims investigator
Barton Keyes (Edward G. Robinson) seems a less morally complex character, audiences are left feeling a bit more comfortable, and the film's critique of American modernity becomes less apparent. (The only Hollywood feature of the period that treated the theme of industrial progress
with greater despair and sophistication was Welles's *Magnificent Am-
bersons,* which also lost its original ending.)

Even in its released form, *Double Indemnity* was an unorthodox film,
challenging nearly a decade of Production Code resistance to James M.
Cain's fiction. Although it contains no explicit sex or violence, it defies
the PCA in at least three ways, which were spelled out by the Breen Office in a March 15, 1943, report to Paramount: first, it depicts an attractive pair of murderers who "cheat the law and die at their own
hands"; second, it deals "improperly" with the theme of adultery; and
third, it is "replete with explicit details of the planning of [a] murder."
The story of how the script eventually gained Joseph Breen's approval
has been told by Leonard Leff and Jerrold Simmons in their useful history of Hollywood censorship, *The Dame in the Kimono,* and the
equally interesting story of Wilder's tense but productive collaboration
with novice screenwriter Chandler can be found in Frank MacShane's
Life of Raymond Chandler.[54] I see no reason to go over this familiar
ground, but I do want to show how the original ending of the film grew
out of the preoccupations of its various writers. For my purposes, the
important point to remember is that Wilder, Chandler, and Cain shared
an outsider's or modernist intellectual's ambivalence toward Los Angeles, where Cain's novel was set. Under Wilder's supervision, this ambivalence was intensified to the point where the city seemed less like the
urban sprawl described by Cain, and more like a dangerously seductive
Eldorado—a center of advanced capitalism, instrumental reason, and
death. The truly controversial aspect of the original film was not so much

its depiction of sex and murder, but its grimly sardonic vision of a "Taylorized" or assembly-line America, culminating in the gas chamber sequence.

Of the three writers connected with the project, Cain was the least inclined to see California in dystopian terms—this despite the fact that he began his career as a journalist and college teacher on the East Coast and served briefly as an editor of *The New Yorker*. Like Dashiell Hammett, Cain was a veteran of World War I who wrote about violence and who published with Blanche and Alfred Knopf.[55] The celebrated first sentence of *The Postman Always Rings Twice* was in fact a quintessential example of the hard-boiled manner: "They threw me off the hay truck about noon." But Cain avoided the pulps and did not write detective fiction; instead, he specialized in Dostoyevskian narratives of criminal psychology, transposed into lower-class America and strongly influenced by the naturalism of Theodore Dreiser, the modernism of Ring Lardner, and the cultural criticism of H. L. Mencken. He was therefore discussed alongside such "serious" writers as John O'Hara, William Saroyan, and Nathanael West, whom Edmund Wilson dubbed "poets of the tabloid murder."[56] Cain himself described his novels as a type of American tragedy, dealing with the "force of circumstance" that drives an individual to the "commission of a dreadful act" (quoted in Hoopes, 551). Actually, he was closer to the spirit of melodrama—not so much the melodrama of Hollywood, but of a certain kind of grand opera, in which the players are swept along on currents of violent desire. He often wrote about opera singers (in his youth he had wanted to become one), and he deliberately set out to "musicalize" emotions. His protagonists spoke in deadpan voices and lived in a world of pure kitsch, but they behaved like lovers in *Carmen*.

Although he was never especially good at writing film scripts, Cain enjoyed Hollywood.[57] In one of his most widely discussed essays, "Paradise" (1933), he attacked Southern California's automobile fetishism, bad food, and lack of organic culture; in the same breath, however, he declared that the state was populated by a more talented class of people than other parts of the country, and that "some sort of destiny awaits this place" (quoted in Hoopes, 226). He especially liked the sunny climate, and at one point he declared that all the great American novels had their roots in western populism. His approach to *Double Indemnity* seemed to confirm these mixed feelings, suggesting a symbiosis between modernity and literary modernism: he offered a darkly satiric account of the California insurance industry, but his style was simple, direct, speedy—perfectly expressive of modern industrial values. *Liberty,* the slick-paper magazine where the novella was serialized, was famous for printing the exact reading times of its stories, and it declared that Cain would require "2 hours, 50 minutes, and 7 seconds," or not much longer than a night at the movies. (According to Maurice Zolotow's *Billy Wilder in Hollywood,* Wilder claimed to have read the story in fifty-eight minutes because he did not move his lips.)

Despite his relatively sanguine attitude toward California, Cain's fiction had nothing to do with successful pioneers or virtuous common folk. The working title of *The Postman Always Rings Twice* was *Bar-B-Que,* which gives a sense of the social world he was trying to delineate. Repeatedly, he focused on the marginal, rootless types who were descended from what H. L. Mencken described as the "morons who pour [into Los Angeles] from the prairies and deserts," giving to "the chiropractic pathology the same high respect that they accord to the theology of Aimee McPherson and the art of Cecil De Mille."[58] Cain's strength as a writer lay in the fact that he treated these characters with Flaubertian detachment, making their destinies seem fatalistic, almost tragic. He also gave his doomed and relatively inarticulate narrators a keen awareness of their surroundings. Here, for example, is insurance salesman Walter Huff describing the Nirdlinger household in the first chapter of *Double Indemnity:*

> All I saw was a living room like every other living room in California, maybe a little more expensive than some, but nothing that any department store might deliver on one truck, lay out in one morning, and have the credit O.K. ready the same afternoon. The furniture was Spanish, the kind that looks pretty and sits stiff. The rug was one of those 12x15's that would have been Mexican except that it was made in Oakland, California. . . . All these Spanish houses have red velvet drapes that run on iron spears, and generally some red velvet wall tapestries to go with them. This was right out of the same can, with a coat-of-arms tapestry over the fireplace and a castle tapestry over the sofa.[59]

A character like Huff is a far cry from Raymond Chandler's Philip Marlowe, just as the mass-produced Nirdlinger home is quite different from the resplendent Sternwood mansion described at the beginning of *The Big Sleep.* (Nirdlinger works for an oil company, whereas Sternwood owns one.) Notice, however, that both dwellings have the same heraldic pretensions, and both narrators know the cost of everything. Given that Cain was under contract to another studio and could not be hired to adapt *Double Indemnity,* Chandler was a logical substitute (he even had the same publisher and eventually the same literary agent as Cain). But

Chandler was a less flat, more spectacular prose stylist, and when he wrote about California, he kept an older world in mind.

Although he was born in Chicago, Chandler was raised amid the property-holding Anglo-Irish of Waterford and London, and he was educated at Dulwich Preparatory School. In a fascinating series of notes on "American and English style" written in the 1940s, he claimed that "all the best American writing has been done by men who are, or at some time were, cosmopolitans. They found [in the United States] a certain freedom of expression, a certain richness of vocabulary, a certain wideness of interest. But they had to have European taste to use the material" (quoted in MacShane, *Life of Raymond Chandler*, 84). When he made this observation, he was obviously thinking of his own style, which is the product of an aestheticized, classically trained sensibility coming into contact with a demotic vocabulary. Notice, too, that all of his detective novels depend upon the narrative voice of Philip Marlowe—a synthesis of tough guy and cultural aristocrat, who views Los Angeles almost like a visitor from abroad. As Jacques Barzun observes, even Marlowe's name connotes "Englishness, Elegance, and Establishment."[60]

Chandler was not exactly a cosmopolitan, but he was not a typical American either. To his English publisher, he wrote, "It is possible that like [Max] Beerbohm I was born a half a century too late, and that I too belong to an age of grace. I could so easily have become everything our world has no use for. So I wrote for *Black Mask*. What a wry joke" (quoted in MacShane, *Life of Raymond Chandler*, 76). His novels have this same wistful tone, suggesting an intense nostalgia for Edwardian gallantry. Describing his attitude toward modern life, he once remarked, "I like people with manners, grace, some social intuition, and education slightly above the *Reader's Digest* level, people whose pride of living does not express itself in their kitchen gadgets and their automobiles. . . . although apart from that I should prefer an amiable drunk to Henry Ford" (quoted in MacShane, *Life of Raymond Chandler*, 77). He did not find many such people in California, and for that reason among others, his work was suffused with loneliness and romantic melancholy.

Even so, Chandler was the greatest of all writers about Los Angeles. He bestowed style upon the place, enabling his readers to enjoy the *flanerie* of driving past its beaches, mountainsides, and vividly contrasting neighborhoods. This experience, moreover, was always tinged with a deliciously Baudelarian atmosphere of decadence, corruption, and decay; hence a novel like *The Big Sleep* sometimes recalls T. S. Eliot's darkest, most reactionary visions of London. Everywhere Marlowe looks, he sees Jews, homosexuals, gangsters, and various pretenders or *arrivistes* from the Midwest. Even the domestic architecture strikes him as fake. "About the only part of a California house you can't put your foot through," he observes when he breaks into Arthur Gwynne Geiger's Laurel Canyon bungalow, "is the front door."[61]

Although Chandler made his living in the popular media, his novels were grounded in a familiar high-modernist belief that the modern world is cheap, insubstantial, and destructive of true culture. His contempt for the urban wasteland was reinforced by his personal frustration with capitalist America. He became a famous novelist late in his life, not long after his career as an executive in the California oil business failed, and he had an instinctive resentment of advertising agencies, slick-paper magazines, or any modernized organization that could pay for his skills. Thus when he came to work in Hollywood, he immediately commented upon "the strange psychological and spiritual kinship between the operations of big money business and the rackets," and he noted that the studio system was designed to "destroy the link between the writer and his subconscious" (quoted in MacShane, *Life of Raymond Chandler*, 123). With relatively little modification, this was exactly the way Philip Marlowe talked. Marlowe was, after all, a symbol of what Mike Davis describes as "the small businessman locked in struggle with gangsters, corrupt police and the parasitic rich (who were usually his employers as well)—a romanticized simulacrum of the writer's relationship to studio hacks and moguls" (38).

Not surprisingly, the Marlowe-Chandler voice was greatly modified in Hollywood movies of the 1940s, especially in Howard Hawks's amusingly sinister but quite apolitical adaptation of *The Big Sleep* (1945). However, that voice can be heard everywhere in the film version of *Double Indemnity*—not least in the affectionate banter between Walter Neff and Barton Keyes, who resemble a couple of writers employed by a film factory. These two men's conversations about the Dietrichson case are similar to a story conference at Paramount, and Walter's attempt to cheat the insurance company is not unlike Chandler's and Wilder's attempt to put one over on the censors and the studio. The implicit parallels between the insurance game and the movies were in fact so amusing to Wilder that he and art director Hal Pereira subtly reinforced them in the set designs: the interior of Walter Neff's apartment was modeled after the one Wilder himself had occupied at the Chateau Marmont when he began working for Paramount; and the offices of the "Pacific All-Risk Insurance Company" were copied almost exactly from the home offices of Paramount Pictures in New York City.

Chandler regarded Cain as a "faux naif" and a "Proust in greasy over-alls" (quoted in MacShane, *Life of Raymond Chandler*, 101). Perhaps for that reason, he and Wilder slightly raised the level of the novella's social atmosphere, making the sex less earthy and the characters more verbally clever. The leading players in the film are literate in a vaguely Hollywoodish way, rather like the sort of people one might encounter at the writer's table in a studio commissary: they use language as a weapon or a mode of seduction, they have a gift for repartee, and their longer speeches have a distinctive cadence and rhetorical flair. Except for the moments of Hitchcockian suspense (such as the scene in which the getaway car fails to start, or the scene in which Keyes shows up at Neff's apartment while Phyllis is there), all the best dramatic effects result from the dialogue. Walter occasionally uses a salesman's corny patter ("That's Neff with two *f*s, like in Philadelphia —you know the story." "What story?" "The Philadelphia Story"), but he also composes the world's most intriguing interoffice Dictaphone message. His narration is filled with self-deprecating wisecracks, and he has a writer's sensitivity to images, as when he walks around the Dietrichson living room, noting the stale ci-gar smoke, the dust motes, and "a bowl of those little red goldfish on a table behind the davenport." Partly because of this language, he some-times resembles Philip Marlowe—a romantic loner who is sentimentally attached to lovable eccentrics like Keyes or innocent waifs like Lola Die-trichson. The difference, of course, is that he lacks Marlowe's inde-pendence, high intelligence, and impossibly heroic integrity. In the final analysis, Walter is little more than a cog in a bureaucracy, and he can-not resist the blandishments of sex and money. With less talent and better looks, he would be the twin of failed writer Joe Gillis in *Sunset Boulevard*.

According to Cain, *Double Indemnity* was inspired by a story he once heard about a newspaper typesetter who, after many years of faithful service, could not resist allowing a salacious error to slip into a headline. A similar idea was carried over into the film: as Chandler might have put it, both versions of the story deal with an organization's attempt to "de-stroy the link" between a worker and his unconscious. In depicting the operations of big business, however, the film creates a much more pow-erful sense of alienation than Cain had done, and it has a greater propen-sity toward gallows humor. The last of these qualities can undoubtedly be attributed to Wilder, who was the true cosmopolitan among the var-ious authors of the project. Wilder had been a journalist in Vienna, a "gigolo" in Weimar Berlin, a scriptwriter for two celebrated German films (*People on Sunday* and *Emil and the Detectives*), and an émigré writer and director in Paris during the early 1930s. Fleeing Hitler, he made his way to Paramount via Mexico—much like the protagonist of his 1941 screenplay, *Hold Back the Dawn,* which, in its original form, was a comedy involving a man in a hotel room who tells his life story to a cockroach. He knew the seamy and the sophisticated sides of both Europe and Los Angeles, and he had been scarred by modern history. The grimmest irony of *Double Indemnity,* which he did not know at the time, was that his own mother had been gassed at Auschwitz only a year or two before the film began production.

Because of Wilder, *Double Indemnity* is profoundly indebted to Weimar Germany—not so much in its photographic style (which reviewers of the time compared with the prewar French cinema), but in its imagery of Fordist Amerika. On the level of language alone, as William Luhr points out, the film is pervaded with grimly deterministic metaphors of modern industry: the lovers promise to remain committed to one another "straight down the line"; Walter devises a clockwork murder involving a train, and when he puts his plan in motion he remarks that "the machinery had started to move and nothing could stop it"; later, looking back over his crime, he claims that fate had "thrown the switch" and that the "gears had meshed." These metaphors are reinforced by equally oppressive visuals; for instance, when we first enter the Pacific All-Risk Insurance Company, the camera tracks over Walter Neff's shoulder and looks down into a dark, cavernous room lined with rows of empty desks, each equipped with identical blotters and reading lamps. The design here is strongly reminiscent of German silent films such as Murnau's *Last Laugh* and of German-inspired Hollywood movies such as King Vidor's *Crowd,* Paul Fejos's *Lonesome,* and the Ernst Lubitsch episode of *If I Had a Million.* (It can also be seen in Welles's *Trial,* and in Wilder's later picture, *The Apartment.*) In all its manifestations, it signifies the tendency of modern society to turn workers into zombies or robots, like the enslaved populace of Lang's *Metropolis.*[62]

The theme of industrialized dehumanization is echoed in the relatively private offices on the second floor of the insurance company, which are almost interchangeable, decorated with nothing more than statistical charts and graphs. Meanwhile, Walter's apartment looks like a hotel room, and the funereal Dietrichson home is described as "one of those California Spanish houses that everyone was nuts about ten or fifteen years ago."[63] The public world is equally massified: when Walter realizes that Phyllis wants to murder her husband, he drinks a beer in his car at a drive-in restaurant; then he goes to a bowling alley at Third and Weston, where he bowls alone in an enormous room lined with identical lanes. The most surreal instance of mechanical reproduction, however, is Jerry's, "that big market up at Los Feliz," where Walter and Phyllis plan their crime. Walter and Phyllis hold sotto voce conversations across aisles filled with baby food, beans, macaroni, tomatoes, and seemingly anything else that can be packaged and arranged in neat rows; they talk about murder in public, but the big store makes them anonymous, virtually invisible to shoppers.[64]

Phyllis (Barbara Stanwyck) is associated with nearly all the locales I have been describing, whereas Lola Dietrichson (Jean Heather) is photographed against the forests of the Hollywood hills and the beaches at Santa Monica. Wilder's melodramatic allegory could not be more obvious: the bad girl represents Culture and the good girl represents Nature. Here again Wilder's indebtedness to Weimar is evident. As I have already indicated, German cinema of the 1920s often used the decadent eroticism of the late nineteenth century to express growing fears of the "new woman." The flapper in *Pandora's Box* and the city woman in *Sunrise* were intended to suggest an urbanized, mass-cultural type that the Germans both loved and hated. Phyllis belongs in the same category; indeed, she is so bad that she seems like modernity and kitsch incarnate—a realist version of the "false Maria" in *Metropolis*.

This implication becomes especially clear when we place the movie Phyllis alongside the femme fatale in Cain's novella, who is an ordinary, rather earthy woman with a "washed out face" and a "shape to set a man nuts" (10). The character portrayed by Barbara Stanwyck is much more blatantly provocative and visibly artificial; her ankle bracelet, her lacquered lipstick, her sunglasses, and above all her chromium hair give her a cheaply manufactured, metallic look. In keeping with this synthetic quality, her sex scenes are almost robotic, and she reacts to murder with an icy calm. "She was perfect," Walter remarks at one point. "No nerves, not a tear, not even a blink of the eye."[65]

Unlike Cain, Wilder and Chandler create a soulless, modernized female whom they can easily kill off (even though she seems to need a lover's embrace in the moment before she dies). They also make Walter's *amour fou* look affectless. Their whole point seems to be that under modernity, lovemaking is reified and "mechanical." As a result, despite all its suggestive dialogue, *Double Indemnity* generates most of its warmth when it dramatizes the platonic relationship between Walter Neff and Barton Keyes. Throughout, these two organization men form a sort of Odd Couple: one is tall and handsome, the other short and plain; one

FIGURE 15. "Jerry's, that big market up at Los Feliz." (Museum of Modern Art Stills Archive.)

smokes cigarettes, the other cigars; one is a "peddler, gladhander, back-slapper," the other a quintessential analyst and statistician; one is a criminal, the other a detective. They are nevertheless alike in their regard for one another's skill and in their mutual contempt for their boss. Keyes enjoys lecturing Walter about the insurance business and at one point offers to recommend him for a promotion to the claims department. For his part, Walter recognizes that behind Keyes's gruff exterior is a sharp intelligence and "a heart as big as a house." One of the ironies of Walter's crime is that in betraying his employer, he is also betraying a friend and a father substitute; hence his interoffice message, which is not only a confession of guilt but also an admission of love.

The last scene of the released print of *Double Indemnity* makes this Chandleresque theme of male friendship and betrayal clear. In classic fashion, it repeats and reverses two motifs from earlier in the picture: Keyes provides Walter with a match, and Walter says "I love you, too," in a more serious tone than he has used before. Notice also that Keyes is given a kind of moral authority. As he predicted in a speech containing one of the film's most vivid metaphors of mechanical destiny, the killers of H. S.

FIGURE 16. "She was perfect. No nerves, not a tear, not even a blink of the eye." (Museum of Modern Art Stills Archive.)

Dietrichson have stepped onto a trolley line, and it's a one-way trip: at the end of the line is death. Keyes becomes a saddened, paternal on-looker—a wise man who, according to Richard Schickel's BFI monograph on the film, should never have been "spurned" by a fatally "mixed up guy" like Walter.[66]

Schickel admires this ending, but he is incorrect when he suggests that Wilder invented it as a substitute for the execution scene (63–64). Actually, there were three possible conclusions to *Double Indemnity,* and none of them involved new material. According to the final drafts of the screenplay in the Motion Picture Academy Library in Los Angeles, the released print is merely a bit shorter than the other two possibilities, omitting not only the execution sequence but also a line of dialogue that was spoken by Walter just after he said "I love you." In the intermediate version, as sirens are heard in the background, the collapsed and bleeding Walter makes a final request: "At the end of that trolley line, just as I get off, you be there to say good bye. Will you, Keyes?" The longest of the three versions went on to show Keyes at the penitentiary, honoring his friend's wishes.

I suspect that Schickel is also wrong when he argues that Wilder's original ending would have been a mistake in tone that would have placed
too great an emphasis on Walter's "criminality" (62). On the contrary,
the execution described in the longest version of the script greatly increases our sympathy for Walter, all the while raising questions about
the criminality of the state. It also provides a tragic recognition scene for
Keyes, who is shaken out of his moral complacency. This last point is especially important, because Keyes functions as a representative of the insurance company. Although he approaches his work with the intuitive
flair of an artist and the intellectual intensity of a scientist, he remains a
loyal agent of industrial rationality—a talented bureaucrat who, in effect, has helped to create the office building, the drive-in restaurant, the
supermarket, and all the other landmarks of modern Los Angeles that
the film relentlessly criticizes.

Early on, Keyes complains that he has been put in charge of making
sure that "fast-talking salesmen" don't foul up the organization. Walter
responds, "You love it. . . . you're so conscientious you're driving yourself crazy." Actually, Keyes's chief problem is that he is too vain about
his abilities. He has served his company for twenty-six years, even though
he knows that the chief executive is a fool; all the while, he carries a "little
man" inside himself, and he tells Walter that "every time one of these
phonies comes along it ties knots in my stomach." One of the many
virtues of Wilder's original ending is that this complex, brilliantly acted
character would have been made to confront his inner demon and to experience poetic justice. Keyes would have been brought face-to-face with
the culminating instance of instrumental reason, the "end of the line"
for industrial culture: the California gas chamber.

Interestingly, one of Joseph Breen's major objections to *Double Indemnity* (voiced in a 1935 letter to L. B. Mayer and repeated in a March
15, 1943, report to Paramount) was that the leading characters are murderers who cheat the law and die at their own hands. Chandler and Wilder
responded by making sure that at least one of the killers would be left
for the law to punish. They borrowed a plot device from *The Postman
Always Rings Twice*, which is narrated by a man who is scheduled to die
in the electric chair, and they provided a detailed execution scene. For
the original version of *Double Indemnity*, Paramount built an exact
replica of the gas chamber, depicting it as a modern, sanitized apparatus
for administering official death sentences. At considerable expense,
Wilder photographed the step-by-step procedure of execution, emphasizing its coldly mechanical efficiency.[67] There was no blood, no agonized

screaming, and, for once in the movie, almost no dialogue. Much of the sequence was shot from Walter's point of view, looking through glass windows at the spectators outside the chamber—an angle creating a subtle parallel between the chamber and the "dark room" of a movie theater. When the fatal pellets dropped, clouds of gas obscured the windows, and we could barely make out Keyes standing amid the witnesses, turning his head away. Soon afterward, a doctor entered the chamber to pronounce Walter dead. According to the script, the original film ended as follows:

THE DEATH CHAMBER

The door connecting with the ante-chamber opens. A guard comes through.
Guard: That's all gentlemen. Vacate the chamber, please.

The guard withdraws and closes the door by which he entered. The witnesses slowly start to file out. A guard has opened the outer door. The witnesses put on their hats as they pass through. A few go close to the windows of the gas chamber to look in at the dead man before they leave.

All the witnesses have now left except Keyes, who stares, shocked and tragic, beyond the door. The guard goes to him and touches his arm, indicating to him that he must leave. Keyes glances for the last time towards the gas chamber and slowly moves to go out.

CORRIDOR OUTSIDE THE DEATH CHAMBER

CAMERA SHOOTING IN THROUGH THE OPEN DOOR AT KEYES, who is just turning to leave. Keyes comes slowly out into the dark, narrow corridor. His hat is on his head now, his overcoat is pulled around him loosely. He walks like an old man. He takes eight or ten steps, then mechanically reaches a cigar out of his vest pocket and puts it in his mouth. His hands, in the now familiar gesture, begin to pat his pockets for matches.

Suddenly he stops, with a look of horror on his face. He stands rigid, pressing a hand against his heart. He takes the cigar out of his mouth and goes slowly on toward the door, CAMERA PANNING with him. When he has almost reached the door, the guard stationed there throws it wide, and a blaze of sunlight comes in from the open prison yard outside.

Keyes slowly walks out into the sunshine, a forlorn and lonely man.

Until someone rescues this scene from the Paramount vaults, we will never know if it is superior to the current version, and even then there may be room for debate. One thing, however, is clear: Keyes's lonely walk out of the prison would have thrown a shadow over everything that preceded it. It was not until *Sunset Boulevard* and *Ace in the Hole* that Wilder would produce such a savage critique of modernity. Although the released version of his famous thriller remains an iconoclastic satire that challenges the censors, it is a lighter entertainment than the original and a

FIGURES 17–18. Two publicity stills from the lost ending of
Double Indemnity (1944). (Museum of Modern Art Stills Archive.)

much easier product for Hollywood to market. (According to the Paramount press book, photographs of Barbara Stanwyck in her wig and tight sweater were circulated to American soldiers overseas, and Edward G. Robinson's performance enabled the studio to obtain a tie-in from the Cigar Institute of America.) No matter how much we admire the film that was exhibited in 1944, the form of cinema that the French described as noir is probably better exemplified by another *Double Indemnity*, which we have yet to see.

FROM DARK FILMS TO BLACK LISTS

Censorship and Politics

> The peculiarity of censorship, and one of its most noticeable
> characteristics—in the absence of which we would never be able to
> grasp its existence—is that things are always managing to get past it.
> CHRISTIAN METZ, *The Imaginary Signifier*, 1982

Hollywood's self-appointed censors have always tried to remain above the factional and potentially unprofitable level of national politics, claiming that their purpose is transcendentally moral. The 1930 Production Code, for example, described commercial movies as *"entertainment"* and *"art,"* as distinct from "pictures intended for churches, schools, lecture halls, educational movements, social reform movements, etc."[1] For his part, Will Hays repeatedly argued that "entertainment is the commodity for which the public pays at the box office. Propaganda disguised as entertainment would be neither honest salesmanship nor honest showmanship."[2]

Hays's logic was typical of the American right wing throughout the 1930s, and it seems remarkably disingenuous. After all, the Production Code itself was a manifestly ideological or propagandistic document, containing prohibitions not only against lustful kissing, visible pregnancy, adultery, prostitution, and "perversion," but also against miscegenation. One of its three "General Principles" was that "law, natural or human, shall not be ridiculed, nor shall sympathy be created for its violation"

(Steinberg, 461). Elsewhere, it contained specific rules against criticism of the police, the clergy, the U.S. government, and officials of foreign nations. Joseph Breen, the chief of the Motion Picture Producers and Distributors of America (MPPDA), and Martin Quigley, the coauthor of the original Code provisions, were both Catholics, and both were anti-Semitic.[3] Breen was a working-class intellectual who sometimes approved of social-problem movies. But such distinctions may not have mattered in the long run, because the process of review itself tended to enforce a conservative "line." Consider the first page of the standard report form used by the Breen Office during the 1940s:[4]

ROLE	CHARACTERIZATION (straight/comic; sympathetic/unsympathetic/indifferent)
Leading Roles	
Professions:	Banker _____
	Lawyer _____
	Doctor _____
	Journalist _____
Public Officials:	Judge _____
	J. P. _____
	Police _____
	District Attorney _____
	Sheriff _____
Religious Workers:	Catholic _____
	Protestant _____
	Jewish _____
Races or Nationalities:	_____
Miscellaneous:	_____

LIQUOR SHOWN AT nightclub__ bar__ saloon__ home__ other__
DRINKING none__ little__ much__
COURT SCENES, how treated? dignified__ comic__
REIGIOUS CEREMONIES, how treated? dignified__ comic__
ADULTERY__ ILLICIT SEX__ DIVORCE__ MARRIAGE__ SUICIDE__
GAMBLING__
TYPES OF CRIMES _____
NUMBER OF KILLINGS _____
OTHER VIOLENCE _____
FATES OF CRIMINALS _____

Given such a form, it seems remarkable that any of the classic films noirs could have been produced at all. In *This Gun for Hire, The Glass Key,* and *Laura,* the line between "sympathetic" and "unsympathetic" characters is blurred, and criminals often seem more appealing, or at least more authentic, than representatives of law and order; in *The Lady from*

Shanghai, The File on Thelma Jordan, and *Where the Sidewalk Ends,* most of the police officers, judges, and district attorneys are corrupt and brutal; in *Ace in the Hole, The Big Clock,* and *While the City Sleeps,* the leading journalists and magazine editors are predatory and murderous. All such films are permeated with alcohol and illicit sex, and in at least one instance—Val Lewton's *Seventh Victim*—suicide is treated as a poetic act.

The censors, however, always saw to it that evil was punished in these pictures and that sin or corruption was depicted with a degree of restraint. The Breen Office policy was evident in the monthly report of May 31, 1941, in which Joseph Breen announced to Will Hays that the MPPDA had just completed reviewing one hundred and ten scripts in five categories: "social problem" (sixteen, including *The Shanghai Gesture*), "crime/horror" (forty-three, including *The Maltese Falcon*), "musical" (fourteen), "western" (thirty-two), and "miscellaneous" (forty-five). Of the total, five were rejected for "illicit sex and drunkenness"—among them, *The Maltese Falcon,* which, according to a PCA report to Jack Warner, required the following revisions: Joel Cairo should not be characterized as a "pansy type"; the "suggestion of illicit sex between Spade and Brigid" should be eliminated; there should be less drinking; there should be no physical contact between Iva and Spade "other than that of decent sympathy"; Gutman should say "By Gad!" less often; and "Spade's speech about District Attorneys should be rewritten to get away from characterizing [them] as men who will do anything to further their careers."

A similar pattern of objections can be seen in the Breen Office reports on other celebrated films noirs. A November 2, 1943, review of *Laura* insisted that Waldo Lydecker must be portrayed as a "wit and debonair man-about-town" and that "there can never be any suggestion that [he] and Laura have been more than friends"; meanwhile, scenes of police brutality had to be downplayed, along with the drinking at Laura's apartment. An April 13, 1944, report on *Farewell, My Lovely* informed the producers that "there must, of course, be nothing of the 'pansy' characterization about Marriott"; by the same token, Mr. Grayle could not "escape punishment" by committing suicide, and the scenes of pistol-whipping, drinking, and illicit sex would have to be reduced or treated indirectly.

If we did not already have the evidence of the films themselves, the censorship reports of the period reveal that classic noir was almost obsessed with sexual perversity. The villains in these pictures tend to be homosexual aesthetes (*The Maltese Falcon, Laura, Phantom Lady*) or homosexual Nazi sadists (*Brute Force*) who threaten the values of a democratic and somewhat proletarian masculinity. Breen Office censors were especially concerned about such characters, just as they were about realistic depictions of heterosexual passion. "When people talk about realism," Joe Breen observed, "they usually talk about filth" (quoted in Leff and Simmons, 145). To gain Breen's approval of love scenes, directors learned the art of omission. In *Double Indemnity,* when Phyllis visits Walter's apartment and kisses him for the first time, he immediately lights a cigarette, mixes a couple of highballs, and begins planning the murder— behavior that seems almost laughable by contemporary standards, with little of the steamy urgency of James M. Cain's novel. Even so, the film manages to imply that Walter and Phyllis go to bed with each other. At one point she puts her head on his shoulder and cries softly, like the rain on the windows. The camera tracks backward and we dissolve to the insurance office, where Walter speaks into the Dictaphone, explaining his motives to Keyes. (These motives have less to do with sex than with a desire to cheat the insurance company and make a great deal of money.) After a few moments, another dissolve returns us to the apartment: time has passed, and Walter and Phyllis are at either end of a sofa; he is reclining and smoking a cigarette while she reapplies her makeup.

Hollywood in the 1940s always depicted sexual intercourse through symbolism and ellipsis. In *The Maltese Falcon,* Spade bends over to kiss Brigid, who is lying seductively on his couch, and the camera moves past him toward an open window, showing the "gunsel" Wilmer on the street outside; the image fades, time passes, and when Spade and Brigid meet a day or so later, they embrace and call each other sweetheart. In *Possessed,* David Sutton (Van Heflin) and Louise Graham (Joan Crawford) have obviously just been to bed together, even though they are shown fully clothed and at opposite ends of a room: David smokes a cigarette and plays Schumann on the piano ("making love" to the instrument, as he says) while Louise moves about ecstatically and contemplates going for a swim in a moonlit lake that we can see outside a window.

Scenes such as these remind us of what Christian Metz calls the "peculiarity" of censorship, which always allows things to pass around it, "like the sluices you sometimes see at the mouths of rivers, where the water gets through one way or another."[5] The censor (whether we are speaking of the state, the church, or the superego) seldom leaves a blank spot or an *X* across a scene. "You can *see* the censor," Metz remarks, much as you can see the workings of secondary revision in dreams; usu-

ally it manifests itself as a slight incoherence or displacement (such as
the water imagery in classic noir), and from the point of view of aesthetics, it sometimes has salutary results. Thus Raymond Borde and Étienne Chaumeton contend that the Breen Office had a paradoxically "pos-
itive" effect on film noir: it helped to make pictures like *The Big Sleep*
and *The Lady from Shanghai* seem confusing and dreamlike, and in many
cases "the necessity for innuendo promoted a type of lighting that could
not but enhance the suggestive power of the images" (19).

Interestingly, the major challenge to Joseph Breen's sovereignty during the 1930s and 1940s came not from gangster movies or stories of
middle-class murder, which usually involved repression and innuendo,
but from costume pictures and westerns.[6] The most notorious instance
of a refusal to obey the Production Code was Howard Hughes's exploitation of Jane Russell as a busty cowgirl in *The Outlaw* (filmed in
1941, released in 1943, and rereleased in 1946). An even more significant breakthrough had already been achieved by David Selznick, whose
multimillion-dollar production of *Gone with the Wind* received Code approval in 1939. Selznick's loud battle to retain the word *damn* was little
more than a clever publicity gimmick; his real victories were in drama-
tizing the pain of childbirth and in retaining the novel's bodice-ripping
sexual conventions. His assistant, Val Lewton, wrote him that preview
audiences loved "what we term the rape scene. . . . They liked to have
Gable compel Scarlett to sit in the chair and listen to him, and when he
picked her up and ran up the stairs with her, the applause was almost
equal to that extended to Babe Ruth when he hit a home run" (quoted
in Leff and Simmons, 106–7).

Hollywood's treatment of sex was only slightly liberalized in 1945,
when Will Hays announced his retirement and Warner Brothers temporarily withdrew from the MPPDA. *Duel in the Sun* (1946), Selznick's
epic tale of *l'amour fou* on the prairie, was ballyhooed in almost the same
fashion as *The Outlaw,* and it attracted most of its viewers because it
seemed daring and scandalous. Among films in this period that might be
classified as noir, Alfred Hitchcock's *Rope* (1948) was unusually controversial; initially banned in Chicago, it was exhibited to "adults only"
in Spokane, Memphis, and Seattle—but only after its opening murder
by strangulation had been cut. Hitchcock escaped broader and more official censorship chiefly because he based *Rope* on a prestigious West End
play and because his treatment of amorality and homosexual love was
every bit as ironic, indirect, and dandified as the two characters who commit the murder. He ruthlessly satirized the bourgeois guests at the film's

dinner party, but he made sure that he never overtly violated the standards of the Production Code. He even cast folksy James Stewart as the man who unmasks the villains, giving him a ringing, last-act speech against evil. Amazingly, advertisements for the film included an endorsement from J. Edgar Hoover, a closeted homosexual and celebrated watchdog against "filth," who proclaimed, "Never such terrific suspense! Leaves you breathless."

Marc Vernet has argued that, "so far as the female body is concerned," postwar American thrillers represented "a return to the *status quo ante,* to the state of censorship prior to 1933."[7] But even the most daring of these movies were noticeably lacking in the forthright bawdiness and sexual display of the Depression years. None of the femmes fatales in classic films noirs could be seen in the braless, seminude costumes that had been worn by gangster's molls, chorus girls, and nightclub sophisticates in films such as *Blonde Venus, Public Enemy,* and *I Am a Fugitive from a Chain Gang.* Joseph Breen refused to approve the rerelease of the 1931 *Maltese Falcon* precisely because "the dame in the kimono" (Bebe Daniels) wore insufficient clothing; as if in response, the 1941 production garbed Mary Astor in a ladylike, almost schoolmarmish dress. Provocative thrillers such as *Double Indemnity, The Postman Always Rings Twice, Gilda,* and *Scarlet Street* relied chiefly on fetishized detail—an ankle bracelet, a white scarf, a glove, or a long sweep of hair.[8] They also slowed down the dramatic action and emphasized the intimate rituals of smoking and drinking in dimly lit rooms. During the period, studio publicists began to treat relatively innocuous kissing scenes as if they were daring. In 1946, MGM claimed that a lengthy kiss between John Garfield and Lana Turner in *The Postman Always Rings Twice* was timed with a stopwatch to make sure it did not exceed censorship regulations. In the same year, the Selznick studio announced that Cary Grant and Ingrid Bergman's extended embrace in *Notorious*—an embrace accompanied by a good deal of low-voiced conversation—was the longest kiss in screen history.

To find truly systemic violations of Breen Office morality or "good taste" in American mass culture during these years, one needs to look not at movies but at paperback books. Beginning around 1948, New York publishers of mysteries and realist novels began to use pulp-style covers; as a result, images of semiclothed women in erotic poses suddenly appeared in bus stations and drugstores all over the country. The trend reached its peak in the early 1950s, and it gradually influenced Hollywood thrillers, including two striking examples of 1953: *Niagara,* a Technicolored saga of passion and murder featuring Marilyn Monroe; and *I, the Jury,* a 3-D exploitation film based on Mickey Spillane's hugely successful paperback novel.[9] Both pictures were situated somewhere between the brooding, repressed eroticism of old-fashioned Bogart movies and the emerging hedonism of *Playboy* and James Bond.

It was violence, not sex, that accounted for the most visible changes in the standards of motion-picture censorship during the 1940s and early 1950s—changes that allow us to speak more accurately of a "return" to 1933. In his September 1946 review of *The Killers,* for example, James Agee remarks that various scenes in the picture are reminiscent of the "calculated violence" that was "commonplace in old gangster films."[10] But the postwar thrillers also seemed more downbeat and perverse, perhaps because the war and its aftermath created a vision of ontological evil and a growing appetite for sadism. Throughout the war, the PCA disapproved of propaganda films that showed explicit scenes of torture; even so, elaborate offscreen whippings and brutal punishments became de rigueur in films such as *Man Hunt* (1941), *Hitler's Children* (1942), *Behind the Rising Sun* (1943), *The Purple Heart* (1944), and *13 Rue Madeleine* (1946). Hollywood regularly portrayed the Germans and Japanese as sexually twisted killers who loved to inflict pain, and this vaguely eroticized, "psychological" imagery contributed to the psychotic villains portrayed at almost the same time by Richard Widmark, Dan Dureya, and Raymond Burr. Because of the war, screen violence also became more frighteningly realistic. Within a few years after the conflict began, unprecedented scenes of maimed and dying bodies could be seen in news magazines and combat documentaries. As the fighting drew to an end, the sense of victory was bound up with a vision of horror. Advertising for the short documentary *With the Marines at Tarawa* (1944) promised audiences "the real thing at last—no punches pulled, no gory details omitted," and in the next year, the Breen Office censored none of the concentration camp footage that the U.S. military supplied to commercial newsreels (see Doherty, 36–57).

Once victory came, feature movies evoked sober memories of the recent carnage, and for a while melodramatic fight scenes no longer looked graceful and bloodless. The newsreel footage of concentration camps made its way directly into *The Stranger* (1946), in which a sheltered daughter of a state supreme court justice (Loretta Young) is given a private showing of Nazi atrocities. In other films, small acts of violence were perversely frightening—as when William Bendix steps on Mark Stevens's thumb in *The Dark Corner* (1946). The tendency toward sadism was especially evident in a series of films about boxing: *The Set-Up* (1949), based on Joseph Marsh's narrative poem of the 1930s; *Champion* (1949), inspired by Ring Lardner's short story of the 1920s; and *The Harder They Fall* (1956), Humphrey Bogart's last screen appearance, from Budd Schulberg's original screenplay. These pictures were scarcely less bloody than Martin Scorsese's *Raging Bull* (1980), but they used violence in a more socially conscious way, fusing prewar images of economic depression with anxiety about fascism and cataclysmic destruction. In political terms, they had an obvious relationship with films made by former members of the Group Theater and the Actors' Studio—films such as *Golden Boy* (1939), *Body and Soul* (1947), *On the Waterfront* (1954), and *Somebody Up There Likes Me* (1956). Indeed, they constitute one of several junctures at which classic film noir is nearly indistinguishable from Odets-style social realism and from the larger history of the proletarian or "ghetto" novel.

All of which brings us to the issue of control over Hollywood's explicit politics. And here again we are involved in a return to the 1930s. As movie historians have frequently remarked, several of the most celebrated films noirs echo the New Deal populism of earlier pictures such as *I Am a Fugitive from a Chain Gang, Fury,* and *You Only Live Once.* This type of social melodrama was by no means the exclusive province of the left wing, but it was inflected by the coalition of liberal and socialist interests that flourished throughout the Depression and World War II—especially by the writers, actors, and directors who worked with the Group or the Mercury Theater, and who were interested in social and psychological "darkness." The connection between noir and the culture of the Popular Front is sometimes deemphasized, however, because critics usually claim that Hollywood's dark cinema expresses an unusually bleak, sardonic, and apolitical attitude toward society. Paul Schrader, for example, argues that the defining quality of noir is a "hopeless" and "relentlessly cynical" mood ("Notes on *Film Noir*," 169); along similar lines, most of the contributors in the Alain Silver and Elizabeth Ward encyclopedia contend that noir is essentially pessimistic or perverse. For these and many other commentators, the noir category as a whole should be kept slightly distinct from both utopian entertainment and every type of social-problem picture.

There are problems with such assumptions. Leaving aside the question of how a supposedly depressing type of cinema could have survived for two decades and then become an object of affection and nostalgia, there is simply no empirical evidence to support the notion that noir involved a cynical rejection of politics. On the contrary, most of the 1940s directors subsequently associated with the form—including Orson Welles, John Huston, Edward Dmytryk, Jules Dassin, Joseph Losey, Robert Rossen, Abraham Polonsky, and Nicholas Ray—were members of Hollywood's committed left-wing community. Among the major crime writers who provided source material for dark thrillers, Dashiell Hammett, Graham Greene, and Eric Ambler were Marxists to one degree or another, and Raymond Chandler and James M. Cain were widely regarded as social realists. Among what Robert Sklar has described as the major "city boy" actors of the period, Bogart and John Garfield, who played veterans of the Lincoln Brigade in *Casablanca* and *The Fallen Sparrow* (1943), were icons respectively of liberalism and leftist radicalism. Meanwhile, the credits for noir screenplays usually included such names as Albert Maltz, Howard Kotch, Waldo Salt, and Dalton Trumbo, all of whom were eventually blacklisted, and these screenplays were often based on literature by such politically engaged figures as Kenneth Fearing, Vera Caspary, Daniel Fuchs, and Ira Wolfert.

There is good reason to conclude that the first decade of American film noir was largely the product of a socially committed fraction or artistic movement in Hollywood, composed of "Browderite" communists (after Earl Browder, head of the American Communist Party) and "Wallace" Democrats (after Henry Wallace, the radical vice president and potential successor to Franklin Delano Roosevelt).[11] This movement is somewhat downplayed by Borde and Chaumeton, who emphasize the anarchic, antisocial qualities of noir and who initially argued that the form died off with the rise of neorealist *policiers* in the late 1940s. The *Cahiers* critics and subsequent American commentators tended to depoliticize noir even further, thereby obscuring the fact that many of the best thrillers of the 1940s and early 1950s were expressions of the Popular Front and the radical elements of the New Deal.[12] A more accurate account would show that although the noir category viewed as a whole has no essential politics, it has formative roots in the left culture of the Roosevelt years— a culture that was repressed, marginalized, and virtually extinguished during the postwar decade, when noir took on increasingly cynical and even right-wing implications.[13] During the 1950s, the congressional hunts for communists in Hollywood were themselves based on a kind of noir scenario and were crucially important to the history of American crime movies, affecting not only their politics and their doom-laden atmosphere, but also their reception by later generations.[14]

Even before the organized attack on left-wing films began, the liberal or anarchic-libertarian elements in Hollywood were closely monitored by guardians of morality and officials of the U.S. government. To fully appreciate the degree to which every type of filmmaking encountered censorship, we should recall that the Breen Office was not the only agency capable of overseeing a movie's content. Throughout World War II, the Bureau of Motion Pictures (BMP) and the Office of War Information (OWI) helped to promote official government policy; the War Department and the various branches of the armed services were charged with protecting military security; and the U.S. Office of Censorship was given the responsibility of reviewing all pictures intended for foreign export. At another level, organizations such as the Writers' Guild of America, the Writers' Mobilization Congress at UCLA, and the secretly conducted Communist Party Writers' Clinics helped to encourage tendentious, antifascist, and relatively upbeat screenplays. After the war, the House Committee on Un-American Activities (HUAC) became strongly interested in movies, and a wide range of quasi-scientific studies of popular culture led to new forms of conservative repression. In fact, when we take into account all the governmental and semiofficial organizations of the Left and the Right who were involved in making judgments about film, the period between 1941 and 1955 was probably the most regulated and scrutinized era in the history of American entertainment.

During this period, Hollywood's darkly psychological thrillers were attacked not only by the Breen Office, but also by prominent Communist Party intellectuals. John Howard Lawson, the first president of the Screen Writers' Guild, argued in 1935 that "the function of revolutionary drama is to circumvent a Freudian escape from truths people wish to avoid" (quoted in Schwartz, 135). He and other members of Hollywood's radical Left criticized films such as *This Gun for Hire* because of their "psychoanalytic" properties and because they made gangsters or hoodlums into heroes of the fight against fascism. After the war, films of a similar type were examined and criticized by an array of liberal "experts" and pop sociologists, who described *The Big Sleep, The Killers,* and *The Dark Corner* as sinister mirrors of American angst and moral decay. In a year-end review for *The Nation* in 1946, James Agee reluctantly admitted that sociological interpretation of these films "as practiced by Dr. Sigfried Kracauer and Barbara Deming" might have a certain value; as far as he was concerned, however, "the most sinister single thing that happened during the movie year was the emergence of just this kind of analysis." It seemed to him that "the function once performed by clubwomen and the nastier kinds of church pressure groups" was now

being taken over "by the kind of people who used most earnestly to op-
pose priggishness" (238).

New forms of "cultural anthropology" and "psychocultural" analysis were being produced, laying the groundwork for a glib and often tau-
tological style of academic criticism that still flourishes today. Even a celebrated amateur like John Houseman got into the act, writing a
think-piece for *Vogue* in which he implicitly criticized his former collaborators Raymond Chandler and Orson Welles for catering to the zeitgeist by making "tough" movies about a "land of enervated, frightened
people with spasms of high vitality but a low moral sense—a hung-over
people with confused objectives groping their way through a twilight of
insecurity and corruption."[15] The cold-war sociologists, however, were
as nothing compared to the Republican-controlled U.S. Congress, which
in 1947 began its purge of the Hollywood Left. In that year, the coalition of radicals and liberals that had been shaped by the New Deal and
World War II was torn asunder, and America's residual Popular Front
came to an end. The conservatives who had been relatively silent during
the war used many of the same "analytic" techniques as the highbrow
sociological critics. Moreover, as Nancy Lynn Schwartz has shown, they
were able to achieve a quick victory through two forms of censorship:
first was an "objective" pressure on filmmakers via organizations such
as the Breen Office, the Johnston Office, the Tenney committee in the
California senate, the Thomas committee in Washington, the Hearst
press, and the Motion Picture Alliance; and second was the creation of
an insidious atmosphere of self-censorship or "before-the-fact editing of
writers and other creators in the industry who found themselves avoiding the controversial" (255).

The conservative strategy paid great dividends in 1947, the *annus
mirabilis* of film noir, which was also the year of the Taft-Hartley Act
(forbidding communists in labor unions); of an executive order from the
White House requiring government employees to take loyalty oaths; of
the HUAC investigations; and of a speech by Eric Johnston, newly elected
president of the Motion Picture Association of America (MPAA), calling for more movies that extolled virtue and "the American way of life."
Hollywood did not stop producing dark thrillers in 1947, but beginning
at about that time, a number of skilled craftspeople who had used such
films for socially critical purposes were either silenced, destroyed, or
driven underground. The purge was made all the more easy by an economic downturn in the industry, which solidified the power of manage-
ment and changed the structure of the old studio system. Looking back

on the period, radical actress Karen Morley commented, "The right wing rolled over us like a tank over wildflowers" (quoted in Schwartz, 253).

Warning signs of the Left's imminent defeat could be seen throughout 1946 and 1947, at the very moment when writers and directors were becoming intensely interested in the fate of returning veterans. In order to demonstrate how the various forces of official repression and artistic resistance operated in those two years, let me pause here to consider the climate of "moral" and political censorship surrounding a pair of representative films noirs, both of which were concerned with home-front readjustment. The first is a Raymond Chandler thriller with liberal overtones, and the second is a manifest social-problem picture. Each production encountered massive intervention from studio bosses, industrial agents, and government bureaucrats. However, each managed to suggest unorthodox or politically "dark" ideas.

BOURBON WITH A BOURBON CHASER

Raymond Chandler wrote the screenplay for *The Blue Dahlia* (1946) as an action vehicle for Paramount's Alan Ladd, whom he regarded as a "small boy's idea of a tough guy."[16] At the same time, he made typically evocative, almost panoramic use of Los Angeles, and he managed to include mordant commentary on postwar America. In keeping with the spirit of his novels, Paramount photographed the exterior scenes in locales such as the Sunset Strip, Malibu, Griffith Park Observatory, the Hollywood bus terminal, and "canteen row" on Cahunega Boulevard. An uncredited writer named "R. McGowan" also worked briefly on the script, but the completed picture is marked by Chandler's distinctive settings and verbal style; it is, in fact, his only original screenplay (not counting the unfilmed *Playback*), and it won him his second Academy Award nomination. Almost from the beginning, however, *The Blue Dahlia* was a troubled project, subject to major revisions and fraught with real danger for its author.

The chief problem, according to producer John Houseman, was Chandler himself, who almost died trying to complete his assignment. In *Front and Center,* the second volume of his charmingly urbane memoirs, Houseman claims that sometime during the last days of 1944, the frail, nearly burnt-out Chandler showed him 120 pages of an incomplete novel that could easily be turned into a film script.[17] Houseman and co-producer Joseph Sistrom immediately persuaded Paramount to buy the property for Alan Ladd, who was only months away from being re-

inducted into the army. Chandler was given the job of screenwriter, and
production began within forty-eight hours of the purchase. Houseman
recalls that Chandler "delivered the first half of his script—about forty-
five minutes of film—in under three weeks, at the rate of four or five pages
a day" (137). The job of casting went smoothly, and shooting was soon
underway, moving along at a much faster rate than expected. As time
passed, the only difficulty was Chandler's slow progress with the second
half of the screenplay. "Ray's problem with the script (as with the book),"
Houseman writes, "was a simple one: he had no ending" (139).

Houseman recalls that during story conferences, Chandler "seemed
only half there, nodding his head, saying little" (140). Finally, the studio's general manager, Henry Ginsberg, arranged a private meeting in
which he announced to Chandler that the entire future of Paramount
Pictures was at stake. Ginsberg offered a large bonus for the completed
script, but this only shook Chandler's already fragile self-confidence and
made him feel that Houseman, whom he regarded as a "fellow Public
School man" (141), was being betrayed. Chandler offered to resign. Not
long afterward, however, he came to Houseman with a bizarre proposal:
he would finish the script if he could arrange to drink whiskey under supervised conditions.

Amazingly, Houseman agreed. He and Chandler went out to a posh
restaurant, where the writer downed three double martinis and three double stingers. The studio then posted two limousines, six secretaries, a
nurse, and a doctor at Chandler's home, where the inebriated author
worked on the script for eight days, never eating solid food but always
keeping a glass of bourbon at hand. He completed the story, but he also
seriously damaged his health. (Significantly, the final script begins with
three characters walking into a bar and ordering "bourbon with a bourbon chaser," and it ends with one of them asking, "Did somebody say
something about a drink of bourbon?")

This anecdote is even more harrowing and suspenseful than the similar one Houseman tells in the first volume of his memoirs, where he recalls nursing the alcoholic Herman Mankiewicz through the writing of
Citizen Kane. Unfortunately, neither story is completely true. Houseman
seems to have forgotten that Orson Welles was the coauthor of the *Kane*
screenplay, just as he forgets that Raymond Chandler had a perfectly good
ending for *The Blue Dahlia* from the moment the film went into production. Chandler's problem was not a writer's block, but the United
States Navy, which refused to clear the project because the killer was a
mentally disturbed ex-serviceman (played in the completed picture by

William Bendix). Because of the navy's objections, Paramount Pictures rejected the closing scenes as they were originally written. In other words, Houseman was collaborating in a process of censorship that required Chandler to change his script and compromise his basic idea. No wonder Chandler became so detached, uninspired, and thirsty.

Houseman's account has been only slightly modified by subsequent historians, even when they acknowledge that Chandler wanted to make a returning naval veteran into an unwitting killer.[18] But records in the Motion Picture Academy Library show that a complete treatment of *The Blue Dahlia,* including suggested dialogue for the closing scene, was submitted by Chandler on January 18, 1945, only a few weeks after he signed an agreement to write the screenplay. This treatment was unusually downbeat and socially realistic, rather like a noir version of *The Best Years of Our Lives;* and although it was written in haste, there is every indication that Chandler was excited by the possibilities it offered. "In less than two weeks I wrote an original story of 90 pages," he told Charles Morton of *The Atlantic Monthly.* "It was an experiment and for a guy subject from early childhood to plot-constipation, it was rather a revelation. Some of the stuff is good, some very much not" (quoted in Mac-Shane, *Life of Raymond Chandler,* 115).

In the opening pages of the treatment, Chandler describes *The Blue Dahlia* as the story of Johnny, George, and Buzz—three returning veterans who represent the sort of cross section of social classes we find in most World War II combat films. The three men are "the last survivors of a bomber crew that made too many missions," and they have been given early discharges because of wounds or stress. Johnny's eyesight is failing, George finds it impossible to concentrate, and Buzz has a silver plate in his skull that gives him headaches and blackouts. To make things worse, the world they return to is hardly better than the one they have left overseas. Before the war, Johnny was a "tester" for a Southern California oil company, living with his wife and child in a five-room house; while he was away, the child died of diphtheria and the wife sold the house and moved to Los Angeles, where she became the occasional lover of a gangster who owns a Sunset Strip nightclub. George was a practicing lawyer, but he was neither well educated nor successful, and his girl has left him. Buzz, the most proletarian of the three, has come home only to discover that his alcoholic father has abandoned his mother, who lives in abject poverty.

The plot Chandler outlines in the original treatment is roughly similar to the one in the completed film, except that Buzz murders Johnny's wife and then suffers a blackout, completely forgetting the incident. Chandler clearly intended to write a Hitchcockian "wrong man" picture, involving an exchange of guilt between Johnny and Buzz; in other ways, however, he was attempting to make all the leading characters seem like scapegoats for a pervasive social malaise. At the end, the nightclub owner, Eddie Ansell (Eddie Harwood in the film), makes a false confession to the murder and allows himself to be shot by the police—all this in order to protect his estranged wife, Joyce, who has already made a false confession to protect Johnny. After Ansell's death, the police close the case, and there is a brief love scene between Johnny and Joyce. On the next day, we see Buzz and George in their apartment, where the sound of a loud radio next door begins to trouble Buzz. Johnny and Joyce arrive; she is wearing one of Ansell's trademark blue dahlias "as a sort of gesture," and as they talk, she picks at the blossom. Seeing this, Buzz grows increasingly distracted. Suddenly he breaks into a crazed monologue and lies down on the couch, rather like a patient under analysis. As his friends watch, he seems to hallucinate the murder scene, ultimately falling into an exhausted sleep. The treatment concludes with the grim reactions of his two wartime buddies:

> They sit watching him. His eyes close and he begins to breathe deeply.
> *Johnny:* (To George) Well—that's it. I hope he never remembers it.
> *George:* He wanted to get his own mother out here and make a home for her. He wanted a lot of things. Now he'll have to live in a room with a barred window.
> *Johnny:* (Quietly) I hope he never remembers.
> THE END[19]

"What the Navy Department did to the story," Chandler told James Sandoe, "was a little thing like making me change the murderer and hence make a routine whodunit out of a fairly original idea" (quoted in MacShane, *Life of Raymond Chandler*, 117). But the navy was not the only censor. The Breen Office was concerned because Chandler depicted Johnny, the character played by Alan Ladd, as a "double" for Buzz— that is, as a trained killer who, under stress, is prone to manic brutality. At one point in the final draft of the script, Chandler carefully describes a beating that Johnny administers to Corelli (Howard Freeman), the night manager of a sleazy Santa Monica hotel. Johnny puts a cigarette out on the back of Corelli's hand, punches him "a staggering blow" in the windpipe, and then "swarms all over him" with a gun. A close-up shows Corelli's face as the gun strikes his nose and cheeks: "Blood spurts.

Corelli's eyes glaze. The gun smashes the side of his jaw. Corelli sinks down out of the shot. There is a thud as he hits the floor" (Chandler, *Blue Dahlia: A Screenplay*, 90). In a later scene, after being knocked out and taken to a deserted farmhouse, Johnny overpowers Leo (Don Costello), one of Harwood's criminal associates, who wears thick eyeglasses:

B-129 CLOSE SHOT—JOHNNY
With his arm curved around Leo's neck . . . Johnny's hand comes up with the thumb extended. It goes toward Leo's eye.

B-130 EXTREME CLOSE UP—JOHNNY'S FACE
Bending down over Leo. It is savage. The muscles of his face are tense as he jabs his thumb into Leo's eye, out of shot. Leo screams. Johnny lets go. There is a heavy thud as Leo falls. He groans. Johnny reaches down for his handkerchief and wipes his hand. (111)

Paramount toned down this action, and elsewhere it omitted several uses of brass knuckles and blackjacks. At the request of the Breen Office, it also cut a scene in which Johnny deliberately sideswipes a sheriff's car, and it dropped a line of dialogue that the PCA felt would be "resented by the police generally." The objectionable line involved Johnny's memories of his youth: "When I was a kid in Chicago, I saw a cop shoot a little white dog to death." In the completed film, the police are benign, and Johnny seems more conventionally middle class; indeed, Alan Ladd is so well groomed and dressed that he looks the economic equal of his rival, the dapper Eddie Harwood (Howard da Silva).

The loss of Buzz as the killer is even more significant, because it turns *The Blue Dahlia* into the sort of entertainment Chandler spent his entire literary career attacking: a classic detective story, bringing all the suspects together in a single room and dramatically revealing one of them as the guilty party. The revised concluding scenes also contain a spectacular moment reminiscent of a circus sideshow: Johnny holds a match in his hand and orders Buzz to light it by firing a gun. What Chandler had wanted to write, as he explained to Sandoe,

was the story of a man who killed (executed would be a better word) his pal's wife under the stress of a great and legitimate anger, then blanked out and forgot all about it; then with perfect honesty did his best to help the pal get out of a jam, then found himself in a set of circumstances that brought about partial recall. The poor guy remembered enough to make it clear who the murderer was to others, but never realized it himself." (Quoted in Chandler, *Blue Dahlia*, 132–33)

FIGURES 19–20. Alan Ladd and Will Wright in the revised
ending of *The Blue Dahlia* (1946).

When Chandler was eventually forced to abandon this idea, the Breen Office, like the navy, was pleased. Hollywood movies were supposed to avoid ambiguities, providing a neat balance sheet of rewards and punishments. Thus in its May 1945 report, the PCA approved of the completed script for *The Blue Dahlia,* describing it as a "murder mystery" of no particular social import and noting that the (civilian) killer was captured and shot by the police. The reviewer also noted, "We have the feeling Joyce and Johnny will find happiness together someday."

The resulting film is nevertheless a better-than-average thriller, enhanced by Chandler's stylization of American speech, and redolent of his original themes. Even if Johnny and Buzz are innocent of murder, the war has turned them into potential killers, and life in Los Angeles makes them disoriented, angry, and paranoid. At the end of the picture, when the true culprit is revealed, his identity hardly seems to matter. As if to compensate for what the studio and the navy had done to his script, Chandler pins the crime on one of the most powerless people in the story— "Dad" Newell, an elderly house detective at the posh Cavendish Court Hotel. Before he dies, Newell expresses his class resentment, and his parting speech gives a rare opportunity to the underrated character actor Will Wright, who makes the most of it: "Maybe I could get tired of being pushed around by cops—and hotel managers—and ritzy dames in bungalows. Maybe I could cost a little something once—even if I do end up on a slab!"

In the last scene of the film, Detective Captain Henderson (Tom Powers) seems troubled about Newell. "I must be getting droopy," he says. "I felt kind of sorry for the old gent at that." In a similar fashion, Chandler enables us to feel sympathy for the film's other ostensible villain, Eddie Harwood, who, because of his criminal record, has been able to stay home during the war and acquire money and women. "I'm not much of a hot shot after all," Harwood says, and throughout the picture he seems trapped and joyless. Matthew J. Bruccoli has described him as an "elegant quasi-racketeer," troubled with guilt over his broken marriage, and continually aware of Johnny's "moral superiority" (Chandler, *Blue Dahlia: A Screenplay,* 132). Leo, his sinister associate, warns him about the dangers of such an attitude: "Just don't get too complicated, Eddie."

Rather like Leo, Hollywood tried to keep Chandler from getting too complicated. But *The Blue Dahlia* is not the sort of movie in which criminals can be brought to simple justice and society restored to order. Chandler always wrote about corruption, or about what W. H. Auden called "the Great Wrong Place." Despite the star system, the Breen Office, and the United States Navy, there is just enough of this theme left in the film to make questions of individual guilt seem trivial and to suggest Chandler's amusement, anger, and romantic fascination at a world gone bad.

THE SNAKES ARE LOOSE

One year after *The Blue Dahlia,* RKO's *Crossfire* managed to depict a homicidal U.S. soldier without encountering objections from the armed services. The film was set in Washington, D.C., at the very end of the war, and it made the humid nighttime streets of the nation's capital seem like a limbo or purgatory, teeming with restless military personnel. A civilian character who is about to be murdered (Sam Levene) comments on the mood of the place; as he puts it, the whole country has been intently focused on the "win-the-war peanut," but now the peanut is eaten and nobody knows what to do. "We're too used to fightin'. But we just don't know what to fight. You can feel the tension in the air. A whole lot of fight and hate that doesn't know where to go."

Crossfire was loosely based on *The Brick Foxhole,* Richard Brooks's 1945 novel about life in the stateside military, which had been published while Brooks was still a private in the marines at Camp Pendleton, California. Despite the novel's awkward characterizations and sometimes painfully sententious prose, it deals powerfully with many subjects that were taboo in Hollywood. The plot centers on Jeff Mitchell, a former animator of Walt Disney cartoons, who has been drafted and assigned to a signal corps studio just outside Washington. Jeff believes that his wife back in California is having an affair, and in frustration he uses a fifteen-day furlough to go on a wild spree. Along the way, he is accompanied by two sergeants: Peter Keely, a much-decorated liberal correspondent for a military newspaper, and Monty Crawford, a former Chicago cop who seethes with hatred for Jews, blacks, foreigners, and civilians—especially when they are 4-F. On the first day of the furlough, the three men attend a boxing match, where Monty enjoys watching a Jewish fighter get beaten. On the second day, Jeff reluctantly joins up with Monty and another soldier, a vicious southern bigot named Floyd Bowers, who has been picked up by a wealthy, effeminate civilian known only as "Mr. Edwards." When Edwards invites them all to his apartment, Floyd nudges Jeff: "We're set, buddy. Set. I ain't beaten up a queer in I don't know how long."

The ensuing events are described from Jeff's drunken perspective, in a kind of hallucinatory internal monologue that suggests the casual humiliations and random violence to which Edwards is subjected. Jeff almost passes out, and just at the point when things are about to turn truly nasty, he leaves Edwards's apartment, assuming that the party is over. On the next day, he wakes up in a prostitute's bedroom, confronted by a strange man who alternately claims to be her husband, her lover, and her pimp. Meanwhile, the police find Floyd Bowers in an alley, strangled with his necktie, and Mr. Edwards in the bathroom of his apartment, beaten to death with the flat porcelain top of a toilet tank.

The reader of *The Brick Foxhole* has no problem guessing who committed the crimes, but the police suspect Jeff, who goes into hiding while Peter Keely searches for Monty. In a highly allegorical conclusion, the liberal tracks down the fascist, confronting his enemy at night in a closed and darkened military museum. The two men regress to primal hostility, and at the end of a protracted bayonet-swordfight, they kill one another. Soon afterward, the police discover that Monty was the murderer of both Bowers and Edwards, and Jeff is allowed to return to his former life in the army. Although Jeff has been temporarily freed of his sexual paranoia, he remains troubled by what he has experienced, and he seems aware that the war being fought in Europe will also have to be fought on some level in the United States.

Almost as soon as it was published, *The Brick Foxhole* was brought to the attention of producer and social activist Adrian Scott, who, together with director Edward Dmytryk and writer John Paxton, had formed a unit at RKO devoted to modestly budgeted, left-wing melodramas. Scott, Dmytryk, and Paxton were strongly identified with *tendenz* films (*Tender Comrade* and *Till the End of Time*), and they had recently achieved major box-office success with a pair of antifascist, hard-boiled thrillers starring Dick Powell (*Murder, My Sweet* and *Cornered*). *The Brick Foxhole* presented an opportunity to combine the two styles; consequently, in the winter of 1945, Scott optioned the novel and proposed a low-budget adaptation at RKO.

Joseph Breen had already declared that Brooks's story was "thoroughly and completely unacceptable, on a dozen or more counts," and the initial response to Scott's proposal at RKO was chilly. But Scott was a proven success at the studio, and he was strongly backed by RKO's incoming production chief, Dore Schary, who had made his own reputation from social-problem movies. With Schary's approval, John Paxton was put to work on a screenplay, which Scott described as a study of "personal fascism" in the character of a brutal United States Army sergeant.[20] To avoid potential objections from censors, Scott and Paxton eliminated all references to homosexuality, emphasizing instead the theme of race hatred. Although the Production Code explicitly forbade the use of racial epithets, and although the studios in general strongly discouraged any suggestion that American society was prejudiced, World War II had made attacks on anti-Semitism topical, safe, and even patriotic. Darryl Zanuck's much-discussed adaptation of *Gentleman's Agreement* was currently in production at Twentieth-Century Fox, and Dore Schary must have realized that Scott's quickie adaptation of *The Brick Foxhole* would anticipate Zanuck and gain considerable prestige for RKO.[21]

Paxton's script, originally entitled *Cradle of Fear,* was a *policier* centering on the colossal irony of a Jew being murdered by a U.S. soldier during the immediate aftermath of World War II. For various reasons, Paxton and Scott also wanted to suggest a broader, more generalized history of racism and to argue that the fascist hatred of minorities was perennial, not confined to the recent war. Their research file contained numerous articles on racial persecution in America, including accounts of the "Protestant Crusade" of the 1840s and 1850s, the subsequent outbreak of "Know-Nothingism," and the rise of the Ku Klux Klan. Paxton's screenplay employed the deterministic, "what-will-have-happened" plot structure of classic detective fiction (including a "lying" flashback), and this structure occasionally allowed him to move further back in time than the immediate story required, depicting the purely historical past. The murder and the search for the killer took place in a little over a day, but the opening of the original script emphasized that the narrative as a whole had vast temporal dimensions:

1. ESTABLISHING SHOT—Washington, D.C., at night, perhaps with the Lincoln Memorial in the background, a soldier and a girl strolling across in the foreground. The feeling is lonely and barren.

   NARRATOR

   This story began a long time ago. It isn't over yet, either. It began in the time of Genghis Khan, in the time of Moses, in the time of Jesus Christ, in the time of Attila the Hun—and in the time before that.

   This part of it happened in Washington, D.C., in 1946.

   DISSOLVE

2. SERIES OF SHOTS. Streetlamps. Each shot is closer, until the tempo is staccato.

   INTERIOR. SAMUELS' APARTMENT—NIGHT.

3. MEDIUM CLOSE-UP—table lamp. There is the brief SOUND of a fierce struggle, o.s., then someone crashes backward into the lamp, sending it to the floor.

Near the end of this version, Detective Finlay's speech on race prejudice to a southerner named Leroy is accompanied by an elaborate montage illustrating the persecution of Finlay's nineteenth-century Irish ancestors. Finlay concludes the speech with a reference to racism in the
American South:

> *Finlay* (quietly): That's history. They don't teach it in schools, but it's history
> just the same. . . . Thomas Finlay was killed in 1850, because he was an
> Irish Catholic. A few weeks ago, a Negro was lynched, because he was a
> Negro. This evening, Samuels was killed, because he was a Jew.

In all subsequent drafts of the script, both the montage of a Boston
race riot and the line about the Negro were dropped, probably because
the studio wanted to avoid giving offense to any particular segment of
the audience.[22] But the film was in danger of being criticized no matter
what course it took. When Scott and Paxton broadened their focus, they
risked alienating specific communities; when they narrowed it, they were
accused of timidity or of catering to the interests of a Jewish-controlled
motion-picture industry. The Breen Office hinted at the last of these motives in its initial report on the screenplay, which noted that "in view of
the speech of the police captain, the story could be defended as being a
plea against all forms of racial and religious intolerance. However, the
basic story is still open to the charge of being a special pleading against
current anti-Semitism."

Following a conference with Scott, Dmytryk, and Paxton in late February 1947, Joseph Breen gave tentative approval to the film (now entitled *Crossfire*) and sent Schary a letter emphasizing five points of un-
derstanding that had emerged from the discussion. One, racial epithets
would be eliminated from the film's dialogue. Two, references to drinking and drunkenness would be toned down "whenever possible." Three,
there would be no suggestion that the girl Ginny is a prostitute, or that
the strange older man in her apartment is her customer. ("Our recommendation," Breen wrote, "is that this man who wanders in should
definitely be indicated as Ginny's divorced or separated husband who is
trying to win her back.") Four, there would be "nothing of a 'pansy' characterization about Samuels or his relationship with the soldiers." Five,
RKO would agree to "make certain that nothing in the finished picture
will cause any complaint from the War Department."

The released film is in technical compliance with most of these agree-
ments: it retains two racial slurs ("Jewboy" and "Mick"), but it uses them
sparingly; it contains only one scene of drunkenness, followed by many

others in which coffee is consumed; it makes Ginny seem a relatively soft-boiled taxi dancer who longs for domesticity; and it invents an army major who makes a climactic speech assuring viewers that the U.S. military disapproves of anti-Semites. But even when *Crossfire* does exactly what the Breen Office and the studio wanted, it enables us to "see" (in Christian Metz's sense) many of the things that censorship was trying to repress. Notice, for example, how it conveys something of the forbidden homosexual content of Richard Brooks's novel even when it works hard to assure us that Samuels, the murder victim, is heterosexual. Sam Levene plays the role without a hint of effeminacy, and when he first appears he is accompanied by an attractive woman (Marlo Dwyer), who asks him to speak with Corporal Mitchell (George Cooper), a troubled young soldier she observes from across a barroom. Mitchell turns out to be a former artist (a former WPA muralist, no less), and he engages Samuels's interest partly because he is such a vivid contrast to his companion, the boorish Montgomery (Robert Ryan). And yet, even though Samuels appears motivated by nothing more than decency and concern for a veteran, and even though we are told that he and Mitchell talk mostly about baseball, the scene has a sexual ambiguity. The effect is heightened because of the Socratic intensity of the conversation, because the actor playing Mitchell is boyishly handsome, and because the bizarre setting creates psychological tension. The city streets, bars, and hotel lobbies are surreally crowded with uniformed men, and Dmytryk's mise-en-scène occasionally resembles an expressionist, militarized locker room. In this place, as one character remarks, "the snakes are loose," and nobody seems purely innocent.

To some degree, the film's quasi-psychoanalytic effect was imposed on Dmytryk because of financial limitations. *Crossfire* was budgeted at a respectable if not extravagant five hundred thousand dollars, but Dore Schary used most of the money on salaries for the star players. (According to the notes in his personal copy of the script, he originally contemplated an even more expensive cast, led by James Cagney as Finlay and John Garfield as Keely.)[23] The picture was shot completely in the studio in a mere twenty-four days, and out of necessity it mixed the conventions of realistic photography (sharp resolution, elaborate depth of field, and plausibly motivated sources of light) with minimalist or black-art devices that eliminated the need for extras or costly sets. The result is a visibly artful and oneiric film, charged with sexual implication or "repressed" meaning, which invites its audience to explore the relationship between movies and dreams.

In the completed film, Dmytryk often relies on symbolism or synecdoche, using a single prop, such as a lamp or a pot of boiling coffee, to convey entire settings and states of mind. The seedy or blankly institutional interiors are broken up dramatically with pools of hard light, and the studio-manufactured streets have no sky overhead, only a pervasive darkness that generates a feeling of entrapment or confinement. This stylized quality extends also to the presentation of the actors. Whenever the important female characters are seen from Mitchell's perspective, they seem momentarily fantastic: Ginny (Gloria Grahame) appears suddenly in close-up, her hair framed by an aureole of light and her entrance announced by a dance-hall band playing "Shine"; Mary (Jacqueline White) is like a ghost or an apparition from suburbia, moving through the smoky beams of a projection booth in an all-night movie theater. Meanwhile, nearly all the males are sinister or strange. Monty, an obvious psychotic, is photographed with a grotesquely distorting 25 mm lens, but even Detective Finlay looks offbeat—a professorial detective who speaks in a weary, alienated monotone from around a pipe or a cigarette that rarely leaves his mouth.

The most Kafkaesque and memorable character in the film is the nameless man in Ginny's room (Paul Kelly), who had troubled Joseph Breen from the beginning. (One of his first lines of dialogue is "You're wondering about this setup, aren't you?") True to their promise to the PCA, the filmmakers never depict this man as a prostitute's customer; instead, taking a cue from Brooks's novel, they make him an enigma without a solution—a chameleon who glibly constructs a series of plausible scenarios to explain his presence and then calmly declares that each explanation is a lie. "I want to marry her," he says to Mitchell at one point. "Do you believe that? Well, that's a lie, too. I don't love her and I don't want to marry her. She makes good money there. You got any money on you?" By turns sinister, pathetic, and comic, he seems to mock the conventions of realist narrative, and as a result he opens his part of the story to all sorts of scandalous interpretation.[24]

On the level of overt politics rather than style, *Crossfire* is a much less unusual film, which may explain why the studio was able to publicize it as a hard-hitting exposé and an important "message" picture. The theatrical trailer featured Dore Schary, who spoke about *Crossfire*'s unconventional theme without saying exactly what the theme might be. Schary claimed that RKO was working in the tradition of *I Am a Fugitive from a Chain Gang* and *The Grapes of Wrath,* and he quoted rave notices from a sneak preview in California, where audiences made sim-

FIGURE 21. Paul Kelly in *Crossfire* (1947).

ilar comparisons. (The preview cards were indeed overwhelmingly favorable, containing only a few objections that the film was "too talka-
tive" or that it amounted to "Jewish propaganda.") By this means, he
tried to situate a potentially controversial production within an easily
recognizable and mostly liberal genre: the Hollywood social-problem
film, which was reaching its apex of respectability at that very moment,
in the postwar work of Elia Kazan.

The key feature of the social-problem film (except in such early Depression cases as *Chain Gang* or the protofascist *Gabriel over the White
House*) is that its problems never appear systemic. And this is exactly the
case in *Crossfire,* which prominently displays a photograph of FDR and
a copy of the Declaration of Independence on the walls behind Captain
Finlay when he makes his speech against racism. (Outside the window,
as the dawn of Enlightenment breaks, we also see the U.S. Capitol for
the first time.) Here and elsewhere, the film suggests that hatred of minorities is contrary to American ideals and to the very foundations of the
government. Unfortunately and perhaps unintentionally, it also implies
that bigots come chiefly from the ignorant, impoverished, and mentally
disturbed lower orders. In his somewhat patronizing speech to Leroy, Finlay says that racism takes different forms, including the "you-can't-join-

FIGURE 22. Robert Ryan in *Crossfire*.

our-Country-Club" type described in *Gentleman's Agreement;* nevertheless, *Crossfire* repeatedly uses codes of social class or educational background to distinguish between the good and bad characters (including
the two women). Robert Ryan, wearing a khaki uniform shorn of in-
signia, makes the villain seem like the United States equivalent of the pe-
tit bourgeois Europeans who had worn black and brown shirts before
the war—a crude bully, ill educated and transparently deceitful, who can
temporarily influence southern farm-boys like Floyd and Leroy (Steve
Brodie and William Phipps), but who is no match for more polished fel-
lows like Finlay and Keely (Robert Young and Robert Mitchum).

If Scott, Dmytryk, and Paxton were indeed communist propagandists,
as the United States Congress later claimed, then the studio must have
been holding them to a relatively conservative vision of the proletariat.
Meanwhile, the War Department and the conventional wisdom of Hollywood may have affected the way *Crossfire* ended. In Scott's final draft
of the script, when Monty tries to escape down a dark alley, a military
policeman with a tommy gun advances methodically, "slowly chewing
gum, expressionless," and shoots him down. For the released picture,
Captain Finlay shoots Monty from the window of the police station. The
new ending was improvised by Schary and Dmytryk, in order to avoid

what Schary called a "storm trooper" attack on Monty. Paxton told film scholars Keith Kelly and Clay Steinman that the film's conclusion was "dramatically crude, in lousy taste and improbable marksmanship," but that "for the idiom of the time, I think it was obligatory to conclude this sort of melodrama in action" (126). Whatever its purpose, the revision causes at least two ideological problems: first, it transforms the New Deal detective into a kind of cowboy; and second, in a quite different way, it undercuts the film's benign rationality, making Monty seem a helpless rat in a maze who is executed from on high by an all-seeing authority. Partly because of the closing sequences, *Crossfire*'s Kafkaesque mise-en-scène overpowers the qualified optimism of its social message. In fact, the last image is similar to the one in *The Blue Dahlia*: two unlikely companions of war, Keely and Leroy, walk off together (this time in search of coffee), but the streets still look grimly shadowed.

It seems important to emphasize that the dark city in the closing shots was intended to evoke social rather than metaphysical anxieties. FDR had been dead for two years when *Crossfire* was made; the film was not merely an expression of angst or alienation, but a partisan statement on behalf of the beleaguered American Left, which viewed the Truman administration and the Republican opposition in especially dark fashion. A month after *Crossfire* was released, John Paxton made this very point in a guest column for the *Los Angeles Daily News,* in which he discussed the future of the country; films like *Crossfire,* he said, were being produced in the hope that "audiences, conditioned by the reality of war, would rise up against the old glittering fairy tales" (27 August 1947). Some of those old fairy tales may have remained in *Crossfire,* but Paxton and his collaborators had certainly not offered a "glittering" view of the world. Despite its many compromises and concessions to censorship, *Crossfire* mounted a strong attack on domestic fascism (a term it never used), and, contrary to what might have been expected, it earned significant profits at the box office. Scott, Dmytryk, and Paxton were nominated for Academy Awards, along with Robert Ryan and Gloria Grahame, and Dore Schary received a special award for "social drama" at the Cannes festival.

After the censors and the studio had modified *Crossfire* to the point where it could be released and awarded, social scientists attempted to measure its effect on audiences.[25] At that very moment, however, the staff of HUAC was also screening the film, which was mentioned during the notorious 1947 investigations into Hollywood communism. On the heels of their greatest critical and commercial success, Adrian Scott and Ed-

ward Dmytryk became members of the "Hollywood Ten" and were ultimately imprisoned for contempt of Congress. To make matters worse,
they and other members of their group were attacked by their bosses.
The 1947 "Waldorf Declaration," a document authored by the most powerful men in Hollywood (including Dore Schary), announced that people
like Scott and Dmytryk had performed a "disservice to their employers"
and had "impaired their usefulness to the industry" (Schwartz, 279). The
balance of political power in American culture was about to shift and
bring an end to the mixture of expressionist theater, popular melodrama,
and left-wing politics that had been nourished during the Roosevelt administration. *Crossfire* was certainly not the last nor even the best social-
problem movie, but it marked the close of a distinctive phase in the national history.

AFTER 1947

The purge of Hollywood leftists was part of a larger right-wing campaign
to rid the country of industrial unions and Roosevelt-style socialism —a
campaign conducted against the background of internal struggles within
the Democratic Party and of growing economic insecurity within the
movie colony.[26] After the war, the Truman administration adopted an increasingly conservative foreign and domestic policy, and in 1946 the Republicans captured both houses of Congress. That same year, Hollywood
experienced some of the worst labor problems in its history, most of which
were unfairly blamed on communists. The widely publicized HUAC hearings, filled with celebrities of the Left and the Right, were paradoxically
useful to the Hollywood moguls, who faced not only picket lines but also
antitrust proceedings and increased competition from television. In this
environment, which was filled with bitter personal animosities that had
been growing over the past decade, it was easy for studio administrators
to exploit the fear of communism and thereby defeat the formation of
an industrywide union. The political, cultural, and economic structure
that had sustained Hollywood during the war was on the verge of collapse; the studios needed to shrink and reorganize themselves, and their
executives must have thought: why not use the blacklist to rid ourselves
of troublemakers?

No historian has been able to show exactly what effect the subsequent
restructurings, blacklistings, and imprisonments had on American culture, but Thom Andersen has intelligently addressed the important question of whether the most famous victims of the blacklist were talented

filmmakers who were responsible for a distinctive kind of cinema. Andersen concludes that during the years between the first HUAC hearings in 1947 and the second in 1951, a group of soon-to-be-blacklisted leftists and their "fellow travelers"—Robert Rossen, Abraham Polonsky, Joseph Losey, Jules Dassin, John Berry, Cyril Endfield, John Garfield, John Huston, and Nicholas Ray—responded to the threat of political repression by creating what amounted to a subgenre. All of the writers and directors in this group relied upon conventions of the film noir, but according to Andersen, they tried to achieve a "greater psychological and social realism." Andersen labels their work *film gris,* because "we have been taught to associate Communism with drabness and greyness" and because their movies are "often drab and depressing" (183). He lists thirteen examples: Rossen's *Body and Soul;* Polonsky's *Force of Evil;* Dassin's *Thieves' Highway* and *Night and the City;* Ray's *They Live By Night* and *Knock on Any Door;* Huston's *We Were Strangers* and *The Asphalt Jungle;* Curtiz's *Breaking Point;* Losey's *Lawless* and *The Prowler;* Endfield's *Try and Get Me;* and Berry's *He Ran All the Way.*

Having made this argument, Andersen confesses that he feels uneasy about his central term and "would be relieved if no one should adopt it" (183). I shall grant his wish, chiefly because *film gris* has already been proposed by other historians, who have something quite different in mind. Charles Higham and Joel Greenberg, for example, distinguish between "the 'pure' black cinema of *Nightmare Alley* and *Double Indemnity* and the excursions into "gray" melodrama of the adapters of Hammett, Chandler, and Graham Greene."[27] And John Tuska complicates things even further when he calls *The Maltese Falcon* a "film gris" and *The Big Sleep* a "film noir." Any new stipulation would only create more confusion. Besides, as I have been trying to suggest, it is usually a good policy to avoid making neat distinctions among Hollywood formulas. It seems undeniably true that a neorealist or documentary grayness infiltrates late 1940s melodrama, but this tendency is not confined to a single political group. As Higham and Greenberg point out, almost 30 percent of the Hollywood films given Code approval in 1947 had a "problem" content and showed a marked departure from the studio-bound expressionism of the previous decade (16); indeed several of the left-wing films in Andersen's list, such as *Night and the City,* are less *gris* in their visual effects than the work of a "friendly witness" like Elia Kazan.

And yet, the filmmakers Andersen places together (to whom we should probably add the original Hollywood Ten, plus Orson Welles, who became a European exile in 1948) do in fact constitute a left-wing school

or community. It also makes sense to distinguish in a general sense between two major branches in the "family tree" of noir—one tending toward cynicism and misanthropy (Hitchcock and Billy Wilder), and the
other toward humanism and political engagement (Welles and Huston).
The second branch became especially militant in the years after the war,
and we can easily identify its politics and aesthetic strategies.[28]

Left filmmakers in the late 1940s and early 1950s often gave a social-
realist spin to familiar noirish plots—as in *M* (1950), a documentary-
style remake of Lang's classic, directed by Joseph Losey and written in
part by the blacklisted Waldo Salt; or as in *The Prowler* (1951), a more
class-conscious version of *Double Indemnity,* also directed by Losey, and
cowritten without credit by the blacklisted Dalton Trumbo. The Left was
also greatly interested in stories about fascist or authoritarian personalities. *Brute Force* (1947), directed by Jules Dassin and scripted by
Richard Brooks, is an attempt to bring *Crossfire's* perverse violence into
the world of prison melodrama, with the sadistic Captain Munsey
(Hume Cronyn) presiding over an enclosed, militaristic state. *Key Largo*
(1947), directed by John Huston and once again coscripted by Brooks,
emphasizes the affinity between a classic Hollywood gangster (Edward
G. Robinson) and the Nazi dictators. Equally notable are two films dealing with protofascist politicians: *Ruthless* (1948), a low-budget variation on *Citizen Kane,* supervised by Robert Rossen and directed by Edgar
G. Ulmer; and *All the King's Men,* adapted and directed by Rossen, which
won the Academy Award for Best Picture in 1949. (This last film has
never been called noir, but it qualifies on many counts.)

As Andersen observes, Red Hollywood's leading personality was John
Garfield, who represented the tough street culture of the Jewish working class. The Left in general was "proletarian" in its concerns, often making films about middle-European or Mediterranean immigrants and repeatedly dealing with the failure of the American dream in the big
industrial centers. Consider Dassin's *Thieves' Highway* (1949), loosely
based on the A. I. Bezzederies novel *Thieves' Market,* which portrays the
struggles of working-class Greeks in the California trucking industry; consider also the Polonsky-Garfield production of *Force of Evil* (1948)—in
many ways the quintessential example of what Andersen means by *film
gris*—which uses Ira Wolfert's *Tucker's People* to create a tragic study of
Jews and Italians in the New York numbers racket. These films and a
few others allowed working-class characters from marginalized ethnic
groups to express themselves in dignified form for almost the first time,
and they offered a vivid contrast to the WASP look of utopian Hollywood.

Racial intolerance was in fact a central issue for the Left. In his initial testimony before the HUAC in 1947, Adrian Scott accused the Republican Congress of being anti-Semitic and antiblack; to prove his point, Scott cited the credits of threatened filmmakers Robert Rossen, Howard Kotch, Albert Maltz, Waldo Salt, Ring Lardner Jr., Herbert Biberman, and Lewis Milestone—all of whom had made pictures attacking racism. During World War II, when black soldiers were fighting overseas, the government had encouraged these and other filmmakers to produce liberal pictures about racial problems, but after the war, with Roosevelt dead and the civil rights movement not yet fully underway, any attempt to discuss such issues on the screen was scrutinized for its potential as "communist propaganda." In response, left-wing Hollywood tended to show the effects of racism indirectly, chiefly through pictures about lynch-mob violence directed against whites. The clearest example is *Storm Warning* (1951), written by Richard Brooks and Daniel Fuchs, which starred two of Hollywood's most prominent anticommunists, Ronald Reagan and Ginger Rogers. Another such film was Losey's remake of *M*, but Losey also managed to overcome intense Breen Office objection to *The Lawless* (1950), a B-picture dealing with a young Mexican in California who is falsely accused of raping a white girl. For all its compromises, this film could not have failed to remind contemporary audiences of recent events in Los Angeles, including the Sleepy Lagoon case and the Zoot Suit riots.

Easily the most disturbing postwar film about lynching was *Try and Get Me* (1950, originally released as *The Sound of Fury*), directed by Mercury Theater alumnus Cyril Endfield, who was blacklisted soon afterward. Inspired by an actual incident that occurred in San Jose, California, in 1933, this picture is in some ways a throwback to Depression-era Hollywood, especially to *Fury* and *They Won't Forget*. It tells the story of unemployed veteran Howard Tyler (played by a perpetually worried-looking Frank Lovejoy), who desperately needs to support his pregnant wife and small son. Tyler grows increasingly resentful because of the TV sets and department stores he sees all around him, and he eventually joins up with a narcissistic petty criminal (Lloyd Bridges). The two men commit a few holdups and then kidnap the son of the richest man in town. But to Tyler's surprise and dismay, his companion in crime turns the kidnapping into a brutal murder.

The film nicely conveys the class structure of a city, and most of its minor characters—such as the "tough" women who go drinking and dancing with the kidnappers—are unusually complex. Although Endfield employs a great many Wellesian compositions, he also gives the action a feeling of authenticity by photographing everything on location in Phoenix, Arizona. The protagonist moves through a world of flimsy bungalows, mom-and-pop groceries, and drab hotels; and the murder is staged at night in a gravel pit, where the victim is bound, gagged, and beaten to death with a rock. Shocking as it is, this initial violence is nothing compared to what happens to the perpetrators after they are captured and arrested. A liberal newspaperman (Richard Carlson) whips up so much public outrage against the killers that a huge mob, led by a group of fraternity boys, descends on the jail and overwhelms the police. The siege is relentless and terrifying, and the two convicted criminals are briskly hauled offscreen to be tortured and killed. At the end, justice and civil order collapse utterly. The stunned newspaperman and the helpless police chief sit in an overturned office, listening all night to savage, carnivalistic whoops from a crowd in the distance.

Try and Get Me occasionally uses heavy-handed Christian symbolism to make its message seem "universal," and in secular terms it often seems preachy. One of its characters is an unintentionally annoying Italian visitor to America who keeps saying things like "Violence is a disease caused by moral and social breakdown. . . . It must be solved by reason." Nevertheless, the film's lynch-mob sequences are profoundly unsettling, and the story as a whole is such a thoroughgoing indictment of capitalism and liberal complacency that it transcends the ameliorative limits of the social-problem picture. Perhaps, as Andersen suggests, Endfield had moved beyond mere problem solving and was trying instead to make a presumptive allegory for the Left's fate at the hands of HUAC.

There is no question that the congressional investigations and the blacklist were treated allegorically in several other films. The situation in the late 1940s was in some ways analogous to what would happen in the late 1960s and early 1970s, when liberal Hollywood avoided direct attacks on U.S. policy in Vietnam but made countless movies about rebellious youth. (History also repeated itself in other ways. John Wayne produced the first Hollywood movie showing U.S. soldiers in Vietnam, and he starred in the first movie showing the HUAC investigations: *Big Jim McLain* [1952], a police procedural in which he played a tough congressional investigator hunting down Reds in Hawaii.)[29] For an example of how the liberals allowed their political concerns to get through in disguised fashion, consider *In a Lonely Place* (1950), starring Bogart as Dixon Steele, an alienated scriptwriter who has been blacklisted by the studios not because of his politics but because of his drinking and brawling. The film makes Steele's problems seem existential and cultural: he is a hard-boiled literary type who is beset by what François Truffaut called "an inner demon of violence" and who despises the trashy taste of Hollywood producers. (As usual, the mass audience is represented by a woman—in this case a hatcheck girl who visits Steele's apartment and tells him the plot of the latest best-seller.) At the same time, *In a Lonely Place* has a densely self-referential or autobiographical quality. It offers a fascinating commentary on Bogart, synthesizing many of his earlier performances and criticizing his tough-guy persona; it alludes to director Nicholas Ray's failed marriage to Gloria Grahame; and it reveals a political unconscious, enabling many of its key personnel to express guilt and anxiety over their professional lives.[30] Significantly, Bogart was under intense pressure from the American right wing when the film was made; after it was released, Nicholas Ray claimed that he was "graylisted," and character actor Art Smith, who plays Dixon Steele's highly sympathetic Hollywood agent, became a victim of the full-scale blacklist.

After 1947, many leftist filmmakers were treated as outlaws, and it is not surprising that they made some of their best pictures from the point of view of criminals. Once again they foreshadowed the "new American cinema" of the 1960s and 1970s: *Force of Evil,* for example, subtly anticipates Coppola's post-Code *Godfather* series (1972–1990) by drawing parallels between organized crime and big business and by placing heavy emphasis on a Cain-and-Abel theme; and *Gun Crazy,* written in part by the blacklisted and uncredited Dalton Trumbo, is a sharply satiric love-on-the-run movie that directly influenced *Bonnie and Clyde* (1967) and a host of other liberal pictures over the next three decades.

Among the best of these influential films was *The Asphalt Jungle* (1950), John Huston's study of what one of his characters calls "a left-handed form of human endeavor," which provoked a whole subgenre of "caper" movies. Remarkably, *The Asphalt Jungle* was made at MGM (where Dore Schary had just become production chief), and it emerged relatively unscathed by either the studio or the censors. The PCA's chief worries, stated in two letters of 1949, were that Huston planned to show a robbery in detail, and that one of the criminals was able to "escape justice" by committing suicide. The completed film, which retained both of these elements, was nevertheless judged to have a "more or less" happy ending. Under the section of the PCA report headed "Portrayal of Professions," the reviewer noted that a lawyer, a private detective, and one policeman out of three were treated unsympathetically; but after the question "Does the story tend to enlist the sympathy of the audience for criminals?" the reviewer answered "no." Ultimately, the film was approved because it appeared to show that "justice triumphs through efforts of law."

One wonders if the censor was looking at the film, or at an early version of Ben Maddow's script, which had gone to some length to throw sympathy toward the police. Like the W. R. Burnett novel upon which it is based, this initial version of *The Asphalt Jungle* focuses on a reformist police commissioner named Hardy, who is attempting to clean up a corrupt midwestern city. Maddow framed the story of the robbery with a "prelude" and "postlude" that show Hardy addressing a group of reporters in his office. In the prelude, Hardy reminds his audience that the only force between the people of the city and an "ominous flood" of crime is the police department; most cops, he asserts, are honest, and without them, "men could plan robbery, mayhem, and death with impunity." In the postlude, which occurs after the death of gang leader Dix Handley in a rainswept river, Hardy returns to the same theme: "The worst police force in the world," he says, "is better than no police force. And ours is far from the worst. . . . Take the police off the streets for forty-eight hours and nobody would be safe. . . . We'd be back in the jungle."[31]

When Huston revised Maddow's script, he eliminated the framing device. His major concession to censorship was the penultimate sequence—a bizarrely staged scene inside a police office, which borrows language from Maddow's original postlude. "It's not anything strange that there are corrupt officers in police departments," Hardy tells the reporters, but at the same time he argues that the overwhelming majority of cops are "honest men trying to do an honest job." He then switches on a bank of police radios in the wall behind his desk and asks rhetorically, "Suppose we had no police force, no matter how bad?" His answer is that "the jungle wins, the predatory beasts take over."[32]

Hardy is played by John McIntire, who has the stern, austere intensity of a Puritan minister addressing his congregation. The most frightening beast in the jungle, he tells the reporters, is Dix Handley—"a hardened killer, a hooligan, a man without human feeling or mercy." But *The Asphalt Jungle* has already gone to considerable lengths to establish Dix as a hero and a man of honor. (Dix is played by Sterling Hayden, a former communist who, together with Huston, was a member of the Hollywood Committee for the First Amendment and who reluctantly named names to HUAC soon after the film was released.) A key scene from earlier in the picture, in which Dix describes how his father's horse farm in Kentucky was destroyed by hard times, is clearly intended to elicit sympathy by evoking popular memories of the Great Depression. As if this were not enough, the last sequence, which directly follows the commissioner's speech, jarringly contradicts everything we have just heard. We see Dix driving frantically toward the Kentucky bluegrass country, where, with hardly enough blood left in his body to "keep a chicken alive," he pulls over to the roadside and struggles out of his car. Trailed helplessly by the woman who loves him (Jean Hagen), he wanders into a field and dies, his body gently nuzzled by thoroughbred horses.

Critics sometimes attribute the lyrical fatalism of scenes such as this to a national zeitgeist. Actually, the atmosphere of death and disillusionment in *The Asphalt Jungle* and most of the other crime pictures of its day has relatively little to do with the nation as a whole, and a great deal to do with a specific community that could no longer maintain its Depression-era faith that America would someday evolve into a socialist democracy. The despairing tone of *The Prowler, Try and Get Me, Force of Evil, Gun Crazy, All the King's Men,* and *In a Lonely Place* is clearly related to the politics and historical circumstances of individual writers, directors, and stars. As Joseph Losey remarked in 1979, the Left in Hollywood was utterly demoralized by Truman, the atomic bomb, and the HUAC investigations, and it was beginning to recognize "the complete unreality of the American dream" (quoted in Andersen, 187).

Paradoxically, the blacklist helped to create some of the finest and most socially outraged examples of film noir, as if the material that government officials and Hollywood censors were trying to repress had managed, in Metz's language, to "get through, one way or another." Even so, an important movement in American cultural history was coming to a dark and destructive end. After *The Asphalt Jungle,* John Huston never again made a film that resonated with the leftist satire of his early work. Between 1945 and 1950, Orson Welles was listed by the FBI as a "threat to the internal security" of the nation, and because he had never been popular in Hollywood, his brilliant career in American entertainment was essentially over.[33] Meanwhile, at least three hundred movie professionals were placed on the blacklist. Many of the younger generation of directors were forced to work abroad, and some of America's best actors had difficulty finding even bit parts. Among the literati, Hammett was in prison, and several key scriptwriters were never allowed to work again. Ironically, the censorship laws regarding sex and violence were slowly being liberalized, but the most popular private eye in American fiction was Mickey Spillane's fascistic avenger, Mike Hammer.

Of course, the film noir itself did not end (Americans did not yet know the term), and many of the people discussed here went on to do excel-

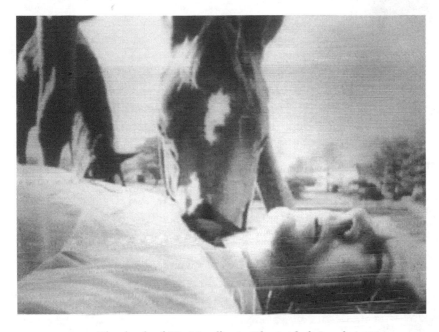

FIGURE 23. The death of Dix Handley in *The Asphalt Jungle* (1950).

lent work on other types of movies. Although Dassin and Losey were better directors of Hollywood genre pictures than of European art films, they obtained a good deal of critical and even commercial success by working abroad.[34] Endfield made two outstanding entertainments in Britain: *Hell Drivers* (1957) and *Zulu* (1964). Dmytryk recanted before HUAC and resumed his Hollywood career, but his best film is the rarely seen social drama *Christ in Concrete* (1949, a.k.a. *Give Us This Day*), based on the radical novel by Pietro de Donato, which was made in England while Dmytryk was still on the blacklist. After the mid 1950s, several of the blacklisted writers, including Carl Foreman, Ring Lardner Jr., Howard Kotch, Albert Maltz, and Dalton Trumbo, slowly reemerged into the light of day, sometimes commenting on their experience through their scripts, and even Abraham Polonsky was allowed to make a revisionist western during the Vietnam years, when protest became fashionable.

Billy Wilder quipped that only two of the original Hollywood nineteen were talented, whereas the rest were merely "unfriendly." But Thom Andersen's research has shown that Wilder was cruelly wrong. Without the Red generation of the 1940s, the tradition of film noir would hardly exist, and whenever a member of that generation returned to the scene of his "crimes," the results were usually interesting. Dmytryk's *Mirage*

(1965) is an antifascist thriller that deserves to stand beside his best work of the 1940s; Rossen's *Hustler* (1961) is a moral allegory of life on the mean streets that improves on *Body and Soul;* and the Hill-Lancaster production of *Sweet Smell of Success* (1957), scripted by Clifford Odets and Ernest Lehman, is the American cinema's most acid commentary on the promoters and show-business types who profited from the blacklist. Burt Lancaster's frightening portrayal of J. J. Hunsecker in the last of these films is intended to remind us of red-baiting newspaper columnists such as Walter Winchell and Westbrook Pegler, but Lancaster is also reminiscent of Charles Foster Kane, the isolated, fascistic personality who stands at the very origins of left-wing noir. Meanwhile, Tony Curtis overturns his pretty-boy persona of the 1950s, making press agent Sydney Falco into an even more repellent and pitiable character than Harry Fabian in Dassin's *Night and the City*. Odets and Lehman further intensify the noirish atmosphere by providing both Hunsecker and Falco with a hipsterish patois similar to the dialogue in Odets's antiblacklist play, *The Big Knife* (adapted for movies by Robert Aldrich and James Poe in 1955).[35] Thus when Falco plants marijuana on a jazz musician whom he also accuses of being a "card-carrying communist," he has a colorful, distinctly hard-boiled way of informing a corrupt cop that the deed has been done: "The cat's in the bag, and the bag's in the river."

The Kennedy generation of writers and directors, especially Stanley Kubrick and John Frankenheimer, were able to continue this tradition, albeit in a less realistic, more coolly self-reflexive fashion. One of Frankenheimer's best pictures, *The Manchurian Candidate* (1962), closely adapted by George Axelrod from a Richard Condon novel, deserves special attention because it functions as a kind of pop-art retrospective of the 1950s, recalling virtually every movie genre and political event of the previous decade, spinning from one mood and narrative convention to another but maintaining a noirlike and highly Wellesian sense of style.[36] Ultimately, this film attempts to outflank the right wing by using their own strategy of cold-war paranoia: a McCarthy-like senator is shown to be an unwitting dupe of the communists, and the red scare itself is revealed as a plot managed by spies from Moscow and Peking.

Although *The Manchurian Candidate* is set in the immediate aftermath of the Korean War, it makes no attempt to visually recreate the 1950s; for example, it depicts a racially integrated military, and it features an African-American psychiatrist (Joe Adams) who behaves like a New Frontiersman. The picture was in fact produced by staunch supporters of John Fitzgerald Kennedy, and it received indirect approval from

JFK himself, who was a great fan of Condon's novel. Perhaps for that reason, its narrative is fully imbued with the ideological strangeness of the time when it was made. To appreciate this fact, contemporary viewers need to recall that Kennedy was able to institute liberal reforms only by maintaining his image as a vigorous champion of the cold war. During his campaign for the presidency, he exploited a supposed "missile gap" between the United States and the Soviet Union, and his greatest popularity in office came as a result of his naval blockade of Cuba. *The Manchurian Candidate* mirrors such contradictions perfectly. It features an explicit endorsement of the American Civil Liberties Union, but at the same time it seems deeply fearful of the Reds; in the last analysis, the only defense it offers against a totalitarianism of either the Left or the Right is the national security state.

In sexual terms, *The Manchurian Candidate* tells an equally bizarre story. As Michael Rogin points out, the film taps directly into cold-war fears of "Momism," which is the "demonic version of domestic ideology," dealing with "buried anxieties over boundary invasion, loss of autonomy, and maternal power."[37] In this case, a communist plot to assassinate the president is masterminded in Washington by a seductive matriarch, who becomes outraged when she learns that the Communist Party has also arranged for her son to act as the killer. The most darkly satiric moment comes when the mother gives her brainwashed son a sexy kiss on the mouth, thereby contributing to his ultimate decision to kill both her and himself.

Like a good many classic films noirs, *The Manchurian Candidate* subscribes to Sigmund Freud's theory that male homosexuality is caused by a son's unresolved romantic attachment to his mother—indeed, it alludes to Freud and to Greek drama during an extended flashback sequence, when the brainwashed son tries to explain his evil mother to Frank Sinatra. This "tragic" determinism is intensified through the casting and acting: the maternal "Red Queen" is played by Angela Lansbury, whose performance skillfully evokes both a vamp and a matron; and the unwilling assassin is played by Laurence Harvey, who exaggerates his prissy, slightly effeminate mannerisms, as if to suggest a young man struggling to maintain a hold on his sexuality. Michael Rogin observes that the Lansbury character is a neat reversal of the sweet mother played by Helen Hayes in Leo McCarey's right-wing spy melodrama of the 1950s, *My Son John*. (She also has something in common with Norman Bates's mom in *Psycho*.) Notice, however, that although *The Manchurian Candidate* creates a maternal dominatrix who threatens to turn her son into a sissy,

FIGURE 24. The mother's embrace in *The Manchurian Candidate* (1962).

it also reasserts the values of domestic femininity and maternal care, chiefly in the form of two "good" women. Janet Leigh nurses Sinatra's wounds after a karate fight and cooks him a spaghetti dinner. Leslie Parrish (who looks rather like a young version of Lansbury) gives Laurence Harvey first aid for snake bite and seems to like it when he slaps her on the bottom and tells her to "act like a housewife." Throughout the film, as Rogin notes, the evil, politically ambitious mother functions as little more than a scapegoat to avoid "having actually to come to terms with politics," and the ultimate irony is that in reviving a cold-war mythology, the picture foreshadows the actual Kennedy assassination, which "brought the cold-war consensus to an end" (17).

The ironies in *The Manchurian Candidate* are in fact so numerous that one cannot be sure whether Frankenheimer and his collaborators were purveying old myths or making fun of them. The picture is remarkably witty and inventive at the level of cinematic technique, exhibiting a rare self-consciousness about its own methods. A dream sequence near the beginning is far more interesting than the equivalent "surrealist" nightmare in a film like *Murder, My Sweet,* because it so cleverly subverts the continuity principle of Hollywood editing and camera movement. In a later sequence, Frankenheimer depicts a television news conference that seems as dynamic and crazy in its own way as the courtroom scenes in Welles's *Lady from Shanghai.* Surrounded by reporters, the bumbling right-wing senator causes a near riot by claiming to have in his hand a list of 207 "card-carrying" communists who work for the Defense Department. As pandemonium breaks out, and as the senator keeps changing the number of communists on his list, Frankenheimer uses the monitors arranged around the room to create split-screen effects, counterpointing "behind the scenes" activity with "managed" images. Eventually, the dizzy crowd, the ubiquitous TV monitors, the wide-angle movie photography, and the discontinuous editing create such a disorienting spectacle that nobody can tell image from reality or truth from fiction.

In the last analysis, Frankenheimer's bewildering liberalism may amount to little more than what Jonathan Rosenbaum describes as "a kind of shadow play, manipulated like the Hollywood clichés for the sake of jazzy effects." One benefit of this procedure, however, is that the film exposes "the deceptive mechanisms of political and Hollywood mythmaking in general" (*Placing Movies,* 120). Rosenbaum correctly observes that whatever its politics, *The Manchurian Candidate* can be bracketed formally with a group of truly adventurous narratives operating on the margins of film noir—among them, pictures such as *Citizen Kane, Breathless,* and *La Jetée* (1963). It also seems to predict a new stage in the history of mainstream crime and espionage movies, brought on in part by the assassination of Kennedy, the Vietnam War, the advent of postmodern visual technologies, and the increasing liberalization of censorship regulations. Film noir had certainly not outlived its usefulness, but its "historical" phase was ending; it was now undergoing a sea change, or perhaps a birth into Hollywood's cultural memory.

LOW IS HIGH

Budgets and Critical Discrimination

A disproportionate number of fondly remembered B pictures fall
into the general category of the *film noir*. Somehow, even mediocrity
can become majestic when it is coupled with death.
ANDREW SARRIS, "The Beatitudes of B Pictures," 1974

Murder stories are easy to produce, and a medium-budget, occasionally
cheesy-looking thriller like *Pushover* (1954) is almost as fascinating to
watch as *Double Indemnity* or *Rear Window,* two expensive films with
which it has a good deal in common. But as Andrew Sarris suggests, there
are also some important cultural reasons for the large number of "fondly
remembered B pictures" in the noir category. The very idea of film noir
took root in America retrospectively, during the heyday of urban art theaters, when Bogart thrillers were especially popular in revival houses and
college film societies, and when advanced film criticism took its inspiration from *Cahiers du cinéma* and the French New Wave. Key examples
of classic film noir (often looking cheaper than they actually were, merely
by virtue of being old and in black and white) were exhibited late at night
in funky venues like the Charles Theater in New York, which also featured 16 mm experiments by the local avant-garde—or in the espresso-
bar surroundings of the Surf Theater in San Francisco, which later became a setting for Woody Allen's *Play It Again, Sam* (1972). Critical
commentary circulated through alternative newspapers and campus film
journals, and from the beginning, aficionados lavished special praise on

B movies or slightly pulpish genre films. It was hip, for instance, to prefer *Murder Is My Beat* over *The Maltese Falcon,* or to argue that *Touch
of Evil* was a better movie than *Citizen Kane.*

Jean-Luc Godard employed a similar strategy: *Breathless* was dedi-
cated to Monogram Pictures, and it deliberately cultivated the grainy,
improvised look of a low-budget production. Like much of the vanguard
photography and painting of the previous decade, it was visibly "imperfect," evoking a jazzy, existential "spirit of poverty" (the phrase is
Jacques Rivette's), which could be set off against Hollywood's glossy il-
lusionism.[1] Its allusions to down-market thrillers were particularly appealing to cosmopolitan audiences: after all, Hollywood films of the type
had been staged on the streets where the bohemian intelligentsia lived,
and they were usually photographed in a style that blended perfectly with
the ambience of the commercially modest yet artistically sophisticated
revival theaters. Hard-boiled pictures like Monogram's *Decoy* (1946) and
PRC's *Railroaded* (1947) still play superbly well at nighttime screenings
in museums or art houses, giving a hallucinated poetry to life in the
"naked city."

Both Godard and the 1960s revival theaters were symptoms of an
emerging postmodernism. To the new generation, the highest sophistication usually involved what Susan Sontag called an "erotics," or an appreciation of surfaces—an intellectual hedonism that dissolved the distinction between highbrow and lowbrow. In a somewhat different way,
Andrew Sarris contributed to this phenomenon.[2] As he wryly observes,
the auteurists were "vulnerable to the charge of preferring trash to art,"
because they took iconoclastic pleasure out of announcing that a film like
Kiss Me Deadly was superior to *Marty;* in effect, they were employing
"the classic highbrow gambit of elevating lowbrow art at the expense of
middle-brow art."[3] But the film critic who most exemplified the new spirit
was Manny Farber, an early advocate of "perceptive trash" (Sarris 24),
who brought a painter's sensibility to bear on male action directors. Farber had a great deal in common with Godard, and for many years he had
been writing in *The Nation* about unheralded pictures from the middle
or lower levels of Hollywood. As we have seen, he never used the term
film noir, but he helped to establish a noir canon through his vivid, sharply
intelligent discussion of Orson Welles, Anthony Mann, and John Farrow.
He also greatly increased critical interest in what he called "termite art"
as opposed to "white elephant art." In his famous 1957 essay "Underground Cinema," he makes the ordinary run of genre movies, many of
which were thrillers, seem like a kind of primitive American poetry:

They are faceless movies, taken from a type of half-polished trash writing, that seems like a mixture of Burt L. Standish, Max Brand, and Raymond Chandler. Tight, cliché-ridden melodramas about stock musclemen. A stool pigeon gurgling with scissors in his back; a fat, nasal-voiced gang leader; escaped convicts; . . . exhausted GI's; an incompetent kid hoodlum hiding out in an East Side building; . . . an underpaid shamus signing up to stop the blackmailing of a tough millionaire's depraved thumb-sucking daughter.[4]

Farber's iconoclasm lay in the fact that he used the idea of the underground, long associated with outlaws and bohemian artists, on behalf of old-fashioned products of the culture industry. Such movies, he argued, have their "natural home in caves: the murky, congested theaters, looking like glorified tattoo parlors on the outside and located near bus terminals in big cities" (15). Offering a powerful antidote to the "banality and pomp" of Radio City Music Hall, they are best viewed in "outcast theaters—the Lyric on Times Square, the Liberty on Market Street, the Victory on Chestnut," where the "cutthroat atmosphere" resembles the action on the screen, and where "the broken seats are only a minor annoyance in the unpredictable terrain" (18).

Ironically, the original French discussion of American film noir, which had helped to validate many of the pictures Farber admired, was stimulated not by fleabag productions, but by a series of major-studio releases that attracted widespread critical attention. Despite their sordid subject matter, prototypical films noirs such as *The Maltese Falcon* and *Laura* were highly publicized events and involved well-paid stars and directors. Howard Hawks, one of Farber's favorite "underground" artists, was in fact one of the most prosperous and respected producer-directors in Hollywood, responsible for a string of box-office hits featuring the leading personalities of his day. What qualified Hawks for membership in Farber's "trash" pantheon was not his working conditions, budgets, or exhibition venues, but his subject matter and style. Hawks specialized in unpretentious action pictures rather than well-made literary adaptations or liberal social-problem pictures; his skillful treatment of ostensibly lowbrow material made him attractive to Farber, who tended to write about some types of film as if they were always as cheap as the worlds they depicted. In other words, like many critics of the French New Wave, Farber blurred the distinction between economics and artistic politics. Ultimately, his notion of the "underground" had less to do with material poverty than with a supposed lack of cultural capital.

This being said, it must also be emphasized that films noirs of the 1940s were symptomatic of a wartime economy and that many of their characteristic visual effects could be immediately duplicated at every level of the industry. Thus a kind of generic cinema grew up around the "original" films and remained in force until the mid 1950s.[5] Roy William Neill's modestly budgeted *Black Angel* (1946), based on a Cornell Woolrich novel, was almost as enjoyable as Hawks's high-profile adaptation of Raymond Chandler's *Big Sleep,* which was released to great fanfare in the same year. William Castle's even cheaper Monogram thriller, *When Strangers Marry* (1944), drew extravagant praise from both Farber and Orson Welles, who admired its innovative use of sparse resources—as when Castle illuminated Kim Hunter's drab hotel room with nothing more than a pulsing neon light from outside the window. (Castle may not have invented this device, but his use of it anticipates many films with bigger budgets, including Michael Curtiz's *Unsuspected* [1947] and Welles's *Touch of Evil.*) Along similar lines, Val Lewton's horror films, which played in bargain-basement theaters without studio promotion, were among Farber's and James Agee's favorite movies of the period.

Throughout the 1940s, there was a stable marketplace for low-budget thrillers, and the noir category itself later became associated with so-called B pictures.[6] But critics often use adjectives like *underground* or *B* quite loosely, in reference to a great many things that were not actually inferior or disreputable. The fact is, most of the respected examples of classic noir belong not to Poverty Row but to an ambiguous middle range of the industry. Very few films about urban darkness and murder in the 1940s and 1950s were among the most expensive Hollywood productions, but neither were they truly cheap. Even when they were not among the industry's leading moneymakers, they were reasonably popular and widely distributed; and although they tended to win awards only when they were perceived as social-problem pictures, most of them were favorably reviewed in the national press.[7] In both economic and cultural terms, therefore, they are best described as liminal products, and it seems appropriate that they eventually came to occupy a borderland somewhere between generic thrillers and art movies.

A sense of middle-to-low-range economic activity was often inscribed in the films themselves—especially in the hard-boiled stories, which depicted white-collar protagonists living in a world of cheap rooming houses and battered offices. Perhaps for that reason, the literature on Hollywood thrillers has tended to foster myths of a cultural underworld. Figures like Dashiell Hammett, Chandler, and James M. Cain are sometimes incorrectly described as low-culture artists, and almost from the beginning, certain films noirs have been mistakenly associated with *art maudit* and

sleazy theaters. For example, in a 1947 essay on exhibition, sociologist
Charles P. Skouras refers to "the grind house, a small theater along a
busy downtown street catering to transients, [which] does its biggest business with action melodramas like *The Killers*."[8] We should recall that
The Killers was a major-studio production based on the work of a prestigious novelist and that it received Academy Award nominations for best
director and screenplay; no doubt it played in "grind houses," but it also
played in expensive ones. Such a film is quite different from Lewton's B-
budget horror pictures for RKO, which were confined to the lower levels of the industry. Lewton's biggest success, *Cat People,* earned a considerable profit and an impressive degree of critical attention; even so,
RKO executive Charles Korner complained, "The only people who saw
that film were Negroes and defense workers."[9]

All of which suggests that we need to look more closely at the complex relationship between economics, reception, and cultural prestige. In
so doing, we shall discover that film noir has a deceptive and somewhat
paradoxical status. Cheapness, after all, is sometimes in the eye of the
beholder, and some forms of lowness are more valuable than others.

B Pictures versus Intermediates

Hollywood has always made low-budget pictures, but the "B" designa-
tion originated in the 1930s, when exhibitors began to offer Depression-
era moviegoers two features for the price of one. Although the palatial
theaters in big cities continued to function as showcases for single at-
tractions, the general audience grew to expect a three-hour program consisting of two movies and several short subjects. In most cases, the first
or "A" picture was a star-filled "quality" production, backed by a major-
studio advertising campaign; whatever its actual budget, it was rented
on a percentage basis, with the producer-distributor sometimes getting
as much as 80 percent of the gross. The "B," or "program," picture was
usually a genre movie from one of the Poverty Row studios and was
rented at a flat rate of $100 or $200.

A wide range of movies fell into the B category, but the cheapest productions in the 1940s were aimed at audiences in the provinces, or at
kids who attended Saturday matinees. To understand the purely budgetary limitations of such films, it may help to note that between 1945
and 1950, when production costs and ticket prices rose almost 60 percent, the average B western from Republic Pictures was made for about
$50,000. Meanwhile, Fritz Lang's *Secret beyond the Door* (1948), a melo-

drama involving the theme of psychoanalysis, was budgeted by the same studio at $615,065.[10] The Lang picture is sometimes described as if it were an example of bargain-basement noir. Certainly it looks inexpensive compared to the Selznick-Hitchcock *Spellbound* (1945); even so, it was intended for the better theaters in the cities, and despite its somewhat tacky production values, it does not actually qualify as a B movie.

In contrast to Lang, most of the house directors and technicians who worked at Republic, Monogram, PRC, and the other Poverty Row companies were held to budgets of under $200,000—which meant that they were given extremely short shooting schedules and only a minimum supply of film stock. They often recycled their sets, their costumes, and even their characters—in part because the most profitable B pictures functioned much like the comic strips in the daily newspapers, showing the continuing adventures of Roy Rogers, Boston Blackie, the Bowery Boys, Blondie and Dagwood, Charlie Chan, and so on. Even a major studio like MGM was equipped with a so-called B unit that specialized in these serial productions. At MGM, however, the Andy Hardy, Dr. Kildaire, and Thin Man films were made with major stars and with what some organizations would have considered A budgets.[11]

The A versus B system remained more or less in place until the late 1940s, but as historian Lea Jacobs has shown, the distinction between the two grades was ambiguous and never dependent on money alone. During the period in question, the vertically integrated studios engaged in a system of "block booking" and "blind selling," whereby ordinary exhibitors were required to accept a certain number of A or B films in advance, without regard to title. The major producer-distributors could therefore use their own theaters to determine how long a given film would be in first-run and in which category it would play. If an A picture did poorly on its initial showing in the big city, it could be immediately assigned B-picture status, and if certain B features had sufficient production values and favorable reviews, they could be marketed as "A's." This last arrangement was especially useful in the case of "intermediates," which cost between $250,000 and $500,000. Such films could not make a profit, Jacobs observes, unless "some exhibitors were persuaded (or coerced!) to pay a percentage of the gross rather than the flat rental fee usual for westerns and other B pictures."[12]

The distinction between A and B was further complicated by the fact that low-budget pictures could sometimes get expensive advertising and high-profile critical attention that raised their cultural capital and their drawing power. Jacobs cites the example of John Ford's *Informer* (1935), which is often described as a B movie, even though its $243,000 budget was only slightly less than that of the average RKO release of its day. A shadowy, fog-shrouded picture about Irish revolutionaries (Raymond Durgnat calls it a film noir), *The Informer* deliberately eschewed stars and spectacle; nevertheless, it had a great many "artistic" qualities, and it received a gilt-edged marketing treatment, premiering at Radio City, attracting the attention of major newspapers and magazines, and ultimately winning several Academy Awards.

In purely budgetary terms, many of the thrillers that historians describe as B or "underground" pictures were actually "intermediates" like *The Informer,* specifically designed to gain a certain amount of critical attention and larger profits from percentage-deal bookings in the cities. These productions typically offered a good deal of sex and violence, along with implicit claims to artistic significance and social realism, usually signified by a mixture of expressionist and documentary techniques. They were shot on dark streets or on inexpensive sets, but they also featured well-known actors from the second tier of the Hollywood star system. Sometimes they had enough impact to become "sleepers" and make a good deal of money. One of the most successful instances of the strategy is *T-Men* (1947), a police procedural about government undercover agents working to crack the "Shanghai Paper Case." This film was distributed by Eagle-Lion, a newly formed company owned by J. Arthur Rank and headed by Brian Foy, who had formerly been in charge of the B-picture unit at Warner. It used the sound stages and physical plant of PRC, one of the leading producers of cheap genre movies in Hollywood, and it employed director Anthony Mann and photographer John Alton because they were both veterans of low-budget action pictures at Republic. *T-Men* was nevertheless provided with a $450,000 budget and a reasonable chance to compete in the A-picture marketplace. Alton, who had always regarded himself as an artist rather than a Hollywood roughneck, responded with a dynamic, wide-angle photography that made especially effective use of expensive locations and night-for-night situations in Detroit and Los Angeles. His brilliant imagery was enhanced by Mann's direction and by the surprisingly tough performance of Dennis O'Keefe, who also specialized in light comedy and low-budget musicals. As a result, the film attracted the interest of critics and trade reporters. *Life* magazine gave *T-Men* a full-scale "Movie of the Week" analysis, and commentators in *Newsweek* and other journals praised it for injecting "realism" into a formulaic plot. (This realism consisted largely of devices borrowed from the successful postwar productions of Louis de Rochemont at Twentieth-Century Fox: newsreel-style narration, location photography, and official cooperation from a U.S. government agency.) Ultimately, the film made $1.6 million at the box office—a profit that would have been impossible under B-picture rental arrangements.[13]

T-Men arrived at the very end of the double feature era, when movie attendance was shrinking, when the studios were reorganizing, and when independent production companies were becoming an industry trend. For a while, its success helped to secure a place in the market for atmospheric, medium-budget thrillers that slightly raised the level of screen violence and perversity. RKO had long specialized in such films, and in the early 1950s Republic and Monogram (which changed its name to Allied Artists) tried to follow suit. Not surprisingly, Mann and Alton were soon hired by Dore Schary at MGM—where, together or separately, they made such modest but technically sophisticated films as Border Incident (1949), Side Street (1949), and Mystery Street (1950). From that point onward, they were free of Poverty Row, and their pictures were seldom rented at a flat rate. Much the same thing could be said of the roughly contemporary work of Samuel Fuller, Jacques Tourneur, and Joseph H. Lewis, who are often inaccurately described as B-picture auteurs. When critics analyze Lewis's career, for example, they barely mention his Bowery Boys films at Monogram in 1940 to 1941, his war movies and westerns at PRC in 1942 to 1944, or his contribution to the Falcon series at RKO in 1945; instead, they concentrate on My Name Is Julia Ross (1946), Gun Crazy (1950), and The Big Combo (1955). These last films were mid-level productions from the era when the Poverty Row system was changing or dying out, and they were all reviewed in the national press.[14] Strictly speaking, they belong not to the world of B pictures but to the more amorphous realm of what Manny Farber described as "faceless" or "half-polished" melodramas, most of which did not become objects of critical fascination until long after they were released.

To see what film noir on a Poverty Row budget looked like, one needs to search out a truly obscure picture such as The Argyle Secrets (1948), an antifascist crime drama written and directed by Cyril Endfield and produced by the Film Classics Studio. The acting, set design, and photography in this movie are not much better than in the standard offering in a Saturday matinee, but the plot is reminiscent of Citizen Kane and The Maltese Falcon, with a couple of scenes from Thirty-Nine Steps tossed in for good measure. Throughout, the dialogue and narration are clever, and the action always moves swiftly. One episode is particularly memorable for its perversity: the protagonist (William Gargan), a tough newspaper reporter searching for the meaning of a rich man's last words, is captured by a gang of villains like the one in *The Maltese Falcon* and subjected to a slow, methodical beating. The torture scene is rendered in the form of an expressionist dream sequence, with the faces of the gang superimposed over the reporter's body and their voices speaking in rhythm with the sound of blows. Soon afterward, the bruised and bloody reporter awakens in a strange bedroom, where he is confronted by a femme fatale (Marjorie Lord). This lady offers him a chance to escape his captors by feigning an attack on her, and he willingly complies, taking an evident sexual pleasure in the job. "It was a funny experience, choking a woman deliberately," he says in his offscreen narration. "I squeezed pretty hard, scuffing bruises at her throat to make it look good. I got so mixed up I didn't know what I was doing, and I stopped once and kissed her pretty hard." Here and elsewhere, one gets the feeling that a movie designed for provincial audiences has been invaded with the dark ironies of big-city entertainment. Even so, *The Argyle Secrets* received no important bookings, and it was given only one review—in *Variety*, which described it as "okay supporting material" for double features. It therefore dropped from sight and has seldom been revived.[15]

The most celebrated director of this sort of "supporting" cinema is Edgar G. Ulmer—who, had he not existed, would probably need to be invented. A true aesthete of the lower depths, Ulmer seems to have taken a pleasure out of blending the sophisticated and the tawdry. He was in fact among the most talented of the many distinguished European émigrés to Hollywood during the 1920s and 1930s. While in Germany, he was a designer for Max Reinhardt; an assistant for F. W. Murnau, Lang, and Ernst Lubitsch; a codirector with Robert Siodmak on *Menschen am Sontag;* and a self-described "art-obsessed" intellectual who felt an affinity with Bertolt Brecht and the Bauhaus. In America, however, he spent much of his time on Yiddish art films, two-bit westerns, instructional films for the Ford motor company, and exploitation movies with titles like *Girls in Chains* (1943). "I knew [L. B.] Mayer very well," he told Peter Bogdanovich, "and I prided myself that he could never hire me!"[16] At the peak of his career, he was dubbed "the Capra of PRC," which meant that he had his own crew and relative freedom at a sub-minor-league studio. His masterpiece, *Detour* (1945), is a genuinely cheap production, photographed in only six days, with a two-to-one shooting ratio, seven speaking parts, and a running time of a little over an hour. As far as I can determine, its only U.S. review was in *Variety*, which said that it was "okay as a supporting dualer" (23 January 1946). It is nevertheless contemporary with the first group of Hollywood movies that the French described as American noir, and it can stand comparison with any of them.

Detour's script, by Martin Goldsmith, is reminiscent of James M. Cain's novels (immediately after the success of *Double Indemnity*, Ulmer wrote a script for PRC entitled *Single Indemnity*), but it also borrows from the doom-laden, slightly crazed fiction of Cornell Woolrich and Frederic Brown, and from the uncanny, twist-of-fate stories that were common on radio during the 1940s. In keeping with these sources, its mise-en-scène is distilled from the essence of hard-boiled cliché. Near the beginning, we see the protagonist, Al Roberts (Tom Neal), wearing a rumpled suit, a snap-brim hat, and a five-o'clock shadow, drinking coffee in a roadside diner just outside Reno. When a truck driver drops a nickel into the jukebox, Roberts's offscreen voice asks, "Why was it always that rotten tune?" This leads to an obligatory flashback and to a bizarre tale of desire and death.

Like Walter Neff in *Double Indemnity*, Al blames his problems on destiny. The flashback begins by showing him in better days, playing a piano in a New York nightclub, where his girlfriend Sue (Claudia Drake) is the featured singer. Al seems to have talent, but when Sue moves to Los Angeles in hopes of becoming a star, he sinks into a black mood. At one point, working solo in the club, he performs a rather violent, boogie-woogie rendition of Brahms, for which he receives a meager tip. Soon afterward, he quits his job and hitchhikes westward. For all his travels, however, he goes nowhere. On the highway, he catches a ride in a flashy convertible driven by Charles Haskell (Edmund MacDonald), who exhibits an old dueling scar from his youth and a vicious scratch that he claims to have received quite recently from an angry woman. That night, while Al takes the wheel, Haskell falls asleep in the passenger seat and dies under mysterious circumstances. Al fears that the police will accuse him of murder, so he buries the dead man and momentarily assumes his identity. After crossing the border into California, he gives a lift to a provocative female hitchhiker named Vera (Ann Savage), who subsequently identifies herself as the woman who scratched Haskell's hand. Vera scoffs at the idea that Haskell's death could have been an accident, and she threatens to expose Al unless he sells the car and gives her half the money. When they arrive in Los Angeles, she accidentally learns that Haskell was the heir of a dying millionaire, and she insists that Al continue his masquerade. She and Al spend the night in rented rooms, drinking heavily and quarreling over her scheme to collect the inheritance. When he refuses to go along, she picks up the telephone and runs into the

FIGURES 25–27. The haunted coffee cup in *Detour* (1945).

bedroom, locks the door, and threatens to call the police. Al grabs the lengthy telephone cord and pulls it hard, trying to snap it free from the connection. When he breaks the door open, he finds that the cord has become entangled around Vera's neck. As he stands over her dead body, a dissolve takes us back to the diner in Reno, where the story began.

Detour is in many ways dated by its mode of production. The lush musical score by Leo Erdoty intensifies this quality, as do the cheap sets and the occasional technical flaws. But Ulmer is no Ed Wood. As only one example of his artistry, consider the early scene in the roadside diner, which involves a clever visual trick. As the jukebox plays "I Can't Believe That You're in Love with Me," Tom Neal is seen in medium shot from across the counter, a coffee cup near his right hand. The camera tracks forward to a tight close-up of his face, and the lights suddenly dim, signaling a transition into a subjective mood. A spotlight hovers around Neal's eyes, giving him a demonic look, and for a moment we can sense a technician behind the camera, trying to aim the light correctly. Neal broods, and the camera tilts down to view his coffee cup; what it sees, however, is a model, several times larger than the original, looming up before him in vaguely surreal fashion. (See figures 25–27.)

Few people will notice that a substitution of coffee cups has occurred; indeed they are not supposed to notice, because Ulmer wants to create a dreamlike close-up of an apparently ordinary object and thus set the stage for the nightmarish flashback. In this regard as in others, he resembles Alfred Hitchcock, who once ordered his technicians to build a huge pair of women's eyeglasses for an important image in *Strangers on a Train* (1950). Not surprisingly, both directors were schooled in the German industry at a time when entire sets were constructed through the viewfinders of cameras. Ulmer had been Murnau's designer on *Sunrise,* one of the most artfully controlled films in history, and *Detour* is quite similar to that production in its studio-based expressionism, its careful attention to camera movement and offscreen space, and its intensely subjective narration.

Ulmer lacked the vast technical resources of Murnau or Hitchcock, but his relative poverty gave him certain advantages. *Detour* is so far down on the economic and cultural scale of things that it virtually escapes commodification, and it can be viewed as a kind of subversive or vanguard art. A radically stylized film, it is photographed almost entirely indoors, overcoming its severe budget limitations by means of process screens, sparsely decorated sets, and expressionistic designs. Ulmer represents his locales with a breathtaking minimalism: New York is nothing more than a foggy soundstage and a streetlamp, and Los Angeles a used-car lot and a drive-in restaurant. Meanwhile, he makes old-fashioned but highly effective use of optical devices such as wipes and irises, and he may be the only Hollywood director of the period—aside from Orson Welles—to deliberately exploit the artificiality of back projection. Notice the scene when Haskell falls asleep while Al is driving his car: behind Al, the white rails or fence posts on the side of the road become hugely magnified, flashing past in a hypnotic blur.[17]

Detour also employs nearly all the modernist themes and motifs described in chapter 2. Not surprisingly, its narrative technique reminds contemporary critic Andrew Britton of both Henry James's fiction and Sigmund Freud's writings on "secondary revision." Britton seems to me to overstate the moral culpability of Ulmer's protagonist, but he is surely correct to argue that Al Roberts is an unreliable narrator who travels through an American wasteland.[18] The last of these themes is particularly important. Like a great many films noirs about the open road, *Detour* represents the western frontier as a desert and the quest for individual freedom as a meaningless circle or a trap. It anticipates the imagery of Hitchcock's *Psycho* by almost thirty years: a barren landscape viewed through an automobile window; a protagonist who drives by day and night, staring into a rear-view mirror and hearing voices from out of the past; a sinister highway patrol officer with dark glasses; a used-car dealership; and a cheap and deadly motel room.

Here again, Ulmer's low budget works to his advantage. *Detour* has no need to indulge in a Hollywood designer's idea of despair, because its own cost-cutting produces an atmosphere of pinched difficulty and claustrophobia. The flimsy sets reinforce the theme of social and cultural impoverishment, and the actors seem to belong to the same marginal world as the characters they play. Everyone in the film is a low-rent pretender or impostor (even Haskell turns out to be a "hymnal salesman"), and nobody has a chance of success.

The most disturbing of these pretenders is Vera, who makes every femme fatale in the period look genteel by comparison. Like Al, she has been hitchhiking across country, and she claims that when Haskell picked her up just outside Shreveport, she fought off his advances, leaving him with an infected hand. In some ways, she is a double for Al, but when she wakes from her brief nap on the passenger seat of the car, she also suggests a ghostly reincarnation of Haskell, come back to wreak vengeance. Al can't figure out what to make of Vera. "She looked as if she'd just been thrown off the worst freight train in the world," he says, but then he notices her "beauty," which seems "homely, but real." Actually, she has dark rings around her eyes, and she suffers from a consumptive cough. ("Hitching rides," she comments, "isn't exactly the way to keep your schoolgirl complexion.") Al compares her with Camille, but clearly she is no wilting, sacrificial heroine of sentimental melodrama; instead, she taps into a raw nerve of greed and exploitation that lies at the core of the film. Ruthlessly hard and half-crazed, she lolls about the Los Angeles hotel rooms in her bathrobe, downing straight whiskey, chain-smoking, and plotting to get rich. She probably knows that she is dying, but she easily dominates Al, first insulting him and then inviting him to bed. A sullen, dangerous, yet sympathetic figure, she leaves an indelible impression, and it is impossible to imagine any A-budget picture that would have been allowed to depict her. When Al sits alone in the Reno diner and recalls her image, he seems to be looking into a void.

On many levels, *Detour* provides justification for the idea that downmarket thrillers are more authentic, less compromised by bourgeois-liberal sentiment or totalitarian spectacle, than the usual Hollywood product. Unfortunately, however, few if any of the most critically respected films of this type were so unsettling, and none were made on such a low budget. The Poverty Row mode of production was given its death warrant in 1948, when the major studios were ordered to divest themselves of theaters; connoisseurship of so-called B film noir began much later, and the use of the term by critics often has less to do with actual costs than with a misperception of poverty—a misperception that involves a particular blend of failed theatricality, artistic sophistication, and subversive implication.

One of the best illustrations of such critical reception can be found in the writing about *Gun Crazy*, another movie about violence on the American road, which inspired several other pictures about outlaw lovers. *Gun Crazy* has much more elaborate production values than *Detour*, and its premiere was held at the somewhat dilapidated but still respectable Palace Theater in New York. Nevertheless, it was produced at a minor studio (Allied Artists); its mise-en-scène creates what Dana Polan accurately describes as "a typology of nonpastoral, wasteland sites";[19] and it lacks the formal coherence of a well-made, major-league feature. Veering back and forth between badness and brilliance, it repeatedly subverts its own earnestness with an anarchic romanticism. As a result, latter-day critics have usually disregarded its actual position in the market and placed it on the level of the pulp sublime.

Shortly after *Gun Crazy* opened, Bosley Crowther gave it a mixed review in *The New York Times*, devoting most of his favorable comments to the script, which was adapted from a story by MacKinlay Kantor in the slickest of all magazines, *The Saturday Evening Post*. Otherwise, Crowther thought the film was "pretty cheap stuff," on a par with "the most humdrum of pulp fiction" (25 August 1950). For later critics, *Gun Crazy* has seemed charming precisely because of its failure to maintain the lofty, sociological tone of Kantor's work, or even the poetic realism of such movies as *You Only Live Once* and *They Live by Night*. Its very title is ambiguous, suggesting both shocked censure and gleeful exploitation, and several of its most enjoyable effects seem unintended. The dialogue, for example, contains lines such as "Two people dead, just so we can live without working!" The two leading players, Peggy Cummins and John Dall, are slightly miscast, and a few of the early scenes are laughable. At one point we see the Dall character as a boy, shooting a chicken in a farmyard; when we cut to an insert of the dead bird, it looks like something that has been lying around the property department for weeks. And yet director Joseph H. Lewis achieves one of the most celebrated sequence shots in the history of movies—a bank robbery in a southwestern town, photographed by Russell Harlan in documentary style from the back seat of the getaway car. This shot is refreshingly free of studioish mannerisms, and the robbery itself (which takes place offscreen) gains considerable tension from being represented as an urgent and partly improvised piece of "real time." Elsewhere, *Gun Crazy* offers a superbly staged holdup of an Armour meat-packing plant, and (for the period) a delightfully forthright eroticism. Although it somewhat villainizes the female, denying her the point-of-view shots it gives to the male, it also inverts the usual sex roles, hinting at John Dall's "feminine" qualities (he had recently played a homosexual for Hitchcock) and allowing Peggy Cummins to play a kind of murderous Annie Oakley. As Alain Silver and Carl Macek point out, most of the film is "atavistic," providing few social or psychological motivations for the outlaw couple; instead, it appears to celebrate their passionate attachment and "basic lawlessness."[20]

Because *Gun Crazy*'s lack of cinematic polish was homologous with the outlaw couple's disregard of bourgeois morality, viewers were given an opportunity to feel irresponsible and discriminating at the same time. The surrealists loved the film, Godard alluded to it several times in *Breathless*, and cinephiles everywhere used it as a weapon against middlebrow critics and major Hollywood studios. However, despite its "underground" appeal, *Gun Crazy* was not a B movie in the same sense as *Detour*. An intermediate production, it was typical of a period when the studio system was undergoing reorganization. Looked at today, what makes it strikingly different from its many big-budget successors—including not only *Bonnie and Clyde* but also *Wild at Heart* (1990), *True Romance* (1993), and *Natural Born Killers* (1994)—is not so much its cheapness but its relative innocence. It belongs to a time before Elvis, before Vietnam, before the collapse of the classic censorship code, before music videos, before the widespread popularity of old movies like *The Wizard of Oz,* and before film noir itself became an idea in the minds of producers. It has no need to allude to most of these things (as its imitators do), nor to devise increasingly spectacular scenes of sex and violence. It simply waivers between entertainment and art, creating a somewhat naive, "good-bad" effect.

A less innocent and slightly more expensive balancing act between pulp formulas and artistic ambition lies behind Robert Aldrich's independent production of *Kiss Me Deadly* (1955)—which, as we have seen in chapter 1, was a crucial event for the French auteurists, signaling the end of Hollywood noir. On one level, Aldrich clearly designed this picture to capitalize on the extraordinary success of lowbrow novelist Mickey Spillane. In the years between 1948 and 1955, Spillane wrote seven of the ten bestselling books of all time and almost single-handedly established a mass readership for the American paperback industry. Despite his worldwide fame, however, Spillane was considered too vulgar and controversial for the major Hollywood producers, and films based on his work were made without A-picture stars or budgets. Meanwhile, intellectuals and cultural critics regularly attacked his private-eye hero, Mike Hammer—a misogynistic, racist, avenging proletarian who deals out brutal punishment to commie traitors and voluptuous dames. Hammer's frankly pornographic adventures involve many of the same formulas that Hammett and Chandler used, but they are devoid of any redeeming social content. Pure masculine fantasy, they resemble an archetypal film noir without the intervening control of the Breen Office or the artistic superego. Here, for example, is the famous conclusion to *I, the Jury,* which was probably inspired by the film adaptation of *Double Indemnity:*

> Slowly, a sigh escaped her, making the hemispheres of her breasts quiver. She leaned forward to kiss me, her arms going out to encircle my neck.
> The roar of the .45 shook the room. Charlotte staggered back a step. Her eyes were a symphony of incredulity, an unbelieving witness to truth. Slowly, she looked down at the ugly swelling in her naked belly where the bullet went in . . . "How c-could you?" she gasped.
> I had only a moment before talking to a corpse, but I got it in.
> "It was easy," I said.

The film version of *Kiss Me Deadly* has a similar atmosphere, although most writings on noir describe it as a critique of Spillane. No doubt it *had* to be critical or revisionist to a degree if it wanted to achieve acceptance among reviewers and mainstream exhibitors; but within the limits of movie censorship in 1955, it also tried to give Mike Hammer's fans a good deal of what they expected. "We kept faith with 60 million Mickey Spillane readers," Aldrich claimed in *The New York Herald Tribune,* where he defended the picture as a work of "action, violence, and suspense in good taste." Scriptwriter A. I. Bezzerides more or less agreed, although he later confessed to cynicism: "I wrote it fast, because I had contempt for it. It was automatic writing. Things were in the air at the time and I put them in."[21]

Bezzerides and Aldrich were in fact liberals, and for that reason, their film has a divided attitude toward the hero, who can be viewed as a conventional tough guy or as a kind of monster. Aldrich himself acknowledged this effect in a 1956 interview: "When I asked my American friends to tell me whether they felt my disgust for the whole mess, they said that between the fights and the kissing scenes they hadn't noticed anything of the sort."[22] The adaptation nevertheless puts an ironic twist on the novel's politics, dispensing with Spillane's first-person narration and right-wing rhetoric and giving the women characters plenty of opportunity to criticize the phallic, self-absorbed private eye (despite the fact that they all find him sexually irresistible). Ralph Meeker, a method-style actor, plays Mike Hammer in Neanderthal fashion, and the film as a whole makes him seem vaguely repellent. A specialist in divorce cases and illegal investigations, he looks rather like a cross between Spillane's character and a *Playboy* male: thus he drives a foreign sports car, he employs a secretary who dresses in tights and does ballet exercises in his office, and he lives in a modernistic apartment with a fancy answering machine built into the wall. In keeping with this proto-Bond ambience, his sphere of operation has been changed from New York to Los Angeles, and he is sent in pursuit of a MacGuffin called "the great whatsit," which turns out to be an atomic bomb stolen by a criminal mastermind named Dr. Soberin. (The criminals in the novel are drug dealers; Aldrich and Bezzerides introduced the mad-scientist cliché because of censorship restrictions against drugs in movies.)

Throughout, *Kiss Me Deadly* alternates between social-realist scenes of urban decay and visions of a souped-up, hypermodern America—a consumerist world of fast cars, pinup girls, monosyllabic tough guys, Bel Air swimming pools, Malibu beach houses, and nuclear fission. The pace and tone are perfectly described by Nick (Nick Dennis), Mike Hammer's auto-mechanic pal (and an alter-ego for scriptwriter Bezzerides), who keeps shouting "Va-va-voom!" In the end, as if to provide an ironic climax to all the explosiveness, Aldrich uses a device worthy of *Dr. Strangelove* (1964): Soberin's hideout at Malibu goes up in an atomic blast, wiping out both Hammer and the villains. (Some prints show Hammer and his secretary, Velda, escaping into the Pacific; their survival is doubtful, however, because they move only a few yards from ground zero.) The final, spectacular shots are brief but stunning, pushing the "lone wolf" myth of private-eye fiction to its self-destructive limit and reducing an entire genre to nuclear waste.[23]

Even before the outrageous, apocalyptic ending, Aldrich and Bezzerides distance themselves from Spillane by filling the movie with signifiers of art, thereby establishing a counterpoint between the callous and the sensitive, the crude and the cultivated. For example, an important clue to the mystery is a couplet from Christina Rossetti's poem "Remember Me." ("But when the darkness and corruption leave / A vestige of the thoughts that once we had.") Elsewhere, the film contains allusions to Cerberus, Pandora, and the Medusa, along with fragments of music by Pyotr Ilich Tchaikovsky and Friedrich Flotow. (One of Mike Hammer's more brutal acts is to destroy a recording by Enrico Caruso; he himself listens to jazz singers like Nat Cole and Madi Comfort.) An even more obvious sign of the film's allegiance to critical modernism is its some-

FIGURE 28. Mike Hammer as *Playboy* male in *Kiss Me Deadly* (1955).

what commercially retrograde visual style. At a time when low-budget movies were increasingly turning to color and wide screens, Aldrich and cinematographer Ernest Laszlo remained faithful to Hollywood's semi-documentary, left-wing thrillers of the late 1940s: they used a grainy, black-and-white film stock that deglamorizes Hammer's world, and they photographed most of the action on location, mapping the shadowy decadence of Los Angeles from Malibu to Bunker Hill. They also borrowed considerably from Orson Welles. No Hollywood movie before *Touch of Evil* so skillfully explores the possibilities of wide-angle tracking shots and deep-focus compositions, and very few create a more jagged, out-of-kilter look. Like nearly all of Welles's best work, *Kiss Me Deadly* is an unusually dynamic and disorienting movie—as in the weirdly reversed crawl that displays the opening credits, where Aldrich seems to be standing Mickey Spillane on his head. Throughout, the film's bizarre settings and wildly opposed cultural codes are set in conflict, and its soundtrack often becomes dissonant, almost hysterical. As a result, it provokes comparison with established forms of serious art. When *Village Voice* critic J. Hoberman reviewed the film for a New York retrospective in 1994, he praised its "crazy, clashing expressionism" and argued that "Hammer's quest is played out through a deranged Cubistic space amid the debris of Western civilization" (43).

FIGURE 29. Turning Mickey Spillane upside down.

Unfortunately, none of these attributes were noted by the Anglo-American critical establishment in 1955. Perhaps Spillane's sensational reputation obscured what Aldrich had done, or perhaps the meaning of the film has changed over time. In any case, when *Kiss Me Deadly* was originally released, *The New York Times* did not review it, the Legion of Decency condemned it, the British banned it altogether, and United Artists had difficulty advertising it in midwestern and southern towns. The French, however, passionately embraced it, and because of their somewhat ironic interpretation, it eventually became one of the most admired films of the decade. Today, in the various culinary guides to classic videos and TV movies, it receives multiple stars. A quintessential example of how a supposedly "cheap" artifact can acquire an aura, it is universally regarded as a masterpiece of noir.

POST-B PICTURES

When *Kiss Me Deadly* was released in 1955, the B-picture industry was already dead, and most studios that financed medium-budget thrillers were in economic trouble. Republic and Allied Artists were unsuccessfully producing intermediate and A pictures, Howard Hughes was in the process of selling RKO to General Tire and Rubber, and Charles Chaplin was divesting himself of one-quarter ownership in United Artists. Two of the most successful mainstream films of that year were Warner Brothers' *Rebel without a Cause* and MGM's *Blackboard Jungle*. Also in 1955, Samuel Z. Arkoff and James H. Nicholson founded American International Pictures. The movies were discovering the youth market, and a new age of exhibition, sometimes called the schlock-exploitation era, was about to begin.

Evidence of the changing times could be seen in two perversely violent, erotically charged thrillers of 1955—neither of them addressed to teenagers, and neither of them especially successful at the box office. First was *The Big Combo,* an intermediate-level production from Allied Artists, directed by Joseph H. Lewis and featuring a number of aging, not-quite stars (Cornell Wilde, Richard Conte, Brian Donlevy). Second was *Killer's Kiss,* a seventy-five-thousand-dollar independent feature distributed through United Artists, produced and directed by Stanley Kubrick, and performed by a small cast of unknowns. The Lewis picture, which was impressively photographed by John Alton, has subsequently acquired a cult reputation because of its skillful treatment of repressed, sadomasochistic relationships; nevertheless, it remains a studioish throwback to the kind of thing Hollywood was doing five years earlier, and it looked dated even when it was released. In contrast, the Kubrick thriller was innovative and virtually handmade, like a protoart film disguising itself as a genre movie and crossing over to the lowest levels of theatrical exhibition.

In its style and mode of production (if not in its sexual politics), *Killer's Kiss* is ahead of its time, whereas *The Big Combo* is relatively antiquated. British critic Chris Hugo observes that it would be almost impossible in the contemporary theatrical marketplace to create a middle-budget, widely distributed equivalent of the Lewis picture. Such a film could succeed, he argues, only as "a minority-interest independent feature, with distribution aimed at art houses," and it would no doubt become "mannered and self-consciously referential to *film noir* of the past, as this 'cultural capital' would be its chief selling point" (Cameron, 253). In comparison, a sophisticated but inexpensive feature like *Killer's Kiss* already has many of the qualities Hugo describes and would be relatively easy to duplicate. In fact, Matthew Chapman's *Strangers Kiss* (1984), a contemporary low-budget movie about the making of a low-budget movie, uses thinly disguised scenes from *Killer's Kiss* for its film-within-the-film, which is directed by a character named Stanley.

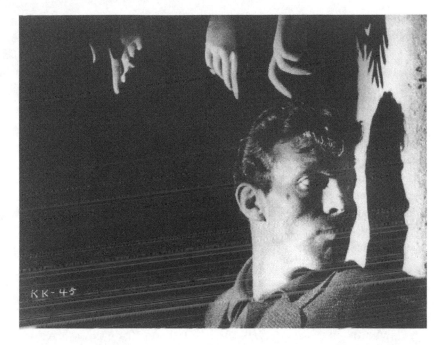

FIGURE 30. *Killer's Kiss* (1955). (Museum of Modern Art Stills Archive.)

Kubrick's perverse story about a triangle of sexual obsession between a gangster, a dance-hall girl, and a prizefighter was produced before the art-theater marketplace had fully emerged, and it was filmed so cheaply that it has almost no direct sound recording or dialogue. The opening sequence borrows a few images from Kubrick's earlier nonfiction short, *Day of the Fight* (1951), and later scenes are photographed with a hidden camera as the players mingle with the nighttime crowds on Times Square. Throughout, Kubrick uses 1940s-style narration as a substitute for speech, and he often composes over-the-shoulder shots in order to hide lip movements. (He also stages conversations on telephones, which makes the work of dubbing much easier.) His cost cutting sometimes results in an abstract or symbolic effect, reminiscent of the avant-garde. Midway through the film, a flashback-within-a-flashback allows the dime-a-dance girl to take over the narration from the prizefighter: her elaborate story is illustrated by nothing more than the image of a ballerina dancing against a black limbo.

The most impressive sequences of *Killer's Kiss* employ the style of artful, New York–school street photography—especially in a protracted sequence in Times Square, where Kubrick digresses from the main action to show a couple of clownish figures in Shriner's hats dancing up and down the sidewalk. On another but equally important level, the film deals somewhat archly with the subject matter of pulp fiction—as when the mulatto-looking gangster gropes at his aristocratic blond employee while forcing her to watch a boxing match on TV; or when a couple of thugs kidnap the woman and tie her up in a Greene Street loft, where she uses her sexual charm to get out of trouble. At certain junctures, Kubrick seems to be gathering motifs from more expensive movies (*Body and Soul, The Lady from Shanghai,* and *Rear Window*) and weaving them into a highly choreographed and rather knowingly sadomasochistic fantasy. One of the most unnerving implications of his approach becomes evident in the climactic fight scene between the hero and the villain, which rivals the mirror-maze in *The Lady from Shanghai* for misogyny and surrealistic invention. The battle takes place in a darkened loft filled with female mannequins from a department store, and the two men throw women's body parts at one another; eventually they seize a spear and a fire ax, but they swing out wildly, impaling stray torsos, chopping off arms and heads, and reducing the nude females to rubble.

At about the time *Killer's Kiss* was released, art-movie noirs began to appear with some regularity on the international scene. Artisanal, somewhat cinema-verité productions, they were usually directed by American independents or by new-wave Europeans, who used melodramatic conventions for atypical purposes. (Orson Welles produced his own low-budget thriller, *Mr. Arkadin,* in 1955, slightly ahead of the art-movie distribution system that might have made it successful.) One of the earliest and best examples was Irving Lerner's *Murder by Contract* (1958), which was photographed in only seven days by Lucian Ballard, and which later exerted a strong influence on Martin Scorsese's *Taxi Driver.* A deadpan black comedy about the American dream, this film starred hirsute TV actor Vince Edwards in the role of a highly disciplined hit man who wants to "improve" himself so that he can buy a home on the Ohio River.[24] At several points, we see the dour, emotionally repressed killer waiting alone in drab hotel rooms for his assignments, passing the time by balancing his bankbook and doing chin-ups and push-ups. After murdering several people (including the man who originally hired him), he is sent by the Mob to Los Angeles, where he is supposed to assassinate a female witness in an upcoming trial. "If I'd known it was a woman," he says, "I would have asked double. I don't like women. It's tough to kill someone who's not dependable." While planning the crime, he swims at Malibu, plays miniature golf, and engages in a long, abusive monologue with a hotel bellboy

FIGURE 31. Irving Lerner's *Murder by Contract* (1958). (Museum of Modern Art Stills Archive.)

who inadvertently brings him a lipstick-stained coffee cup. He also visits a gun shop, and he tells one of his fellow gangsters that the place seems crazy because it doesn't sell antitank weapons to anyone from off the street. "To get that gun you have to have a license and be a civilized country," his companion says defensively. "Are you a civilized country?"

Films in the tradition of *Murder by Contract* are still made today, but since the 1960s they have become increasingly self-reflexive. The trend may have started with Peter Bogdanovich's New Wave–inspired *Targets* (1968), a disturbing commentary on Vietnam-era violence, starring Boris Karloff as an aging actor who feels alienated from both contemporary America and the new Hollywood. Bogdanovich filled this inexpensive picture with references to Hawks, Fuller, and other "underground" auteurs; he inserted footage from an unreleased Roger Corman movie; he cast himself as a director; and he staged a suspenseful, Hitchcockian climax at a drive-in theater where Karloff was making a personal appearance. The result was an unusually sophisticated, densely allusive film, worthy of comparison with the best work from Europe. An even more celebrated instance of similar techniques, marking the development of an American art cinema, is Martin Scorsese's *Mean Streets* (1973), which

repeatedly quotes from old gangster pictures, even while it borrows camera techniques from Godard and François Truffaut. Consider also such
later examples as the Coen brothers' *Blood Simple* (1984), which uses a
Steadicam to create hyper-Wellesian tracking shots, or Scott McGehee and
David Segal's *Suture* (1993), which takes its imagery from John Frankenheimer's *Seconds* (1966) and its central metaphors from poststructural-
ist theory. (It even has a female character named Renée Descartes.)

By the 1990s, a relatively secure place had been established in the urban theatrical market for self-consciously artful thrillers, whose budgets
can sometimes be astonishingly low. Robert Rodriguez's *El Mariachi*
(1992) was shot for only seven thousand dollars, and its well-publicized
cost (which did not include distribution and advertising) helped to fuel
its critical and commercial success. Meanwhile, old-fashioned pulp novelists like Woolrich, David Goodis, and Fredric Brown—all of whom were
discovered and canonized by the French, and all of whom are now published in designer paperbacks from Viking Press—had become favored
sources for slightly upscale productions. A recent vogue for *maudit* author Jim Thompson began in Paris with Bernard Tavernier's *Clean Slate*
(1981), traveled to the American independent cinema with Maggie
Greenwald's *Kill-Off* (1989) and James Foley's *After Dark, My Sweet*
(1990), and finally arrived in big-budget Hollywood with Stephen
Frears's *Grifters* (1990) and Roger Donaldson's remake of *The Getaway*
(1994). (Orson Welles anticipated these events by coscripting an adaptation of Thompson's *Hell of a Woman* in 1977. Unfortunately, the film
was never produced.)

Meanwhile, the old Poverty Row and intermediate noirs have been
remade for media-conscious viewers. (We even have a new version of
Breathless [1983].) Many of the "original" films noirs were also remakes,
but they did not acknowledge their status as latecomers, nor did they
treat B movies as art. Today, because the theatrical market for assembly-
line genre movies no longer exists, and because we have a fully developed noir canon, any attempt to reproduce the low-budget past inevitably
involves a certain excess of style or allusiveness. Contemporary noirs
therefore oscillate between elaborately designed, star-filled productions
such as *Heat* (1996) and art movies such as *Bullet-Proof Heart* (1995).
The best of the noir remakes, including Tamra Davis's *Guncrazy* (1992)
and Steven Soderbergh's *Underneath* (a 1994 version of *Criss Cross*, discussed in chapter 7), tend to belong in the second category; unfortunately,
however, all varieties of remade noir usually suffer from too much ambition. When Hollywood converts its old thrillers into art, it gives them

more significance than they can bear; when it turns them into spectaculars
—as in *D.O.A.* (1988) and *Cape Fear* (1991)—it overstates their most
interesting qualities.[25]

Nowadays, even the low-budget movies seem technically slick, and
any kitsch is subject to sophisticated if cynical appreciation. The particular form of cinephilia associated with critics such as Godard, Farber,
and Sarris has almost disappeared—partly because it was dependent upon
a genre system that was vanishing from theaters at the very moment when
its auteurs and underlying logic were being discovered. Where can we
find the "faceless," unselfconscious movies of the present day and an iconoclastic critic who champions them? Certainly not in regular theaters or
in alternative journalism. To see how far we have come since the days of
Manny Farber, consider "Joe Bob Goes to the Drive-In," a syndicated
column written by Dallas cineaste "Joe Bob Briggs," who enjoys thumbing his nose at liberal intellectuals and who has recently become a commentator on Ted Turner's TNT network. Joe Bob regularly lists the number of bare breasts and dead bodies in his favorite movies, and he makes
frequent use of the all-purpose but relatively negative suffix *Fu*, meaning "an act of senseless or random violence, usually inflicted upon the
viewer," as in "Disco Fu." He seems to be making fun of both the establishment and the Bible Belt yahoos, but in reality his cultural politics
are quite safe. He is an ersatz good old boy—a carefully constructed persona who enjoys redneck camp and who writes about a "drive-in" culture that no longer exists (if it ever did). His true beat is the ever-
expanding but relatively anonymous world of DTV (direct-to-video
production), and his mission is to provide a consumer's guide to the soft-
core, white-male pornography that fills the average video store: sadistic
horror movies, violent adventure pictures, and "erotic thrillers"—films
that seldom play theatrically except in foreign countries and that ordinary critics barely notice.

During the mid 1990s, DTVs became a seventeen-billion-dollar-a-year
industry, involving more money than all the major studios combined.
Their average production budgets, however, have remained in the one-
and-a-quarter- to two-million-dollar range, at a time when theatrical
movies often cost somewhere between fifteen and eighty million. One
reason for their low cost is that DTVs require no promotional hype; they
attract customers chiefly on the basis of video-box art, much as the old
pulp novels relied on cover paintings, and they build followings through
word of mouth. Then, too, they are inherently cheap to make. According to Lance Robbins, vice president of Saban International Pictures, they

use limited locations and only a few basic characters: "(Think a blonde, a detective, a gun and a car.)."[26]

Barbara Javitz, president of Prism Pictures, which was responsible for the hugely successful and quite noirlike *Night Eyes* series of DTV films, explained to the *Los Angeles Times* that "we have been able to fill a niche that the studios weren't attending to. . . . As major features have become more costly, and as society has become more voyeuristic, we've been able to come up with more of these erotic thrillers, what used to be called B-movies." Javitz's allusion to Poverty Row is in many ways appropriate, although the typical erotic thriller also functions a bit like *Playboy* magazine, providing luxurious backgrounds and masturbatory fantasies for lonely men with VCRs. Such films often feature former *Playboy* models like Shannon Tweed or Shannon Whirry, and their plots usually involve some combination of voyeurism, striptease, lesbian sex, two-on-one sex, and mild bondage. Playboy Films, a subsidiary of Paramount, has even begun to produce its own DTVs, including two noirlike pictures of 1995: *Cover Me* ("a female undercover cop descends into the steamy sex underworld to crack the case of a cover girl killer") and *Playback,* which has no connection to Raymond Chandler's novel of the same name ("passionate partnerships and dangerous deals are on the agenda in this sexy corporate thriller").

Like the B movies of yesteryear, DTVs sometimes imitate the plots of more lavishly produced pictures. But in an era when videotape has become the dominant form through which people see feature films, it is difficult to say whether the big-budget theatrical market actually determines the important stylistic or generic trends. Major-studio films such as *Basic Instinct* (1992), *Sliver* (1993), *The Color of Night* (1994), *Showgirls* (1995), and *Striptease* (1996) were almost certainly made in imitation of DTVs, hoping to capture their particular section of the home-video market. In most cases, however, the equivalent DTVs achieved a higher percentage of profit. The difference, as Lance Robbins explains, is that DTV producers "are doing *Sliver* without the $10-million actress attached" (quoted in Willens, 25).

DTV thrillers provide audiences with a special kind of narrative pleasure, paying somewhat more attention to what Linda Williams calls the lovemaking "numbers" of pornographic cinema than to the goals or enigmas of mainstream theatrical narrative. For this reason, they are regularly distributed in alternative versions, allowing viewers a choice between "softer" and "harder" scenes of sex and violence. The major studios have responded by offering "director's cut" videos of such big-budget pictures

as *Basic Instinct, Sliver, The Color of Night,* and *The Getaway,* which
contain an extra few seconds of frontal nudity. But the audience's curiosity about the bodies of celebrated movie stars seems limited, and the
DTV market has continued to grow. DTV has even created its own star
system, without the benefit of press agents. In addition to women like
Tweed and Whirry, who are reliable and effective thespians, erotic
thrillers feature such male players as Andrew Stevens (also a writer, director, and auteur for the *Night Eyes* films) and the critically underrated
Eric Roberts.

In recent years, the cable networks have begun to imitate DTVs, producing woman-in-distress melodramas like *Apology* (1986), shady-cop-
and-sexy-lady mysteries like *Deceptions* (1990), and low-budget remakes
of classics such as *This Gun for Hire* (1991), *Night of the Hunter* (1991),
and *Notorious* (1992). *Gotham,* the story of a Manhattan detective investigating a woman who is supposed to be dead, was Showtime's highest-rated made-for-TV movie in 1988. *Third-Degree Burn,* an erotic mystery about a cheap private eye hired to follow a beautiful blond, was
HBO's highest-rated production in 1989. By 1990, according to *Time*
magazine, these and other types of "film noir thriller" had become the
"hottest new ticket on the cable dial," and they are probably the closest
the contemporary market has come to the old-style program pictures of
classic Hollywood. *Time* reporter Richard Zoglin describes them as "a
bit more graphic in sex and violence than network movies" but as a valid
and "unsettling" form of popular art: "The cable networks may get more
attention for their high-minded docudramas (*Mandela*) and gourmet remakes (Charlton Heston in *A Man for All Seasons*), but these unpretentious B movies are their doughy bread and butter" (23 July 1990).
Zoglin's language is similar to what we find in most of the critical literature on hard-boiled movies from the 1940s and 1950s. Media critics
have always defended certain types of ostensibly disreputable, formulaic
thrillers by appealing to their moral ambiguity and their lack of bourgeois sentimentality or "high-mindedness," and such a defense is valuable to the movie industry because it enhances the films' crossover potential, allowing them to play at the higher end of the market. No wonder
that varieties of dark cinema have proliferated in video stores, where low
and high levels of production meet, and where upscale cable-noirs and
DTV erotic thrillers mingle with stylish theatrical films like *Casino* (1995)
and *Seven* (1995).

Most of the profits in contemporary cinema are generated in video
stores, which are melting pots of American film culture. But critical at-

FIGURE 32. Tommy Lee Jones in *Gotham* (1988), a made-for-TV thriller that helped inspire the trend toward "cable-noir."

tention, publicity, and professional cachet are derived almost exclusively from theatrical exhibition. It has therefore become commonplace for both DTV and cable producers to slightly raise their budgets, aiming for a more discriminating or intermediate audience and hoping to play at least marginally in another medium. Sophisticated, expensively produced British television exports, such the *Prime Suspect* and *Cracker* films that have appeared on PBS and the Arts and Entertainment channel, sometimes find rental outlets in America, and there is a growing collector's market for all sorts of TV nostalgia; in general, however, made-for-TV noir acquires no cultural capital and little chance of video distribution unless it takes the form of high-profile, subscription-network shows like *Fallen Angels*, which is a series of medium-budget anthology films involving some of the best-known actors and directors in Hollywood (including an excellent adaptation of a Jim Thompson story directed by none other than Tom Cruise). For similar reasons, DTVs get more attention from large chains like Blockbuster if they receive big-screen showing, no matter how brief or inconsequential. Mark Damon, producer of at least ten DTVs a year during the early 1990s, argues that thrillers must have "a good look, and be shot with some quality." He also gives exhibitors a financial incentive if they book his films in limited theatrical runs—not because he expects box-office success, but because "it gives the film a bit more clout in the stores, overseas or in the cable markets" (quoted in Willens, 25).

Mainstream studios are better situated to take advantage of the different ways a movie can be sold or rented, and as a result they have begun to develop their own DTV subsidiaries, negotiating easy crossovers between theaters and video outlets. Organizations like Columbia Tri-Star and Live Home Entertainment make a policy of financing independent, medium-budget movies that play in theaters but at the same time are "video protected." Among recent films, John Dahl's *Red Rock West* (1994) is a good example. When executives at Columbia Tri-Star decided that this modestly produced mixture of film noir and western would not play well in theaters, they quickly sold it to HBO and to video stores as an "erotic thriller." But it did good business in European theaters, and on the strength of a showing at the Toronto Film Festival, it was booked into a San Francisco art house, where it broke all box-office records. Columbia Tri-Star suddenly executed a complete about-face and arranged for a nationwide release in selected cities. The new strategy paid off, even though copies of the film had already found their way into video stores. *Red Rock West* acquired theatrical profits, favorable reviews in the *New Yorker* and other journals, and greatly enhanced video rentals; indeed, it was such a success that Dahl's next film, *The Last Seduction* (1995), which had been intended for cable TV, went straight to art theaters across the country, earning major profits and greatly boosting the career of actress Linda Fiorentino.[27]

From the purely commercial point of view, the most notable "sleepers" or crossover noirs in the American market during the past decade have been *The Crying Game* (1992) and *Reservoir Dogs* (1992). The first is a British production containing an elaborate allusion to Welles's *Mr. Arkadin* and a sensationally clever plot development; critically overrated, it nevertheless provoked a good deal of debate over racial, national, and sexual politics, and it became a fashionably scandalous date movie, playing mainstream theaters and winning a screenplay Oscar for writer-director Neil Jordan.[28] The second is a stylish and equally shocking "caper" picture by Quentin Tarantino, financed with DTV money. *Reservoir Dogs* bristles with allusions to Godard, Kubrick, and others and is in many ways a dazzlingly innovative picture, but it also works at the level of "drive-in" entertainment, offering enough graphic, eroticized violence to please Joe Bob Briggs. Both *The Crying Game* and *Reservoir Dogs* earned substantial profits in video rentals, and they acquired large enough followings to be rereleased several times in urban theaters. Like *T-Men* in the late 1940s, they mixed generic conventions with artistic effects, blurring the line between exploitation and sophistication. Their success reveals that despite many differences between the past and the present, certain aspects of the marketplace have not changed. Filmmakers still transform inexpensive movies about sex and violence into hot properties that earn critical respect. This project inevitably attracts them to the film noir—or at any rate to the particular economic and discursive space where noir has always been appreciated.

OLD IS NEW

Styles of Noir

The visual style of film noir is often associated with low-key lighting, un-balanced compositions, vertiginous angles, night-for-night exteriors, extreme deep focus, and wide-angle lenses. These and other noirlike camera effects have been discussed in a well-known essay by Janey Place and Lowell Peterson, who do an excellent job of explaining how certain familiar images of the 1940s and 1950s were created. But Place and Peterson base their analysis on a small sample of films, and several of their generalizations seem questionable—for instance, their claim that "camera movements are used sparingly in most *noir* films."[1] All the stylistic features they describe can be found in pictures that have never been classified as noir. By the same token, relatively few can be found in a certifiable hard-boiled classic such as *The Big Sleep,* which creates its night-world of rain, mist, and smoke entirely within a studio, with the camera always at eye level. A somewhat Hitchcockian thriller such as *The Big Clock* is closer to the model Place and Peterson seem to have in mind, but the most effective scenes in that film are designed to convey the diffuse, fluorescent lighting of a Manhattan office building during working hours. Notice also that much of the action in *The Big Clock* is based on long takes or sequence shots requiring complicated camera movements—as when Ray Milland secretly enters the kitchen door of a luxury apartment, discovers a dead body in the living room, rearranges the evidence, retraces his steps through the kitchen, holds a brief conversation with a man in the hallway, and exits via the elevator.

Historical film noir is in fact a more stylistically heterogeneous category than critics have recognized. Certain famous noir directors (Orson Welles, John Farrow) moved their cameras a great deal; others (Edward Dmytryk, John Huston) relied on cutting between dynamic compositions; still others (Howard Hawks) were straightforward, almost invisible storytellers who avoided baroque flourishes. Although the available film stocks and camera technology had a strong influence on style, and although there was a broadly shared notion of what "mysterious" or gothic films should look like, there were no hard-and-fast rules for noir imagery. Dark crime dramas such as *The Big Sleep, The Big Clock, The Big Steal, The Big Heat,* and *The Big Combo* may have had a good deal in common, but not so much as we commonly think at the level of photography.

Our collective memory of noir style probably has less to do with a camera technique than with a kind of visual iconography, made up of what Geoffrey O'Brien describes as "a nexus of fashions in hair, fashions in lighting, fashions in interior decorating, fashions in motivation, fashions in repartee."[2] As we have seen, however, Raymond Borde and Étienne Chaumeton placed relatively little emphasis on such things; instead, they stressed the emotional or psychological effects of noir, arguing that latter-day pictures such as *Death Wish* and *Dirty Harry,* which are quite different both politically and visually from the studio films of the 1940s, amounted to a kind of "rebirth" of the form.[3] In contrast, a great many subsequent critics and viewers have understood film noir chiefly as a way of dressing actors, designing sets, and photographing urban life. Many of its supposedly essential motifs—which were created not only by photographers but also by costumers, art directors, and production designers—have managed to persist, undergoing subtle transformations and returns in contemporary movies. In certain respects, these archetypal images help to maintain a sense of continuity with the old studio system, but they also enable filmmakers to produce new forms through quotation or allusion. Jean-Luc Godard and Martin Scorsese evoked them in some of the most innovative pictures of the 1960s and 1970s; Bernardo Bertolucci and Roman Polanski used them to create retro-styled historical films; and in succeeding years, many directors have transformed them into a vehicle for nostalgia and parody, available to anyone who wants to engage self-consciously with the traditions of American cinema.

Later in this chapter I discuss retro stylishness and noir parody, which link the present with the past in complex ways. Before approaching these matters, however, it seems necessary to address another, somewhat related question: how has film noir managed to become a "neo" commodity, in spite of the vast technical and cultural changes that have occurred in the movie industry since 1945? In other words, how do the many noir styles manage to reproduce themselves and at the same time evolve into different forms? In my view, the answer to this question lies in iconography or fashion as much as in camera technique. A complete answer, moreover, involves the changing look of America itself. Edward Dimendberg argues that the style of Hollywood crime pictures was profoundly influenced by the shift from "centripetal" to "centrifugal" forms of urban development in the period between 1949 and the present; the traditional metropolis, he notes, "with its fabric of neighborhoods, familiar landmarks, and negotiable pedestrian spaces," gave way to "an increasingly decentralized America knitted together by highways, television, and radio"—resulting in the apparent demise of classic noir, and its rebirth in "centrifugal" movies of the postmodern era.[4] I would agree, but in order to impose reasonable limits on my own discussion, I need to bracket the issue of the actual city, along with the general history of technology and its relation to film style.[5] In the first section of this chapter, I want to focus on a specific technical revolution: the film industry's shift from black-and-white to color photography, which affected one of the most common signifiers of "noirness" and our general perception of the world.

BLACK AND WHITE AND RED

[I]f you are above a certain age, you tend to think
that real movies are black and white. . . . I mean the
movies that formed me and that are deepest in my
unconscious are black and white, by and large.

MICHAEL CHAPMAN, photographer of *Taxi
Driver*, *Raging Bull*, and *Dead Men Don't Wear
Plaid*, interviewed by Dennis Schaefer and Larry
Salvato, 1984

Between 1941 and 1952, most of the purely mechanical images in the world—including snapshots, magazine and newspaper illustrations, newsreels, feature films, and television programs—were in black and white. In the same period, most of the hand-assisted or purely imaginary images—including easel paintings, billboard advertisements, paperback book covers, comic books, and Sunday cartoon strips—were in color.

The camera was supposed to view things realistically, and black and white was strongly associated with empirical or documentary truth. Its power to depict major historical events and the patterns of everyday life was so great that it influenced fine art; thus one of the world's first black-and-white paintings was Pablo Picasso's *Guernica* (1937), which evokes the documentary or graphic feeling of both newsprint and contemporary newsreels.

Despite the ubiquity of black-and-white images, the technology of color film was fairly well advanced by the early 1940s. John Ford shot his World War II documentary, *The Battle of Midway* (1943), in 16 mm Kodachrome, blowing it up into 35 mm Technicolor for theatrical distribution. The United States Navy made several wartime short subjects in color, and the military personnel who made training films seemed to agree that color photography was a more useful medium for reconnaissance work or medical diagnosis; it could "see" through battlefield camouflage, and, in the words of a navy medical officer, it made flesh wounds "far more vivid and realistic."[6] In most cases, however, moviegoers and filmmakers regarded Technicolor as inappropriate for the grim realities of combat. The only film genres in which color was not merely acceptable but also de rigueur were cartoons, travelogues, and musical comedies; in other words, color was associated with what Tom Gunning describes as the "cinema of attraction," or with carnivalistic films involving fantasy and utopian spectacle.[7]

Throughout the period, color was also relatively expensive and commercially unproven. Despite the success of Selznick's *Star Is Born* (1937) and *Gone with the Wind* (1939), the industry as a whole did not believe that the Technicolor process had important effects on box-office receipts.[8] According to some filmmakers, it could actually harm the more serious pictures by undermining the values of classical narrative; thus British cameraman Guy Green argued that "photography for dramatic subjects . . . must not be a glorious spectacle all on its own. . . . It must be suppressed and made to lend itself to the subject."[9] In part for such reasons, the movies in general were less concerned with the contrast of vibrant hues than with the play of light and shadow. Even projects such as *Yellow Sky* (1948), a spectacular western filmed in Arizona, and *The Prince of Foxes* (1949), an elaborate historical pageant filmed in Italy, were shot in black and white.[10] Notice, moreover, that in certain quarters, black and white had long been regarded as a stylized medium—a sign not merely of realism but also of abstraction, bohemia, aestheticism, and avant-garde taste. As we have seen in chapter 2, darkness was central to modernist art of every kind. European poets such as Charles Baudelaire reveled in black moods; James McNeill Whistler entitled his famous painting of his mother "Arrangement in Grey and Black"; and the International Futurist Exhibition of 1915 featured a "black square against a white background" composed by Casmir Malevitch. In our own day, black has been described by the painter Louise Nevelson as "the most aristocratic of colors."[11] Another contemporary artist, Ad Reinhardt, seems to agree, although he thinks of black as a noncolor. "It's aesthetic," he says—unlike red or yellow, which have to do with "vulgarity or folk art or something like that" (quoted in Wodek, 193).

The aesthetic use of black and white is evident in most forms of art photography, which in turn influenced the American abstract expressionist painters of the late 1940s and early 1950s—a group that includes Arshile Gorky, Willem deKooning, Barnett Newman, Clyfford Still, Franz Kline, Robert Motherwell, Jackson Pollock, and Robert Rauschenberg. At the peak of their influence (which coincides with the so-called film noir), this group produced images that looked rather like 1930s art photos reduced to a purely graphic, nonrepresentational level. Hence the art critic David Anfam speaks of Franz Kline's *photographic* sensibility" and compares him to Walker Evans and Edward Weston.[12] Anfam also notes that Kline's interest in black and white can be related to the ethos of the New York School of street photographers—including Robert Frank, Richard Avedon, and Ted Croner—who flourished in the same period, and whose work was similarly evocative of the "chill, steely glare of a Manhattan vista" (24).

In *Reframing Abstract Expressionism* (1993), Michael Leja goes further, arguing that Hollywood film noir belongs on the same broad cultural terrain as well-known abstract paintings by Kline, Pollock, and other members of the New York group. The "claim to significance" in both noir and the new painters, he observes, was "grounded in the presumption of a complicated subjectivity under stress, suffused in (primitive) terror and tragedy." Both forms "posited the complex white male individual and his cosmic situation as the proper focus for analysis," and both were relatively existential or "outside history."[13] This argument may seem excessively philosophical where Hollywood is concerned, but there can be little doubt that a modernist ideology involving male subjectivity and urban darkness or primitivism helped to condition a great deal of art in the postwar decades.[14] Notice also that during the same period, the center of international modernism shifted from Paris to New York.[15] Black-and-white cityscapes of the Manhattan skyline became virtually syn-

onymous with the artistic sensibility, and they began to appear with increasing regularity throughout the visual culture—in the younger generation of street photographers; in films such as *The Naked City, The
Window,* and *Detective Story;* and in the graphic, monochromatic effects
of nonrepresentational paintings. "As a native New Yorker," Richard
Kostelanetz remarked, "two colors are worthy of art—black and white;
all other colors are appropriate for illustrations" (quoted in Wodek, 24).

The black-and-white photographic style that we associate with film
noir was therefore given legitimacy by virtue of the fact that it suggested
both gritty realism and the highest aesthetic refinement. (Even today,
black-and-white photography implies stylishness and sophistication—as
in a recent American television commercial that shows an Infinity automobile on a wet city street at night, parked outside a jazz club.) There
was considerable irony in this situation, because hard-boiled fiction,
which had been a source for many postwar films, was associated with
the lurid color illustrations on the covers of pulp magazines. During and
after the 1940s, the movies divested such fiction of its potential vulgarity, giving it slightly more upmarket or serious connotations—in part by
the simple act of converting it into a more abstract visual medium.

As we might expect, the contradictory implications of black-and-white
photography—its claims to both realism and artistic stylishness—are evident in prototypical noir cameraman John Alton's "textbook" for non-
professionals, *Painting with Light* (1949, reprinted 1995). Throughout
this book (which in its original edition contained several color illustrations), Alton insists that audiences "are getting tired of the chocolate-
coated photography of yesterday" and that "mystery" movies should "go
realistic."[16] He claims that World War II has made audiences reject "sweet
unreal photography," accustoming them to black-and-white scenes in
which there are "no boosters, no sun reflectors, no butterflies, and no
diffusers" (134–35). Since 1947, he says, movies have become "starkly
real," and pictures such as *Boomerang* and *T-Men,* which were filmed
on location, have proven that "realistic photography is popular" (135).
Elsewhere, however, Alton spends a good deal of his time explaining how
to light close-ups of glamorous women and how to make "beautiful"
outdoor compositions with the aid of diffusers, filters, and reflectors. Even
when he argues that the illumination of sets "should be as realistic and
true to life as possible" (67), his real purpose is to create a heightened
dramatic atmosphere, especially in films that involve "mystery lighting."
He loves "slums, bars, gambling joints, where the filament of a lamp is
the only bright spot" and where "a few photoflood bulbs strategically

placed" will provide sufficient illumination (49). He emphasizes the importance of "Jimmy Valentine lighting," or the positioning of a key light directly below the faces of villains, so that they take on a grotesque look. He also provides helpful hints for creating moody images of rain or fog in urban environments. "When shooting neon or other electric lights," he notes, "wet the pavement to get reflections of the light sources in the picture" (49). The particular fascination of these shots, he observes, is the result of "*light-play*—reflections on the shiny, wet surfaces of the street. They are music" (59).

Despite the title of his book, Alton is different from most painters, who tend to associate black and white with the technology of printing. Like all cinematographers, he instinctively thinks of the photographic image as a theatrical or stagelike space, filled with dramatic highlights and cast shadows. The technique of "mystery lighting," he suggests, derives from a long-standing tradition of gothic stage plays and magic shows that illuminate sinister figures from below. He is quite good at showing how this tradition might enable Hollywood to photograph sudden flares of light amid surrounding darkness; at one point, he even composes a sort of extended haiku or imagist poem on the topic:

> Ship-wrecked figures on a raft, in complete darkness, with only the
>   phosphorescence of the ocean waves breaking the ink-black of
>   the pictures; in the distance, the fluctuating light of a lighthouse
> The effect of passing auto headlights on the ceiling of a dark interior
> Fluctuating neon or other electric signs
> The light of a passing streetcar on an otherwise dark street
> The hanging light on the ceiling of a cheap gambling joint
> Searchlights of prisons or concentration camps
> Flashes of guns in absolute darkness
> The opening and closing of a refrigerator that has a light inside, in a dark
>   kitchen
> The well-known street lamp.
>
>   (47–48)

These and many other hypnotic moments of light-in-darkness were put to excellent use in the medium-budget thrillers that Alton photographed for Anthony Mann during the late 1940s. In *Raw Deal* (1948), for example, the doomed hero fights with the villain in a firelit room at night and then dies near an alleyway in a slum neighborhood, lying on wet pavement beneath the "well-known street lamp." And in *He Walked by Night* (1949), a killer is cornered by police in the Los Angeles sewer system, where, as in a similar episode of *The Third Man,* the only sources of illumination are police searchlights, the "flash of guns in absolute darkness," and "a few photoflood bulbs strategically placed." Such examples might seem commonplace on paper, but both films manage to avoid cliché through the almost tactile quality of the lighting effects; the fog in *Raw Deal,* for instance, has a glaring, clammy look that makes every other studio-made fog of the period seem fake.

Curiously, Alton's book downplays the techniques of camera perspective, concentrating almost exclusively on codes of glamour and "realism" in the lighting of studio sets and star close-ups—this despite the fact that radical camera angles, wide-angle lenses, and deep-focus compositions were especially important to his "mysterious" pictures. (He was also good at composing eerie, off-center compositions in which an isolated figure is briefly glimpsed at the extreme lower corner of a frame.) Director David Bradley, who came to Hollywood after filming a series of independently produced literary adaptations (*Peer Gynt, Julius Caesar,* and *Othello*), recalls that he and Alton had an especially good working relationship on *Talk about a Stranger* (1952) because they both believed in Wellesian or baroque uses of low-level cameras and sharp depth of field.[17] Nearly all of Alton's black-and-white work with Mann was filled with such techniques: in *T-Men,* for example, two men hold a conversation over a lampshade, and Alton photographs them from below the lamp, aiming straight upward at their chins and using an extreme wide-angle lens that makes them look grotesquely elongated. From the evidence of his book, however, Alton seems to have regarded studio lighting, not framing or perspective, as his transcendent concern. Perhaps he was always more of a Sternbergian aesthete than a tough guy.[18] Even in a criminal melodrama like *Raw Deal,* he is especially interested in the "color" or lighting palette of black and white. Consider the opening scenes of that film, in which we see Claire Trevor visiting Dennis O'Keefe in prison: the photographic drama is largely a matter of the subtly graded spectrum of light and dark, ranging from the steely gray exteriors and the purgatorial diffusion of the interior establishing shots to the beautiful close-ups of Trevor, who wears the hint of a black veil, and whose eyes sparkle like diamonds because of a cleverly placed reflector.

A similar preoccupation with the tonal qualities of black-and-white imagery can be found in other celebrated films noirs of the 1940s, most of which are neither starkly realistic nor purely expressionistic. These films usually try to achieve a balance between documentary and art, mixing locations with studio sets and creating an eroticized treatment of underworld settings. Their charm has something to do with the purely

graphic qualities of the film stock, but it also depends on subtle variations of light, enhanced by arc lamps and a wide array of new lenses that
provide sharpness and resolution. In general, they are films that brilliantly
exploit the darkness of cinema, replicating the effect of a projector beam
splitting through the gloom of an auditorium; again and again, they remind us that the medium itself originated in shadow play, or in the primitive fascination of hot fire gleaming in cold blackness.

A particularly good example of these effects is RKO's *Out of the Past*
(1947), which derives some of its most captivating moments from the
fact that it was produced at a studio where nearly everything was composed of rich, India-ink blacks and silvery highlights. Photographer
Nicholas Musuraca and director Jacques Tourneur, who had collaborated
on the Val Lewton pictures at that same studio, were especially good at
creating a lyrical or sensuous play of shadow, and their considerable talents are evident throughout. Interestingly, Musuraca's work involves no
night-for-night scenes, no distorting lenses, no extreme deep-focus compositions, no "choker" close-ups, and very few radical angles—in other
words, it manifests almost none of the traits that Place and Peterson claim
are essential to the visual atmosphere of film noir.[19] The photography of
Out of the Past nevertheless seems definitively noirlike, chiefly by virtue
of its low-key, deeply romantic "painting with light."

Let me pause here to offer a few illustrations of lighting technique in
Out of the Past, because this particular film represents such an impressive use of what had become standard Hollywood procedures. The best
place to begin is with the major technical problem that affected Musuraca
or any studio photographer who worked in low-key black and white: the
need to keep the various objects on the screen from blending into one another. Because of the limited "color spectrum" available to the camera,
an actor in a beige trenchcoat standing against a gray wall could almost
disappear, and sets looked flat if they contained no contrasting points of
illumination. One solution to the problem was to make sure that the foreground and the background were lit differently. Consider the moment
when Jeff Bailey (Robert Mitchum) exits the manager's office of the Sterling nightclub, where he has just stolen some papers: first he stands against
a dark area outside the door, his body illuminated by an overhead lamp;
then he walks down the hallway, silhouetted against a bright background;
then he descends the stair, moving past an overhead light just as the wall
ahead grows dark (figures 33–35). An even more striking example of the
same effect can be seen early in the film, when Kathie Moffat (Jane Greer)
enters the story. Wearing a pale dress and a matching straw hat, she walks

FIGURES 33–38. Contrast lighting in *Out of the Past* (1947).

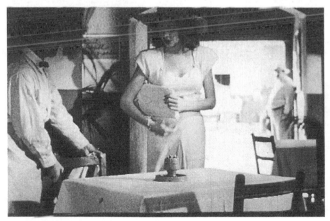

out of the Acapulco sun, moving through a dark archway and into the cool shadows of a cantina. Her light clothing makes her almost invisible on the brilliant plaza, but when she steps into the room she seems to materialize out of brightness, becoming first a silhouette and then a visible figure against a shaded wall (figures 36–38).

The same rules apply whether we are speaking of low-key or high-key scenes, although it should be emphasized that clothing itself can be as important as lamps or reflectors. Notice the "framing" episodes of *Out of the Past,* which were filmed in the crystal-clear daylight of Lake Tahoe, Nevada—an atmosphere that seems more appropriate to a western than to a thriller.[20] When gangster Joe Stephano (Paul Valentine) enters this world, he wears a black hat and a black trenchcoat. Late in the movie, when he drives into the mountains and attempts to kill Jeff Bailey, he is silhouetted against the sunny landscape or against the sparkling waters of a mountain stream. To borrow a line from Raymond Chandler, he looks as conspicuous as a tarantula on a slice of angel food.

In the darkened scenes of the film, the actors are often lit with a single hard light from the side, so that part or all of their faces are in deep shadow. Whenever the audience needs to read the expressions on silhouetted or partly obscure faces, Musuraca uses a soft fill light—as in figure 41, which shows Jeff and Kathie looking out of a bright room and into the night. In cases where the foreground and the background have roughly the same degree of illumination, he uses a rim light or a "liner," usually positioned to the side and slightly to the rear of the actors and either above or below the camera—as in figures 42–43. This sort of lighting had been commonplace in Hollywood since the 1920s, not only because it created a separation between figure and ground, but also because it gave faces a three-dimensional quality. Wide shots of dark city streets usually involved similar techniques, because architecture needed to be picked out of the gloom and given a certain dimensionality or sculptural effect. Figure 44 shows an RKO set representing San Francisco at night, with its darkness strategically broken by a neon sign, several glowing windows, a streetlamp, and a pair of automobile headlights reflecting off wet pavement: a key element is a single floodlamp hidden in an alley, which creates a sense of depth and separation between two of the buildings. Figure 45 shows a studio mock-up of a courtyard behind an apartment house on Telegraph Hill: Robert Mitchum is silhouetted against a bright patch of "sky," and the surrounding darkness is broken chiefly by rays of "moonlight" striking a low wall and a clothesline.

Musuraca's chief method of giving depth and atmosphere to interior

FIGURES 39–40. Clothing as contrast in *Out of the Past*.

FIGURES 41–43. Fill lighting and "liners" in *Out of the Past.*

FIGURES 44–45. Lighting "exterior" sets in *Out of the Past*.

scenes was to use a modified form of what Alton called "Jimmy Valentine lighting." With the assistance of art director Jack Okey and set decorator Darrell Silvera, he gave the below-eye-level key light an ostensible source, such as a fireplace or a table lamp, which threw slightly high shadows on the walls and lent a gothic quality to faces. Meanwhile, he situated one or two indirect lights close against the walls, so that the edges of picture frames and other furnishings cast their own dramatic shadows. This technique often created a sinister or perversely violent mood, as in the early scenes in which Whit Sterling (Kirk Douglas) hires Jeff to find Kathie (figures 46–47). Notice, however, that the same lighting arrangement is used when Jeff and Kathie first spend the night together. The setting is Kathie's bungalow on a rainy evening in Acapulco: "It was a nice little joint with bamboo furniture and Mexican gimcracks," Jeff recalls. "One little lamp burned." We see Jeff and Kathie dash into the room from a thunderstorm, and a solitary lamp, situated low in the foreground, motivates high shadows on the walls. After drying Kathie's hair with a towel, Jeff passionately embraces her and tosses the towel across the lamp, which pitches over in a gust of wind from the open doorway. The camera then drifts outdoors, gliding along the veranda in the backlit rain. A few moments pass, and we return to the darkened room. The lighting now seems to come from the moon, which shines through a pair of French windows (impossibly, since the rain still falls), silhouetting Jeff's figure against the wall as he rises to shut the door.

Here and elsewhere, the codes of erotic lighting have an affinity with the codes of mystery lighting—and appropriately so, because *Out of the Past* is a film about fatal attraction or the fear of a woman's sexuality. Nowhere is the intertwining of eroticism and danger more apparent than in a sequence near the end of the picture, when Jeff secretly investigates Kathie's San Francisco apartment. Once again high shadows are cast by a single lamp, and the luxurious furnishings are sculpted by hidden background lights. When a telephone rings, Kathie enters from a party next door, and Jeff steps into a darkened bedroom, observing her conversation from the shadows (figure 48). After Kathie hangs up, she crosses to a liquor cabinet. Jeff steps out of the bedroom doorway, his face lit by a sinister, low-level light (figure 49). Kathie turns and starts to run, but Jeff grabs her arm and pushes her down into a chair (figure 50). The reverse angle shows her landing roughly, her mink coat falling off and lamplight spilling across her bare shoulders; her black dress is outlined against the gray upholstery of the chair, and her seductive body functions almost like a return blow, countering Jeff's violence (figure 51).

FIGURES 46–47. "Jimmy Valentine" lighting in *Out of the Past*.

FIGURES 48–51. Eroticism and "mystery light" in *Out of the Past*.

More could be said about Musuraca's contributions to *Out of the Past,* but these examples suffice to outline a basic repertory of techniques that were central to a great many Hollywood films of 1947, when the so-called noir style was at its height. During that year, it was estimated that only 12 percent of U.S. films were photographed in color. The increasingly sophisticated technology of lenses and film stocks made black and white seem an extremely flexible medium that was suited to both locations and studio sets and adaptable to every genre in the industry. The situation for photographers, however, was about to change. In the early 1950s, Eastman Kodak introduced a single-strip color film and a dye-coupling process that eliminated the need for expensive Technicolor equipment. The new Eastmancolor stock (derived from the German Agfacolor and renamed Warnercolor, Metrocolor, or anything else the studios liked) required no special cameras, no monopolistic laboratory, and no "color consultants"; it appeared when the movies were attempting to differentiate themselves from television, and it resulted in a sudden, massive reduction in the amount of black-and-white photography. By 1954, at least half the films produced in Hollywood were shot with Eastmancolor. This figure dropped slightly when the movie industry became more interested in selling its product to television, but soon afterward, television itself became a color medium. Over the next decade, broadcasters used color videotape to document the ghastly combat in Vietnam, astronauts took color pictures of the earth, families assembled photo albums out of color snapshots, and a tourist with a home-movie camera photographed the assassination of John F. Kennedy on color film. By the early 1970s, most people regarded color as the normal or "realistic" way of seeing, and black and white as an abstract or stylized medium, redolent of the past.[21]

Because of the relative brightness of the Eastmancolor photography, the transitional years between 1955 and 1970 were ill suited to atmospheric color movies about murder and psychological violence—even though these themes had never been limited exclusively to black-and-white pictures. "Whether rightly or wrongly," Borde and Chaumeton observed in 1954, "color has been used only in the limit works of the noir series, in 'darkened' movies, but always in extremely interesting ways" (179, my translation). One of the most notable and uncharacteristically flamboyant of the "limit works" was *Leave Her to Heaven* (1945), a quasi-Freudian melodrama starring Gene Tierney as a beautiful but murderously jealous heiress. Photographer Leon Shamroy won an Academy Award for the film, chiefly because of the way he combined "mysterious" elements—lamplit rooms, extreme deep-focus compositions, low angles that brought ceilings into view—with spectacular Technicolor scenery from locations such as Monterey, California, and Flagstaff, Arizona. His dominant color, as Meredith Brody and Lee Sanders have observed, was an orange or amber hue that suggested "the same sickness and corruption as the high contrast photography of black-and-white film noir" (Silver and Ward, 170). But *Leave Her to Heaven* also took advantage of a symbolic contrast between "cold" and "hot" colors. At one point, Tierney decides to abort her pregnancy: nicely coiffured and wearing a pale blue nightgown, she deliberately falls the entire length of a grand staircase; a dissolve takes us to a sunny beachfront several months later, and she emerges from the surf, wearing a blood-red swimsuit that clings to every line of her body.

Another "limit work," much more in keeping with the repressed or "darkened" quality Borde and Chaumeton describe, was Alfred Hitchcock's *Rope* (1948)—which, according to the Warner Brothers pressbook and *The New York Daily News,* was also the first film in history to use color "for a suspenseful story of murder and detection." Although a great deal has been written about the long takes in this film (like the Patrick Hamilton stage drama on which it is based, *Rope* is performed in "real duration"), relatively little has been said about the fact that Hitchcock was making his first picture in Technicolor. One of the cinema's purest aesthetes (almost as Wildean as the two killers in the story), he seems to have been intensely preoccupied with the lighting effects and the color scheme, even to the point of firing his photographer, Joseph Valentine, who had worked with him previously on *Shadow of a Doubt* (1943). As he explained in his interview with François Truffaut, he thought that Valentine lacked "artistic taste" where color was concerned:

> I was determined to reduce the color to a minimum. We had built the set of an apartment, consisting of a living room, a hallway, and a kitchen. The [windows] overlooked the New York skyline, and we had that background made up in a semicircular pattern. . . . Toward the last four or five reels, in other words, by sunset, I realized that the orange in the sun was too strong, and on account of that we did the last five reels all over again. . . . [Valentine] simply said to himself, "Well, it's just another sunset." Obviously he hadn't looked at one for a long time, if ever at all, and what he did was completely unacceptable; it was like a lurid postcard.[22]

Hitchcock made sure that color in *Rope* would be subdued, in keeping with the upper-class, artistic-intellectual world in which the drama takes place. Notice that the framed pictures on the walls of the tastefully decorated Manhattan apartment are mainly pen-and-ink drawings or monochromatic, gray-and-white paintings. The opening shot—showing two well-dressed young men strangling a third with a rope—seems to comment on this absence of brightness: it begins in a dark room with the shades drawn and with all three characters wearing dark suits and ties, so we see only their faces, hands, and white shirt fronts, together with an expanse of beige curtains that barely admit sunlight. After stuffing the dead body in a trunk, one of the killers (John Dall), switches on a lamp, which creates a golden sidelight. "Don't!" says his companion (Farley Granger). Dall switches off the lamp and lights a cigarette. "It's the darkness that's got you down," he remarks cheerfully. "Nobody feels safe in the dark." He turns and crosses to the drapes, pulling them open to reveal the steel-gray skyline of Manhattan, which is topped by a few pinkish, late-afternoon clouds. The room is now fully illuminated with a cool, muted light. "Pity we couldn't have done it with the curtains open," Dall says, "in the bright sunlight!"

As the two killers discuss their crime and prepare for a dinner party, they walk through the foyer, the dining room, the kitchen, and then back into the living area, which is decorated in relatively discreet, somber colors. (The camera follows them, but here and elsewhere, Hitchcock never allows it to turn 180 degrees from the original establishing angle; in other words, he avoids what would have been the equivalent of a "suturing" reverse shot, deliberately preserving the effect of fourth-wall proscenium theater.) With each successive long take, Hitchcock's technicians slightly rearrange the pattern of lights over the entire set, until the skyscrapers outside are silhouettes. In shot number 5, the horizon is amber, the tops of the buildings are almost lost in darkness, and there are shadowed areas in the room; James Stewart turns on a table lamp over the piano, but Farley Granger becomes irritable: "Would you mind turning that off?" he snaps, and Stewart complies. In shot 6, the apartment has become so dark that the maid needs to turn on most of the lights as she extinguishes candles and cleans up after the party; at this point, there is a thin rosy line on the horizon, and, amid the lighted windows of the skyscrapers, a tiny neon sign is blinking red. Finally, in the last shot, when complete darkness has fallen outside and a glow of electric light outlines the horizon, we have the most colorful effect in the film. James Stewart takes a rope out of his pocket and accuses Dall and Granger of murder; as the camera pans to show their reaction, the giant letter S on a neon sign just outside the window to the right begins blinking. When Stewart opens the trunk at the center of the room, the neon shades his face with a sickly green and then with a bloody red.

This last shot is a good example of how a familiar motif from black-and-white thrillers could be given spectacular new life through the expressive power of colored light. Hitchcock prepares his audience for the moment by maintaining a restrained color scheme through most of the picture, but also by dispensing with the high contrasts and dramatically cast shadows of a film like *Out of the Past*. "When I saw the initial rushes," he told Truffaut, "my first feeling was that things show up much more in color than in black and white" (Truffaut, 132). He immediately recognized that he could do without "liners," or back lights, because color tends to create an obvious separation between foreground and background. Despite strong resistance from studio technicians, he completely avoided flamboyant shadows on walls or faces. The result is a film that maintains a polite, drawing-room atmosphere until the climactic moment, when repressed color breaks free in almost garish form.

Very few directors who worked in color during the next decade were tempted to follow Hitchcock's example. In fact, the best color films about murder and suspense always reverted to the chiaroscuro effects of black-and-white lighting. A case in point is *Niagara* (1953), directed by Henry Hathaway and photographed by Joe MacDonald, which features post-card views of Niagara Falls and vivid images of Marilyn Monroe in a red dress, but which also provides a number of atmospheric scenes involving venetian blinds and inky shadows.[23] Another example is *Slightly Scarlet* (1956), a loose adaptation of James M. Cain's *Love's Lovely Counterfeit*, directed by Alan Dwan and photographed in Technicolor and "Superscope" by John Alton. Much of this picture is shot in high-key style, and it exploits the growing market for cheesecake by featuring a pair of voluptuous redheads (Rhonda Fleming and Arlene Dahl). In the sinister or mysterious scenes, however, Alton arranges the lights exactly as he would for a black-and-white production. He often photographs silhouetted or half-lit faces, and he makes extensive use of back-lighting and indirect light to create a sense of depth in darkened rooms. Whenever the crime boss (Ted de Corsia) enters a scene, we see a baroquely exaggerated form of "Jimmy Valentine lighting" that throws spooky shadows all the way to the ceiling.

There were only isolated experiments with muted color in this period— among them, William H. Clothier's Cinemascope and Eastmancolor photography for *Track of the Cat* (1954), a western set in the north woods, where nearly everything except the flesh tones of the actors and Robert Mitchum's red jacket was depicted in shades of black and white. At another extreme, elaborate black-and-white lighting and deep-focus compositions were put to effective use in two sumptuously colored pictures about women in distress: Ross Hunter's *Midnight Lace* (1960) and *Portrait in Black* (1960), both photographed by Russell Metty, who previously worked with Orson Welles and Douglas Sirk. But Metty's work was becoming an exception to the rule in an industry whose product was, at least temporarily, growing brighter and brighter. By this time, the old masters of black and white were nearing retirement or were finding new careers in television. Karl Freund, for example, invented multiple-camera techniques for *I Love Lucy*, and Nicholas Musuraca became the chief photographer for the *Jack Benny Show*.

Eventually, the techniques of what John Alton called "mystery lighting" fell into disuse—a phenomenon that was hastened by portable cameras and sound equipment, but most of all by color television. Don Seigel's remake of *The Killers* (1964), originally intended as a TV movie, is pervaded with noirlike sadism and double dealing but is photographed in band-box colors; significantly, its bloody conclusion takes place on a sunlit, suburban lawn. A similar brightness can be seen in two of the most expensively produced private-eye movies of the 1960s: *Harper* (1966, based on Ross MacDonald's *Moving Target*) and *Marlow* (1968, based on Raymond Chandler's *Little Sister*). Whatever their incidental virtues, neither of these films was able to provide a visual correlative for the shadowy, decadent romanticism of the 1940s. Even in the 1970s, color films dealing with noir subjects were sometimes flatly and brightly lit, using few points of illumination and relying on color alone to create separation; *The Laughing Policeman* (1974), for example, is an extremely gritty police procedural about the mean streets of San Francisco, but it contains relatively few dark areas or cast shadows.

The early 1960s were years of crisis for old-style mystery photography, but they were also the last years in which black and white could be shown in the United States without seeming like a parody or a deliberate allusion to the past. The Beatles made their film debut in black and white, and because of the huge commercial success of Hitchcock's *Psycho,* horror films in particular seemed to resist a complete move toward color. Notice also that the period was a golden age for U.S. art theaters. Although the major European directors eventually became interested in experimental uses of color, they were at first identified with a kind of visual austerity.[24] The most influential imports—Ingmar Bergman's *Seventh Seal* (1957), Michelangelo Antonioni's *L'Avventura* (1960), Federico Fellini's *8-1/2* (1963), Joseph Losey's *Servant* (1963), and the early work of the French New Wave—were shot in black and white. Raoul Coutard's early work for Godard and Truffaut was especially noteworthy because of its lack of studioish gloss and its freewheeling use of available light. A few European thrillers—such as René Clément's *Purple Noon* (1960) and Michael Powell's *Peeping Tom* (1960)—offered vibrant and expressive color images, but they attracted comparatively little critical attention in the United States, in part because they looked too much like mainstream commercial products. Change became evident only in the second half of the decade, especially in two "art" thrillers by European directors, both of which used color schemes reminiscent of pop-art painting: Antonioni's *Blowup* (1966), and John Boorman's *Point Blank* (1967).

Even today, black and white is sometimes associated with intellectual abstraction and the kind of artistic integrity that rejects big budgets—despite the fact that it has become the most expensive film stock a director can use. Perhaps one reason why its aura of art and authenticity survives is that a generation of moviegoers born in the 1950s and 1960s have a nostalgic memory of classic Hollywood. Not surprisingly, some of the most respected American films of the past twenty-five years involve a deliberate regression to black and white. Peter Bogdanovich's *Last Picture Show* (1971), photographed by Robert Surtees, evokes the dirt-poor life of a small Texas town in the 1950s, at a time when the town's black-and-white movie culture is slowly dying. Woody Allen's *Manhattan* (1979), photographed by Gordon Willis, pays enraptured tribute to sophisticated New York's black-and-white taste in nearly everything. Martin Scorsese's *Raging Bull* (1980), photographed by Michael Chapman, unifies contemporary camera technology with the great tradition of black-and-white movies about boxing. And Steven Spielberg's *Schindler's List* (1993), photographed by Janusz Kaminsky, terrifyingly recalls the gray skies and black horrors of the concentration-camp newsreels, disrupting the colorless atmosphere only once, with a breathtaking use of red.[25]

Meanwhile, prompted by a generation of largely New York–based directors and photographers who reached maturity in the 1970s, Hollywood has learned that color films about murder can be as somber and shadowy in their own way as anything from the 1940s.[26] New Yorker Gordon Willis, who photographed *Klute* (1971) and parts 1 and 2 of *The Godfather* (1972 and 1974), became famous as the "Prince of Darkness" because of his use of color with extremely low levels of illumination. His two *Godfather* films often show the actors as silhouettes or as dim presences hidden in gloom, and the interior scenes tend to be monochromatic, suffused with an amber, incandescent glow that established a widespread fashion.[27] Another photographer in the same tradition is Willis's former camera operator, Michael Chapman, who recalls that before he began work on *Taxi Driver,* he and Martin Scorsese looked at a variety of old movies, including "New York movies, *film noir, Sweet Smell of Success,* things like that." The completed film contains especially dense and mysterious blacks, which were achieved by underexposing half a stop on the exposure meter, "pushing" the development process, and making sure that at least one point of light within the frame was overexposed. "You know," Chapman told an interviewer, "you can shoot with no lights at all in the taxi as we did, as long as there's some point somewhere in the frame that's over-exposed, really burned. If you do that then your blacks will be acceptably dense. . . . [When you work in the] classic style—what you think of as the New York style of one lightbulb in the john and nothing else and everything is dark and shadow—well, that one light bulb should be there."[28]

Taxi Driver is memorable not only for its blacks but also for its neon, steam, and smoke. In still other ways it is indebted to the postclassical, documentary effects of the French New Wave, and its highly mobile cameras and Panavision lenses create a nervous but spectacular *flanerie* that would have been impossible to achieve in the classical period.[29] Perhaps equally important, its lurid world of porn theaters and child prostitutes is illuminated with colored lights (similar to the ones used for barroom scenes in Scorsese's earlier *Mean Streets*), which create a very different effect from the chaste, artful blacks and whites in even the grittiest earlier films about urban crime. This technique (partly derived from the "blaxploitation" films of the 1970s) was so crucial to *Taxi Driver* and other movies of its day that it has become a mannerism in all types of post-1970s noir. In Lawrence Kasdan's *Body Heat* (1981), for example, photographer Richard H. Klein augments the shadowy effects of the 1940s with colored gels, which often divide rooms or faces into "hot" and "cold" areas. And in Wim Wenders's period movie *Hammett* (1983), Philip Lathrop and Joe Biroc, assisted by production designers Eugene Lee and Dean Tavoularis, employ gels and painted walls to create a fusion of pulp illustration and German expressionist theater (which, we tend to forget, was often garishly colored, much like European expressionist painting).

A great many retro or "neo-noir" films use colored light not only to heighten the atmosphere of sex and violence, but also to evoke the monochromatic tradition of high-contrast, black-and-white thrillers. (Stephen

Soderbergh's *Underneath* frequently shoots whole sequences through red, blue, or green filters.) But because color has become normalized, the conventional effects of black-and-white lighting can also be integrated smoothly into recent films that have no retrospective or nostalgic intent. Consider Michael Mann's *Thief,* photographed by Donald Thorin, which was released in the same year as the deliberately retro *Body Heat. Thief* begins with a night-for-night shot in which the camera drifts slowly down between two buildings to reveal a black car sitting in an alleyway during a rainstorm; backlit rain falls through a dramatically silhouetted network of fire escapes and gathers in shiny puddles on the asphalt. This sort of tried-and-true "mystery" imagery soon gives way to a quite different style: daytime scenes in windowed offices are photographed with tungsten filters, so that the world outside becomes a bluish haze; lighting in diners and various institutional settings is unremittingly flat; and in most of the intimate sequences, telephoto close-ups reduce the backgrounds to a blur. But whenever the protagonist (James Caan) holds a meeting with his sinister employer (Tom Signorelli), everything once again becomes shadowy and atmospheric. Their first conversation is shot against the background of the Chicago River at night, with the skyscrapers reflected in the water; to make the moral perspective clear, every close-up of Signorelli is lit from below, whereas every close-up of Caan is lit from slightly above.

The old black-and-white lighting style is therefore still with us, and not only in color movies. The classics of the 1940s are regularly shown alongside letterboxed spectaculars as objects of nostalgia on TV, and a variety of young filmmakers still enjoy using black-and-white stock. In our brave new world, black and white can suggest Hollywood or Europe, glamour or seediness, realism or aestheticism, poverty or affectation, archival evidence or clever stylization. It is often seen in commercials or MTV videos, where it functions merely as one form among others, jumbled up in a wild mixture of aspect ratios and computer technologies. In response, an increasing number of feature films in color have begun to use black and white for expressive or symbolic purposes (just as the silent directors once used elements of hand-tinted color in the midst of black and white). Kenneth Branagh's dreadful *Dead Again* (1991) is one example, but consider also Oliver Stone's *Natural Born Killers* (1994), which is probably the most systematically discontinuous movie ever produced in Hollywood, radically switching camera speeds, lenses, lighting styles, and film stocks within individual sequences.

Despite its many connotations, black and white is most frequently used to signify the past—especially the past inhabited by our parents and grandparents, which we can see in old movies but never experience directly. A highly intelligent commentary on this phenomenon is independent filmmaker Mark Rappaport's thirty-six-minute *Exterior Night* (1994), made for high-definition color TV (HDTV), which combines original color imagery with archival footage of sets or backgrounds from *The Maltese Falcon, The Big Sleep, Mildred Pierce, Possessed, Dark Passage, The Fountainhead, Young Man with a Horn, Strangers on a Train,* and a score of other black-and-white movies. Using a blue-screen technique, Rappaport and HDTV cameraman Serge Roman frequently pose contemporary actors against studio nightclubs and streets from the 1940s. Even when the action is staged on colored sets representing the present day, the black-and-white imagery is never far away: we glimpse it through windows or on TV screens, and the characters talk about it constantly.

Exterior Night is narrated by a young man named Steve (Johnny Mez), who wears black jeans, a black leather jacket, and bright red Converse sneakers. An "old-fashioned guy," Steve is fond of composers like Rogers and Hart, and he feels an intense ambivalence toward classic movies like *The Damned Don't Dance,* which is based on a novel by his grandfather, Biff Farley, the most famous mystery writer of the 1940s. Each night in his dreams, he finds himself walking along dark streets that "I had never seen before, yet knew intimately—you know, the way dreams are." Hoping to understand this recurring mise-en-scène, he pays a visit to his parents, an archetypal couple from a 1950s sitcom. "Dad was the only clue," he thinks. "In fact, he was a prime suspect." Also during his wanderings, Steve encounters Sylvie, a young singer who shares his love of old jazz standards and who bears a striking resemblance both to his mother and to Biff Farley's girlfriend, the legendary Mona, also known as the "chanteuse in chartreuse" (all three women are played by Victoria Bastel). Sylvie works in a tiny bohemian dance club, and, like the more glamorous Mona, she sings a haunting tune called "Deja Vu" ("a song from the past that continues into the present"). Steve immediately falls in love with her, but when they spend the night together he is troubled by "every dream in the book." For the remainder of the film, he finds himself walking through a black-and-white world—wandering along Times Square at night, riding in taxicabs against the background of process screens, standing on deserted streets lit by solitary lamps, and visiting a posh nightclub called "The Golden Orchid," where Biff Farley met his mysterious death.

FIGURE 52. Actors posed against an empty set from Michael Curtiz's
Young Man with a Horn (1950) in Mark Rappaport's *Exterior Night* (1994).
In the film, the two actors are in color. The young man (Johnny Mez) wears
red sneakers, and the woman (Victoria Bastel) wears a chartreuse gown.

"I was caught up in the nostalgia for a memory I never had," Steve
says, and the film as a whole illustrates this point. Like a sweetly romantic
version of *Last Year at Marienbad, Exterior Night* creates a paradoxical, Möbius-strip relationship between the past and the present—an eternal round of "noirness" that has no particular beginning or end. Hence
the blue-screen process has an affinity with the back-projection techniques
of classic Hollywood, heightening the oneiric quality of stock imagery.
Meanwhile, the color has the same yearning, moody qualities as the black
and white. Actors are lit with colored gels that split their faces into symbolic areas of red and blue; Steve's present-day bedroom has venetian-
blind shadows running along its walls; and the black-and-white dream
imagery sometimes metamorphoses into the vivid covers of old paperback books, reminding us that the hard-boiled past was in some ways
more colorful than the present. At the end of the film, Steve recovers a
package containing what he believes to be the lost manuscript of Biff Farley's last novel. When he unwraps his treasured discovery, it turns out
to be nothing more than an album of black-and-white photographs. "A
book of souvenirs," Biff's offscreen voice calls it. "Places where I lived
my life, places which you've visited. It's all we have in common. . . . Don't
say I never gave you anything." Inside are photographs of a cityscape at
night. As Steve gazes at the pictures, they become animated: cars move,
mists circulate, and something appears to have just exited the scene. The

effect is surreal, as if Atget had wandered onto an empty back lot in the Hollywood of the 1940s. As Humphrey Bogart would say, images such as these are the "stuff that dreams are made of." *Exterior Night* captures their special beauty, showing how they function in the collective unconscious of filmmakers born after 1940 and helping us to understand why certain directors and cinematographers—even when they work in color—repeatedly aspire to the condition of black and white.

PARODY, PASTICHE, FASHION

If anything characterizes postmodern art, it is what Peter Wollen describes as a relentless "historicism and eclecticism, which plunders the image-bank and the word-horde for the material of parody, pastiche, and, in extreme cases, plagiarism."[30] But postmodern movies have a very short historical memory, usually limiting their "image-bank" to the period since 1930. The so-called film noir occupies an especially important position among the available styles; hence at least three generations of young, artistically ambitious directors have made it a favored object of quotation and imitation.

A metafilm like *Exterior Night* is one example of this tendency. Working outside Hollywood, Rappaport uses elements of burlesque, parody, and "plagiarism" to comment on a lingering fascination with a genre or style, creating his effects not only with cinematography but also with the entire "nexus of fashion" that constitutes the popular conception of film noir. Rappaport's attitude toward the material he borrows or imitates is fairly typical. Although comic parodies of noir can be seen everywhere in our culture (appearing in such different contexts as Dennis Potter's *Singing Detective,* Garrison Keillor's "Guy Noir," and specific episodes of TV shows like *Sisters* and *Parker Lewis Can't Lose*), they seldom have a purely analytic, deconstructive, or critical purpose. Parody in any form is both a conservative and an evolutionary mode; even in Rappaport's case, it seems Janus-faced, expressing affection for the things it mocks, enabling certain motifs to survive and enter into new combinations.[31]

Perhaps for this reason, parody and its more blank-toned cousin pastiche, which are the ludic forms of what Gerard Genette describes as "hypertextuality," are as old as high culture itself. The Greek tragedies were accompanied by the burlesques of Aristophanes, and the history of the novel has been shaped by authors such as Miguel de Cervantes, Henry Fielding, Laurence Sterne, Gustave Flaubert, and James Joyce, who use parody or pastiche both to distinguish themselves from earlier models and to form complex links with tradition. Notice, furthermore, that parody has the same kind of importance to the fashion system and the consumer economy. Where film noir is concerned, there are recent TV commercials that use comic parodies of film noir to sell Hellman's mayonnaise and Colombian coffee; there is even an elaborate, black-and-white parody of neo-noir, starring Julliette Lewis and Harry Dean Stanton, which advertises Guess Jeans.

Consider also an article "Fashion Noir" in the fashion section of the November 3, 1993, *Los Angeles Times,* where Betty Goodwin writes a regular column, "Screen Style." In a short piece devoted to Carl Reiner's comic parody *Fatal Instinct,* Goodwin notes that the film's costume designer, Albert Wolskey, is "purposely inconsistent in his retro references" and mixes contemporary accessories with a wide range of older styles. Detective Ned Ravine (Armand Assante) wears "22 suits, all a generic blue model with the same black tie." Femme fatale Lola (Sean Young) "comes off like a tacky 50's starlet in tight, draped, pulled, cinched and cutout dresses." Wife Lana (Kate Nelligan) is an "amalgam of Barbara Stanwyck, Bette Davis, and other '40s stars," cavorting around in "silk peignoirs with feather boas and matching slippers." Secretary Laura (Sherilyn Fenn) has "the pouf-sleeved innocence of Judy Garland in her 'Andy Hardy' days." The movie as a whole, Goodwin says, is "intentionally dopey," but it nonetheless offers its female viewers something to imitate: "While you might hold the fluffy feathers," Goodwin tells her readers, "try the silk robes—they act as undeniably divine lounging garb." She notes with pleased amusement that the costumes for Lola are "pure Frederick's of Hollywood, circa the 1950s catalogs," and she quotes Wolsky's observation that "the '40s and '50s are the last great period for clothes." In fact, she says, some of Lola's outfits can be obtained at "Repeat Performance," a trendy Los Angeles clothing shop specializing in antique designer fashions.

It might seem odd that film noir, which is commonly associated with seedy hotels, all-night diners, and the haunts of the underworld, should be capable of starting a fashion trend, even in parodic form. But as Clifton Webb says about one of his cocktail parties in *The Dark Corner,* such movies are also composed of a "nauseating mixture of Park Avenue and Broadway." They usually depict nightclubs, café society, and the homes of the extremely rich. By their very nature, they are deeply concerned with sleek clothing styles, and they repeatedly give us women who signify what Laura Mulvey describes as "to-be-looked-at-ness." Thus when RKO's *Murder, My Sweet* was released in 1945, it prompted the *Holly-*

wood Citzen News to run a long article entitled "It's Murder, but Gowns Are Sweet," by fashion correspondent Florabel Muir, who spends two full columns lovingly describing the costumes worn by Claire Trevor. Rather like Betty Goodwin in 1993, Muir suggests that the bad-girl outfits are a bit excessive and shouldn't be slavishly imitated. The attractive playsuit Trevor wears in her opening scene, for example, is excellent for the beach, but unsuitable for "receiving guests in a stately drawing room"; moreover, Trevor should have avoided wearing a gardenia in her hair, because "gardenias and playsuits do not go together." One of the best costumes, Muir says, is a black dinner gown, "which would be the perfect little black dinner gown for you, or for anyone, if only it didn't have quite so much glitter" (2 April 1945).

The deliberately flashy noir fashions of the 1940s were by no means limited to women, nor were they simple by-products of studio design. Dashiell Hammett was one of the most dapper literary figures of the late 1920s and early 1930s (as the photograph on the cover of the first edition of *The Thin Man* was designed to show), and like his character Ned Beaumont, he knew that you were not supposed to wear silk socks with tweeds. Raymond Chandler, who never made such a fashion error, took Hammett's interest in clothing even further. In the second sentence of *The Big Sleep,* Philip Marlowe tells us, "I was wearing my powder-blue suit, with dark blue shirt, tie and display handkerchief, black brogues, black wool socks with dark blue clocks on them." Whether he was speaking of Moose Malloy (who wore "a shaggy borsolino hat, a rough grey sports coat with white golf balls on it for buttons, a brown shirt, a yellow tie, pleated grey flannel slacks and alligator shoes with white explosions on the toes"), Orfamay Quest (who carried "one of those awkward-looking square bags that made you think of a Sister of Mercy taking first aid to the wounded"), or Leslie Murdock ("a slim tall self-satisfied looking number in a tropical worsted suit of slate blue"), Marlowe recognized that apparel was a precise index of taste and social position. No wonder he was played in the movies by a former boy-crooner like Dick Powell, who was fastidiously tailored. And no wonder that Chandler himself once picked Cary Grant as the ideal Marlowe.[32]

According to Borde and Chaumeton's first edition of the *Panorama du film noir américain,* noir began to die off at exactly the moment when these and other fashions became dated and accessible to parodists. The coup de grâce, they argue, was lovingly administered by Vincente Minnelli, one of the cinema's most dress-conscious directors, who staged the "Girl-Hunt Ballet" at the climax of MGM's *Band Wagon* (1953). An

FIGURE 53. The "Girl Hunt" ballet in *The Band Wagon* (1953). (Museum of Modern Art Stills Archive.)

eight-minute Technicolor dance number presented in the form of a 1940s-style dream sequence, "The Girl Hunt" stars Fred Astaire as hard-boiled detective Rod Reily and Cyd Charisse as both a blond ingenue and a raven-haired femme fatale. The most stunning moment occurs in a smoky barroom, where Reily, wearing a cream-colored suit, a black shirt, and a yellow tie, dances a steamy number with the "dark" Charisse, who wears scarlet, sequins, and black mesh tights. In a switch on the usual formula, the blond turns out to be the villain whom Reily must pump full of lead. He wanders off at the end with the brunette. "She was bad," he tells us. "She was dangerous. I wouldn't trust her any further than I could throw her. But she was my kind of woman."

For Borde and Chaumeton, "The Girl Hunt" captures the "very

essence" of the noir series, submitting it to a "poetic transformation."
Minnelli, they argue, is both a commercial surrealist and a "tortured aesthete," whose "lucid complicity" with the 1940s is made possible by the
fact that noir itself had become little more than a "memory." The sump-
tuous ballet, they suggest, ought to be preserved in a kind of "imaginary
cinémateque," as a memorial to a dead form (138). The problem with
such arguments, however, is that "The Girl Hunt" was nothing especially
new. Minnelli had staged similar parodies in his Broadway revues of the
1930s, and one of the first pictures he wanted to make when he went to
Paramount in 1937 was *Times Square,* a parodic "mystery chase" set to
Broadway show tunes. He also knew the smash hit *Guys and Dolls*
(1950), in which dapper gangster Sky Masterson sings "Luck Be a Lady,"
dressed in a costume similar to Astaire's in *The Band Wagon*. This and
many other musical shows about the underworld were clearly an influence on "The Girl Hunt," which satirizes not only Hollywood but also
the most successful American author of 1953, Mickey Spillane.

The example of Spillane helps to underscore the fact that showbusi-
ness parody often has less to do with the ridicule of a dead style than
with an attempt to capitalize on a wildly popular trend.[33] Consider the
many cartoon parodies released by Warner Brothers in the 1940s and
1950s. One of these is a Fritz Freeling production of 1944, involving a
wolf in a zoot suit who visits a theater to see *To Have and Have Not*.
(The Zoot Suit riots in Los Angeles had occurred only a year earlier.) The
cartoon itself is in Technicolor, but what the wolf sees is a perfectly executed black-and-white caricature, filled with absurdly comic exaggera-
tions—as when Bogart lights Lauren Bacall's cigarette with a blowtorch.
A later Warner cartoon by Chuck Jones, timed to coincide with the studio's release of *Dragnet* (1954), casts Porky Pig and Daffy Duck as
Sergeants Joe Monday and Shmoe Tuesday, who work as cops on a futuristic space station. The cartoon imitates Jack Webb's popular TV show,
but at the same time it resembles an old-style film noir, with Porky and
Daffy talking around the cigarettes in their mouths.

A similar desire to ape current fashions lies behind films such as *Fatal Instinct,* which was designed to satirize not only the classics of the
1940s, but also *Body Heat, Fatal Attraction, Cape Fear*, and *Basic Instinct*. Much the same thing could be said about Carl Reiner's more effective and technically brilliant parody, *Dead Men Don't Wear Plaid*
(1982), which was made possible by the fact that vintage films noirs still
circulate as commodities on TV. In other words, even when parody
ridicules a style, it feeds on what it imitates. I would go further: much

like analytic criticism, parody helps to define and even create certain styles, giving them visibility and status. "We murder to dissect," William Wordsworth once said of critics, and parodists could be charged with a similar crime; but scholars and mimics also preserve what they destroy, transforming it into an idea that can be revived by later artists. (This would explain why a series of film-noir burlesques, including *The Black Bird* [1975] and *The Cheap Detective* [1978], were roughly contemporary with the rise of neo-noir.)

It seems obvious that both parody and criticism have helped to shape the popular conception of film noir, enhancing its strength as an intellectual fashion and as a commercial product. Even so, we cannot say exactly when parodies of noir began, and we cannot distinguish precisely between parody, pastiche, and "normal" textuality. Samuel Goldwyn's *They've Got Me Covered* (1944), starring Bob Hope, contains at least one sequence (photographed by noir cameraman Rudolph Mate) that mimics all the visual conventions of the dark thrillers of its day. A later Hope film, Paramount's *My Favorite Brunette* (1947), features Alan Ladd in a cameo appearance as a tough private eye. Are these parodies, or clever tributes? Notice also that both Dashiell Hammett and Raymond Chandler occasionally wrote subtle burlesques of their own fiction. Frank MacShane argues that Chandler was a comic novelist and that at least one of his stories, "Pearls Are a Nuisance" (published in *Dime Detective* in 1939), is a "parody from start to finish" (*Life of Raymond Chandler*, 56). According to MacShane, some of the more flamboyant aspects of Chandler's prose, such as his description of a violent beating in "Bay City Blues" and his famous opening to "Red Wind" ("On nights like that every booze party ends in a fight. Meek little wives feel the edge of the carving knife and study their husbands' necks. Anything can happen. You can even get a full glass of beer at a cocktail lounge."), were intended to suggest that "much of what he was writing was rubbish" (*Life of Raymond Chandler*, 56–57).[34]

Even a classic film noir like *Out of the Past* derives much of its charm—at least for contemporary viewers—from the fact that it verges on self-parody (a quality it shares with *The Lady from Shanghai*, which was released in the same year). The basic ingredients are almost too familiar: a trenchcoated, chain-smoking private eye; a gorgeous femme fatale; a flashback narrative; a world-weary, first-person narration telling a story of murder, betrayal, and sexual obsession; a downbeat ending; and a haunting theme song played not only by the studio orchestra but also by every jazz band and barroom pianist in sight. (This same tune had been used in *Crack-Up,* another film noir produced at RKO in the previous year.) The plot, derived from Daniel Mainwaring's *Build My Gallows High,* is strongly influenced by *The Maltese Falcon,* and the dialogue (the best of it written by the uncredited Frank Fenton) is rich with quasi-Chandleresque wit. Some of the lines could have been used for an intentional parody like "The Girl Hunt." At one point, for example, the good girl (Virginia Huston) remarks that Jane Greer "can't be *all* bad— nobody is." Mitchum wryly mutters, "She comes the closest." Mitchum's offscreen narration has a similar quality. "I never saw her in the daytime," he says of Greer. "We seemed to live by night. What was left of the day went away like a pack of cigarettes you smoked." All the while, the film as a whole seems intelligently self-reflexive or artful in the way it treats its secondhand atmospherics. When we hear the lines I have just quoted, we see the private eye seated at an outdoor café in a Mexican plaza at dusk, directly across from a neon-lit theater called the "Cine Pico," which is showing Hollywood movies. From this very spot, the *belle dame sans merci* makes her mysterious entrance, like a creature of the pop-culture imagination.

The European auteurs of the 1960s and 1970s, who helped create the idea of film noir, were even more self-conscious than a director like Jacques Tourneur; they grounded their work in allusion and hypertextuality rather than in a straightforward attempt to keep a formula alive. Godard and Rainer Fassbinder were especially notable for the way they eschewed melodramatic plots and realistic sex and violence, reducing the private eye and the gangster to comic-book stereotypes (sometimes, as in *Breathless* and *The American Soldier,* via characters who imagined themselves as heroes but were actually playing stereotypical roles). Even Truffaut's more lyrical *Shoot the Piano Player* keeps the old conventions at a playful distance: when Charles Aznavour and Marie Dubois walk down the Paris streets in trenchcoats, the effect is vaguely comic, as if they were on their way to a costume party. The German Wim Wenders, who began his career as an avant-garde artist, and who briefly became a sort of crossover phenomenon, took a somber approach. His most commercially successful film, *The American Friend* (1977), is a loose adaptation of a Patricia Highsmith novel, written half in English and half in German, which can be read as a straight thriller modeled on Hitchcock and Nicholas Ray, as a pastiche of certain Hollywood conventions, and as an allegory about the relationship between America and West Germany two generations after World War II.[35] Here and elsewhere, the idea of film noir tends to bridge a gap between Europe and America, between mainstream entertainment and the art cinema. Thus American film noir of the "historical" period was largely a product of ideas and talent appropriated from Europe, and neo-noir emerged during a renaissance of the European art film, when America was relatively open to imported culture. The second of these two phases was affected not only by the French and German New Waves, but also by an Italian tradition of philosophical noir—as in Antonioni's pop-art *Blowup* and Bertolucci's retro-styled *The Conformist* (1971). It was also strongly influenced by European directors who made English-language thrillers that were aimed partly at the American market: not only Antonioni, but also Polanski (*Repulsion*), Boorman (*Point Blank*), and eventually even Wenders (*Hammett*).

In America, however, it was difficult to turn far away from commercial entertainment. The younger generation of Hollywood directors tended to incorporate New Wave techniques or retro style into spectacularly violent crime pictures, both attacking and preserving traditional values. Most of their films can be described as parodic in a loose sense— that is, they openly borrow from a large and diverse body of earlier movies, establishing a more or less ironic filiation with a supposed classical norm. There are, of course, many important exceptions to this rule: crime pictures such as *The French Connection* (1971), *The Killing of a Chinese Bookie* (1976), *Straight Time* (1978), and *Miami Blues* (1990) can be called noir, even though they make no special attempt to reproduce stylistic conventions of the 1940s and 1950s. I am speaking here of latter-day noirs that have a quality of deliberate allusiveness, as if they were trying to display a certain wit or sophistication about the cinematic past.

One of the most interesting if problematic American attempts to follow in the path of the Europeans is Robert Altman's revisionist production of *The Long Goodbye* (1973), which subjects the Chandleresque detective film to offbeat casting and a certain amount of derisive parody, all the while making Brechtian jokes about Hollywood. The underlying concept is intriguing: Elliot Gould is intentionally miscast as Philip Marlowe, and the setting is updated to contemporary, dope-crazed Los Angeles, where the private eye becomes a ridiculous anachronism. (Altman referred to the character as "Rip Van Marlowe," and at one point in the film we hear a policeman remark, "Marlowe with an *e*. Sounds like a fag name.") The feeling of historical dissonance is especially strong at the level of style, which involves Panavision, zoom lenses, improvised dialogue, unorthodox sound recording and mixing, and a rather diffused, pastel-colored photography by Vilmos Zsigmond, who "flashed" the film

stock to degrade contrasts. On many levels, the picture completely reverses the values we associate with Chandler and classic noir: in place
of witty dialogue and wry offscreen narration, it gives us inarticulate characters and a mumbling private eye who incessantly talks to himself; in
place of carefully framed, angular compositions, it uses a roving, almost
arbitrary series of panning and zooming shots that continually flatten
perspective; and in place of romantic music, it employs a 1940s-style
theme (composed by John Williams) that undergoes countless re-
arrangements—including versions for door chimes, a sitar, and a mariachi band.

Altman turns Marlowe into a chain-smoking slob and a nerdy sentimentalist, and novelist Roger Wade (Sterling Hayden) into an aging Hemingway type who brutalizes his wife (Nina van Pallandt). The theme of
macho brutality, which is in some ways the flip side of Marlowe's and
Chandler's chivalrousness, finds its most disturbing expression in a scene
that the old Breen Office would never have allowed: gangster Marty Au-
gustine (Mark Rydell) smashes a coke bottle into the face of a beautiful
young woman. In other respects, however, *The Long Goodbye* is faithful to its source. Significantly, its initial script was written by veteran pulp
novelist Leigh Brackett, who also worked on Howard Hawks's version
of *The Big Sleep* and who tried to achieve a more or less straightforward
adaptation. Much of its commentary on the chaos and soulessness of
Southern California is perfectly in keeping with the original novel, and
despite the fact that it creates a new ending, it preserves Chandler's basic plot.[36]

Although *The Long Goodbye* has an impressively hallucinatory effect and a good deal of satiric edge, it seems to me to work best at a fairly
traditional level. When Altman tries to send up the novel, introducing
alienation effects and snide jokes about classic Hollywood, he usually
achieves very little; after all, hard-boiled fiction always skirted close to
satire or burlesque, and Chandler himself was already a savage critic of
the movies. Significantly, Chandler was also far more critical than Altman of the Los Angeles police; the film merely makes a few jokes about
the corruption of small-town Mexican cops. Notice, too, that certain of
Altman's more freewheeling inventions—such as the coke-bottle attack
and the running gag about the stoned, bare-breasted girls who live in an
apartment across from Marlowe—seem designed to exploit a new style
of misogyny and violence under the cover of a smugly superior attitude
toward private-eye stories.

These problems are especially evident in the last scenes, when Altman

employs a sophomoric trick reminiscent of the football game at the end
of *M*A*S*H* (1970). Marlowe discovers that his friend Terry Lennox
(Jim Bouton) has committed murder. Lennox says, "What the hell, nobody cares," and Marlowe replies, "Nobody but me." Then, in a gesture that runs completely against the grain of his character, Marlowe
shoots Lennox, who falls dead in a lake. Marlowe turns and walks off
down a long road lined with trees, passing Eileen Wade, who is riding
toward him in a Jeep from the opposite direction. The image is an obvious allusion to *The Third Man*, but on the soundtrack, instead of romantic music, we hear "Hooray for Hollywood." In this shot and at several other junctures, it is difficult to determine exactly what Altman is
satirizing. Is his film a Chandleresque attack on L.A.'s gangsters and hip-
pies, or is it a pot-induced attack on Chandler's novel? Audiences at the
time were unsure what to think, and the initial advertising campaign did
not help, because it made viewers expect a classic thriller. When the film
did poor business in Los Angeles and other cities, United Artists withdrew it from circulation and designed a new set of trailers and posters
to emphasize its parodic aspects. Surrounded by these cues to interpretation, it was rereleased eight months later in New York, where it received good reviews but continued to perform poorly at the box office.

An almost completely opposite and more successful use of the hard-
boiled tradition can be seen in *Chinatown* (1974), a lavishly produced
picture that opens with the 1940s Paramount logo and closes with the
new logo of the 1970s. The contrast between this film and Altman's is
remarkably systematic: *The Long Goodbye* completely dispenses with
an art director, but *Chinatown* depends heavily on the production designs of Richard Sylbert; *The Long Goodbye* engages in jokey, New Wave
digressions from its central narrative, but *Chinatown* is an engrossing,
classically constructed thriller; *The Long Goodbye* inhibits identification
with the protagonist, but *Chinatown* encourages it; *The Long Goodbye*
treats old Hollywood derisively, but *Chinatown* returns wholeheartedly
to the past, recreating 1930s Los Angeles in meticulous detail and acknowledging its indebtedness to *The Maltese Falcon* by casting John Huston in an important role.

Though *Chinatown* makes use of Panavision and highly mobile camera equipment that enables an operator to walk with characters through
doorways and into tight spaces, it cleverly adapts the new technology to
the feel of the old studio films; throughout, the framing is tight and re-
strictive, and the color scheme is relatively muted and monochromatic.
Scriptwriter Robert Towne and director Roman Polanski, the chief au-

thors, were obviously devoted to old movies. "I love the cliches," Polanski told *Newsweek* magazine when the film was released. But Towne borrowed more from Hammett than from Chandler, and Polanski went back
to even earlier models, bringing *Chinatown* close to the tale of gothic
horror. Ostensibly a nostalgia or retro film, *Chinatown* is actually a critique of the American past, inflected by Marxist and Freudian themes
that were latent in some varieties of classic noir, and inspired to some
degree by Bertolucci's *Conformist*. Its particular qualities arise from a
tension between Towne's socially acute, melancholy private-eye story and
Polanski's slightly perverse, absurdist tastes. These two attitudes can be
sensed in nearly every aspect of the production, even in Jerry Goldsmith's
theme music: a low, plaintive trumpet solo counterpointed by an eerie
string passage. Between them, they give considerable shading and dimension to the film's protagonist, J. J. Gittes (Jack Nicholson), who is
an ethically compromised character, even less conventionally heroic than
Sam Spade.

Gittes is a hothead and vulgarian; he overdresses, he horselaughs at
dirty jokes (which he thinks his secretary shouldn't hear), and he can't
talk to a rich lady client without accidentally falling into profanity. Even
so, he uneasily insists that his small business is an "honest living," and
in a barber shop he almost starts a fight with a banker who sneers at
him. He also tells a couple of self-righteous cops that he would never
stoop to extortion. During the course of the film, he emerges as a slightly
more believable version of a fantasy Bogart sometimes embodied—the
tough man whose exterior disguises compassion and an outraged sense
of justice. From indirect references in the dialogue, we learn that he was
once a policeman in Chinatown, where his job was "puttin' Chinamen
in jail for spittin' in the laundry." His orders were to do "as little as possible" because, as the district attorney once said, "you may think you
know what's going on, but you don't." Gittes complains, "You could
never figure out what was happening." Something tragic happened in
Chinatown—the movie never tells us what, but it concerned a woman
Gittes was trying to help. Now, during the course of his present investigation, his history repeats itself with a vengeance. He becomes involved
with the wealthy and enigmatic Evelyn Mulwray (Faye Dunaway) and
tries to help her out of trouble. Events begin to take on affinities with
those in *Vertigo* (1958): the upper-class woman in the present becomes
an echo of a woman in the past, and after the detective has peeped into
other people's lives and found the keys to a murder and a political scandal, he is crushed under the very guilt he was trying to overcome. But

the solution to the mystery also has profound social consequences. By the end, the Chinese ghetto has become the symbol of an epic corruption and irrationality—a disease that spreads as wide as the city and is about to spread into the surrounding valley.

The crimes depicted in *Chinatown* include not only murder and political chicanery, but also incest and pedophilia between the almost mythical tycoon Noah Cross (Huston, a myth himself, who had recently played Noah in *The Bible*) and his daughter Evelyn. Even so, the movie would probably be less disturbing if Polanski had not subtly linked its dark sexual themes to the psychology of Gittes. In an interview at the American Film Institute, Polanski revealed that he had greatly heightened the subjectivity of the narrative—in fact, he shot nearly everything from Gittes's point of view, showing him peering through camera lenses or windows and constantly spying on the other characters. Largely because of this device, *Chinatown* becomes a study in the sadistic gaze, and it ends when Gittes finds himself an unwitting accomplice in the death of the woman he is spying upon—indeed, he is handcuffed to the man who fires the gun.

The theme of universal guilt and sexual malaise is typical of classic noir, but *Chinatown* benefits from the relaxation of censorship codes, and despite its underlying emphasis on voyeurism, its treatment of Evelyn Mulwray is relatively unusual. Given the deep ambivalence toward women in movies such as *The Maltese Falcon, Out of the Past,* and *The Lady from Shanghai,* we expect her to be a vessel of evil sex; in fact, she turns out to be a victim. *Chinatown* is also unusual in its forthright treatment of greedy capitalists and crooked politicians. Towne based his script on an actual scandal that hit Los Angeles in the early decades of the century, when rich men bought cheap farmland and had it incorporated into the city, thus acquiring control over the area's water supply. As Mike Davis observes, "The windfall profits of these operations welded the ruling class together and capitalized lineages of power (notably, the *Times-Mirror* empire) that remain in place today" (114). In the last analysis, therefore, 1930s L.A. becomes a metaphor for the whole of Richard Nixon's America.

Meanwhile, Polanski's European sophistication comes through, giving the movie a decadent, voluptuous pace and a subterranean horror. The violence of the film is understated and largely repressed, but occasionally it surfaces, especially when Polanski himself appears, playing Elisha Cook Jr. to Nicholson's Bogart. Nicholson calls Polanski a "midget," whereupon the little man administers a symbolically appropriate retaliation; inserting a switchblade into the private eye's left nostril, he neatly

slices the wing of the nose. Polanski is probably also responsible for making the world of the film resemble the fiction of Nathanael West. The
slick-haired men and heavily made-up women are attractive, but the nostalgic effects sometimes have a disquieting effect. Even Faye Dunaway,
who remains passionate and sexy, is not quite the glamorous figure we
associate with this kind of movie. Her face is powdered, her eyes are red,
and her teeth are stained from lipstick. Her hair, which she compulsively
brushes back from her forehead, is stiffened with permanent waves. She
is frequently dressed to the neck in gray or black, but in one scene she
wears riding clothes and her throat is sweaty. Her every gesture suggests
frustrated sexuality and incipient madness, and Polanski, who was always more interested in the pathology of sex than in romance, seems to
have encouraged her nervousness by keeping the camera close to her
face.[37] Again and again, he juxtaposes her suffering with that of a spot-
lessly innocent-looking girl (Diane Ladd) whom she is trying to hide from
Gittes. The image is diabolically clever, because the girl's innocence
turns out to have been born out of the corruption that threatens to destroy her.

Much of *Chinatown* has a quiet, ghostly feel, as when Gittes stands
outside the Mulwray estate and hears the faint squeak of chamois
against a yellow Packard. The movie is also filled with Asian servants
and Latino workers who glide around the edges of the scenery, watching the white world decay. The houses and settings are nicely selected
and designed to evoke the period, and yet they seem vaguely embalmed,
in part because of John Alonzo's anamorphic, often extremely low-key
photography, which hides interiors in gloom and emphasizes dry, yel-
lowish colors. The air of grotesquerie extends even to minute details that
register almost subliminally: vaguely funereal flowers in vases or on
lawns; a picture of a black sailing ship on a wall behind two doomed
women; a pattern on a bedspread that I momentarily took for a blood-
stain; and a girl's summer dress and wide straw hat lying incongruously
in a dark living room. In one shot late in the movie, Gittes bends over
to look at a shiny object at the bottom of a pond. Off in the corner of
the screen, something stirs—the reddish fin of a goldfish, looking for an
instant like a monster. (Earlier, we recall, Polanski promised to feed the
hero's nose to a goldfish.)

This sinister ambiance prepares us for the climactic moments, when
Gittes finds himself back in Chinatown. Here again the film invites comparison with *The Maltese Falcon* and other dark thrillers of the 1940s,
many of which came to ironic, somewhat joyless conclusions, based on

FIGURE 54. Retro style in *Chinatown* (1974).

a deep-seated sexual paranoia. The note of failure in classic noir, however, was frequently softened by a qualified attempt to assert some kind of justice or return to social equilibrium. In contrast, *Chinatown* is truly pessimistic. Because it is a Vietnam-era film, contemporary with the Watergate scandals, its hero does not walk away from chaos like Welles in *The Lady from Shanghai* ("Maybe I'll live so long that I'll forget her—maybe I'll die trying"); instead, he is helped offscreen by two of his business partners. The ordinary institutions having failed, he remains locked in a world of irrational greed and sickness, and his consciousness of that world has left him so numb he can barely move.

In Towne's original script for *Chinatown*, Noah Cross was killed and Gittes carried Evelyn Mulwray's daughter to Mexico, presumably heading off to a Latin shelter that was sometimes suggested in Sam Peckinpah's westerns. Such an escape is myth, of course, a pastoral, but at least it provides relief from Amerika. Polanski's version is just the opposite, offering no possibility for meaningful action, not even flight. Gittes sees Evelyn slumped over the wheel of her Packard, her eye exploded by a bullet; the daughter screams, while Noah Cross embraces her and tries to shield the view. As Gittes stumbles off, the camera rises above a Chinatown street, with Goldsmith's theme music creating a languorous mood in keeping with the art-nouveau posters that advertised the movie. At this point, the only consolation anyone might have would be in opium dreams.

Despite all the terror and despair he creates, however, Polanski seems to relish the sight of a boogeyman swallowing a baby. Furthermore, despite all its social and psychological corruption, the film as a whole inspires a sentimental fondness for old Hollywood, giving the 1930s a fascinating sleekness, intimacy, and plenitude. My own reaction to the ending of *Chinatown* is therefore a bit like Lionel Trilling's toward *Heart of Darkness:* I'm not sure whether to recoil, or to take subtle pleasure in the elegance of "the horror." To be sure, no scene in a detective melodrama is more troubling than the one in which Gittes confronts the patriarch Noah Cross, baffled by the man's fathomless lust and greed; and no scene is more emotionally charged than the one in which Gittes slaps Evelyn to make her confess her past: with each swift blow, the effect changes dizzily, moving from shock to repulsion to deep compassion. Nevertheless, if we want to believe that Polanski is serious, then we must suspect that he sometimes identified with Gittes—a man engulfed in a corrupt world. The only major director of the period who worked in both the East and the West (for what Godard used to call Mosfilm-Paramount and Nixon-Paramount), he may have felt that life was beyond corruption —that it was merely absurd, and that a cool and brilliant style was the only recompense. The ending of *Chinatown* carries the hint of such an attitude. At the same time, it makes the movie hypnotically beautiful, almost a flower of evil.

Writing in 1979, cultural historian John G. Cawelti offered *Chinatown* and several other Hollywood films of its day (especially those by Robert Altman and Arthur Penn) as evidence that the old generic system was "exhausted" and on the verge of transformation into pictures "more directly related to the second half of the twentieth century."[38] In his view, the "doomed burlesque" and "tragic parody" in such movies as *Bonnie and Clyde* and *The Long Goodbye* suggested that audiences were becoming increasingly sophisticated about film history and that American pop culture was undergoing a renewal, bringing it closer to "the mainstream of postmodernist literature" (190–91). Although *Chinatown* was more nostalgic than truly parodic, Cawelti argued that it was one of the most important works of the period—a new type of movie that "deliberately invokes the basic characteristics of a traditional genre in order to bring its audience to see that genre as the embodiment of an inadequate and destructive myth" (194). Three years later, in the wake of *Star Wars* (1977), *Raiders of the Lost Arc* (1981), and the election of Ronald Reagan, Fredric Jameson saw postmodern style and the vogue for nostalgia quite differently. Consumer society, Jameson pointed out, was highly conducive of "stylistic diversity and heterogeneity," especially where pastiche or any form of "blank parody" was concerned. In a wide-ranging indictment of late capitalism, he noted a similarity between pop artists like Andy Warhol and retro movies like *Body Heat*—which, even when they were set in the present, seemed to occur in "an eternal '30s." Although he admired *Chinatown,* Jameson claimed that such films in general were "an alarming and pathological symptom of a society that has become incapable of dealing with time and history" ("Postmodernism and Consumer Society," 117). They also suggested that writers and artists of the present day no longer felt capable of creating new styles or traditions; it was as if the whole weight of "sixty or seventy years of classical modernism" were pressing down on the younger generation like what Marx had called an historical "nightmare" ("Postmodernism and Consumer Society," 115).

In greater hindsight, neither of these views is exactly correct. It is particularly difficult to view *Chinatown* in Cawelti's terms, when most critics argue that historical noir was already a rebuke to classic Hollywood's dominant mythology. (We should recall that *Double Indemnity, Detour,* and *Out of the Past* end with the protagonists either dead or about to be executed and that *Kiss Me Deadly* explodes the entire cast.) For his part, Jameson sounds overly pessimistic. Nostalgia may be pervasive in the new film noir, but it is also a theme in the "original" pictures—which, as Paul Schrader points out, usually involve the sort of protagonist who "retreats into the past" (58). Furthermore, any discussion of nostalgia needs to ask: nostalgia for what? A good deal of postmodernist noir involves a conservative, ahistorical regression to the pop culture of the 1950s, or to a glamorous world before that, where people dressed well and smoked cigarettes. But this is by no means always the case. Feminist critic Barbara Creed observes that the "missing past" in most films noirs seems to be a past that "once validated the paternal signifier"; even so, she notes that three of the nostalgia films mentioned by Jameson—*Chinatown, Body Heat,* and *The Conformist*—involve a male protagonist who fails precisely because "the patriarchal symbolic, the Law, has also failed."[39] Clearly the past has different constituencies and different uses, and we need to consider the retro films on an individual basis. To cite only one exception to the general rule, the nostalgia in *Devil in a Blue Dress* (discussed in chapter 6) has slightly different implications than the nostalgia in *Chinatown,* even though the two films are in many ways quite similar.

Granting these complications, Jameson may be closer to the truth where the general run of movies is concerned. Unquestionably, *Chinatown* was an innovative film, made possible by an increasing awareness of old movies on TV, a liberalized censorship code, and a disillusionment with certain American myths. Its immediate legacy, however, was purely stylistic, at the level of cameo roles, moody photography, and male fashion; and it may have taught the advertising industry how to sell products by making them look stylishly moderne. It spawned two British remakes of classic noir, both starring the aging Robert Mitchum as Philip Marlowe: *Farewell, My Lovely* (1975), photographed by John Alonzo in a cloyingly arty, wide-angle fashion, and *The Big Sleep* (1978), updated to contemporary London, with James Stewart miscast in the role of General Sternwood. Such films were heavy with nostalgia, and their treatment of history was entirely superficial. The same kind of shallowness and conservatism can be seen more recently in a retro thriller like *Mulholland Falls* (1996), whose production design (also by Richard Sylbert) and music score (by Dave Grusin) are lifted more or less directly from *Chinatown*. Although it supposedly takes place in the 1950s, and although it seems vaguely influenced by James Ellroy's historical novels about Los Angeles, *Mulholland Falls* is visually indistinguishable from the world imagined by Towne and Polanski. Like *Chinatown,* it deals with police violence and official corruption (the murder is committed inside the United States Army's nuclear testing program), but it nevertheless remains sympathetic toward the Los Angeles Police Department—especially toward the "hat squad," an elite quartet of plainclothesmen who drive around the city in a convertible, beating up gangsters. Aside from administering vigilante justice, the chief function of these four tough guys is to light cigarettes with Zippos and model a peacock collection of suits and accessories.

Even the comic parodies of noir in the 1980s and 1990s have usually been conservative, given to a kind of window-shopping through the past.[40] A qualified exception is Robert Zemeckis's *Who Framed Roger Rabbit?* (1988), which deals with a scandal in the L.A. transit system, and which joins the dark world of *Chinatown* with the anarchic violence of the old Warner cartoons. A more typical example is a TV show like "The Dream Sequence Always Rings Twice," first broadcast in 1985 as a special black-and-white episode of ABC's hit series *Moonlighting*. This show is introduced by none other than Orson Welles (in one of his last performances), who also makes a brief announcement before each commercial, reminding viewers that nothing is wrong with their color sets.

FIGURES 55–56. "The Dream Sequence Always Rings Twice" (1985).

The program itself offers the audience a *Rashamon*-like narrative, in which Mattie and David (Cybill Shepherd and Bruce Willis), the two bickering private eyes, have separate dreams about a case involving an L.A. developer who plans to revive a 1940s-style nightclub. Mattie becomes Rita, a singer with a big band, and David becomes Chance, a young man with a horn. The major joke has to do with small variations in the content and style of the two fantasies. Mattie's "movie" contains a number of flowery, soft-focus shots, whereas David's is filled with tilted angles, offscreen narration, and seedy locales. The overriding aim of the entire episode is to create a fairly traditional screwball comedy, giving the audience an opportunity to watch contemporary stars recreating yesterday's fashions—art-moderne nightclubs, smoky bars, Vorkapitch montages, big-band music, turned-down hats, slinky evening gowns, suits with shoulder pads and suspenders, pomaded hair, permanent waves, and wise-cracking dialogue, all of it photographed in shadowy black and white. This nostalgia extends even to the hard-boiled elements of David's dream, as the show itself acknowledges. At one point, we see David sitting in the window of a dingy apartment facing onto a neon "Hotel" sign, wearing an undershirt and playying a trumpet into the hot night air. His offscreen voice comments: "I always play my horn with my shirt off, late at night by an open window, next to a flashing neon light. I know I look good that way."

A roughly similar, albeit noncomic approach to old-fashioned noir can be seen in one of contemporary cinema's purest examples of what Jameson means by pastiche: Joel and Ethan Coen's *Miller's Crossing* (1990), which borrows selectively from the long tradition of Hollywood gangster movies, and more extensively from Dashiell Hammett. The Coen brothers mix together ideas from *The Glass Key, Red Harvest,* and *The Maltese Falcon,* all the while carefully avoiding direct quotation from the novels. Although their film involves a certain amount of burlesque, it is in one sense deeply true to the imaginative world created by Hammett. It shows us a city ruled by gangsters, filled with sadomasochistic violence and ambiguous sexual relationships; it captures the exact feel of pulp dialogue ("What's the rumpus?" the characters say whenever they greet one another); and it skillfully evokes Hammett's typical settings and decor. As one instance of this last effect, notice the hero's apartment, which is a synthesis of the high-windowed rooms inhabited by Ned Beaumont in *The Glass Key* and the sets for Sam Spade's living room in both the 1932 and 1941 movie versions of *The Maltese Falcon*.

And yet, despite its many horrific and satiric elements, *Miller's Cross-*

ing is "about" little more than wide-angle lenses, low-level compositions, tracking shots, and the monochromatic look of masculine rooms with leather upholstery and parquet flooring. It is "about" smoking a cigarette in the dark while sitting next to a black telephone, with oriental rugs spread over hardwood floors and gauzy curtains wafting in the night breeze. Perhaps most of all, it is "about" the glamour of men's hats. It begins with a surreal black hat blowing through the woods, and it repeatedly shows us gangsters peering beneath the downturned brims of their fedoras. The protagonist (Gabriel Byrne) wears a particularly dashing hat that he likes to hang on his foot when he sits in a chair with his legs crossed; at one point, making an emergency exit from his room late at night, he behaves like a latter-day cowboy, grabbing his hat and his gun rather than his shoes. Such attention to fetishistic detail is appropriate to the genre, but *Miller's Crossing* differs strikingly from any of its predecessors in its refusal to engage seriously with American political or social history. Unlike Hammett, unlike the Warner gangster films, and unlike 1970s movies such as *Chinatown* and *The Godfather*, it is incapable of (or uninterested in) creating a sense of tragedy. Moreover, in contrast to even the most conservative forms of comic parody, it does not even make us laugh at the things it imitates.

Something else again is happening in *Pulp Fiction* (1995), which, according to Quentin Tarantino, "isn't noir. I don't do neo-noir."[41] This claim is in one sense justified, because the style of Tarantino's work has relatively little in common with the films I have just described. *Pulp Fiction* is staged in a sharply observed contemporary Los Angeles, made up of cheaply remodeled, mission-style apartment houses; condos with swimming pools and keypad alarm systems; frilly, ranch-style homes in the valley; strip-mall gun stores decorated by Confederate flags; and theme restaurants like Jack Rabbit Slims, a "wax museum with a pulse," where the menu includes "Douglas Sirk steak." Notice also that the narrative structure is contingent rather than paranoid. Unlike classical film noir, this picture does not resolve its nonlinear plot by attributing causality to some overriding social or psychological determinant. Instead, it strings events together in an amusing pattern of random or coincidental relations, in a style more in keeping with Richard Linklater's *Slacker* (1991) or TV's *Seinfeld* than with a modernist text like *Double Indemnity*.

On the other hand, *Pulp Fiction* has an obvious source in tough-guy literature, and it creates a montage out of the interrelated fragments of four hard-boiled "short stories," which are woven together in a complex time scheme. It contains allusions to *The Big Sleep*, *Gun Crazy*, *Kiss Me*

Deadly, and even *Chinatown.* ("After you, kitty cat," one of the characters says, echoing Polanski in the last of these films.) Its original title
was *Black Mask,* and its script (cowritten by Roger Avary) was influenced by second- or third-generation noir writers like Jim Thompson,
Charles Willeford, and Elmore Leonard. It could hardly be described as
a psychoanalytic movie, but it is filled with sardonic jokes about anal-
ity. Its disorienting plot, its atmosphere of "criminal adventure," its disdain for socially responsible messages, and its fascination with B-movie
violence would surely have appealed to many of the French critics who
invented American noir in the 1940s and 1950s.

Ultimately, the difference between *Pulp Fiction* and other types of neo-
noir has less to do with its structure and sensibility than with its specific
"nexus of fashion." For example, its two hit men, Vincent and Jules (John
Travolta and Samuel L. Jackson), dress in black suits and pencil-thin ties,
like Lee Marvin in the remake of *The Killers.* Both men eschew hats, and
instead of slicked-back hair, they adopt the styles of the 1970s: Vincent
has long tresses, and Jules has jheri curls. The film's novelty therefore
lies in the fact that it draws upon a slightly different range of antecedent
texts than the usual dark thriller. Instead of simply harking back to the
1940s and 1950s, Tarantino takes most of his inspiration from the period when both auteurism and the idea of noir gained a strong foothold
in America and when a fairly sophisticated film culture coexisted with
"bubblegum" music and color TV. He uses old-fashioned materials in
much the same way as the *Cahiers* group in the early 1960s, but his nostalgia extends forward to movies like *Mean Streets* and *Saturday Night
Fever* (1977), and his cinephilia is combined with a "screen memory" of
TV kitsch.

It is well known that Tarantino acquired his knowledge of film history from a video store rather than a *cinémateque.* Even so, he makes
densely hypertextual movies that reproduce the "underground" quality
of 1960s criticism. His *politique* consists of tributes to European auteurs
such as Godard, Fassbinder, and Jean-Pierre Melville; Americans such
as Scorsese, Schrader, and Sam Peckinpah; old-fashioned tough guys such
as Hawks and Samuel Fuller; and contemporary specialists in blood melodrama such as John Woo and Abel Ferrara. *Pulp Fiction* alludes to these
figures, but also (as the title indicates) to a kind of pantheon of junk,
similar to the "over-the-top" horror movies and peplum favored by the
surrealists. Among its touchstones are Italian exploitation movies like
Zombie (1980), blaxploitation flicks like *The Mack* (1973), and Roger
Corman B pictures like *Shock Confessions of a Sorority Girl* (1957). In

FIGURE 57. Retro killers in *Pulp Fiction* (1994). (Museum of Modern Art Stills Archive.)

fact, it ultimately becomes a comic, almost encyclopedic celebration of every sort of male-adolescent trash over the past fifty years. For example, it pays homage to cheap cartoons (*Clutch Cargo*), profoundly obscure combat-on-motorcycle movies (*The Losers*), and a series of kiddie culture heroes (Lash LaRue, Fonzie, and Charlie's Angels). At various junctures, it even contains learned conversations about the relative merits of mass-produced cheeseburgers.

Not surprisingly, the narrative events in *Pulp Fiction* are borrowed indiscriminately from other movies. In the episode called "The Gold Watch," a prizefighter named Butch (Bruce Willis) has an absurdly funny nightmare starring Christopher Walken, who parodies his famous role as a Vietnam veteran in *The Deer Hunter*. Butch wakes from the dream to find himself in a situation that resembles noir boxing movies such as *The Killers, The Set-Up,* and *Body and Soul*. After killing his opponent in the ring, he jumps out of his dressing room window and into the back seat of a taxicab, which is driven by a beautiful woman just like the one in *The Big Sleep* (through the windows of the cab, we see a black-and-white process screen). Over the next fifteen minutes, he keeps lurching from one scary movie to another, including *Psycho, Deliverance,* and even *Reservoir Dogs*. The frenzy of allusion reaches a climax when he chooses a series of possible weapons from the wall of a pawn shop: first he's Buford Pusser in *Walking Tall*, then he's Leatherface in *The Texas Chainsaw Massacre,* and finally he's Robert Mitchum in *The Yakusa.*

This use of mostly lowbrow materials is strongly reminiscent of the original auteurists. And indeed the early Godard is especially important to Tarantino, who likes the feeling of "movies commenting on themselves, movies and movie history" (quoted in Woods, 74). Godard's influence can be seen everywhere in *Pulp Fiction*—in Uma Thurman's hairdo (which recalls Anna Karina), in the scene where Thurman and Travolta dance the twist (which was inspired not only by *Saturday Night Fever* but also by *Bande à part* [1964]), in the comic intertitles, and in the very spirit of the film's allusiveness. The important point to note, however, is that even though *Pulp Fiction* is filled with references and cross-references to a variety of texts (including an important quote from the Book of Ezekiel, which incidentally evokes *Night of the Hunter*), it is light years from a movie like *Breathless* in the range of material it brings together and the demands it places on an audience. For all his talent, Tarantino's "hypertext" is relatively narrow, made up largely of testosterone-driven action movies, hard-boiled novels, and pop-art comic strips like *Modesty Blaise*. His attitude toward mass culture is also much less ironic than that of a director like Godard. In effect, he gives us Coca-Cola without Marx. "I get a kick out of the fact that you can buy Coca-Cola all over the world," he told an audience at Britain's National Film Theatre. "It's little things like that, like Coca-Cola and Big Macs and Madonna and Elvis Presley and Muhammad Ali and Kevin Costner, that make us part of a world, whether we like it or not" (quoted in Woods, 73). *Pulp Fiction* therefore remains entirely within the sphere of entertainment and postmodern capitalism, never requiring us to rethink or criticize the nature of movies. The result, for all its youthful vigor and inventiveness, is an unintentionally parodic repetition of classic auteurism, in keeping with the less political and more commercial atmosphere of MTV and mainstream Hollywood.

In less direct ways, *Pulp Fiction* also seems to grow out of a kind of parodic repetition of European nightlife in 1945. Tarantino had written part of the film in Amsterdam, and he was well acquainted with the trendy, drug-filled culture of Los Angeles, where international artists and rebellious young movie stars mingled in clubs such as Tatou in Beverly Hills. One inevitably thinks of Tabou in postwar Paris, although the American version has a more hazy philosophical justification, and its drug of choice is different. According to a 1995 item in *Playboy* magazine,

Tatou achieved a certain status because its fashionable clientele wore dark clothes and experimented with heroin. The owner told reporter Mark Ehrman that his patrons were obsessed with a "new film noir mentality" that involved an attempt "to experience in real life what film noir is about—that certain bliss which will inevitably lead to doom" (May 1995, 144). Whether Tarantino knew of such places or not, they seem appropriate to his outlaw characters in *Pulp Fiction.* "Coke is dead," Eric Stoltz tells Travolta at one point in the movie. "Heroin is coming back in a big fucking way." Not long afterward, we see Travolta (a night club trendsetter in *Saturday Night Fever* and *Urban Cowboy*) mainlining heroin and going for a nocturnal drive in a red T-bird.

In still another sense, *Pulp Fiction* could be said to parodically repeat the history of Hollywood as a marketplace for crime movies. Far too dark a picture to please the industry establishment, it lost the Academy Award to *Forrest Gump,* just as *Double Indemnity* lost to *Going My Way* in 1944. But here again, certain obvious differences between the past and the present need to be observed. Tarantino and Avary won an Oscar for their screenplay, probably because their film was less threatening than Billy Wilder and Chandler's. Ultimately, *Pulp Fiction* lacks the seriousness and originality of the best of the historical films noirs; it repeats history as bloody, inconsequential farce rather than as tragedy or cutting-edge satire.

Of course *Pulp Fiction* remains an exciting departure from the typical special-effects blockbuster or sentimental comedy. It shows the seamier side of Hollywood's utopian mythology and demonstrates what I have been trying to suggest all along: that film noir, like any other style or genre, tends to evolve by repeating old ideas in new combinations. Even so, after seeing this picture and a good deal of other postmodernist noirs, I find myself wishing it were possible for directors to follow the advice that Orson Welles once gave to Peter Bogdanovich:

> [F]ilms are full of good things which really ought to be invented all over again. Again and again. Invented—not repeated. The good things should be found— *found*—in that precious spirit of the first time out, and images *discovered*— not *referred* to. . . . Sure, everything's been done, but it's much healthier not to know about it. Hell, everything had all been done when *I* started.[42]

THE OTHER SIDE
OF THE STREET

In previous chapters, I argue that film noir occupies a liminal space somewhere between Europe and America, between high modernism and "blood melodrama," and between low-budget crime movies and art cinema. As an idea in criticism and as a market category in mainstream entertainment, the term has a similar quality; it describes both action pictures and "women's" melodramas, problematizing the usual generic or gendered distinctions. Still other kinds of liminality are depicted in the films themselves. The stories frequently involve characters who have an ambiguous social position between the law and the underworld, or who seem in danger of losing their respectability and falling into a world of crime or madness. The action sometimes moves back and forth between rich and poor areas of town, or it takes place on a borderland—as in *Touch of Evil,* where an unstable, confusing boundary between the United States and Mexico becomes the locus of hysterical violence between nationalities, social classes, races, and sexes. In such cases, noir offers its mostly white audiences the pleasure of "low" adventure, having little to do with the conquest of nature, the establishment of law and order, or the march of empire. The dangers that assail the protagonists arise from a modern, highly organized society, but a society that has been transformed into an almost mythical "bad place," where the forces of rationality and progress seem vulnerable or corrupt, and where characters on the margins of the middle class encounter a variety of "others": not savages, but criminals, sexually independent women, homosexuals, Asians, Latins, and black people.

Radical film critics have responded to this situation in mixed fashion. In the 1970s and 1980s, for example, Anglo-American feminists analyzed film noir in two important and interconnected ways: as an instance of what Laura Mulvey calls the patriarchal mechanisms of "visual pleasure" and as a reflection of male hostility toward women in the postwar economy. The Hitchcockian eroticism of classic suspense movies was shown to rest upon a sadistic gaze that could sometimes become troubled and ironically self-reflexive but that ultimately served a perversely masculine need for social and sexual control; meanwhile, the misogyny of hard boiled, pop-Freudian scenarios was made vividly apparent. Interestingly, however, feminists have been unable to agree about film noir's specific sexual politics. This conflict is especially apparent in E. Ann Kaplan's introduction to the influential anthology *Women in Film Noir* (1978), which points out that the various contributors share no single position "on whether film noir as such is progressive or not."[1] The problem of arriving at a broad agreement has something to do with the impossibility of defining film noir "as such," but it also has to do with the inherently contradictory nature of Hollywood entertainment and with the in-between-ness of the films in question. As Kaplan points out, women characters in film noir are often evil, but because they are "central to the intrigue," they take part in an important "ideological work" normally assigned to males (2). Some of the best-known noir narratives involve displacement of the patriarchal family in favor of lone wolves and spider women. Although the noir femme fatale is usually punished, she remains a threat to the proper order of things, and in a few cases, the male protagonist is "simply destroyed" because he cannot resist her charms (3). Hence a picture like *Double Indemnity,* for all its evident misogyny, usually leaves feminist critics in a position of arguing about whether the ideological glass is half full or half empty.[2] As a moderator for these arguments, the most Kaplan can say is that film noir provides an intriguing "interplay of the notion of independent women *vis a vis* patriarchy" (3).

An equally mixed set of responses can be found in critical discussions of masculinity and homosexuality in film noir. Despite the fact that the Production Code of the 1940s explicitly forbade the depiction of homosexuals, the repressed "returned" in genres such as the horror movie or the psychological thriller, where implicitly gay characters were treated with a mixture of contempt and fascination. The novels of Dashiell Hammett and Raymond Chandler were filled with latently homosexual situations (such as the odd relationship between Philip Marlowe and "Red" Norgaard in *Farewell, My Lovely*), and veiled stereotypes of gays were everywhere apparent in the crime pictures derived from those novels. In *The Maltese Falcon,* for example, the band of criminals is rather like a gay family, and in *The Big Sleep,* Humphrey Bogart imitates a lisping bibliophile. In many films, such as *The Big Heat,* the villain was a homosexual type, though he was never openly acknowledged as such. One of the most curious instances of Hollywood's attempt to conceal the obvious is *Laura,* an unusually feminist narrative for its day, which casts Clifton Webb as a Wildean aesthete named Waldo Lydecker, but which asks us to view the character as a murderously jealous heterosexual who suffers from a kind of Pygmalion complex. Here and in several other important noirs, a covert homophobia is linked with a populist attitude toward social class: the villainous Lydecker is depicted as a parasitic dandy, in contrast to the more proletarian tough guy who is the hero of the narrative. Notice, however, that Lydecker plays an important role, and at some points he seems like the hero's double. Merely by acting as the villain, he is a much more complex and significant presence than the equally closeted homosexuals in the average Hollywood comedy.

It would appear that the ideology of mainstream melodrama is threatened when women, artistic intellectuals, and vaguely homosexual characters appear as villains, or when the action takes place in an excessively "abnormal" milieu. This phenomenon has led Richard Dyer and several other critics to argue that the noir category in general expresses "a certain anxiety over the existence and definition of masculinity and normality" (Kaplan, 91). As Dyer observes, film noir "abounds in colorful representations of decadence, perversion, aberration, etc." (Kaplan, 92), and its typically rootless, unmarried heroes provide a somewhat tenuous standard of normative masculine behavior. In many cases, the noir protagonist's ability to serve as a role model is undercut by his quasi-gay relationships with men, by his masochistic love affairs with women, and by his more general weakness of character (see *Gilda, Double Indemnity,* and *Strangers on a Train*). Given such protagonists, Frank Krutnick concludes that 1940s noir deals with "traumatized or castrated males" who cannot function as the fantasy objects of an ideal masculine ego. The noir form as a whole, he says, is devoted to a "dissonant and schismatic representation of masculinity" and is "perhaps" evidence of a "crisis of confidence" in the male-dominated culture.[3]

Whether or not one accepts Krutnick's argument about American society in the 1940s, it seems clear that Hollywood thrillers of the period tended to center on both male and female characters who were morally flawed, neurotic, or psychologically "damaged." In a general sense, these films were attempting to inflect melodrama with what I have elsewhere described as an air of modernist ambiguity and psychological determinism. Influenced by American fiction during the 1920s and 1930s, they injected a degree of irony, antiheroism, and perverse violence into adventure stories, thereby expressing what Dyer calls an "anxiety" about normality. This does not mean, however, that they were inherently homophobic or misogynistic: as we have seen, Richard Brooks's novel *The Brick Foxhole,* which was filmed in 1947 under the title *Crossfire,* is an explicit attack on homophobia, and a few traces of the original theme remain in the adaptation. Notice also that the noir sensibility strongly affected various forms of domestic or "women's" pictures in the 1940s, undercutting the usual formulas. As R. Barton Palmer observes, *Possessed* (1947) and *Cause for Alarm* (1947) are somewhat different from an equally "psychoanalytic" but less noirlike melodrama such as *Now Voyager* (1942), because they do not provide a "compromised yet satisfying wish fulfillment—that is, the heroine put back in her place but offered a different, rewarding life."[4]

Even when film noir is openly hostile toward women or homosexuals, it solicits the psychoanalytic and potentially deconstructive critical discourse that has grown up around it. Moreover, like other Hollywood formulas, it has depended upon contributions by female or gay artists. The only important woman director of the 1940s, Ida Lupino, was responsible for several movies that could be classified as noir, as were women writers such as Daphne du Maurier, Vera Caspary, Dorothy B. Hughes, and Leigh Brackett. One of the most prolific American writers of noir fiction, Cornell Woolrich, was a homosexual, as were directors George Cukor and Vincente Minnelli, who were frequently drawn to noir themes or motifs. In our own day, there have been many examples of hard-boiled detective novels with female, gay, or lesbian protagonists, as well as a number of films noirs directed by women. In the latter group are Maggie Greenwald's *Kill-Off* (1990), Kathryn Bigelow's *Blue Steel* (1990), and Lizzie Borden's *Love Crimes* (1992). The Bigelow and Borden films are intriguing applications of the "exchange of guilt" formula to women characters, but unfortunately their social criticism is undercut by a clichéd and overly deterministic psychology.[5] A much more interesting exploration of a similar theme is *Captives* (1996), a British production directed by Angela Pope, which offers a complex study of a love affair between a middle-class woman who has separated from her husband and a prison convict who has killed his wife. On a different level, consider Claire Peploe's lovely tribute to *Out of the Past* in the comic, magical-realist production of *Rough Magic* (1997).

As we might expect, film noir's treatment of race leads us to similar conclusions, for if noir is preoccupied with femmes fatales and homosexuals, it is equally preoccupied—and for many of the same reasons—with people of color. I have previously observed that movies of the type often depict Anglo protagonists who visit "exotic" places like Latin America and Asia or who frequent Harlem jazz clubs, the Casbah, and Chinatown. But film noir is not merely an occasion for whites to engage in racist fantasies. Noir flourished in America during the period between World War II and the beginnings of the civil rights movement, when a number of liberal and left-wing filmmakers were attempting to make pictures about racial prejudice and lynchings; moreover, when noir is viewed in a larger historical and cultural perspective, it is not exclusively the product of a white imagination. Virtually every national cinema in the world has made at least a few movies that fall into the category, and in the United States, many African-American writers have specialized in noir fiction. In recent years especially, African-American stars and directors have shown an interest in noirish conventions, thereby broadening the implications of the form and opening up the possibility for what Manthia Diawara has called "new and urbanized black images on the screen."[6]

These racial, ethnic, or national issues have received comparatively little attention from critics, and I want to emphasize them here. Unfortunately, because the topic is so large, I shall need to limit myself to a few relevant motifs, gesturing toward the need for further work by other writers. In the following pages, I offer a brief historical survey of Asian and Latin themes in film noir and devote most of my critical attention to pictures that involve black people. I try to give a fairly comprehensive treatment of the topics I discuss, but I avoid theoretical speculation about the political or racial "unconscious" of noir. I merely want to observe several recurring patterns or themes, chart relatively obvious social changes, and offer a glancing commentary on the ways in which America's dark cinema has both repressed and openly confronted the most profound tensions in the society at large. Although my remarks emphasize the racism and national insularity of Hollywood, my chief purpose is to show that noir, like the popular cinema in general, has a potential for hybridity or "crossing over"—a potential enhanced by noir's tendency to create styles out of the mixed racial or national identities in the metropolis. The pictures by African Americans strike me as particularly good illustrations of this effect. By appropriating certain traditional formulas, such movies also reveal one of the most important and seldom recognized implications of the term *film noir*.

ASIA

The Shanghai Gesture, The Lady from Shanghai, Macao, The House of Bamboo, The Crimson Kimono, The Manchurian Candidate, Chinatown, The Killing of a Chinese Bookie, The China Lake Murders, China Moon—these and other well-known titles would appear to suggest that film noir has a deep affinity with the Far East.[7] The Asian theme can in fact be traced back to Dashiell Hammett's earliest hard-boiled stories for *Black Mask,* which are saturated with a low brow Orientalism reminiscent of the Yellow Peril years before and after World War I. In "The House in Turk Street," the Continental Op encounters a gang of killers led by Tai Choon Tau, a wily Chinese man who wears British clothes and speaks with a refined English accent. According to the Op, "The Chinese are a thorough people; when one of them carries a gun he usually carries two or three or more," and when he shoots, "he keeps on until his gun is empty" (*The Continental Op,* 105). In "Dead Yellow Woman," the Op finds himself trapped on a stairway in the secret passageway of a house in Chinatown; below him is a beautiful girl with a "red flower of a mouth" and four Tong warriors reaching for their automatics; above him is a Chinese wrestler with "a foot of thin steel in his paw."[8]

The Maltese Falcon involves a search for an Orientalist object, and the 1932 film adaptation contains a scene in which Sam Spade receives an important clue to the mystery of who killed Miles Archer from a resident of Chinatown. There is no equivalent scene in John Huston's remake of 1941; but in the next year, Huston filmed *Across the Pacific,* a *Falcon* spin-off, in which Humphrey Bogart and Mary Astor battle Japanese spies in Panama. This film was, of course, produced during World War II, when images of deceitful and violent Asians from earlier pulp fiction were easily incorporated into anti-Japanese propaganda. (The popular Charlie Chan series of B movies, featuring Anglo performers, remained in production throughout these years, but the Mr. Moto series, starring Peter Lorre, dropped from sight. The Moto pictures had been quite noirlike in their visual style; in fact, when Orson Welles saw *Thank You, Mr. Moto* [1937], he hired the film's director, Norman Foster, to work on *Journey into Fear* [1942].)

If the Far East was repeatedly associated in film noir with enigmatic and criminal behavior, it was also depicted as a kind of aestheticized bordello, where one could experience all sorts of forbidden pleasures. Thus when Philip Marlowe visits an exclusive Hollywood nightclub in Chandler's 1942 novel, *The High Window,* he notices a "check girl in peach-bloom Chinese pajamas," who has "eyes like strange sins" (*Stories and Early Novels*, 1083). Josef von Sternberg's *Shanghai Gesture* (1940), which Raymond Borde and Étienne Chaumeton regard as a key work in the emerging noir "series," is specifically about this theme of forbidden pleasure. The film was derived from a 1925 Broadway play that took place in a Chinese house of prostitution. To avoid problems with censors, Sternberg shifted the action to a gambling casino, but he intensified the atmosphere of exotic perversity, casting Gene Tierney and Victor Mature as Poppy and Omar, a pair of half-caste lovers who become connoisseurs of vice. Orson Welles's *Lady from Shanghai,* which the director himself described as "an exercise in eroticism," had a similar effect. A delirious mixture of misogynistic romance and dark social satire, the film stars Welles's ex-wife Rita Hayworth as the Sternbergian temptress Elsa Bannister, who was born in Macao ("the wickedest city in the world") and exerts control over a band of gangsters in San Francisco's Chinatown.

Propaganda images of sadistic Asians persisted through the cold-war decades, when China became communist and America became involved in a series of military adventures throughout the Asian Pacific. In *The Manchurian Candidate,* Henry Silva plays the evil Chunjin, a North Korean spy masquerading as a houseboy, who infiltrates the highest levels of Georgetown society and engages in a vicious karate fight with Frank Sinatra (a fight later parodied by Blake Edwards in the *Pink Panther* films). During the same period, however, the United States also wanted to put a human face on its Asian allies. American soldiers stationed abroad were marrying Asian women, and at home the civil rights movement was under way. As a result, Hollywood addressed the themes of interracial romance and marriage in such big-budget productions as *Love Is a Many-Splendored Thing* (1955), *Sayonara* (1957), and *South Pacific* (1958). At almost the same time, low-budget auteur Samuel Fuller made a series of tough, unorthodox films involving Asian themes—among them, *The Crimson Kimono* (1959), a noirlike police melodrama that was far more daring than any of the pictures listed so far. The plot of *The Crimson Kimono* involves Los Angeles police detective Joe Kojaku (James Shigeta), who feels uneasy about his Nisei background and wants to assimilate into modern American life. During an investigation into the murder of a stripper, Joe and his partner, Charlie Bancroft (Glenn Corbett), meet a beautiful young artist (Victoria Shaw), to whom they are both attracted. When the woman gravitates toward Joe, Charlie grows jealous, and the two men fight one another in traditional Kindo style. Throughout, Fuller plays interesting variations on the stereotype of Asian inscrutability, showing how all the characters fail to "read" one another. The personal story and the murder investigation are linked through the theme of sexual jealousy, and both problems are resolved after a documentary-style chase through the streets of Little Toyko at the peak of the Japanese New Year celebration. The film ends strikingly, with a kiss between Joe and his Caucasian lover.[9]

By this point, the moody Orientalism of the 1940s seemed passé and did not resurface in any significant form until Robert Towne and Roman Polanski's retro-styled *Chinatown*, which once again associated the Asian district of an American city with mystery, violence, and perverse sex. However, one of *Chinatown*'s distinctions lay in the fact that it treated the old-fashioned motifs ironically, as a kind of white projection. The Chinatown street at the end of the film is not a center of evil but an oppressed ghetto controlled by the Los Angeles Police Department and the city's ruling class; the story's true perversity originates elsewhere— mostly in the dark heart of Noah Cross, who ultimately enters the Chinese community to kill off one of his children and to enclose another in his creepy embrace. Unfortunately, *Chinatown*'s many imitators tended to employ Asian titles or motifs merely to create an exotic atmosphere. During the 1980s, the most ambitious attempt to explore a Chinatown setting in the context of a thriller was Michael Cimino's *Year of the Dragon* (1985)—a neogangster film starring Mickey Rourke, which offered a contemporary version of the old-fashioned Tong wars. By the end of the decade, as Tokyo became an economic rival of the United States, old stereotypes began to reappear in thrillers such as *Black Rain* (1989) and *Rising Sun* (1990), which reproduced the classic images of mystery and Eastern decadence, clothing them in sleek postmodern dress and giving them an air of liberalism by virtue of multiracial casts.

When we actually cross over to the perspective of films directed by the "other," we can find plenty of noirlike elements but no Asian exoticism. The best examples of film noir in the Japanese art cinema have been two pictures by Akira Kurosawa: *The Bad Sleep Well* (1960), which fuses *Hamlet* with a Warner-style crime movie, and *High and Low* (1962), an adaptation of an Ed McBain *policier*, which makes brilliant use of widescreen, black-and-white photography. At an entirely different level, the Japanese pop cinema is filled with cathartically violent genre pictures that have noirish settings or themes. One of the most flamboyant auteurs in this field is Seijun Suzuki, a B-movie contract director for Nikkatsu Pictures in Tokyo during the period between 1956 and 1967, who made bizarrely stylized movies about prostitutes and contract killers, somewhat comparable to the tabloid thrillers of Samuel Fuller (see, for example, *Toyko Drifter* [1966] and *Branded to Kill* [1967]).

In America, the Chinese-American director Wayne Wang's *Slamdance* (1987) is filled with visual references to noir classics such as *Rear Window* and *The Lady from Shanghai,* although it has no specifically Asian themes. A much more interesting picture along these lines is Wang's earlier, low-budget *Chan Is Missing* (1981), which employs an investigative plot structure and a style reminiscent of the early New Wave in order to depict a Chinese-American community from the "inside."[10] Peter Feng has described this picture as a "revisionist Charlie Chan film," although he points out that Wang skillfully eludes any attempt to be pinned down with the usual terminology of generic classification, commercial categorization, or ethnic essentialism. Ironically, the success of *Chan Is Missing* in both art houses and video stores led Hollywood producers to offer Wang the chance to remake *In a Lonely Place,* a project he eventually rejected because the script contained "all American characters, except for one Asian."[11]

More recently, Hong Kong cinema has been in vogue on the American market. One of the most artistically complex of these pictures is Wong Kar-Wai's *Chungking Express* (1995), which seems to be inflected by the French New Wave's fascination with noir. Far more influential, at least in commercial terms, are the films of action director John Woo, who describes himself as "un-Chinese," and who has become a major cult success. Woo's highly stylized productions, such as *The Killer* (1989), synthesize generic conventions from Hollywood thrillers (especially the crime story motivated by revenge, guilt, or male bonding) with over-the-top flourishes from martial arts movies and Far Eastern musicals. I suspect that many of his youthful fans in America, not unlike Dashiell Hammett's early readers, are indulging in fin de siècle Orientalism. In any case, his work in Hollywood has been largely confined to hard-body action films suitable to stars like Jean-Claude Van Damme, or to adventure spectaculars such as *Broken Arrow* (1995), which are designed for a worldwide market. Unfortunately, except in the karate-style fight sequences, these movies suggest very little Asian influence; the violence is less bloody than in the Hong Kong productions, and the action centers on the sort of swashbuckling trial by combat that Borde and Chaumeton regard as the antithesis of noir. Even in *Face/Off* (1997), where Woo employs many of the signature elements of his Hong Kong thrillers, the effect is relatively conventional. As Julian Stringer has pointed out, Woo's non-

Hollywood films are strongly affected by the recent history of China and are filled with an unusually melodramatic, "weeping" style of masculinity.[12] Neither of these qualities can be seen in *Face/Off*, which transforms the noirlike theme of the "double" into a high concept for a pair of macho white male stars and weighs down the big-budget actions with clumsy, implausible exposition. At best, the picture appears to have been shot and edited by a mainstream director who was imitating John Woo.

LATIN AMERICA

Significantly, Woo's *Killer* ends in a scene of melodramatic excess, involving fireworks and a bloodbath in and around a bizarre Christian church. The Christian symbolism in an Asian setting seems weirdly exotic, but in one sense it is merely an appropriation and reversal of the cultural semiotics in the typical Hollywood thriller. Notice how *Chinatown* employs a traditional Asian enclave to create a baroque, carnivalistic ending, in which the characters' repressed passions come to the surface. A similar technique can be seen in many other Hollywood noirs involving Asian themes—for example, in the Chinese theater at the end of *The Lady from Shanghai*, in the amusement-park shootout at the end of *House of Bamboo*, and in the Japanese New Year at the end of *The Crimson Kimono*. But the atmosphere of carnival is not limited to Orientalist settings. Where noir is concerned, almost anywhere will do—the suburban U.S. town in *Strangers on a Train*, where Guy and Bruno fight one another on a runaway carousel, or even postwar Vienna, where Holly Martins and Harry Lime confront one another on a Ferris wheel. The point is to find a relatively festive locale that symbolizes the Place of the Unconscious or of psychological catharsis and gives the director sufficient opportunity to stage a spectacle. In Hollywood pictures, Latin American cities and villages have been especially useful for such purposes, because they can be so easily associated with baroque celebration. Hence we have the Day of the Dead parade and the tiovivo carousel in *Ride the Pink Horse* (1947) and the eroticized, Sternbergian carnival in *Gilda*.

During the 1940s, noir characters visited Latin America more often than any other foreign locale, usually because they wanted to find relief from repression. This phenomenon was no doubt overdetermined by various geographic, political, and economic factors: California's proximity to Mexico; Hollywood's support for the Roosevelt government's "Good Neighbor" policy; the postwar topicality of stories about Nazi refugees in Argentina; the RKO-Rockefeller interests in Western Hemisphere oil fields; the general importance of Latin America as an export market; and so on. But it also had to do with the purely symbolic value of south-of-the-border settings, which provided a visual counterpoint to the Germanic lighting and modernist architecture in most varieties of dark cinema. In *The Lady from Shanghai,* for example, Latin America becomes the "bright, guilty place," contrasting vividly with the dark skyline of Manhattan and the murky avenues of Central Park at the beginning of the story. And in *Out of the Past,* Jeff Bailey's pursuit of Kathie Moffat takes him to a series of sun-baked Mexican towns that offer a temporary escape from the forbidding shadows of a northern metropolis.

The Latin backgrounds in classic films noirs take a variety of forms, ranging from the sleazy border crossings in *Where Danger Lives* (1950) and *Touch of Evil* to the sophisticated capitals and resorts in *Notorious* (1946) and *His Kind of Woman* (1950). Sometimes Latin America is indirectly evoked through California's mission-style architecture, as in *In a Lonely Place* ("Sorta hacienda-like, huh?" a hatcheck girl remarks when she sees Bogart's apartment). Sometimes it is suggested in nightclub scenes, as in *Mildred Pierce,* when a singer imitates Carmen Miranda. In the darkly claustrophobic *Double Indemnity,* it hovers about the edges of the narrative like the perfume that Phyllis Dietrichson tells Walter Neff she bought in Ensenada, where people drink "pink wine" instead of bourbon. No matter how the Latin world is represented, however, it is nearly always associated with a frustrated desire for romance and freedom; again and again, it holds out the elusive, ironic promise of a warmth and color that will countervail the dark mise-en-scène and the taut, restricted coolness of the average noir protagonist. In *Double Indemnity,* Fred MacMurray almost escapes to Mexico; in *Raw Deal,* Dennis O'Keefe tries unsuccessfully to escape to Panama; in *In a Lonely Place,* some of Humphrey Bogart's most disturbing scenes with Gloria Grahame are set off against a framed reproduction of a Diego Rivera painting; and in *Ride the Pink Horse,* the embittered war veteran played by Robert Montgomery finds brief refuge by hiding in the tiovivo carousel.

Interestingly, many of the classic films noirs were made during a time of increased racial tensions in the Latin communities of Los Angeles. The Sleepy Lagoon case of 1943, in which a group of Chicanos were framed for the "Lover's Lane" murder of a white couple, may have been an indirect influence on Joseph Losey's postwar, social-realist thriller, *The Lawless,* and later on Welles's *Touch of Evil.* For most filmmakers, however, the Latin world was imagined as a place located on the other side of the country's borders. Notice also that when classic Hollywood's noir characters traveled to Latin America, they took all their neuroses with them, and in a sense they never really left home. (This effect was heightened by the fact that Hollywood movies tended to use foreign settings merely as decor, staging most of the action on studio sets.) In *Notorious,* the Rio enclave of Nazis and U.S. spies is situated apart from the city, which is glimpsed in a few postcard views and functions as a sensual backdrop for a network of jealous obsessions among foreigners. In *Gilda,* the Buenos Aires casino is owned by a Nazi, and it bears a strong resemblance to the European-U.S. nightclub in *Casablanca.* In *His Kind of Woman,* Robert Mitchum and Jane Russell find themselves in a Baja California resort that looks as if it had been designed by Frank Lloyd Wright; the resort functions as a playground for rich Yankees, and the Mexicans themselves are in evidence only as strolling musicians or bumbling cops. And in *Out of the Past,* there is a moment when a corner of Mexico suddenly becomes New York: "There's a little cantina down the street called Pablo's," Jane Greer says. "It's nice and quiet. A man there plays American music for a dollar. You can shut your eyes, sip bourbon, and imagine you're on 59th Street."

These half-seen, barely experienced Latin locales give a picturesque quality to the films and perpetuate stereotypical images of passionate lovers and quaint peasants. In at least two cases, the Latin background heightens the sexy aura of Rita Hayworth, whose real name was Margarita Carmen Cansino. It also enhances the feeling of sophistication in films that are already imbued with an urban sensibility; the 1940s were, after all, a period when Latin and Afro-Caribbean motifs were all the rage in café-society nightspots like the Mocambo and the Trocadero, and when dances like the samba and the rumba were popular among the upper classes. Hollywood's vision of Latin America was therefore largely confined to a mélange of sentimental pastoralism and chic primitivism. Even so, the movies were careful not to associate the ownership of casinos and nightclubs with Latin Americans (usually the owner is a fascist émigré or a deported gangster), and they occasionally hinted at Yankee imperialism. Welles's *Lady from Shanghai* and *Touch of Evil* are especially notable for the way they show rich northerners using the Latin world as a kind of brothel and for their brief glimpses of poverty on the Mexican streets—a theme that was much more evident before Columbia reedited the first picture.

In the 1960s and 1970s, when Latin America became a battleground between socialist revolutionaries and the CIA, some of the more romantic imagery of Latin countries began to temporarily disappear from U.S.

screens. At the same time, urban life in the United States was being increasingly Latinized. Los Angeles in the years between 1920 and 1960 had the highest proportion of native-born white Protestants of any major city in the country; but after 1960, there was a great influx of Latino and Chicano Catholics. This phenomenon was repeated in other metropolitan centers of the Southwest and Florida, to the point where certain politicians demanded that a wall be built around the southern U.S. border and that English be established as the official U.S. language. Perhaps Hollywood was equally nervous about the population change. The new demographics are barely noticeable in the original release print of the futuristic *Blade Runner* (1982), which is set mostly in L.A.'s Chinatown and expresses a deep ambivalence about aliens or hybrids. (As Rolando J. Romero points out, the prerelease version featured a character played by Edward James Olmos, who provided a kind of synecdoche for the Chicano population.)[13]

The population growth in certain cities of North America eventually led to new kinds of noir settings. One of the most significant developments was the emergence of "Miami noir," a term that applies equally well to *Body Heat,* the *Miami Vice* TV show, and *Blood and Wine* (1997). Unfortunately, few pictures in this vein have made significant use of Latin characters. Almost the same thing might be said of the Miami-based, hard-boiled fiction of Charles Willeford and Elmore Leonard, who have not been adapted as often as one might expect. During the 1980s, Jonathan Demme and Fred Ward produced an intelligent film version of Willeford's *Miami Blues,* and *Jackie Brown,* Quentin Tarantino's adaptation of Leonard's *Rum Punch,* was released as this book went to press. So far, the best movie derived from Leonard's Florida novels is the lightly comic and not terribly noirlike *Get Shorty* (1996). (The protagonist of this last film is a Miami gangster named "Chili" Palmer, but he is played by John Travolta. Other important details are treated in similarly cavalier fashion; when Palmer makes a charming and admiring speech about *Touch of Evil,* he gets most of the facts wrong.)

The situation today is all the more ironic because, as I note in chapter 1, Latin America has a strong tradition of film noir: consider, as only two examples of many that could be listed, Julio Bracho's *Distinto amanecer* (Mexico, 1943) and Jorge Ileli's *Mulheres e Milhões* (Brazil, 1961), the last of which has many things in common with *The Asphalt Jungle* and *Rififi*. Such pictures usually represent the Latin world as a dark metropolis rather than as a baroque, vaguely pastoral refuge from modernity, and as a result, they indirectly reveal a mythology at work in

Hollywood. Two of the more effective recent examples include *Foreign Land* (1995), a Brazilian-Portuguese coproduction directed by Walter Salles and Daniela Thomas, and *Deep Crimson* (1997), a Mexican remake of *The Honeymoon Killers* (1970), directed by Arturo Ripstein. Both of these films are sharply attuned to the noirlike themes of moral culpability and doomed love, and have more poetic resonance than most of the neo-noir features from Hollywood. Unfortunately, we have no Latino versions of such North American "border" films noirs as *Border Incident, Touch of Evil, The Border* (1982), and *Lone Star* (1996), all of which center on racism and economic exploitation in the Southwest. The closest approximation is Robert Rodriguez's *El Mariachi* (1992), a comic, "wrong-man" thriller, in which everyone except the Anglo villain speaks Spanish.

Meanwhile, the classic implications of the Latin world have tended to reappear with little modification in Hollywood neo-noir. In *Body Heat,* the sultry femme fatale is last seen on a beach in Rio, reclining next to her Latin lover. In *The Wrong Man* (1994), repressed sexual tensions break out among a group of North Americans traveling in Mexico. In *The Juror* (1996), a chase begins in New York and ends in a remote Guatemalan village during a carnival; the concluding scene shows the heroine (a single mom who designs postmodern art) gunning down the psychotic bad guy (a Mafia hit man with sophisticated artistic taste) inside an ancient Mayan temple, assisted by villagers wearing carnival masks. Elsewhere, especially in gangster movies, the South American drug lord now rivals the Italian mobster as a favorite villain—a trend established by the remake of *Scarface* (1983), which smoothes the transition from the Mediterranean to the Caribbean by casting Al Pacino in the role of a Cuban. In such pictures, Latin America continues to be represented in the form of a garish nightclub. The only difference is that the place is filled with colored light and is supposed to be owned by the Latins themselves.

AFRICA

The first private eye of the pulps, Carroll John Daly's "Race" Williams, made his debut in a story called "Knights of the Open Palm," which was published in a special Ku Klux Klan issue of *Black Mask.* (Lee Server points out that Daly, who was a relatively clumsy writer, at least had the distinction of authoring one of the anti-Klan entries.) Notice also that one of Raymond Chandler's earliest stories, "Noon Street Nemesis," originally published in *Detective Fiction Weekly* in May 1936, is set almost entirely in a black section of Los Angeles. When the story first appeared, the editors of the journal deleted all references to the race of the characters, but Chandler made sure that the deletions were restored for the reprinted version, "Pickup on Noon Street," in *The Simple Art of Murder.*

Perhaps more importantly, the complex plot of Chandler's 1940 novel, *Farewell, My Lovely,* is set in motion by ex-con Moose Malloy's killing of a black man in an all-black bar on L.A.'s Central Avenue. The investigation of the crime is assigned to a worn-out white policeman named Nulty, who does nothing. Even Philip Marlowe, who twice uses the word *nigger* in casual conversation, seems resigned to the fact that the murder of black people is of no concern to the legal system. As the novel proceeds, other corpses (belonging to the white race) pile up quickly, and it is easy for most readers to forget the first death. In a sense, however, the neglect of the black man is precisely the point. Chandler's major theme is that "law is where you buy it," and the novel as a whole is designed to illustrate that crime is treated differently in different areas of town. During a period when high-modernist fiction was usually centered on the isolated consciousness of middle-class characters, Chandler used the lowly private-eye formula to map an entire society; and in *Farewell, My Lovely,* he shows that crime on the lowest social level of Los Angeles is on a single continuum with crime on the highest level. Hence the evocative opening chapters of the book, which give us closely observed pictures of a black community on Central Avenue, are linked by cause and effect to the later chapters, which take us to Jessie Florian's decrepit house on West 54th Street, to Lindsay Marriot's smart residence above the Coast Highway, and to Lewin Lockridge Grayle's stately mansion near the ocean. We also meet a series of detectives who represent different constituencies: the ineffectual, incompetent Nulty, who works in the poorest district; the sinister Blaine and his dull-witted partner "Hemingway," who are the hired minions of the gangsters and con men in Bay City; and the intelligent, persistent Randall, who investigates crimes for Central Homicide.

This social geography was not entirely lost in the Scott-Dmytryk-Paxton film adaptation of the novel, entitled *Murder, My Sweet.* Indeed the Scott unit at RKO had been established for the purpose of making social-realist movies. However, given the Hollywood censorship code and the racial climate of 1944, it was impossible for RKO to show the police as corrupt or to put Chandler's original opening on the screen. The film therefore devises a sinister scene in a police station, which looks vaguely like a third-degree interrogation, and it shows Moose Malloy breaking up a working-class bar filled with white men in hard hats. Not until 1975, in the Dick Richards version of *Farewell, My Lovely,* did the movies attempt a reasonably faithful reproduction of what Chandler had written, but even then, Hollywood seemed nervous about the tone of Chandler's work. The Richards film is only mildly critical of the cops, and it insists that Moose Malloy killed the black man in "self-defense." It also turns Philip Marlowe into an overt liberal who befriends an interracial couple and their small son.[14]

The idea that blacks and whites might be brothers under the skin had already been suggested more indirectly on the first page of *The High Window,* the novel Raymond Chandler wrote immediately after *Farewell, My Lovely.* Marlowe encounters a lawn ornament in front of Elizabeth Bright Murdock's pretentious house in the Oak Knoll section of Pasadena: "a little painted Negro in white riding breeches and a green jacket and a red cap," who looks a bit sad, as if he were becoming "discouraged" from waiting so long. Each time Marlowe enters or exits the house, he pats the ornament on the head, and occasionally he speaks to it. During his initial visit, he turns to the figure and says "Brother, you and me both" (*Stories and Early Novels,* 988). On his way out after first meeting Mrs. Murdock, he mutters, "Brother, it's even worse than I expected" (1002). At the end of the novel, one of his last gestures is to give the ornament a farewell pat.

For some readers today, a joke of this kind may seem condescending; but the lawn ornament tells us everything we need to know about the ruthless, repressive Mrs. Murdock, and it helps to establish Marlowe's class position as a paid servant of the vulgar rich. (For a manifestly racist treatment of black people in hard-boiled literature of the period, see the novels of Chandler's contemporary Jonathan Latimer.) Furthermore, there is an intriguing historical circumstance that makes the comparison between Marlowe and a black man not entirely inappropriate. The heyday of tough-guy realism, which produced Chandler, James M. Cain, Horace McCoy, and the other white writers whom Edmund Wilson describes as "poets of the tabloid murder," was also a major period of social-protest literature by African Americans, and the black social-protest novelists—especially Richard Wright and Chester Himes—were intensely and necessarily preoccupied with murder and mean streets. Wright's *Native Son* and *The Outsider* were plotted like thrillers, and so was Himes's *If He Hollers, Let Him Go;* in fact, as Mike Davis points out, Himes's skillfully crafted early work could be placed among the finest examples of

Los Angeles noir, offering a "brilliant and disturbing analysis of the psychotic dynamics of racism in the land of sunshine" (43).

Himes was rarely discussed in such terms during his lifetime, but at the suggestion of Marcel Duhamel, editor of Gallimard's *Série noire,* he eventually became a successful writer of tough detective fiction. In the years after the war, French critics saw a connection between the white tough guys and the black protest writers, who could be assimilated into a left-existentialism that Jean-Paul Sartre and many of his followers believed was at the very heart of the American novel. Hence both groups were given a cultural acceptance in France that they had not fully received in the United States. Significantly, Wright himself was living in Paris, and *The Outsider,* which he wrote during those years, has a good deal in common with Sartre's own novel about crime, *Les jeux sont faits.* Himes, too, moved to Paris in the early 1950s, and most of his early crime novels were first published in French; his most commercial work was done for the *Série noire,* and he was the first non-French author to receive the *Grand Prix de la litérature policière,* which was awarded in 1958 for *La reine des pommes (A Rage in Harlem).*

It would be wrong to fully equate either the hard-boiled school or the black social-protest novelists with European existentialism. The overwhelming sense of alienation, entrapment, and paranoia in Wright's and Himes's fiction rises out of a relentless social fact rather than a Kafkaesque abstraction, and the somewhat similar themes in the white writers can be traced back to the main tradition of naturalism and social realism in the American novel. But even though the three distinct cultural formations have separate histories, they share a common ground. The tough school of literature and film is filled with motifs that can be explained in vaguely existentialist terms; and as Roger Rosenblatt observes, the single place where "modern black and white heroes come closest to each other in terms of common atmosphere and situations is in the literature of the existentialists."[15] Wright and Himes therefore might have had as much to contribute to the French discourse on film noir as Chandler and Graham Greene.[16] If they did not, the reason is that Hollywood in the 1940s and 1950s did not adapt black novelists, or even show many black characters on the screen.

Most films noirs of the 1940s are staged in artificially white settings, with occasional black figures as extras in the backgrounds. The African-American writer Wanda Coleman has commented on this phenomenon in an article for *The Los Angeles Times Magazine* (17 October 1993), in which she also admits that she loves to watch old thrillers on TV. "Nothing cinematic excites me more than film noir," she remarks; even so, there often comes a moment when her suspension of disbelief is shattered. The black Pullman porters, musicians, shoeshine boys, janitors, maids, and nightclub singers in these films are created out of a narrow range of stereotypes, and they painfully remind Coleman that, "like murder, the cultural subtext will out": "My husband groans and my son laughs. Someone black has suddenly appeared onscreen. My stomach tightens and I feel the rage start to rise. . . . To enjoy that sentimental journey back to yesteryear, I have to pretend I live in a perfect world. . . . I have to force myself back through the door, back into the movie" (6).

Some black players in the 1940s were treated in relatively dignified ways, in part because the movie industry and the U.S. government were attempting to liberalize race relations during World War II. But in the era before the full-scale civil rights movement, film noir made no overt attempt to criticize the segregated society, and it never presented anything from a black point of view. Even a breakthrough actor like Canada Lee, who gave impressive but rather Uncle Tomish performances in *Lifeboat* (1944) and *Body and Soul* (1947), was never allowed to appear in a film version of his greatest stage role, as Bigger Thomas in Orson Welles's 1940 production of *Native Son*.[17] Welles, in fact, was the one white director in the period who might have made racial blackness more consistently and disturbingly present for white audiences. His incomplete documentary, *It's All True* (1942), was abandoned by RKO largely because it paid too much attention to the black population in Brazil.[18] At about the same time, he wanted to produce a film based on *Native Son*, but the project was much too controversial for the studios. For similar reasons, he was forced to put aside his fascinating adaptation of *Heart of Darkness*—which, had it been produced in 1940, would probably be regarded today as the first example of American film noir.

As we have seen, Conrad's novella was already a kind of *roman noir*, and it served as an inspiration for Graham Greene's thrillers, especially *The Third Man*. Welles's screen version would have updated the African materials in the original text, placing the opening narration against the background of a sound montage and a series of dissolves that took the viewer through contemporary Manhattan at night, ending with a Harlem jazz club. When the action moved to the Congo, the exploitation and murder of the black population would have been carried out by modern-day fascists. "This shouldn't surprise you," one of them says. "You've seen this kind of thing on city streets."[19] RKO executive George Schaefer wrote to Welles that the script "[lost] something" because of these references to contemporary politics, but Welles's proposed method of shooting the film was equally troubling.[20] He intended to use an expensive, mobile camera equipped with a gyroscope, and he organized his technically detailed, camera-specific screenplay in terms of long takes representing Marlow's point of view.[21] Where the politics of spectatorship were concerned, the technique was especially controversial, because it so often brought the viewer and Marlow into face-to-face contact with black characters.

To fully appreciate what Welles's screenplay achieves, we need to understand that he did not plan to make a mere recording of what the narrator sees, as in Robert Montgomery's unintentionally comic *Lady in the Lake* (1947), or as in the opening sequences of Delmer Daves's *Dark Passage* (1947). The camera he describes is impressionistic and subjective in a more complete sense, often showing us what Marlow thinks or feels. Like Conrad's prose, it is capable of shifting its focalization within a single take, moving from literal point-of-view shots to poetic omniscience—as when it suddenly tracks backward out of the manager's office in the Congo Station, tilts down to look at a sick man on the floor, passes through the front entrance, cranes over the roof to show the jungle beyond, and then tilts up to a starry sky. Ultimately, it creates a kind of white dream or hallucination about blackness, and one of the many reasons why it might have been effective on the screen (contrary to what most people have said) is that, unlike Chandler's Marlowe in *Lady in the Lake,* Conrad's Marlow is a relatively passive and highly imaginative witness. Welles never treats the camera as an action hero who is periodically socked in the jaw by a gangster or kissed by a gorgeous woman; instead, he gives us an eerie narrative presence who stands by and watches, occasionally being confronted by grotesque sights and sounds. His script describes a bewildering variety of characters who bob in and out of the frame, and it is filled with precise instructions for a delirious, overlapping dialogue that helps to convey Marlow's mounting confusion and disorientation. The uncanny effect would have been enhanced by a sophisticated, expressionistic use of process screens, showing bizarre images of the journey downriver toward the Central Station. On a more immediate level, however, the camera would have administered mild shocks in the form of characters who sometimes look back at the lens, arresting Marlow's attention and making both him and the ordinary white viewer feel slightly uncomfortable or self-aware. These characters would have included not only the dictator, Kurtz, and his minions, but also the Africans themselves. Soon after Marlow's arrival at the Outer

Station, for example, the script tells us that he sees a "big, ridiculous hole in the face of [a] mud bank. In it, frying in the sun, are about thirty-five dying savages and a lot of broken drain pipes. Into some of these pipes the natives have crawled, the better to expire. . . . As Marlow looks down, CAMERA PANS DOWN for a moment, registering a MED. CLOSEUP of a negro face, the eyes staring up at the lens. The CAMERA PANS UP AND AWAY."

According to Frank Brady, Welles planned to hire three thousand "very black" extras, and he resisted all of RKO's suggestions that he save time and expense by putting greasepainted figures in the distant background. Two of the black characters would have been especially significant: a solitary, "half-breed" employee of the European ivory traders (scheduled to be played by Jack Carter, the star of Welles's Harlem stage production of *Macbeth*), and an extremely dark-skinned woman who is Kurtz's lover at the Central Station. The half-breed is described as "an expatriate, tragic exile who can't remember the sound of his own language," and he is repeatedly given the opportunity to look Marlow in the eye. The dark woman is seen only once, near the end, when she stands on the bank of the river, looking toward Marlow and stretching out her arms in grief. Here and elsewhere, relatively marginalized black people provide important dramatic moments—as when one of them looks at the camera and makes the famous announcement, "Mister Kurtz, he dead."

All of the black characters in Welles's film are racial stereotypes, and the script as a whole never escapes from the ideological contradictions at the heart of Conrad's story. As Patrick Brantlinger observes, the original novella "offers a powerful critique of at least certain manifestations of imperialism and racism, at the same time that it presents that critique in ways that can only be characterized as imperialist and racist."[22] Where the film is concerned, Welles's liberalism is frequently undercut by his use of primitivist and racist fantasies. Notice, too, that his camera would have represented a mixture of three exclusively white subjectivities: an "average" male in the audience; the fictional Marlow; and Welles himself, who not only plays Marlow but also, in the manner of *Citizen Kane*, fills the story with autobiographical details. Even so, *Heart of Darkness* would have been unique, providing the only occasion in the history of classic Hollywood when the white gaze was troubled by a returning black gaze and the imaginary spectator was made sharply conscious of racial difference.

By comparison, the ordinary run of films noirs in the 1940s made black people almost invisible, like the briefly glimpsed figures who carry Wal-

FIGURE 58. Theresa Harris and Caleb Peterson in *Out of the Past* (1947).

ter Neff's bags or wash his car in *Double Indemnity*.[23] Close-ups of these figures were especially rare, except in brief scenes involving jazz in such pictures as *Out of the Past, D.O.A.,* and *In a Lonely Place*. There were, however, occasional attempts to give brief speaking roles to black people, and a conscious effort was made to avoid depicting them as the minstrel-show caricatures or comic illiterates of the 1930s. One scene in *Out of the Past* illustrates the new trend: Jeff Bailey visits a black dance club, where he locates Kathie Moffat's former maid, Eunice, and asks her if she knows anything about Kathie's whereabouts. The role of Eunice is acted by Theresa Harris, who had previously given a fine, unstereotypical performance in Jacques Tourneur's *I Walked with a Zombie* (1942). She responds to Jeff's questions without a trace of subservience, all the while conveying a wry intelligence. Her male companion (Caleb Peterson) is an unusually dignified presence—unsmiling, silent, and slightly on guard. The scene as a whole is played without condescension, and whether it intends to or not, it makes a comment on racial segregation.

Here and in several other films of the kind, black extras or bit players also give the protagonist an aura of "cool," so that he resembles what Norman Mailer once described as the "White Negro." This effect is especially apparent in Robert Aldrich's 1956 adaptation of *Kiss Me Deadly,* which, as I indicate in chapter 4, seems to have a divided and

somewhat incoherent attitude toward Mike Hammer. In some respects
Aldrich criticizes Mickey Spillane's hero, but in others he slightly revises
the character, making him a relatively sympathetic embodiment of urban liberalism. Thus when we first meet Hammer, he is listening to Nat
Cole on the radio; later, we discover that he is a regular customer at an
all-black jazz club, where his friendship with a black singer (Madi Comfort) and a black bartender (Art Loggins) helps to indicate his essential
hipness.

At about this time, Hollywood began to produce films that involved
a full-scale "buddy" relationship between male blacks and whites, thus
allowing the black actors to become true characters. The phenomenon
originated as early as *Casablanca,* but it became a formula after the 1950s,
influencing such postclassical, quasi-noir pictures as *In the Heat of the
Night* (1967), *Lethal Weapon* (1987), and *The Last Boy Scout* (1991),
all of which are instances of what Thomas Bogle identifies as the "huckfinn fixation." Bogle remarks that, traditionally, "darkness and mystery
have been attached to the American Negro, and it appears that the white
grows in stature from his association with the dusty black." Thus in the
classic huckfinn scenario of the 1950s, a white male's companionship
with black people signifies his opposition to the corruption and pretense
of bourgeois society and enables him to acquire a measure of "soul"; the
important qualification, as Bogle observes, is that the black character
"never competes with the white man," functioning instead as a kind of
"ego padder."[24] At first glance, the situation in *Lethal Weapon* is a bit
more complicated, because the black character is portrayed as a middle-
class suburbanite and the white character as a social outcast. The film
reverses the usual structure of racial patriarchy, showing an alienated
white man who is restored to health by a black father-figure; meanwhile,
it depicts the black family in the utopian style of a television sitcom, surrounded by commodities and enjoying the comforts of the American
dream. Notice, however, that the white male emerges as the true phallic
hero—the "lethal weapon" who saves the black bourgeoise and maintains a traditional ideology. As Robyn Wiegman remarks, the film "allows the white figure to be healed by the same familial unit that he himself is responsible for preserving."[25]

A much more intriguing reversal of the huckfinn relationship can be
seen in Robert Wise's much earlier, independently produced noir classic,
Odds against Tomorrow (1959), written without credit by the blacklisted Abraham Polonsky. Operating on one level as an allegory about
racial conflict, the film explores the deadly tensions that break out be-

FIGURE 59. The private eye as "White Negro." Ralph Meeker, Madi Comfort, and Art Loggins in *Kiss Me Deadly* (1955).

tween three bank robbers: an aging ex-con (Ed Begley), a southern racist (Robert Ryan), and a black jazz musician who is also a compulsive gambler (Harry Belafonte). These last two figures are unwillingly bound together by the crime, but they never learn to cooperate with one another. Throughout, Wise and his collaborators are unsentimental in depicting the wounds of race and social class, and they create a number of impressively unorthodox minor characters—including a homosexual thug (Will Kuluva) and a sex-starved, pathetically masochistic woman who lives upstairs in Ryan's apartment building (Gloria Grahame). At the end of the film, during the brief, failed bank robbery, Begley is killed, and the picture climaxes with a gun battle between Ryan and Belafonte, who chase one another across a series of oil storage tanks. When the tanks explode in a fashion reminiscent of *White Heat* (1949), the two men's bodies are so broken and charred that an investigating fireman asks a police officer, "Which is which?"

In the years following the civil rights movement, films made by black people became more widely visible. Significantly, the first important commercial breakthrough by a black director in Hollywood was Ossie Davis's *Cotton Comes to Harlem* (1970), an adaptation of the Chester

FIGURE 60. Harry Belafonte in *Odds against Tomorrow* (1959).

Himes's *roman noir* about Harlem police detectives Grave Digger Jones
and Coffin Ed Johnston. In place of Himes's sinister, subversive irony,
Davis employs an old-fashioned ethnic humor, in much the same way that
Hollywood in the 1930s tried to play Hammett and Chandler in broadly
comic style. Partly as a result of *Cotton Comes to Harlem,* however, a
truly radical transformation of black images suddenly appeared in 1971,
when a pair of low-budget crime pictures directed by black men became
surprise hits. Melvin Van Peebles's *Sweet Sweetback's Baadasssss Song*
and Gordon Parks's *Shaft* were grounded respectively in the themes of
criminal adventure and private-eye fiction, but they gave new life to old
forms by turning the black male into a sexually potent hero. Both had
crossover appeal for young white audiences of the Vietnam era, and both
were symptomatic of a broad countercultural reaction against liberal
stereotypes. Of the two, the independently produced *Sweet Sweetback*
was by all odds the most threatening; it gave full vent to separatist black
rage, allowing its criminal protagonist (Van Peebles) to fulfill every nightmare of white society and to emerge unconquered. *Shaft,* which was produced at MGM, was a straightforward entertainment, accepting the legal establishment in the qualified manner of a typical private-eye movie.

Its eponymous hero (Richard Roundtree) laughed at the law but was unwilling to join a group of black-power revolutionaries; he was also mildly cooperative with the one white policeman in New York who seemed not to be a racist.

One of the striking differences between these last two films and the standard noir thrillers of the 1940s was their refusal to depict the male hero as in any way flawed, compromised, or even vulnerable. Responding to decades of emasculated or nearly invisible black people on the screen, Van Peebles and Parks created black supermen, and they spawned a brief series of low-budget imitations that can be listed among the most phallocentric pictures this side of Mickey Spillane or James Bond. In one of the *Shaft* sequels, the hero tries to resist being typed as a sybaritic stud: "I'm not James Bond," he insists. "I'm Sam Spade." He nevertheless remains a Bond-like, leather-coated warrior who lives in a sophisticated Village pad and is irresistible to women. The hero of *Sweetback* is not only sexually prodigious but also downright ruthless, and he was clearly an influence on Gordon Parks's next film, *Superfly* (1972), a highly successful criminal adventure featuring a slick cocaine dealer who dresses and behaves like a Harlem pimp.

Thomas Bogle observes that Van Peebles and Parks "assiduously sought to avoid the stereotype of the asexual tom," but in doing so, they reproduced an equally old and distorted image of the "wildly sexual" black hedonist (240). They also tended to glamorize the dark side of town. Parks was especially good at photographing downtrodden New York locales, such as the porn movie theaters along 42nd Street and the gloomy alleys of Amsterdam Avenue, in ways that made the urban ghetto look pregnant with adventure. In fact, his neorealist color photography and night-for-night chase sequences had a strong influence on Martin Scorsese's *Mean Streets* and *Taxi Driver,* thereby helping to establish a visual style for American neo-noir as a whole. Despite their broad influence and their escapist fantasies, however, Van Peebles and Parks could not be completely absorbed into the mainstream; their early work still seems refreshingly different from Hollywood, if only because of its rough, documentary texture and its unusually angry, rebellious tone.

By the 1990s, the black middle class had grown sufficiently to provide greater opportunities for black stars and directors; nevertheless, various forms of de facto segregation still existed, and the black underclass in the cities had reached crisis proportions. In the face of these circumstances, the urban thriller or *policier* emerged (for better or worse) as the form of popular movie entertainment that most consistently dealt with

FIGURE 61. Richard Roundtree in *Shaft* (1971). (Museum of Modern Art Stills Archive.)

black issues. The two white directors who were most influenced by black film noir in the 1970s—Scorsese and Quentin Tarantino—showed an interest not only in black themes but also in the most powerful word in the English language. In Scorsese's case, the term *nigger* is often spoken by Italian working-class characters who suffer from a racial inferiority complex and feel a compulsive need to identify themselves as white. In Tarantino's, the effect is somewhat different. The gangsters and tough guys in *Pulp Fiction* use the term over and over again (along with *bitch*), while at the same time the film tries to protect itself against charges of racism by means of the plot and the casting: John Travolta and Samuel L. Jackson are linked together like Huck and Jim; Bruce Willis saves a black man from being raped by a couple of white southern racists; and Tarantino himself plays a gangster's accomplice who is married to a black woman. Audiences probably respond to the racial epithets in mixed ways, much as they once responded to Archie Bunker on TV. Some liberal viewers may regard the repeated *nigger* as a daringly realistic gesture, or as an attempt to divest a repressed word of its ugly power; racist viewers, however, are likely to experience a secret thrill.

If many of the old images of blackness persist in Hollywood noir, there is also a new kind of African-American presence. A wide range of hip-hop or "gangsta" films directed by African Americans depict a black criminal milieu in a fashion similar to traditional rogue-cop or caper movies, and the black actor Larry Fishburne has performed impressively in a series of ambiguous roles derived from classic noir—most notably as the undercover narcotics agent who is drawn to crime in *Deep Cover* (1992) and as the ex–CIA operative in *Bad Company* (1994). This chapter cannot do justice to all the recent "noirs by noirs," and for that reason among others, I recommend Manthia Diawara's essay on the topic in *Shades of Noir* (1993). Diawara uses Chester Himes as a paradigmatic African-American author of noir fiction, and he makes an important distinction between two types of crime movies by African-American directors: on the one hand are more-or-less-traditional romance narratives and gangster films such as *A Rage in Harlem* (1991) and *New Jack City* (1991); and on the other hand are realist, socially critical pictures such as *Boyz N the Hood* (1991), *Juice* (1992), and *Clockers* (1995). Both types combine noir motifs with rap music, but the socially critical pictures tend to appropriate the highly commodified youth culture and its associated black nationalism on behalf of "an ideology of black progress and modernism."[26]

For my own part, I would note that two of the most impressive African-American movies about crime—Charles Burnett's *Glass Shield* (1995) and Carl Franklin's *Devil in a Blue Dress* (1995)—avoid black nationalism and the new music almost completely. In most respects, these pictures are quite different from one another: *The Glass Shield* is a low-budget feature based on the true story of the first black sheriff's officer in L.A. county's notorious Edgemar station; *Devil in a Blue Dress* is a twenty-million-dollar adaptation of Walter Mosley's best-selling 1990 private-eye novel, featuring star-performer Denzel Washington, who co-produced the film with the assistance of Jonathan Demme and other important Hollywood names. What the two movies have in common is a high degree of artistry, plus a tendency to refigure or transform the familiar patterns of noir. Both did relatively poor business in their initial theatrical release, but they remain worthy of serious attention.

The Glass Shield reverses the rogue-cop formula by centering on an idealistic young officer who is assigned to a rogue unit. The basic plot situation recalls Sidney Lumet's *Serpico* (1973), but Burnett's approach is expressionistic, bringing us much closer to the look of historical noir. *The Glass Shield* also has something in common with Mike Figgis's entirely fictional *Internal Affairs* (1990), which pits a group of honest police detectives—a Latino, a lesbian, and a black man—against a corrupt white officer and his well-armed colleagues. *Internal Affairs,* however, is a slickly produced "psychological" thriller dealing with kinky sex and an exchange of guilt between a Latino good guy and a white bad guy. *The Glass Shield* shows no interest in doppelgängers, and it never indulges in subtly pornographic "entertainment values." Moreover, its austere, beautifully controlled technique makes Figgis's far more expensive production seem as empty as a magazine ad.

Burnett's protagonist, John Johnson (Michael Boatman), is a token black policeman who undertakes his job at Edgemar with a youthful ardor. Even so, his colleagues treat him coolly or contemptuously. His only friend is Deputy Fields (Lori Petty), a former law student from Minnesota, who encounters abuse not only from the other officers but also from people on the street. Johnson and Fields quickly become disillusioned, and at virtually the same moment they realize that the station as a whole is guilty of excessive violence. The uniformed patrol unit, known as the "Rough Riders," has a reputation for beating criminals; two officers are being sued for wrongful death in a recent case; and when Johnson is called to the scene of a robbery, he is ordered to stand outside a building while a group of club-wielding police and their attack dogs converge on an unarmed suspect in an empty room. Johnson himself participates in the dubious arrest of Teddy Woods (Ice Cube), a young black man who is stopped and searched without probable cause. and Johnson's involvement in this case leads ironically to his expulsion from the force. In the film's closing shot, we see him standing outside a courthouse with his fiancée, bashing a fist through his car window in frustration.

The Glass Shield nevertheless holds out some hope for justice. Moreover, unlike many examples of classical film noir, it treats Johnson's family not as a locus of repression but as a relatively calm center of love and dignity. In a 1989 essay, "Inner City Blues," Burnett places strong emphasis on this theme, denouncing entertainment movies—including movies by black directors—that deal with gangsters and "the worst of human behavior." What America needs, he argues, is a socially conscious cinema that can give black audiences a sense of community and offer what he calls (not unlike Raymond Chandler) "an element of redemp-

tion."²⁷ *The Glass Shield* is therefore designed to suggest the familial, religious, and legal structure of a black neighborhood, showing how Johnson's career isolates him from the people he most loves or respects—including his mother, his father, his fiancée, and the black priest and lawyer
who struggle against white officialdom. Meanwhile, Burnett also depicts
a diverse gallery of whites in complex terms: the intense Deputy Fields,
who remains on her job a bit too long; the sallow-faced, expressionless
Mr. Greenspan, who has probably murdered his wife; the sleazy yet somehow pathetic "Rough Riders," who gather each week for a bowling game;
the racist station commander, who breaks into tears when his unit gives
him a deep-sea fishing rod for his birthday; the aging plainclothes detective in the Woods case, who continues to frame people even while he
is dying of cancer; the slick young prosecutor, who expertly coaches the
police on how to disguise their racism; the decent but frightened desk
sergeant, who ultimately turns against his colleagues; and the woman
judge at the Woods trial, who adopts a black child.

In these and many other ways, *The Glass Shield* is an impressive social commentary, but it would not be such a memorable film if it lacked
Burnett's subtly measured and dreamlike style. The opening shots, for
example, juxtapose a comic-strip fantasy of Johnson's life as a policeman with a flat soundtrack composed entirely of sirens and traffic noises.
A series of drawings shows Johnson and Fields chasing down a couple
of white thugs, with dialogue and gunshots rendered in bold lettering:
"There's no way out!" "Don't try to be a hero!" "Kapow!" Johnson is
wounded, and as the medics arrive, Fields holds him in her arms and announces, "You proved yourself. Your shield is made of GOLD!" From
this panel, we dissolve to a live-action shot of an adventure comic pinned
to the door of Johnson's police academy locker. The camera pans to Johnson's ecstatic face as he listens to an overhead loudspeaker calling his
name and ordering him to report to Edgemar station. He seems euphoric,
but the shot is photographed in slow motion, and it creates a bizarre effect: in the background, we can see an out-of-focus police cadet who is
dreamily juggling a pair of nightsticks.

Occasionally, Burnett and photographer Elliot Davis employ the
"mystery" imagery of classical noir. For example, in the scene in which
Edgemar detectives question Teddy Woods, we see venetian blind shadows on the walls, and everything is shot from an extremely low level with
a wide-angle lens. Elsewhere, the film makes use of tilted, *Third Man*
camera angles—as when Johnson steps outside his front door and is presented with a subpoena by the sheriff's department. In most cases, how-

ever, a sense of isolation and fear is created through relatively unorthodox means. The scenes in the Edgemar station seem eerie because the pace of the acting is calm and deliberate, and because the rooms look unusually empty. Here and in the courtroom, the background music is understated, and the soundtrack is cleverly mixed to create a dimly heard ambience of random, institutional, and ghostly chatter. In exterior scenes, the mise-en-scène is even more strange. Night-for-night sequences are bathed patterns of orange and blue light, and the city streets are weirdly deserted. Crimes occur in antiseptically empty spaces: clean but underpopulated strip malls, lonely gas stations, vacant warehouses, abandoned houses, and streets devoid of cars. Each time Johnson and Fields are called to investigate, they find themselves in a quiet, deserted spot, where the silence is suddenly broken by a swarm of black and-white police cars and uniformed troopers arriving en masse. In scenes such as these, Burnett takes advantage of his low budget to create an oppressive void, a neo-Kafkaesque vision of fascist repression and racist brutality. He seems to have no particular model in mind, but on a relatively subtle level, his work has something in common with a classic social-problem picture such as *Crossfire*.

In contrast, Carl Franklin's *Devil in a Blue Dress* invites direct comparison with *Chinatown* and the tradition of hard-boiled private-eye literature. Like Walter Mosley's novel, the film begins in 1948 Los Angeles, near the spot on Central Avenue where Raymond Chandler placed the opening scenes of *Farewell, My Lovely*. As in Chandler, the plot involves a search for a missing woman who has changed her identity, and it leads to a fairly typical disclosure of sexual perversion and political corruption. But because the action is viewed from a different social, economic, and racial perspective, familiar motifs of urban noir are either intensified or neatly reversed.

Although the film's protagonist, Easy Rawlins (Denzel Washington), is both a private eye and something of a knight errant, his motives are far more realistic than Philip Marlowe's, and his life is placed in much greater jeopardy. Marlowe's skin color and social polish enable him to move with relative ease through every level of the city, whereas Rawlins faces barriers each time he steps outside his immediate community. In the course of his investigation, he narrowly escapes being beaten or killed by college kids on Santa Monica Pier; he is sadistically roughed up by the white gangsters who hired him; and he is brutally assaulted by the Los Angeles Police Department, who give him a single day to solve a murder or die. He uses every skill at his command merely to stay alive, and in attempting to solve a mystery, he defamiliarizes the entire city. As Paul Arthur observes, in this film, "the white districts and their bases of individual and institutional domination . . . serve as the heart of darkness."[28] The dance clubs and pool halls along Central Avenue are shadowy and sometimes violent (especially when they are invaded by whites), but they seem more accommodating than Santa Monica Pier and the Ambassador Hotel. Throughout, the white world is a dangerously alien territory at the margins of "normal" life, and poor and semirural areas that were never represented by the classic studios are given an aura of peace and dignity.

Like most noir heroes, Easy Rawlins is a loner with a "dark" past, which is represented in the film by a brief flashback to his life of crime in the prewar South and by several references to the dead bodies he saw in Europe while fighting for the United States Army. Unlike his predecessors, however, Rawlins does not suffer from guilt or quasi-existential angst. He wants nothing more than a steady job, so that he can satisfy the American dream of having a home with a bit of lawn attached. Hence the normative locale of the story is not, as in Chandler, a detective's lonely, rented office in Hollywood, but a privately owned bungalow in working-class Watts, where we see children at play in the streets. "I guess maybe I just loved owning something," Rawlins tells us in his offscreen narration, as we see him driving up to his mortgaged, one-bedroom house—a sunny dwelling with hardwood floors, a breakfast nook, and a pleasant front porch looking onto a patch of grass. The film's production designer, Gary Frutkoff, has skillfully selected and decorated this house, in the process giving a new twist to the theme of male domesticity in private-eye fiction: Rawlins lives in self-sufficient, Marlowe-like isolation, but he is also a housekeeper and a benign embodiment of capitalist progress, who enjoys planting rose bushes and communing with his neighbors.

When the film opens, a downturn in the postwar economy has deprived Rawlins and other African Americans of employment. (We see some of his neighbors loading up their autos and beginning a Joad-like migration back to the South.) In a bar on Central Avenue, Rawlins is approached by a white gangster (Tom Sizemore), who offers him a large sum of money to search the black side of town for a mysterious white woman named Daphne Monet (Jennifer Beals). According to the gangster, the woman has a "predilection for the company of Negros; she likes jazz and pig's feet and dark meat, so to speak." But when Rawlins succeeds in finding Daphne, he discovers that she is passing for white. The

FIGURE 62. Denzel Washington in *Devil in a Blue Dress* (1996). (Museum of Modern Art Stills Archive.)

sister of a black gangster from Lake Charles, Louisiana, she has become involved in an interracial love affair with one of the most influential white men in Los Angeles; moreover, she is in hiding because she has proof that a leading candidate for mayor is a pedophile. Two people who know her have already been murdered by the politician's thugs, and she and Rawlins are next in line.

The film cleverly uses the noir femme fatale to comment on the themes of racial passing and the "tragic mulatta," which were typical of American literature and film in the 1930s and 1940s. Not unlike the white Velma Valento in *Farewell, My Lovely*, Daphne conceals her identity by heightening the signifiers of social class and sexuality; in this case, however, a spectacular "female" body helps to draw attention from a "racial" body.[29] When the secret is uncovered, Rawlins must save both Daphne and himself from the increasingly powerful forces arrayed against them. Eventually, he enlists the financial help of Daphne's white lover, and his visit to this man, reminiscent of so many encounters between Marlowe and the Los Angeles plutocracy, has a truly iconoclastic quality. He also gets assistance from "Mouse" (Don Cheadle), a psychotic criminal he once knew in the South, who brings a frighteningly comic, graceful violence to every situation. The film climaxes in a bloody, nighttime shootout with the gangsters, which director Franklin stages with great brio. (In his previous film noir, *One False Move* [1992], he was as good as Howard Hawks or Anthony Mann at constructing lean, suspenseful action sequences; in this picture, the death of Sizemore is vaguely reminiscent of Bob Steele's elaborate death scene in *The Big Sleep*.) But even though Rawlins shoots the bad guys, unravels the mystery, and rescues the woman in the blue dress, the "color line" of postwar Los Angeles remains in force. Daphne cannot be reconciled with her lover and must return to Louisiana.

The color line may also have affected the film itself. Washington and Beals exchange sexual glances on the screen, but (like Washington and Julia Roberts in *The Pelican Brief* [1995]) they never make actual contact. In contrast, Walter Mosley's novel contains explicit, passionate love scenes between Easy and Daphne, who is described as a near blond, and who is not nearly so innocent as the character in the film. The novel also makes Mouse a far more threatening figure, and it provides several details about Easy's past in World War II, where he killed many white men. (Mosley is in fact partly Jewish, and World War II and the Holocaust are significant elements in his fiction.) Perhaps equally important, the novel is concerned as much with incest as with miscegenation; indeed, its theme of pedophilia extends to Daphne's own father, who abused her when she was a girl.

In "crossing over" to mainstream cinema, *Devil in a Blue Dress* became a softer, less troubling text. In many ways, however, the film provides a strong cinematic equivalent to the novel, rewriting *Chinatown* in much the same way that Mosley rewrites Chandler. The Polanski film is specifically recalled in Tak Fujimoto's low-key, wide-angle photography, in Jerry Goldsmith's romantic score, and in the crucial recognition scene in which Rawlins discovers Daphne's true identity. ("Scream, so I can tell the police about your boyfriend Frank Green!" Rawlins shouts. "Frank is my brother," she replies.) But *Devil in a Blue Dress* depicts a more recent history, and its nostalgia has a different effect. Although it reveals the corruption beneath sleek, art-moderne Los Angeles in the same manner as any retro-styled film noir, it is designed to celebrate the resilience and tenacity of the postwar black community and to recover a lost or underrepresented culture. The beautifully orchestrated crane shots of Central Avenue show us both the neon-lit dens of iniquity and the vibrant, crowded life on the street. At the Regent Theater, we glimpse a marquee advertising Oscar Micheaux's *Betrayal*, and in other scenes we hear snippets of music designed to reveal that black Los Angeles in 1948 was a center not so much of jazz as of early rhythm and blues. (The film makes excellent use of "race" records never heard in classic Hollywood, including T-Bone Walker's "West Side Baby," Amos Milburn's "Chicken Shack Boogie," and Pee Wee Clayton's "Blues after Hours.") Most of all, Franklin and the other contributors give a pastoral feeling to the Watts neighborhood where Rawlins lives, conveying both its fragile economic condition and its pride of accomplishment.

Chinatown and most of its imitators are pessimistic stories, involving the disillusionment or death of an alienated white male, a crisis of "family values," and an implicit critique of capitalism. In contrast, *Devil in a Blue Dress* is optimistic, involving a black protagonist who moves upward toward the middle class and who becomes stronger at the end. This character must confront a tragic personal and social history, but, in the tradition of the mainstream detective novel, he is not crushed by what he sees; in fact, the closing shots depict him as a hero who strides confidently down the sunlit street in front of his house, smiling at mothers and children. (The buoyant effect is heightened by Denzel Washington, who, like all the great movie stars, has a distinctive bodily signature—a razor grin and a relaxed, rolling walk.) Easy Rawlins is clearly no Jake Gittes, and he is quite different from the angry antiheroes in the African-American protest novels of the 1940s. In many ways an improbable construction, he has more in common with a "redemptive" figure like Chandler's Marlowe. It is as if Mosley, Franklin, Washington, and the other creators of *Devil in a Blue Dress* were looking back across history, from the vantage point of another side of town, to give a somewhat ironic salute to the classic private eyes of white Hollywood. "You and me, too, brother," Rawlins might say—or, in the words of Ralph Ellison, "Perhaps on the lower frequencies, I speak for you."

THE NOIR MEDIASCAPE

"There is nothing but trouble and desire."
HAL HARTLEY, *Simple Men*, 1992

One day in 1993, Emmy Award–winning filmmaker Ara Chekmayan visited a Pennsylvania fleamarket, where he discovered a statuette that looked exactly like the Maltese Falcon. Chekmayan purchased the black bird for eight dollars, and not long afterward, believing it to be one of two identical props that had been used in the famous 1941 Warner Brothers movie, he offered it up for auction at Christie's, who estimated its value at fifty thousand dollars. Before an auction could take place, however, a Los Angeles collector pointed out that identical copies of the statuette could be purchased at forty-five dollars apiece from a book dealer in Long Beach, California. (In that same year, my wife bought one in a Westwood bookstore and gave it to me as a Christmas present.) Chekmayan immediately withdrew his rara avis from sale, and the entire unhappy adventure was noted in *People* magazine.

The central irony of this story lies in the well-known fact that the "original" Maltese Falcon was itself a fake. Dashiell Hammett's novel can be read as a parable about art and surplus value, showing how a fetish object is created through the sheer power of myth. (Notice also that many of the villains in films noirs of the 1940s were dealers or collectors of fine art.) The irony deepens, however, when we realize that a similar myth has now accumulated around the classic Hollywood cinema. Contrary to what Walter Benjamin hoped in the 1930s, mechanical reproduction has not destroyed the "aura" of exhibition art; instead, the transitory but highly fetishized images of a bygone movie industry have become collector's items or museum pieces. Even the property warehouses of the old studios contain valuable objects. A kitschy statuette originally intended to represent a worthless imitation has been transformed into "the stuff that dreams are made of," if only because Humphrey Bogart touched it.

There is nothing new about this process. The twentieth century offers many examples of mass-produced trivia that become rare and valuable with the passing of time. (Walter Benjamin himself was a collector of popular children's books that eventually became prized items.) But Chekmayan's falcon illustrates two points about the film noir that are worth emphasizing: first, the falcon provides concrete evidence that Hollywood thrillers of the 1940s have become historical artifacts, possessed of a certain artistic or cultural cachet; and second, it reveals that these same thrillers can spread their aura across different media, becoming valuable as other things besides movies. *The Maltese Falcon* may have begun as a book and a couple of films, but it can become a statue in a museum, or practically anything else.

In effect, the idea of film noir spreads so widely that it helps to constitute what anthropologist Arjun Appadurai calls our "mediascape," which is made up of both the "capabilities to produce and disseminate information" (newspapers, magazines, television stations, film production studios, computers, and so on), and the images created through such media.[1] We might even say that noir itself is a kind of mediascape—a loosely related collection of perversely mysterious motifs or scenarios that circulate through all the information technologies, and whose ancestry can be traced at least as far back as ur-modernist crime writers like Edgar Allan Poe or the Victorian "sensation novelists." Of course, not everyone in the world is aware of the term *film noir*, and people find different uses for the things they read or see. Even so, self-conscious forms of noirish narrative continue to appear all around us, blurring the line between our fictional and real landscapes and contributing profoundly to the social *imaginaire*.

This phenomenon is especially evident in the postmodern environment, where dark Hollywood pictures of the 1940s and 1950s provide motifs, images, plots, and characters for every sort of artifact. For example, the slightly upscale regions of the leisure market frequently draw upon the memory of noir. Bernard Herrmann's music scores have been adapted into concert pieces by prestigious conductors; ambitious novelists such as William Gibson, Don DeLillo, Martin Amis, J. P. Ballard, Paul Auster, and Susanna Moore self-consciously allude to the noir literary tradition; the lurid illustrations for pulp magazines provide inspiration for the cover art on the annual "fiction issues" of *The New Yorker;* Raymond Chandler, Cornell Woolrich, and other crime writers of the 1940s have been published in fine editions by the Library of America; and in March 1993, the O. K. Harris Gallery in New York featured an exhibit by artist Arson Roje, who executed a series of hyperrealistic, eerily colored paintings of publicity stills and lobby cards from the 1941 version of *The Maltese Falcon.* Nor is this borrowing limited to middlebrow, institutional, or "authentic" arts. Film noir served as a minor reference point for Guy Debord and the situationists in Paris, who entitled one of their most famous manifestations *The Naked City.* More recently, the moods and images commonly associated with noir have influenced such cult TV shows as *The X-Files* and *Millennium.* The CD-ROM industry offers guides to Chandler, as well as interactive narratives such as *The Dame Was Loaded* (1996), which allows the male viewer to play the role of a private eye. Meanwhile, the World Wide Web is filled with information sites about every variety of pulp fiction and psychological melodrama.

The vaguely subcultural world of American comic books has shown an especially marked interest in retro-noir fantasies. Paradox Press, a special division of DC Comics, publishes "graphic novels" in a noir format, and Frank Miller, whose *The Dark Knight Returns* helped to fuel the Batman craze of the 1980s and 1990s, has produced a series of Mickey Spillane–inspired strips entitled *Sin City.* (Miller has probably exerted a strong influence on neo-noir as a whole—chiefly because of the way he fuses the black-and-white lighting patterns of the 1940s with the hard-body, exaggeratedly sexual poses in contemporary action movies.) Ironically, Mickey Spillane also inspired *Ms. Tree,* one of the longest-running private-eye comic books in history, which features a feminist private investigator and single mother named Michael Tree. Indeed, the amazingly durable Spillane, who began his career in the comic trade, has written futuristic versions of his original "Mike Danger" stories for a company called Tekno Comics, and in 1996, these illustrated tales of sex and vengeance were being discussed as a movie from Miramax pictures.

If Miramax were to distribute a Mike Danger film, it would be contributing to the low end of a motion-picture cycle that began in 1989 with *Batman* and threatens to die off in the late 1990s with productions like *Barb Wire* (a sort of noir *Barbarella*). Over the past decade, Hollywood has regularly issued summertime adventures based on the dark side of comic strips. The formula has not always been profitable, but it accounts for such mildly entertaining if extravagant movies as *Dick Tracy* (1990), *The Shadow* (1994), and *Batman Forever* (1995), all of which are aimed at an audience of older children and adults. The major films in the cycle are derived from slightly infantile and outmoded sources, but in true postmodern fashion, they create glossy, show business "events," featuring award-winning actors like Jack Nicholson and Al Pacino and lavish sets by Anton Furst and Joseph Nemec III, who employ a style known in the business as "noir lite." High production values and straightforward comic-book heroics are mingled with over-the-top performances, double-entendre dialogue, dystopian satire, and a good deal of directorial self-consciousness (as in *Batman*'s allusions to Alfred Hitchcock and Fritz Lang). The result is a pop-art spectacle that tries to provide something for almost everybody, enabling the more sophisticated adults to feel knowledgeable while they regress into nostalgia and childhood fantasy.

As we have seen, modestly budgeted and somewhat nostalgic versions of feature-length film noir have also become a staple of cable television. A typical 1996 picture, *Café Society* (distributed theatrically in 1997), is described as follows in the Showtime program guide: "The year is 1952. New York City's El Casbah nightclub, where Manhattan's fabulously wealthy gather to wallow in the gluttonies of success. One of them, Mickey Jelke (Frank Whaley), is heir to a tremendous fortune when he turns 25. Ask undercover agent Jack Kale (Peter Gallagher) about him, however, and he'll tell you he believes Jelke to be part of a big pornography ring. Then there's Patricia Ward (Lara Flynn Boyle), another society kid who's probably not what she seems to be. Three characters, one *film noir* triangle. Coffee?" In some cases, a similar nostalgia (if it is, in fact, nostalgia) extends even to the city streets, which are transformed by the tourist industry into simulacra of old Hollywood sets. The San Francisco tourist office provides a "Dashiell Hammett walking tour" to complement its "Victorian Architecture tour" and "Flower Power tour." Fans of *The Maltese Falcon* can visit a dark alley near Union Square, where a brass plaque memorializes the scene of a famous crime. "On approximately this spot," the plaque reads, "Miles Archer, partner of Sam Spade, was done in by Brigid O'Shaughnessy."

In one sense, the circulation and transformation of noir motifs is merely an exaggerated expression of modernity itself. The various aspects of the leisure economy have always been related, and film styles or genres have always tended to mirror or influence other types of entertainment. The pulp fiction magazines of the 1930s offered many of the same things—

westerns, melodramatic "love stories," tales of crime and horror—that could be seen in theaters or heard on the radio during that decade. Even in the 1940s and 1950s, the barely articulated noir sensibility was not confined to movies or literature; on the contrary, it spread across every form of narrative or protonarrative communication. As one instance, consider Entertainment Comics, better known as EC, which in the early 1950s took direct aim at the libido of adolescent boys, specializing in black comedy (*Tales from the Crypt* and *The Vault of Horror*), grotesque "speculative fiction" (*Weird Science*), and anarchic satires of pop culture (*Mad* and its short-lived clone, *Panic*). At one point, EC adapted a number of dark short stories by Ray Bradbury, and it nurtured a group of stylish, groundbreaking illustrators who borrowed conventions from noirlike movies and pulp magazine covers. The entire EC line was unusually sexy, violent, and iconoclastic. Its two most obviously noir venues, *Crime Suspenstories* and *Shock Suspenstories,* were filled with restless suburban marriages, neurotic killers, and corrupt police who administered third-degree punishment to innocent civilians. Drawn in an angular, chiaroscuro style, EC's ten-cent crime anthologies often showed voluptuous women being murdered or tortured, but they also gave vivid treatment to controversial issues such as race prejudice and drug addiction.

Not surprisingly the success of EC prompted an outcry from guardians of morality. In 1954, at the height of the McCarthy era, psychiatrist Fredric Wertham wrote a best-selling exposé of the comic industry, *The Seduction of the Innocent,* which led to a full-scale Senate investigation headed by Estes Kefauver of Tennessee.[2] EC's major competitors quickly appointed a censorship board administered by moral czar Judge Charles F. Murphy, which denied an official "seal of approval" to any comic that used words such as *crime, horror, terror*, and *weird*. In response, EC killed off its leading titles and experimented briefly with a melodramatic but "educational" volume called *Psychoanalysis*. In 1955, it converted its most popular genres into twenty-five-cent "picto-fictions" for adults— among them, *Crime Illustrated: Adult Suspense Stories* and *Shock Illustrated: Adult Psychoanalytical Tales*. The company disappeared at about the same time as classic film noir, although its most popular offering, the parodic *Mad,* metamorphosed into a relatively sanitized and uninventive "magazine." Then in the 1980s, with the relaxation of censorship and the reconfiguration of the marketplace, some of its original volumes began to resurface as expensive reprints for nostalgic older adults and affluent teenagers; the volumes were a strong influence on Stephen King, and they eventually inspired a movie and a cable TV series called *Tales from the Crypt* (1989–1996). Nearly a third of the shows in the series were adapted from the original EC crime comics and were directed by such figures as John Frankenheimer, Walter Hill, and Robert Zemeckis.

Television and radio have also been crucial to the history and dissemination of noir taste. EC was inspired in part by the dark or horrific radio dramas of the 1940s—especially by CBS's *Suspense*, which featured the major Hollywood stars of its day. Following in a tradition established by Orson Welles at the same network, *Suspense* devised ingenious ways to motivate retrospective forms of first-person narration: a dead man (Robert Taylor) leaves a manuscript in a shoe box; an invalid (Agnes Moorehead) makes desperate telephone calls to several people because she suspects that she is about to be murdered; and a killer (Peter Lorre) breaks into a police station and holds the cops at gunpoint, forcing them to listen to the weird story of his crimes. The series often adapted novelists such as Cornell Woolrich and James M. Cain, and at least two of its original scripts —Cyril Endfield's "The Argyle Inheritance" and Lucille Fletcher's "Sorry, Wrong Number"—were later turned into films noirs. Many of its episodes (marketed today as nostalgia radio, with the commercials intact) still have a power to entertain. Among the more compellingly bizarre shows of 1949, for example, were "Consequence," starring James Stewart as a doctor who tries to escape a bad marriage by faking his death; "For Love or Murder," starring Mickey Rooney as a murderous, romantically infatuated jazz musician who hears drums in his head; and "The Bullet," starring Ida Lupino as a career woman whose success causes her jealous, ex-convict husband to threaten to shoot her.

Suspense was the immediate forerunner of Alfred Hitchcock's hugely successful TV shows of the 1950s and 1960s; indeed, one of its most admired episodes, a 1942 adaptation of Cornell Woolrich's novel *The Black Curtain*, was filmed by *The Alfred Hitchcock Hour* in 1962, under the direction of the young Sydney Pollack. Meanwhile, film noir's most celebrated character type, the hard-boiled private eye, remained a staple of entertainment programs on both radio and television from the 1940s through the 1980s. On radio in the period between 1948 and 1952, Dick Powell was singing-detective Richard Diamond, and Howard Duff was a particularly effective Sam Spade. One of the earliest examples of such characters on TV was *Charlie Wild, Private Eye* (1950–1952), a production of CBS, ABC, and Dumont, which freely adapted Dashiell Hammett's Sam Spade adventures, concealing the literary source and changing the hero's name because of the HUAC investigations into Hollywood communism (Kevin O'Morrison played Wild, and Cloris Leachman was featured as Effie Perinne). Later in the decade, David Janssen was *Richard Diamond, Private Detective* (1957–1960), Philip Carey was *Philip Marlowe* (1959–1960), Darren McGavin was *Mickey Spillane's Mike Hammer* (1957–1960), and Craig Stevens was *Peter Gunn* (1958–1961).

The best-known police procedural on U.S. radio and television from 1949 until the early 1970s was Jack Webb's increasingly bland and conservative *Dragnet,* which evolved from *He Walked by Night* (1949), and which, in its later episodes, costarred Webb and Harry Morgan, who had acted together as a pair of heavies in another film noir called *Appointment with Danger* (1951). (Webb's wide-screen and color movie version of *Dragnet* in 1954 was also inflected with noirlike photographic and performance conventions, as was his 1955 movie and radio series entitled *Pete Kelly's Blues.*) Other TV productions derived from classical noir include *Naked City* (1958–1963), the BBC's *Third Man* (1959–1964), and *Mike Hammer*, who resurfaced in a successful series featuring Stacy Keach (1984–1987). In the same years as the last of these shows, ITV in London produced a series of artful, atmospheric adaptations of Raymond Chandler's short stories, featuring Powers Boothe as Philip Marlowe. At this point, the classic private eye was becoming an antique, but he could be brought up to date by transforming him into a somewhat yuppiefied, postfeminist type, as in Robert B. Parker's *Spencer* novels and TV show (1985–1988) and in John Sayles's exceptionally good series of TV dramas entitled *Shannon's Deal* (1989–1991). He could also become a certified born loser, as in a made-for-cable thriller like *Third-Degree Burn* (1989).

It would require a small book merely to list all the burnt-out police officers and philosophical private eyes in American pop culture over the past three decades. Both genders and nearly all sexual inclinations have been represented by such figures, and every large city in the country has been mapped by them. Among the cop shows and criminal adventures on U.S. television, *The Fugitive* (1963–1967) and *Miami Vice* (1984–1989) are particularly important to the history of noir.[3] Consider as well two expensively produced British exports, *Cracker* and *Prime Suspect*, which not only depict a society in decay but also make the detective protagonists seem almost as darkly compulsive as the criminals. These and some of the other examples I have mentioned are sometimes only remotely noirlike, but we should recognize that they all have familial connections with the classical thrillers of the 1940s, which they often acknowledge. The eponymous hero of *Cracker*, for instance, has a Bogart poster on the wall in his house. When producer-director Blake Edwards turned his highly successful *Peter Gunn* TV series into a rather bad movie called *Gunn* (1967), he staged the climax in a hall of mirrors that was reminiscent of *The Lady from Shanghai*. In one episode of the *Mike Hammer* TV series in the late 1980s, director Ray Danton did the same thing, achieving somewhat better results than Edwards on a lower budget.

At the very least, we need to recognize that noir is a much more flexible, pervasive, and durable mood, style, or narrative tendency than is commonly supposed and that it embraces different media and different national cultures throughout the twentieth century. Contrary to what Alain Silver and Elizabeth Ward tell us on the first page of their indispensable encyclopedia of Hollywood noir, the form in question does not constitute "a self-contained reflection of [post–World War II] American cultural preoccupations," and it is certainly not "the unique example of a wholly American film style."[4] The term *film noir* was used in France in the 1930s (if not earlier), and it was first applied to the American cinema by the French; in fact, a great many of the Hollywood films designated by the term were remakes of European pictures, made by émigré directors and writers. Certain of the characteristic expressions of film noir—especially the never-ending cycle of *policiers* and criminal adventures—have been produced by virtually every medium and every cinema in the world, and no doubt they will continue to be produced. If, as Jean-François Lyotard and others suggest, postmodernity is merely a restaging of modernist preoccupations on the grounds of contemporary technology and economics, then noir is likely to be with us for a long time to come.

This being said, the contemporary American scene has distinctive features that mark it off from the past. We can never know exactly how audiences in the 1940s and 1950s viewed the dark movies of their day, but it seems obvious that we view those same films differently, in contexts far removed from the ones for which they were originally intended. The postwar films noirs now occupy the same shelf space in video stores and the same time slots on TV as last year's Hollywood thrillers; their reception, furthermore, is mediated by an extensive critical discourse (as in the case of this book), which gives them a certain status. Some people regard them as artistic visions of paranoia and entrapment; others view them in a spirit of Reaganite nostalgia for the glamour and simplicity of pre-Vietnam America.

In certain instances, the classic films noirs also provide contemporary audiences with material for what Barbara Klinger calls "mass camp." Anyone who has watched *Laura* or *Out of the Past* in a crowded uni-

versity auditorium will know that such movies require a suspension of
disbelief best achieved at home or in a select revival theater. Some of the
most serious lines of noir dialogue, written in the spirit of hard-boiled
poetry or psychoanalytic profundity, have become unintentionally funny.
(Peggy Thomson and Saeko Usukawa have published two amusing and
nostalgic volumes made up entirely of dialogue from classical noir: *The
Little Black and White Book of Film Noir* [1992] and *Hard-Boiled*
[1994].) Where *Laura* is concerned, the camp effect is at least partly intended—any movie that puts Clifton Webb, Judith Anderson, and Vincent Price in the same drawing room is inviting a mood of fey theatricality. In the 1940s, however, camp was a marginal or subcultural style,
risking criticism or censure. Today, as Klinger observes, the camp sensibility has been fully democratized by changes in social attitudes about
gender and sexuality, by the liberalization of censorship rules, by the critical legitimization of pop art, and by the culture industry itself, which
has learned how to market old products in new ways. Camp in the late
twentieth century has therefore acquired a kind of "mainstream chic-
ness," especially evident in the *Batman* blockbusters, which is grounded
in the audience's sense of superiority over outdated conventions. An almost completely ahistorical mode of reception, it is marked by a strong
tendency "to embrace what is perceived as mediocrity for a transient,
disinterested form of recreation without group affiliation or political
bite."[5]

The only classical films noirs that seem relatively immune from mass-
camp readings are pictures such as *The Asphalt Jungle,* which take place
largely outside the studio, in a virtually all-male milieu, and convey an
astringent, somewhat ironic attitude toward heterosexual romance—
hence a more serious cult following can develop around a postmodern
caper movie like *Reservoir Dogs.* It should be noted, however, that even
the most condescending forms of mass camp involve affection for the
things they mock. Contemporary audiences who laugh at *Mildred Pierce*
or *Double Indemnity* remain at least partly under the spell of the films.
The naïveté of these viewers lies not so much in their amused attitude,
but in their implicit assumption that contemporary pictures based on
similar themes are somehow more realistic, less burdened by artifice or
sentimentality.

In point of fact, most examples of neo-noir are less artistically sophisticated and politically interesting than the films they emulate. Lawrence
Kasdan's *Body Heat* treats sex in a manner appropriate to the post-Code
era, employing naturalistic acting and a somewhat elliptical cutting style;

even so, its narrative structure is conventional, its characters familiar, and its Florida location merely decorative next to *Double Indemnity*'s Los Angeles. In comparison, a picture like David Mamet's *House of Games* (1987) might seem different. An oneiric, sinister, and sometimes radically ambiguous movie, *House of Games* is filled with oddly lobotomized performances and artfully repetitious dialogue that echoes Ernest Hemingway without trying to copy him ("I'm a writer. I'm a sort of writer." "Oh, so you're a writer. What do you write when you write?"). It nevertheless provides a classically proportioned, "three-act" drama with a strong sense of closure, and most of its themes and stylistic effects are taken straight from Hitchcock. The story centers on an arctic, upper-class female who suffers from more neurotic compulsions than Marnie; the editing combines Kuleshovian effects and omniscient, "bird's-eye" perspectives; and the entire staging is designed to create an expressionist atmosphere of eroticized suspense and impending violence. No doubt *House of Games* is a more fastidious and ostentatiously experimental picture than anything by Brian DePalma, but in the last analysis it is vulgarly Freudian, lacking the passion that makes a director like Hitchcock something other than a superbly skilled, misogynistic technician.

The same adaptation of traditional formulas, with a slightly revisionist twist, can be seen in *Fatal Attraction* (1987) and *Basic Instinct* (1992), the two most commercially successful films noirs ever made. Interestingly, the two pictures have a good deal in common: both are directed by Europeans; both star the actor-producer Michael Douglas, who has a talent for portraying angry white males (he even makes the ruthless tycoon Gordon Gekko in *Wall Street* seem vaguely sympathetic); and both, despite their patriarchal implications, feature stunning performances by women. Alex, the psychotic one-night stand in *Fatal Attraction,* and Catharine, the Sadeian woman in *Basic Instinct,* are among the most frightening femmes fatales in the history of movies—chiefly because they are viewed without the constraints of old-fashioned censorship and without the mollifying romanticism of Hollywood in the 1940s. Neither film, however, represents an advance over earlier models in terms of style or sexual politics.

Glenn Close has said that she regards *Fatal Attraction* as a film noir, especially in its original version, which ends with Alex's suicide.[6] Unfortunately, because of negative reactions from preview audiences, Paramount and director Adrian Lyne reshot the grim conclusion, turning Alex from a vulnerable character into a *Psycho*-style killer, and then restoring Douglas's family to a secure if chastened happiness. (Paramount and

Billy Wilder also softened the ending of *Double Indemnity,* but the more
superficial and commercially adroit Lyne had certain advantages over
Wilder: after the theatrical release, his "director's cut" was marketed to
video stores in laserdisk and VHS formats, adding to the studio's rev-
enue.) The first version of *Fatal Attraction* is in fact an unsettling study
of a disturbed woman who at first seems menacing but eventually becomes a scapegoat for the bourgeois family. The film cleverly invites its
audience to identify with Michael Douglas, and then shifts the point of
view and emotional emphasis toward Close, who gives Alex a plausi-
bility and psychological complexity beyond anything imagined in the
script. And yet, despite these virtues, and despite considerable narrative
tension and technical sheen, the director's cut of *Fatal Attraction* is in
many ways a less ironic and morally ambiguous treatment of infidelity
than André de Toth's modestly budgeted *Pitfall* (1948), a classic noir
grounded in a staunchly conservative view of the nuclear family. *Pitfall*
relentlessly supports conventional morality, causing its restless protagonist (Dick Powell) to pay for the rest of his life because of a single, twenty-
four-hour indiscretion. At the same time, it uses the married man's involvement with another woman to reveal tensions between social classes,
and it portrays the ostensible femme fatale (Lizabeth Scott) in quite sympathetic terms. Perhaps more significantly, it makes suburban America
seem like an iron cage for both the wife and the husband.

Basic Instinct was also marketed in two versions, but the video release was designed merely to give the audience an extra forty-two seconds of nude sex. Few mainstream Hollywood films have so deliberately
flaunted their aspirations to soft-core pornography, and few have provided a clearer instance of how the masculine gaze generates fantasies of
desire and castration. *Basic Instinct* is filled with explicit, foregrounded
instances of what Laura Mulvey calls "sadistic voyeurism" and "fetishistic scopophilia"—most obviously in the early scene in which the sexy
young Catharine Trammell (Sharon Stone) sits on a raised, spotlit plat-
form and allows a group of male detectives (representing the point of
view of the audience) to look up her dress. Predictably, this scene initi-
ates a narrative that is both Hitchcockian and Sternbergian, oscillating
between the protagonist's need to investigate and punish the woman and
his equally important need to adore her and be destroyed. (Director Paul
Verhoeven previously explored similar themes in *The Fourth Man,* a 1984
film noir made in Holland, in which a brief moment of male frontal nudity reveals the need to protect the phallus in both its real and symbolic
senses.)

Throughout, *Basic Instinct* wears its noirlike sexual qualities on its sleeve, mixing psychological drama with pure spectacle. Like a perverse musical, it uses a deadly love affair between a rumpled, chain-smoking detective and a wealthy, provocative murderess to motivate a series of sadomasochistic "numbers" and several theatricalized displays of decadence. Also like a musical, it celebrates the union of a male and female who come from different worlds—a policeman and a criminal who are trying to achieve the "fuck of the century." Although the policeman is a fairly conventional antihero, the criminal is a decidedly postfemme fatale, resembling a cross between Sade's Julliette and Madonna. Catharine Trammell is not only a great beauty but also a hedonist, an intellectual, a bisexual, and a serial killer who openly mocks Freudian attempts to explain her behavior. She is, moreover, a pure machine woman in the tradition of Phyllis Dietrichson, her evil redeemed only by Stone's witty performance and by the film's refusal to condemn her transgressions. At the end, she and the detective (who shares her taste for violence) are suspended in a moment of infinite erotic deferral, with an ice pick hidden under the bed. As R. Barton Palmer observes, this conclusion is reasonably complex in its treatment of sex and gender and "very much in the tradition of Hitchcock's *Vertigo*."[7] But the comparison with Hitchcock (which Verhoeven deliberately encourages) also serves to remind us of important differences: *Basic Instinct* offers its audience a distinctly latter-day form of surrealism, without the equivalent risk of censorship, without the swooning cult of romantic love, and virtually without the Freudian unconscious.

Such films come dangerously close to the kind of cultural recycling and transformation described in a well-known passage from Thomas Pynchon's *Vineland* (1990), in which the daughter of a 1960s left-wing filmmaker (lately turned FBI agent) visits the newly constructed "Noir Center" shopping mall in lower Hollywood. Designed to resemble the Bradbury Building, the mall contains, among other things, a mineral-water boutique called "Bubble Indemnity" and a perfume store called "The Mall Tease Flacon." To the young woman, it seems as if yuppification has run to "a pitch so desperate" that she can only hope the whole process is "reaching the end of its cycle." She grows particularly angry because of what film noir represents in her own historical memory:

> She happened to like those old weird-necktie movies in black and white, her grandfolks had worked on some of them, and she personally resented this increasingly dumb attempt to cash in on the pseudoromantic mystique of those particular olden days in this town, having heard enough stories . . . to know

better than most how corrupted everything had really been from top to bottom, as if the town had been a toxic dump for everything those handsome pictures had left out.[8]

Pynchon is correct when he says that the "weird-necktie" style died sometime in the late 1950s, concurrent with the passing of the old studio pictures, only to be replaced by a variety of ahistorical, slickly commodified, and often "dumb" imitations. Except on television and in direct-to-video formats, the highly rationalized genre system gave way to a kind of shopping-mall cinema made up of superproductions for the masses and boutique pictures for specialized audiences. Most of the big pictures in the neo-noir category have been filled with comic-strip villains, loud explosions, and dialogue that consists mainly of "Fuck you" and "No, fuck *you!*" For their own part, the boutique movies are often less about characterization and social milieu than about seductive production designs, flamboyant camera effects, and spectacular sexual violence. One example is Peter Medak's *Romeo Is Bleeding* (1993), which features Lena Olin as the sexiest one-armed dominatrix in the history of cinema, but which never rises above the level of a clever pastiche. A slightly more effective case in point is Larry and Andy Wachowski's *Bound* (1996), which takes its visual cues from Frank Miller's artfully self-conscious *Sin City* comic books. (Cinematographer Frank Pope creates a starkly graphic palette of black, white, and gray for this film, adding occasional touches of red for blood and green for money.) On the surface, *Bound* is sexually unorthodox, inviting us to fully identify with a lesbian couple who are seeking revenge on a distinctly unpleasant male; what is really at stake, however, is a fairly conventional male pleasure of watching two beautiful actresses as lovers—something that *Bound* does far better than the big-studio remake of *Diabolique* in the same year.

But the current situation may not be quite so dumb as Pynchon suggests.[9] The category of noir has a long and complex history, and it provides images, moods, and stylistic techniques that can be adapted and transformed by good, bad, and indifferent pictures from every level of the marketplace. Speaking purely of the American commercial cinema, it would be difficult to find a better treatment of the doppelgänger theme than David Cronenberg's *Dead Ringers* (1988), a more disturbing depiction of criminal violence than Martin Scorsese's *Goodfellas* (1990), or a more disconcerting presentation of a psychopath than Jonathan Demme's *Silence of the Lambs* (1991). These pictures may be subject to criticism on aesthetic or political grounds, but so are the classic films noirs.

Whatever we might say about the 1940s and 1950s, the better contemporary thrillers seldom leave out the "toxic dump" of social or moral corruption; indeed, some element of anger, fear, cynicism, pessimism, or *nostalgie de la boue* seems necessary to the form. Notice also that film noir has always been subject to appropriation by a variety of constituencies; in the past few decades, it has affected high-end productions such as *Batman*, independent pictures such as John Dahl's *Kill Me Again* (1989), and imports such as Bill Bennett's *Kiss or Kill* (1997)—the last of which represents a particularly effective use of old formulas. Noir has also been a favored subject of vanguard or deconstructivist filmmakers. Sally Potter's *Thriller* (1979) and Manuel DeLanda's *Raw Nerves: A Lacanian Thriller* (1980) are indebted to classic models, as are a number of "crossover" projects, including David Lynch's *Blue Velvet*, Hal Hartley's *Simple Men* (1992), and Atom Egoyan's *Exotica* (1994).

The best contemporary films noirs seem to me to come from the middle range of the industry, represented by the last few pictures I have mentioned, where modest production values and a relative lack of hype allow directors to explore art-cinema values within the context of familiar narratives. In the United States, the somewhat incestuous relationship between the Sundance Film Festival, *The New York Times,* and distributors like Miramax and Fine Line has encouraged movies of this type. Each fall and winter, independently produced, noirlike pictures are shown at Sundance, written about in the Sunday *Times,* and distributed to big cities, where they usually share the same venues with English or Australian imports, Masterpiece Theater–style adaptations, and the few subtitled offerings that manage to find exhibitors. Such films are roughly analogous to the "hybrid" thrillers of the 1950s, and they generate reasonable profits because they fill at least two niches in the market: they appeal to a sophisticated audience, but at the same time they serve as general entertainment in the video stores.

There are so many of these hybridized films that I cannot list them all here. As a way of concluding my description of the noir mediascape, let me offer a brief discussion of three recent examples, which might be termed "independent" or "art-film" noir. In a sense, the three have little in common, but that fact should not trouble us. The idea of noir, after all, can accommodate many different things.

Example 1: The Grammercy Pictures–Universal release of Steven Soderbergh's *Underneath* (1995) is a remake of Robert Siodmak and Mark Hellinger's more elaborately produced *Criss Cross* (1949). While he was working on this film, Soderbergh explained to a reporter from *The New York Times* that "the ideas behind noir . . . are interesting to me, not pastiche or homage." He had no special desire to imitate Siodmak, he said, nor to prove "my shadow's longer than yours"(6 February 1994). Perhaps for that reason, *The Underneath* is most effective at the points where it diverges from the earlier film. Soderbergh, who is the uncredited author of the screenplay, changes the locale from Los Angeles to present-day Austin, Texas, thereby replacing the 1940s urban jungle with a slightly eerie background of suburban houses and nondescript streets. He also gives more emphasis to the working-class characters' domestic relationships and marginal jobs than to the suspense plot, which involves a botched armored-car robbery. Most strikingly, he transforms the drifter-protagonist (Peter Gallagher) from a romantically obsessed and rather stolid type (originally played by Burt Lancaster) into a weak-willed *homme fatale*.

Soderbergh's antihero, Michael Chambers, is a compulsive gambler who has run away from home to escape his debts. As the film begins, we see him returning after a long absence, finding a job as an armored-car driver, reading self-help books, and attempting to reestablish connections with the people he left behind. His policeman brother (Adam Trese) envies and despises him; his widowed, still attractive mother (Anjanette Comer), who has always favored him, is about to marry a boring but dependable man (Paul Dooley); and his former lover Rachel (Alison Elliot), whom he abandoned, is living with a sadistic and intensely jealous small-time gangster (William Fichtner). As in the 1949 production, the plot concerns a deadly triangle between Michael, Rachel, and the gangster, who become duplicitous allies in a robbery scheme. In this case, however, a fourth character is introduced—a sweetly pretty young woman named Susan (Elizabeth Shue), who is attracted to Michael, and with whom he has a casual affair. Soderbergh also adds a new development to the conclusion, making the film seem a bit more in tune with the 1990s: Rachel tricks Michael into killing the gangster and then leaves Michael behind to die, reminding him before she goes that he once abandoned her. After all these years, she says, she has begun to understand "the appeal of walking away."

Michael Chambers emerges from the film as an ineffectual, superficially attractive character who finds himself sliding into a trap of his own making. In several respects, he resembles his mother and Rachel, both of whom are caught in unhappy, small-town relationships, and both of whom are petty gamblers, obsessively playing the Texas lottery. Actually, everyone

FIGURE 63. Noir remade: Alison Elliot, William Fichtner, and Peter Gallagher in *The Underneath* (1995). (Museum of Modern Art Stills Archive.)

in the film lives a life of quiet desperation, grasping at vague hope for a jackpot. If this malaise is not immediately apparent, that is because *The Underneath*, like *Criss Cross*, presents most of the action from Michael's point of view, using flashbacks and bizarre camera angles to heighten the sense of individual neurosis. The hospital sequence creates a truly Kafkaesque atmosphere of paranoia and black comedy, with the characters at Michael's bedside viewed subjectively through an extreme wide-angle lens, and the set designed in asymmetrical, *Caligari* fashion.[10] (At one point during the subsequent kidnapping, the world turns completely upside down.) Although Soderbergh abandons the 1940s convention of subjective, voice-over narration, he experiments quite effectively with a visual stream of consciousness, creating a good deal of spatial and temporal disorientation. In the opening sequence, for instance, we see Michael through the green windshield of an armored car as he drives along a highway; then we see him in the back seat of a taxicab, gazing unhappily out the window; then we see a conversation between him and Susan aboard a Greyhound bus, where he once again sits alone beside a window. The chronology of these images is not clear, and there is a disjunction between sound and visuals; thus we hear the conversation aboard the bus before it appears on the screen, and we continue to hear it over a shot of Michael and Susan as they part company at their destination.

Throughout, *The Underneath* keeps its audience slightly off balance, joining the conventions of historical film noir with the more complex modernism of a New Wave director like Alain Resnais. Soderbergh's greatest strengths, however, are at the level of realist character and mood (especially in scenes involving repressed sexual tension), and for that reason the mechanics of the crime-movie plot keep overriding or frustrating his film's more interesting qualities. The problem is especially evident in the last scene. As she drives off with the stolen loot, leaving Michael to ponder his wasted life, Rachel stops at a convenience store to buy groceries and a lottery ticket; in the parking lot, we see the boss of the armored-car company (Joe Don Baker), who has been secretly responsible for financing the entire robbery scheme and who now plans to murder Rachel. This blatantly ironic twist is out of keeping with the wit and obliqueness of the earlier parts of the film. Even though it reinforces the recurring themes of gambling and failure, it makes the narrative as a whole seem too pat or generic—in one sense, too faithful to noir.

Example 2: No such problem affects Billy Bob Thornton's *Sling Blade* (1997), which was not marketed or reviewed as a noir, although it easily could have been. Thornton, the writer, director, and star of the film, previously cowrote and acted in *One False Move* (1994), an exciting low-budget thriller set in rural Arkansas. He also wrote and acted in "Some Folks Call It a Sling Blade" (1993), a sinister, black-and-white short subject directed by George Hickenlooper, which was rephotographed in color and with different camera angles to make up the opening sequences of *Sling Blade*. Reviewers have described the completed feature-length version of this story as "Faulknerian"—a somewhat strained comparison that nevertheless properly evokes Thornton's interest in southern gothicism. (We should recall that William Faulkner himself was a noir novelist and that some of the classic films noirs, including Frank Borzage's *Moonrise* [1949], are set in the rural South.) Indeed, had the Miramax distribution company been given their way, *Sling Blade* would probably have looked even more noirlike. It was shot in only twenty-four days for a cost of 1.3 million dollars and was originally intended as a sort of regional art movie for the video stores; Miramax, however, paid ten million for the rights and wanted to speed up the action along more commercial lines. Fortunately, Thornton resisted; as a result, he was able to explore certain "dark" motifs in a theatrical venue while avoiding a generic classification.

Sling Blade is a straightforward narrative performed at a deliberate,

FIGURE 64. Art film or neo-noir? Billy Bob Thornton in *Sling Blade* (1996). (Museum of Modern Art Stills Archive.)

contemplative pace that seems anathema in contemporary Hollywood. Using long takes and a relatively static camera, photographer Barry Markowitz shoots the film chiefly with available light, immersing the interiors in a musty gloom and often illuminating figures with a single table lamp. This style is perfectly keyed to the central character—a slow-witted loner named Karl Childers (Thornton), who, when he was quite young, murdered his mother and her lover with a garden tool. During his childhood, Karl was locked in a shed by his parents and at one point was forced by his father to bury the still living body of his newborn brother. At the beginning of the film, he is pronounced "cured" and is released from the state mental hospital into the town where he was born, his only possessions a set of books that he has read over and over: the Bible, a story by Dickens ("that 'un about Christmas"), and some practical repair manuals. What follows is to some degree a sweetly comic wild-child story, involving Karl's attempt to adjust to the "big world" of laundromats, fast food, and low-budget supermarkets. During his wanderings about town, he befriends a small boy named Frank (Lucas Black), and he forms a bond with Frank's divorced mother, Linda (Natalie Canerday), and her closest friend, the gay manager of the store where she works

(John Ritter). But Linda has an alcoholic boyfriend (Dwight Yoakam) who repeatedly bullies the group; as this character becomes more violent toward Frank, Karl's history threatens to repeat itself.

The suspense in *Sling Blade* derives from our awareness of Karl's past, but the tension is intensified by Thornton's performance. Frowning, stooped, and plodding, his speech filled with grunts and nervous twitches, he seems rather like an unsentimental Forrest Gump. Unless he tells us through sudden bursts of guttural dialogue, we cannot know what he is thinking; and even after we become aware of his innate sweetness, we can never be sure what he might do if he were to become intensely disturbed. As Doyle, the vicious, self-loathing boyfriend, Yoakam is equally remarkable. A construction worker and would-be leader of a surf-rocker band, Doyle spends much of the film lounging in Linda's house, drinking beer and abusing not only Linda but also the boy, the "retard," and the "queer." He exudes a lazy, feline charm, but like most bullies he is a transparent manipulator and a bit of a coward. Karl's response to his accelerating threats is determined and almost passionless. After a touching farewell to Frank, he goes to the repair shop to fashion a "sling blade" out of a broken lawnmower. Late at night, while Frank and Linda are away, he walks to Linda's house and confronts Doyle—who, as usual, is reclining in an easy chair. The scene is played quietly, in a discreet long shot, and Doyle offers no resistance, even instructing Karl on how to dial 911 after the killing. The physical relationship between the two men— one of them standing at the left and the other seated at the lower right— reminds us of an earlier moment, when Karl pays a visit to his aging father (Robert Duvall), who sits in an easy chair and feebly, contemptuously flicks his tongue at his son. Karl says that his father is beyond execution because he is "already dead." But in slaying Doyle, Karl is obviously reaching deep into his own past. The fatal blows are simple and swift, aimed outside the frame, at a figure whose body we never see. Karl then goes into the dimly lit kitchen, where, after calling the police, he eats a few of Linda's biscuits, first smearing them with mustard.

Sling Blade is not without flaws (it makes the southern town look improbably nice and almost completely white), but it creates an unusual moral fable, rendered in an austere, sometimes amusingly digressive style. Clearly, such a film does not need to be called noir. Even so, *Sling Blade* tells an oedipal story involving murder; it deals with a character who cannot escape his past; and it uses low-key lighting to generate a gothic mood. If nothing else, it shows that familiar motifs of noir can be given new and mildly unorthodox applications. Perhaps for that reason, and

FIGURE 65. Noir as a dream: Patricia Arquette in *Lost Highway* (1997). (Museum of Modern Art Stills Archive.)

perhaps because it was something of a populist movie, it became a surprise hit. At some point, Miramax must also have recognized that an actor-director from Bill Clinton's Arkansas (with a name like "Billy Bob," no less) could be highly marketable; in any case, Thornton was suddenly transformed into a celebrity, and his screenplay won an Academy Award.

Example 3: David Lynch's *Lost Highway* (1997) makes a vivid contrast to both of the foregoing pictures and is somewhat easier to describe because its plot does not depend upon the achievement of a goal or the solution to an enigma. A thoroughgoing pastiche, this film brims with allusions to three decades of noir, which it uses to create a dream narrative. Significantly, the screenwriter is Barry Gifford, who worked on Lynch's earlier pastiche, *Wild at Heart,* and who once wrote an entertaining book about film noir, *The Devil Thumbs a Ride* (1988). Between them, Lynch and Gifford seem determined to evoke a sense of pure "noirness." Almost every image and every character in the film has an archetypal quality: a nocturnal road out of *Detour* and *Psycho;* a "Lost Highway Motel," where a woman may or may not be dead; an exploding house on stilts like the one in *Kiss Me Deadly;* an alienated jazz musician who might be a killer; a brooding rebel-without-a-cause who lusts after a gun moll; a sadistic gangster who is obsessed with porn movies and prostitutes; a woman's mutilated body, reminiscent of the Black Dahlia; and not one but two femmes fatales—the first a redhead like Gilda, the second a blond like Phyllis Dietrichson.

These allusions are treated skillfully, but they did not please American critics, who felt that *Lost Highway* was excessively dehumanized and self-reflexive. To some extent, I would agree. The film can also be criticized because it relies too much upon the nowadays predictable methods of postmodernist art and because it clearly indulges in a semipornographic, male-adolescent fantasy.[11] Even so, it seems to me an intelligent and weirdly beautiful picture that generates a powerful atmosphere of desire, terror, and dread. Throughout, Lynch's control of sound and image is worthy of his work in *Blue Velvet,* but in this case he takes greater risks with his audience, completely suspending narrative logic and never abandoning the feeling of a dream. His characters abruptly change their identities or become doubles, his plot twists back upon itself like a serpent, and his cool technique transforms familiar generic motifs into something almost musical or poetic. The total effect is closer to the avant-garde poetry of *Eraserhead* (1978) than to any of Lynch's subsequent work, and it has the audacity to run against the formally conservative grain of the contemporary art cinema.

To a certain extent, Lynch returns us to the issues in chapter 1 of this book. Whether he intended to or not, he has created something very close to the ideal film noir as the surrealist-inspired French might have imagined it in the decades after World War II. In other words, he gives us Hollywood sex and violence (suggesting far more than he shows) without the excuse of a realistic narrative; he mixes black, deadpan humor with horror; he utterly disorients his audience, never giving them an explanation for bizarre events; and he fetishizes everyday life, making a series of California living rooms and anonymous roadways seem truly uncanny. In the process, he also creates twin femmes fatales (both played by Patricia Arquette), who occasionally metamorphose into a creepy and rather androgynous male (Robert Blake). In "female" shape, this composite figure is the ultimate fetish object—a voluptuous, fleshy tease with vampire teeth, as stylized and heartless as an American automobile from the 1950s. Even when she is nude, she never removes her wigs or her six-inch heels.

No American thriller has ever gone so far to achieve the "disappearance of psychological bearings or guideposts" that Raymond Borde and

Étienne Chaumeton regard as the main objective of film noir. And yet, despite all its disquieting effects, *Lost Highway* merely takes us where we have already been. Unlike the ideal cinema of surrealist criticism (or the work of a director like Luis Buñuel), it looks backward to an imaginary past, preoccupied with pop art and the dream imagery of affluent America in the last decade of film noir. It deals impressively with primal anxieties, but it seems to have no destructive anger, no specific politics, no purpose other than regression. Both the filmmakers and the characters keep circling around the same familiar bank of images, drawn like moths to a flame. Thus, for all its horror, sexiness, and formal brilliance, *Lost Highway* ultimately resembles all the other retro noirs and nostalgia films of the late twentieth century: it remains frozen in a kind of cinématheque and is just another movie about movies.

Whatever their limitations, the films I have described are more true to their initial premises than Curtis Hanson's slickly directed adaptation of James Ellroy's *L.A. Confidential* (1997)—a big-budget, highly publicized, and critically overrated feature that begins in darkly satiric fashion and then segues into crowd-pleasing melodrama. The three policemen who function as antiheroes in this picture—a "celebrity crime-stopper" who moonlights as advisor for a TV show called *Badge of Honor*, a brooding roughneck who beats up suspects, and a gung-ho idealist who cleverly manages his career—are eventually transformed into righteous avengers, and are much more sympathetic than the equivalent characters in Ellroy's novel. In the concluding scenes, the good guys dangle the bad guys out of office buildings or mow them down with shotguns, and vigilante justice triumphs over official corruption. Hanson and co-scriptwriter Brian Hegeland even devise a happy ending in which the battle-scarred roughneck drives off into the sunset with his true love, an ex-prostitute with a heart of gold.

Unlike *Chinatown*, which it vaguely resembles, *L.A. Confidential* uses the past superficially and hypocritically. On the one hand, it attacks Hollywood of the 1950s, making easy jokes about the "reality" behind old-style show business; on the other hand, it exploits every convention of the dream factory, turning history into a fashion show and allowing good to triumph over evil. The film's primary appeal seems to be its stylish "look," and this may explain why, upon its release, the tributary media of the consumer economy—magazines, trade bookstores, radio shows, and CD recordings—were flooded with reminiscences of noir, all of them designed to profit from a trend. Even so, *L.A. Confidential* was only a modest commercial success. The man in charge of marketing the picture for Warner Brothers had a concise way of explaining why it never became a box-office bonanza: "The bulk of the audience who enjoys film noir are directors, film students, critics and the most ardent, generally upscale film enthusiast" (quoted by David Ansen, *Newsweek*, 27 October 1997). Another, equally good explanation is that *L.A. Confidential* is merely nostalgia, lacking the complex historical relevance that Roman Polanski and Robert Towne were able to achieve in the pre-blockbuster years at the end of the Vietnam War.

Questions of value aside, both *L.A. Confidential* and the intermediate-budget films noirs are deeply symptomatic of today's cinema. Art pictures like the ones I have described, some better and some worse, will continue to appear on theater screens, as will the noirish blockbusters and the hard-boiled action movies. If this diverse mixture of things does not exactly constitute a genre, it nevertheless coheres around a taste and a set of market strategies that are ongoing and relevant. It might help if I could end my survey of the late-twentieth-century mediascape with a spectacular insight into why such tastes are important—a Rosebud in the heart of the furnace, as it were, followed by a slow tilt upward to reveal the smoke of corruption in the sky. But the truth is, the history of noir is not over, and it cannot be given a single explanation. No doubt movies of the noir type have always appealed strongly—but not exclusively—to middle-class white males who project themselves into stories about loners, losers, outlaws, and flawed idealists at the margins of society. The different manifestations of noir, however, can never be completely subsumed under a single demographic group or psychological theory.

Given the current situation, debates over whether specific films are "truly" noir, or over the problem of what makes up a film genre, have become tiresome. There is, in fact, no transcendent reason why we should have a noir category at all. Whenever we list any movie under the noir rubric, we do little more than invoke a network of ideas as a makeshift organizing principle, in place of an author, a studio, a time period, or a national cinema. By such means, we can discuss an otherwise miscellaneous string of pictures, establishing similarities and differences among them. As I argue throughout this book, every category in criticism or in the film industry works in this fashion, usually in support of the critic's or the culture's particular obsessions. If we abandoned the word *noir*, we would need to find another, no less problematic, means of organizing what we see.

But I would also argue that even if noir is only a discursive construction, it has remarkable flexibility, range, and mythic force, maintaining our relation to something like an international genre. In America, the musical hardly survives except in animated cartoons, and the last important western was Clint Eastwood's distinctly noirlike *Unforgiven* in 1992. (Perhaps significantly, the urban-centered romantic comedy remains a popular form and sometimes functions like the flip side of noir.) All the while, the themes of the old thrillers—one-way streets and dead ends, mad love and bad love, double crosses and paranoid conspiracies, discontents in the nuclear family and perverse violence in every corner of the society—are as topical as ever and still productive of good films. We may feel a special melancholy when we view the seductive black-and-white films of the 1940s; such films, however, contribute to a recurring pattern of both modernity and postmodernity. The dark past keeps returning. It will do so long after this commentary has ended and the theatrical motion picture has evolved into some other medium.

Noir in the
Twenty-first Century

Legends and Lists

One purpose of this book has been to dispel certain prevailing ideas about the American film noir. Almost a decade after the book's initial publication, however, some of the ideas still circulate. Here, for example, from *The New York Times* of August 22, 2006, is the opening of Dave Kehr's review of a special DVD edition of *Double Indemnity:*

> The simplest way of describing film noir is as a collision between the visual conventions of German Expressionism and the lurid plotting of the American pulp novel. "Proto" film noirs, like Joe May's 1929 "Asphalt," filmed in the Babelsberg studios in Berlin, usually found social causes for their heroes' problems, but the American noir, derived from the pulp fiction that began to appear in the detective magazines of the 1930s, was more delirious and psychological in nature. It expanded the German notion of the "femme fatale," like Marlene Dietrich in Josef von Sternberg's more grubbily naturalistic than Expressionist "Blue Angel" (1930), into extravagant masochistic fantasies with devouring, far larger than life figures who lured men to their doom . . . much more for the pleasure of sadistic destruction than for material gain.

I've singled out Kehr because he provides a concise, straightforward statement of widely held opinions that can be found in many other places. Let me emphasize that he's a well-informed critic whose taste and intelligence I greatly respect—indeed the connection he suggests between noir and naturalism is interesting and worth pursuing.[1] I also sympathize with the problem he faces in having to define noir in fifty or a hundred words for a daily newspaper. For the most part, however, it's almost as if he were following the advice of a journalist in John Ford's *The Man Who Shot Liberty Valance:* "When the legend becomes fact, print the legend."

As we've seen in the first two chapters of this book, the first films to be called "noir" were made in France in the 1930s, not in Germany or Hollywood, and the film version of *Double Indemnity,* though partly scripted by Raymond Chandler, was derived not from pulp fiction but from a slick-paper magazine serial and best-selling novel written by a man who never published in the pulps. The "femme fatale" was memorably played in Germany by Dietrich and Louise Brooks, but she, too, gets her name from France; her most important ancestors can be found in the pornographic fantasies of the Marquis de Sade and in the novels of Emile Zola and the naturalists. It's no accident that Fritz Lang's *Scarlet Street* (1945), which features one of the most disturbing of the noir femmes fatales, is based on the work of a Zola-like French novelist, or that Lang's *Human Desire* (1954), which involves another dangerous female, is based on a well-known novel by Zola himself. Where James M. Cain is concerned, the plot of *The Postman Always Rings Twice* is lifted from Zola's *Thérèse Raquin* (1867).[2] Cain's innovation in both *Postman* and *Double Indemnity* was to abandon the heavy prose of the naturalists and to tell the story in a first-person, hard-boiled style redolent of Hemingway. In this regard he contrasts sharply with a naturalist such as Theodore Dreiser, whose *American Tragedy* also provided a source for films noirs. (The influence of Dreiser on noir persists down to the present day: Woody Allen's *Match Point* [2006], the story of a tennis pro who murders his lover in order to maintain his upper-class marriage, could be described as a fusion of *American Tragedy* with Patricia Highsmith's *The Talented Mr. Ripley.*)

Like many other critics who have written in the wake of Paul Schrader's "Notes on Film Noir," Kehr argues that the visual style of dark thrillers in the 1940s derives from German expressionism. A few of the key pictures in the category may indeed have been made with an eye on the Germans: Huston's *The Maltese Falcon,* for example, was filmed almost entirely in a studio, using visual techniques that vaguely suggest the UFA style; nevertheless, *Falcon*'s wide-angle, deep-focus photography also creates a "realistic," sharply detailed effect, quite different from German films of the Weimar period. While it's true, as has often been observed, that a number of important directors of Hollywood film noir came from Germany, the very existence of a full-scale German expressionist cinema has been questioned by some scholars. Even if it did exist, nobody has offered

convincing evidence that it was an important influence in the 1940s. Fritz
Lang denied that his work had anything to do with expressionism, and
unless we assume that shadows and staircases were invented by the Germans, Wilder's *Double Indemnity* has no specific connection to German
photography or design. In an essay that convincingly debunks all the usual
arguments about the German émigrés and film noir, Thomas Elsaesser has
reminded us that most of the Weimar directors who came to America
weren't particularly identified with thrillers or street films when they
worked in their native country; he points out, for instance, that the most
famous German film by Wilder, Siodmak, and Ulmer was *Menschen am
Sonntag,* from which, he amusingly suggests, one might deduce a German influence on Italian neorealism.[3]

A reasonably plausible case can indeed be made that the visual qualities of Wilder's first film noir were a product of his early experience as
a news reporter. In an intriguing coffee-table volume of photographs entitled *New York Noir,* Luc Sante and William Hannigan have recently
demonstrated that *Double Indemnity*'s night-for-night photography has
something in common with the nocturnal crime photos that appeared in
the *New York Daily News* and other tabloids in the period between the
1920s and 1940s.[4] Indeed the lurid, low-brow material that most interested both Wilder and James M. Cain, who had also been a reporter,
wasn't pulp fiction but tabloid journalism. Cain's novel was inspired by
one of the most sensationally publicized and photographed murder cases
of the 1920s, in which Ruth Snyder was convicted of bludgeoning, strangling, and poisoning her unwanted husband. Snyder became the first
woman to be executed in the electric chair, and as the fatal switch was
thrown, a reporter from the *Daily News* used a hidden camera strapped
to his ankle to snap her picture. The headline on the next day (Friday,
January 13, 1928) was a single word—"DEAD!"—accompanied by a
full-page, low-angle photo of the youthful Snyder in a dark, open-necked
dress, her body fastened to the chair. "This is perhaps the most remarkable exclusive picture in the history of criminology," the caption read.
"It shows the actual scene in the Sing Sing death house as the lethal current surged through Ruth Snyder's body at 11:06 last night. Her helmeted
head is stiffened in death, her face masked and an electrode strapped to
her bare right leg. The autopsy table on which her body was removed is
beside her."

In my own view, an even stronger argument can be made that the style
of classic film noir was influenced by the more generalized growth of urban street photography in the 1940s and 1950s—a period associated with

tabloids such as *PM,* with slick-paper magazines such as *Life* and *Look,* and with the photographic movement known as the "New York School." After World War II, when Hollywood began to shoot films outdoors and on location, the scenery in crime films increasingly resembled the black-and-white photos of working-class areas or densely packed commercial districts that were also being shown in newspapers, magazines, and art galleries. The most famous New York street photographer of the imme-diate postwar years was Arthur Felig, better known as "Weegee," whose best-selling book of gritty images, *Naked City,* inspired Jules Dassin's 1948 crime film, *The Naked City.* Weegee was hired as a visual consult-ant on the Dassin picture and subsequently on Robert Wise's noir box-ing film, *The Set-Up,* in which he makes a cameo appearance.[5] Holly-wood also borrowed from the city pictures of the European surrealists and the imagery of metropolitan architecture that extends back at least as far as Alfred Steiglitz. Although New York was a favored location for such images, it was by no means the only iconic noir city; Robert Siod-mak's *Criss Cross,* Rudolph Mate's *D.O.A.,* and Robert Aldrich's *Kiss Me Deadly* made especially good use of downtown Los Angeles, and Phil Karlson's *Kansas City Confidential* and *Phenix City Story* gave raw atmo-sphere to smaller, less familiar locations. Perhaps the most obvious con-nection between still photography and noir, however, was former *Look* magazine photographer Stanley Kubrick's *Killer's Kiss,* which provides a kind of survey of visual subjects associated with New York—people on the subway, nighttime crowds in Times Square, grubby boxing gyms, street vendors, silhouetted skyscrapers, the façade of a sleazy dance hall, the interior of Pennsylvania Station at dawn, and so forth. Far more than studio expressionism, this was the style that came to suggest "noirness."

As Kehr points out, the initial cycle of Hollywood films noirs often involved sadomasochistic stories about femmes fatales (or, as in *Shadow of a Doubt* and *The Third Man,* hommes fatals). Nevertheless, we should keep in mind that almost two-thirds of the films usually described as noir have nothing to do with fatal women. The list includes such different pictures as *Laura* (despite the fact that Dana Andrews is haunted by Gene Tierney's portrait), *The Big Sleep* (despite the presence of a few bad girls), *This Gun for Hire, The Glass Key, Crossfire, The Big Clock, Kiss of Death, The Set-Up, The Window, The Asphalt Jungle, Union Station, Night and the City, In a Lonely Place, Pickup on South Street, His Kind of Woman, Odds against Tomorrow,* and *The Sweet Smell of Success.* Several of these films deal with "perverse" or neurotic sexuality, but as I've argued in chapter 3, an equal number are as much if not more concerned with so-

cial issues. There are many themes, moods, characters, locales, and stylistic features associated with noir, no one of which is shared by all the
films that have been placed in the category. Moreover, as I've previously
noted, many stylistic qualities usually described as noir can be found in
films that don't belong to the category. Consider David Lean's *Brief Encounter* (1945), the poignant story of an unfulfilled, potentially adulter-
ous romance between two "ordinary" married people, which is told in
flashback using a great deal of offscreen narration and virtually every
nocturnal setting and "expressionist" technique known to black-and-
white movies: wet city streets, dramatic staircases, elegant restaurants,
shabby pubs, dark train stations, tilted camera angles, moody shadows,
dreamlike lighting effects, and so forth.

   All this is not intended as a scandalous revelation, nor as an argument
that there is no such thing as noir; obviously, there are many filmmakers, critics, and audiences that recognize a film noir when they see one.
I'm merely attempting to acknowledge the complex structure of art styles
in general, which are always discursively constructed and inevitably
branch out in different directions, taking on a variety of filiations according to the characteristics we choose to emphasize or ignore. What
is true of culture is also true of science. In *The Order of Things,* Michel
Foucault, whom I've earlier quoted in a slightly different context, is especially interesting on the subject of biological classification systems and
their attempt to "tame the wild profusion of existing things."[6] The classical field of natural history, Foucault argues, was "nothing more than
the nomination of the visible" and was able to name and pigeonhole the
various elements of the biological world only by excluding certain bits
of information and making sure that "everything that presents itself to
our gaze is not utilizable" (133). The very category of "natural life," he
points out, is "relative, like all the other categories, to the criteria one
adopts. And also, like them, subject to certain imprecisions as soon as
the question of deciding its frontiers arises" (161). When the dimension
of time or history is added to the dimension of spatial or tabular arrangements, the problem is exacerbated. Most writing about classification,
Foucault contends, is "utopian" in its desire to maintain orderly similarities and differences and is always threatened by a "heterotopia" of
data that undercuts orderly language, "not only the syntax with which
we construct sentences but also that less apparent syntax which causes
words and things (next to and also opposite one another) to 'hold together'" (xviii).

   I'm not so much a relativist as Foucault (if he is a relativist), but in recognition of the inherent instability of generic classifications I've tried to avoid excessively neat definitions of *film noir*. I've also deliberately pushed against the frontiers of the term, discussing a few pictures that my readers may feel aren't noir at all. (I often wonder if I should have included *Sling Blade*.) I've done so in part because writings on noir seem to me to derive part of their fascination from their tendency to define the form ostensively, by simply listing or pointing to different films. The best way to define film noir, Peter Wollen once remarked to me, is to say that it's any film listed in Borde and Chaumeton's *A Panorama of American Film Noir*. Indeed, the device of the list, which is important for cinephiles everywhere and especially for the French in the 1950s, is crucial to that seminal book. Fortunately, *A Panorama* has at last been translated into English by Paul Hammond, and more of us now have access to its 1954 appendix, which contains Borde and Chaumeton's chronological enumeration, confined to "major titles–post 1940,"of eighty films grouped into six subcategories, which they describe as an "index of the main series."[7] Here are the six categories and a few of the titles:

1. "Film noirs," including *The Maltese Falcon, Journey into Fear, Phantom Lady, The Mask of Dimitrios, Gilda, Out of the Past, Sorry, Wrong Number,* and *The Window*
2. "Criminal psychology," including *Rebecca, King's Row, Double Indemnity, Under Capricorn, Gun Crazy,* and *House of Strangers*
3. "Crime films in period costume," including *Dr. Jekyll and Mr. Hyde* (1941), *Gaslight,* and *Ivy*
4. "Gangsters," including *The Killers, White Heat, The Asphalt Jungle, The Enforcer,* and *The Big Heat*
5. "Police documentaries," including *Kiss of Death, Crossfire, Where the Sidewalk Ends,* and *Panic in the Streets*
6. "Social tendencies," including *The Lost Weekend, Crossfire, Thieves' Highway, The Set-Up, The Big Carnival, The Enforcer, The Big Heat,* and *The Wild One*.

In some ways this listing is puzzling. Do the films that are not grouped under "Film noirs" occupy a space outside the central category? If so, then Borde and Chaumeton must feel that the Warner adaptation of Eric Ambler's *A Coffin for Dimitrios* is somehow more noirlike than the Paramount adaptation of Cain's *Double Indemnity*. There are also some odd or at least unexpected titles: *King's Row? The Wild One?* Why are *Double Indemnity* and *Gun Crazy* listed under "Criminal psychology" while

Gilda is listed under "Film noirs"? The problem of how to manage the groupings is indicated by the fact that three titles—*Crossfire, The Enforcer* and *The Big Heat*—appear twice, each time under a difference rubric. Despite these problems, however, there remains a certain coherence and imaginative power in the list as a whole, suggesting currents of eroticized violence, instrumental surveillance, and social and psychological malaise running through some of the best American films of the 1940s and 1950s. (It's remarkable how few of the films originally listed in *A Panorama* are still regarded as core examples of the form. In 2006, Wikipedia listed thirty-five "film noirs of the classic period"—twenty from the 1940s and the rest from the 1950s. The list, derived from films noirs that had received the highest ratings by users of the Internet Movie Database, makes for instructive comparison with Borde and Chaumeton.[8])

Although Borde and Chaumeton treat noir as an American phenomenon, one of their chapters deals with French crime movies made in imitation of Hollywood. They grumble about the 1950s vogue for thrillers starring Eddie Constantine as superheroic private eye Lemmy Caution (Godard later used Constantine in *Alphaville* [1965], thereby commenting on the Americanization of French culture), and they describe most of the recent spate of French tough-guy pictures as "caricatures" of noir manufactured by producers who "work with film the way some women work the streets" (130). Among the Paris-produced films they strongly admire are *Du rififi chez les hommes* (1954, directed by American expatriate Jules Dassin), *Les diaboliques* (1954, Henri-Georges Clouzot), and *Razzia sur la chnouf* (1955, Henri Decoin). In its totality, however, their book ranges more widely both within and without Hollywood than this chapter or the 1954 appendix might suggest. For the American edition, Paul Hammond provides a useful filmography of every film Borde and Chaumeton mention, which gives a better idea of the taste that guides their project; the filmography reaches back to the 1930s and extends forward to the last edition of *A Panorama* in the 1970s, including not only a large number of American films noirs but also a miscellany of somewhat distantly related, more or less "dark," pictures of various genres (*They Gave Him a Gun* [1937], *Blind Alley* [1939], *Cobra Woman* [1944], *Colorado Territory* [1949], *The Thing* [1951], *Beat the Devil* [1953]). In addition, it lists many titles from other nations (*Die Dreigroshenoper* [Germany, 1931], *The Thirty-Nine Steps* [UK, 1935], *La bête humaine* [France, 1938], *Bila Tma* [Czechoslovakia, 1948], *The Blue Lamp* [UK, 1950], *Los olvidados* [Mexico, 1950]).

Writings on noir after Borde and Chaumeton have increasingly crossed generic lines, national boundaries, and historical periods, confirming Mark Vernet's often-quoted remark that noir is a "collector's cinema," one of the charms of which is that "there is always an unknown film to be added to the list" (Copjec, 26). Most historians seem to enjoy recruiting titles at the outer edges of the concept. One of the most impressive and consistently intelligent examples of this tendency in recent years was a 2005 film exhibition entitled "You Can't Win," at the Vienna Filmmuseum in Austria. Curated by Alexander Horvath and extending over two months, the exhibition gathered together nearly all the canonical examples of American film noir plus several of its close cousins (*M, The Blue Angel, Citizen Kane*) and lesser known European ancestors. Among the films in the latter group were Anthony Asquith's *A Cottage on Dartmoor* (1930), which rivals Hitchcock's *Blackmail* for cinematic inventiveness, psychological ambiguity, and eroticized violence; Robert Siodmak's *Pièges* (1939), which deals with an attempt to trap a serial killer in Paris;[9] Pierre Chenal's *Le dernier tournant* (1939), which is the first film adaptation of *The Postman Always Rings Twice*; and Franz Schnyder's *Wilder Urlaub* (1943), which is a Swiss production concerning a deserter from the German army. The series also presented important non-Hollywood noirs from the peak years of the form: Alberto Cavalcanti's *They Made Me a Fugitive* (1947), Henri-Georges Clouzot's *Quai des Orfèvres* (1947), and Peter Lorre's impressive and only film as director, *Der Verlorene* (1951).

Given world enough and time, the Vienna exhibition could have ranged even more broadly. As I've indicated previously, films we can describe as noir have never been confined to America and can be found in most national film industries. (Exceptions to the rule, though someone will surely prove me wrong, are Nazi Germany, the Soviet Union, and China in the period of socialist realism.) Recent examples from Latin America include the late Argentine director Fabian Bielinsky's *Nine Queens* (2000), a darkly witty story of a con man and his pupil (remade in the United States as *Criminal* [2004]), and *Aura* (2006), a heist movie involving a meek taxidermist; Brazilian director Nelson Pereira dos Santos's *Brasilia 18%* (2006), which concerns crime and political corruption in high places; and Thai director Sananjit Bangsapan's *Hit Man File* (2005), a somber yet sensual action movie about an ex-revolutionary soldier turned contract killer. From France, there is Benoît Jacquot's *A tout de suite* (2006), another in the long tradition of love-on-the-run movies. One of the best examples from Norway is Erik Skjoldbjærg's *Insomnia* (1997), a psychological study of a guilty detective, which in 2003

was transformed by Christopher Nolan into a much less eerie and ambiguous Hollywood remake. In a fine monograph, Adun Englestad has
shown how the Skjoldbjærg version uses the uncanny daylight of a Nordic
summer to create a twist on the usual noir atmosphere, meanwhile de-
constructing the detective's search for a killer in even more radical fashion than Arthur Penn's *Night Moves* (1975); Englestad also reveals a long
history of Norwegian film noir, dating back to 1937 and involving at
least fourteen significant pictures.[10]

FURTHER RESEARCH

At almost the same moment that this book was originally published, Rick
Altman and Steve Neale authored separate studies of film genre, both of
which make points similar to my own about the discursive nature of
generic categories.[11] In the years following, a good many new scholarly
writings on noir have also been published, to the point where we can speak
of an academic industry devoted to the subject. Among the recent books
are several anthologies of essays by various hands, including Mark T. Conrad's *The Philosophy of Film Noir* and three additional volumes of Silver and Ursini's extremely useful *Film Noir Reader*. Individually authored
volumes include Jans B. Wager's *Dames in the Driver's Seat,* which deals
with gender and racial issues; Sheri Chinen Biesen's *Blackout,* which examines the Hollywood industry during World War II; John T. Irwin's *Unless the Threat of Death Is Behind Them,* which offers a critical analysis
of hard-boiled novels and films; and, most intellectually sophisticated
and ambitious of all, Paula Rabinowitz's *Black and White and Noir,*
which describes a "pulp politics" running through the culture of twentieth-
century America and expressing itself in every possible medium. To these
volumes one might add Alexander Nemerov's more specialized *Icons of
Grief: Val Lewton's Home Front Pictures,* an intriguing study of the most
respected producer of B pictures in the era of historical film noir.[12]

A number of important journal articles have also appeared. Of special note where my own research is concerned are two items: First, David
Andrews's "Sex Is Dangerous, so Satisfy Your Wife: The Softcore Thriller
in Its Contexts," which provides a scrupulously documented history of
the nontheatrical, erotic thrillers briefly discussed in chapter 4 of this
book. Andrews's paper nicely complements Linda Ruth Williams's book-
length study of such films, demonstrating how the direct-to-video industry
has responded to cultural change, growing more "feminized, pornographic, and consumerist" while also becoming cheaper to produce and

less like the theatrical films noirs of the 1940s and the neo-noirs of the
1980s and 1990s.[13] Second, Vivian Sobchack's "Chasing the Maltese Falcon: On the Fabrications of a Film Prop," tells the engrossing story of a
bevy of "original" falcons that have become collector's items.[14] Sobchack
reveals that Ara Chekmayan's flea-market discovery of the black bird,
which I've described in chapter 7, ultimately became a prosperous find:
his rara avis was "authenticated" by Profiles in History, a dealer in mem-
orabilia, and was sold at auction in March 2000 for $92,000. Sobchack
also notes several other profitable falcons: Dr. Gary Milan, a Los Angeles dentist, purchased a copy of the bird from the former head of the
Warner Property Department for $70,000 and has loaned it to various
exhibition spaces, among them the Pompidou Center in Paris, MoMA
in New York, and the Turner Classic Movies retail store in Los Angeles.
Another copy, given by Jack Warner to actor-producer William Conrad
and presumably bearing the knife cuts made by Sydney Greenstreet during the scene when he discovers the statuette is made of lead, was sold
to jeweler Ronald Winston in 1994 for the record price of $398,000.
(For other fabulous and amusing details, I refer readers to Sobchack's
lengthy account.)[15]

During the past decade a number of historians have produced especially significant work dealing with the cinematic representation of
cities—an issue at which this book only glances but one that has obvious relevance for the history of film noir. Edward Dimendberg's *Film Noir
and the Spaces of Modernity*, referred to in chapter 5, is now available,
and we have the benefit of its wide-ranging discussion of the "built environment" in crime films, showing how old movies preserve images of
subsequently destroyed public spaces and how films are affected by the
historical shift from "centripetal" to "centrifugal" cityscapes.[16] Other
discussions of the topic have tended to focus on the movie capitol itself.
For instance, in the context of a wide-ranging study of Hollywood's imaginary treatment of Los Angeles, Robert Carringer has interesting things
to say about *Point Blank*, a key instance of what he describes as a "pathological" form of movie cityscape, which uses an even larger number of
Los Angeles locales than *Kiss Me Deadly*. Director John Boorman gives
us color, wide-screen views of the Santa Monica beaches, the Hollywood
boulevards, the downtown high-rises, the Forest Lawn cemetery, and numerous other exterior and interior spaces, all of them chosen to create
an Antonioni-like sense of emptiness and alienation. " 'I wanted my setting to be hard, cold and in a sense, futuristic,'" Boorman remarked when
the film was made. " 'I wanted an empty, sterile world, for which Los

Angeles was absolutely right.'"[17] One of the most impressive sequences
is photographed in the concrete channel that was built along the bed of
the Los Angeles River in the 1930s. For most of the year only a rivulet
of water runs through the eight-mile-long, hundred-yard-wide structure,
giving an opportunity for movie crews to stage spectacular car-chase sequences; as Carringer points out, however, Boorman and his editor use
the weird emptiness of the concrete basin to create a Hitchcock-style set
piece involving three characters on foot: the revenge-seeking protagonist, a gangster, and a concealed hit man with a rifle. Carringer nicely
describes the emotional dynamics of the sequence: "By alternating between distant views from outside the riverbed that shrink the figures in
relation to their surroundings, and eye-level views from below that
heighten the sense of enclosure, Boorman invests the space with not one
but two pathologies, agoraphobia and claustrophobia" (260).

According to writer and filmmaker Thom Andersen, "People who hate
Los Angeles love *Point Blank.*" Speaking as a midwesterner who has lived
only briefly in Los Angeles, I love both the city and Boorman's film. On
the other hand I also love Andersen's *Los Angeles Plays Itself* (2003),
from which the above quote is taken. This 169-minute video documentary, made up chiefly of clips from more than two hundred films of every
imaginable genre and level of production, is one of the most effective
video essays ever produced, giving the sometimes opinionated Andersen
an opportunity to explore in fascinating detail the various ways his native city has been pictured by both Hollywood and independent directors. Like André Bazin, Andersen believes that cinema should manipu-
late time and space as little as possible; he dislikes films that play editing
tricks with geography or that use Los Angeles to represent Chicago, New
York, or simply an anonymous urban space. (A film he admires is *Kiss
Me Deadly*, which has a somewhat neorealist style.) Nevertheless, he
shows how all types of movies have unintentionally documented major
changes in the city simply by virtue of photographing them. The demolition of Bunker Hill, a prominent setting in such films noirs as *Criss Cross*
and *Kiss Me Deadly*, destroyed what once was a vibrant working-class
neighborhood and transformed it into downtown canyons of office buildings and condominiums more suitable for later movies about futuristic
dystopias. Angel's Flight, the trolley that once ran up Bunker Hill, has
been moved to another location nearby and serves as a quaint curiosity
for tourists. Elsewhere, architectural landmarks such as the Pan Pacific
Auditorium and the Ambassador Hotel are preserved only in old movie
footage. (In 2002, prior to its demolition, the Ambassador became the

subject of a remarkable experimental film by Pat O'Neill—*The Decay of Fiction,* in which ghostly figures from films noirs, shot in black and white and double-exposed against color footage of empty corridors and rooms, seem to haunt the hotel.)

Andersen repeatedly insists on the importance of being true to the city's ethnic complexity and turbulent political history. One of his many insights is that films noirs or related movies have "almost systematically denigrated" the great examples of modernist architecture in Los Angeles by associating them with sleazy crooks or the corrupt rich. In *L.A. Confidential,* the celebrated Lovell House, built in 1928, becomes the home of a pornographer—this despite the fact that architect Richard Neutra, who designed the house, was a progressive and the house was used as a center for left political activity in the 1930s. In *The Big Lebowski* (1998), the John Lautner House, atop Benedict Canyon, dating from 1972, also becomes the home of a pornographer; and in *Lethal Weapon,* Mel Gibson gleefully destroys Lautner's Chemosphere House, constructed in 1960, which the movie turns into a hangout for South African gangsters. Frank Lloyd Wright's 1924 Ennis House has been used more often than any of the modernist structures; transplanted by the movies to different nations, cities, and time periods, it nearly always provides a setting for decadence or evil, as in *Blade Runner.*

At one point Andersen identifies a subgenre of paranoid, socially critical, but also cynical films about the "secret history" of Los Angeles that began to appear in the wake of the Watts riots. The most notable of these are *Chinatown* and *Who Framed Roger Rabbit?,* both of which, Andersen points out, alter or distort the city's history for dramatic purposes, effectively projecting present-day disillusionment onto the past and helping to create urban legends. More recent examples, released after Andersen's documentary, are Brian De Palma's *The Black Dahlia* (2006), based on James Ellroy's novel about the sadistic 1947 murder of Elizabeth Short, and Allen Coulter's *Hollywoodland* (2006), from a script by Paul Bernbaum about the apparent suicide in 1959 of TV actor George Reeves. The latter film is by far the more interesting, in part because it never really uncovers a secret conspiracy. Its center of consciousness is Louis Simo (played by the slightly miscast Adrian Brody), a disgraced former policeman with a broken marriage who operates a private detective agency out of his tiny apartment. One of his former colleagues on the police force sneers at this new job and jokes that the world doesn't need "another Ralph Meeker." Hired by Reeves's mother, Simo opportunistically seizes on the case, drumming up sensational newspaper publicity to embarrass the LAPD. As his investigation proceeds, he suffers the usual threats and a bloody beating, but he also tries to repair his relationship with his troubled son and overcome various addictions. Meanwhile, a series of flashbacks tells the sad story of how Reeves (Ben Affleck) tried to establish an acting career. His life in Hollywood began with a bit part in *Gone with the Wind,* led up to a starring role as Superman in a cheesy but successful TV series, and ended in failure and violent death. Was he shot through the head by a hired minion of his jilted lover, Toni Mannix (Diane Lane)? By a minion of her ruthless husband, the legendary MGM executive and "enforcer" Eddie Mannix (Bob Hoskins)? By the gimlet-eyed and apparently greedy young woman who had replaced Toni Mannix in Superman's bed (Robin Tunney)? Or did he commit suicide, as the police ruled?

Hollywoodland has a *Rashomon*-like narrative that keeps all the possible solutions in play, allowing Simo to imagine four different scenarios for Reeves's death. But the most likely conclusion to be drawn from the evidence and from Simo's last vision of the shooting is that the public story was true after all—the death was a suicide. Ultimately, the film is less about scandal, corruption, and the exposure of a secret history than about the shadiness, desperation, and loneliness in ordinary lives. Reeves emerges as a would-be leading man who suffers a series of awful indignities: he becomes the kept lover of an older woman, an actor in a padded Superman suit, and a former comic-book hero who is laughed at when the audience spots him in a brief role in *From Here to Eternity.* When we last see him, he is making "celebrity" appearances alongside Lash LaRue at kid shows and auditioning in a home movie for a job on the wrestling circuit. Although the film as a whole has a stylish, sinister atmosphere, its approach to this story is morally realistic: Reeves and nearly all the other characters (exceptions include Reeves's mother and one of Simo's deranged clients) are flawed, pitiable, but sometimes likable people whose lives are in disarray. There are almost no pure villains or victims, and nearly everybody is treated with compassion—all of which makes *Hollywoodland* a fairly unusual film noir.

MORE STYLES OF NOIR

Although the digital revolution has led some writers to proclaim the death of cinema, the movies, much like God and the novel, haven't disappeared. I've argued elsewhere that the replacement of celluloid with digital images is no threat to the aesthetics of motion pictures and that we needn't fear that an art form is vanishing;[18] nevertheless, the immense growth of home entertainment and digital technology (including such things as Avid editing equipment, high-definition video, and CGI) has affected the style of film noir and all other types of movies in ways beyond the matters discussed in chapter 5. The conjunction of digital editing systems with television-style shooting techniques, in which scenes are photographed with multiple cameras and long lenses, has created a tendency toward what David Bordwell calls "intensified" continuity editing, especially in large-budget Hollywood features. "Continuity cutting," Bordwell observes, "has been rescaled and amped up, and the drama has been squeezed down to faces—particularly eyes and mouths."[19] Big-budget movie directors strive for close-up "coverage" of each nuance in a scene, using multiple cameras and small wireless microphones attached to the bodies of actors. As a result space is flattened, backgrounds are blurred, and the average shot length has been shortened—most images are held on the screen for somewhere between two and eight seconds. Examples abound in recent, vaguely noirlike thrillers. As two instances see Tony Scott's *Man on Fire* (2004) and *Domino* (2005), in which every blink of an eye, every swig of booze, and every gunshot is given a massive close-up.[20]

In addition to accelerated cutting and tight framing of details, most contemporary films employ spectacular camera movements. At the opening of *Hollywoodland,* for example, the camera seems to spiral slowly down from the clouds over Los Angeles and zero in on a crime scene on a residential street. This sort of reframing would have been impossible before computer animation, but the shot also involves footage photographed by a Steadicam—a camera mount that has changed the quality of all types of traveling shots, creating a rapid sailing or floating of movements over long distances and facilitating "walk and talk" scenes or shots that involve dynamic 360-degree turns around a figure. Some movies playfully flaunt the combination of Steadicam movements and digital visual effects. Early in Matthew Vaughn's black-comic thriller, *Layer Cake* (2005), the protagonist (Daniel Craig) walks into a drugstore and fantasizes about the day when his criminal vocation will become legitimate. "One day," his offscreen voice says, "all this drug money business will be legal." The camera glides past store shelves filled with trendy-looking bottles of ecstasy and cocaine, all of them labeled "fcuk" and inscribed with advertising slogans ("Feel the Love" and "Intensify your Life"). We see Craig walking 180 degrees around the store, and as he moves the bottles behind him begin to morph into ordinary products such as mouthwash or aspirin. The pace of the transformation gradually increases until it gets ahead of him just at the moment when he picks an item off a shelf and hands it to a druggist behind a counter.

On the other hand, some digital effects are completely undetectable. The photographic print of *Layer Cake,* for example, was subjected to a Digital Intermediate (DI) process that subtly polishes the look of the images, manipulating color tones and facial details. This and similar processes are increasingly employed by Hollywood to give a glossy look to every sort of production. Meanwhile, certain pictures shot on digital video have become virtually indistinguishable from traditional photography. A particularly interesting case in point is Michael Mann's *Collateral* (2004), 80 percent of which was shot on high-definition video, blending Panavision with HD24P Widescreen. The film's story takes place on a single evening in Los Angeles, between late afternoon and sunrise, when a cabdriver named Max (Jamie Foxx) inadvertently picks up a hit man named Vincent (Tom Cruise) and is forced to chauffer him to a series of killings. Most of the action is staged in the flat basin between Pico Rivera and Hollywood, where the neighborhoods, freeways, and downtown skyscrapers look weirdly beautiful. Unfortunately, the plot is often weakly motivated, and at the climax Vincent turns into a super villain more appropriate for a horror movie like *Halloween* or a science-fiction picture like *The Terminator.* Where the film succeeds is in the tense performances of Foxx and Cruise as a pair of quasi-Hawksian professionals who almost bond with one another and in the unusually impressive color HD video images of the city.

In the wake of *Los Angeles Plays Itself,* Thom Andersen wrote a mixed review of *Collateral,* generally praising its nocturnal imagery and its use of various ethnic areas of the city that seldom appear in Hollywood movies.[21] During an early scene at a Latino gas station painted with a vivid mural, Max speaks Spanish, and in other scenes we visit a black jazz bar in Leimert Park, a Latin dance club in Pico Rivera, and a Korean disco in Koreatown. "Whenever I'm here," Vincent says to Max, "I can't wait to leave. Too sprawled out and disconnected." But the film belies this statement. The numerous helicopter shots give the Los Angeles freeways spectacular form, and the ever-present, changing views outside the cab windows create a sense of automotive *flanerie* similar to the one I've already noted in the novels of Raymond Chandler. Eventually, affinities and significant coincidences begin to emerge from apparent disconnectedness. Vincent, a lone wolf who occasionally reveals a sense of embittered and even fearful isolation, develops an attachment to Max

FIGURE 66. Tom Cruise and Jamie Foxx in *Collateral* (2004).

on the grounds of their mutual pride in their work. We learn something about both men's histories, and one of Max's passengers (played by Jada Pinkett Smith) turns out to be one of Vincent's targets. Early on, Vincent says that he's heard about someone who died of a heart attack on the Los Angeles subway and sat on the train for six hours before anyone noticed "his corpse doing laps" around the city (a story usually associated with New York). At the end Max watches Vincent collapse into a seat on the Blue Line train and die.

One of the cinema's great colorists, Mann seems acutely sensitive to the palette of the film. He repaints the Los Angeles taxis a lipstick orange, and in an early sequence inside a taxi terminal he shows everything in telephoto close-ups that flatten space and create a nearly abstract pattern of red-oranges, yellows, and browns. (This color scheme contrasts with the first sequence of the film, also shot in telephoto, showing Max arriving at LAX, where everything is in shades of gray.) As the sequence develops, we see tightly framed close-ups of Max preparing for work like a pilot getting ready for takeoff—cleaning the interior of the cab, checking the signal lights, and attaching an azure and green picture-postcard of a Pacific island to the sun visor. When Max exits the terminal, we're given the first wide shot: a telephoto image of the cab silhouetted against a sunlit mural on a wall across the street, so that it seems to be driving into the flat surface of a California landscape painting. Then we cut to an exhilarating helicopter shot of the sparkling clean taxi cruising swiftly along a nearly empty freeway in the bright, late-afternoon sun to the sound of music from its radio. The feeling of driving as adventure—utterly different from Travis Bickel moving through a New York waste-land in *Taxi Driver*—is enhanced by subtle variations of light and color. A good many of the shots from inside the cab give us deep views out the windows (it's impossible to tell which of these shots were special effects), and we become aware of how the artificial light of the city affects the night sky. In production notes for the film, Mann noted that "there is a unique mood to the skies above LA at two or three a.m. Streetlights reflect off the clouds. Even in darkness you can see into the distance" (quoted in Andersen, "Collateral Damage"). The film sometimes uses this phe-nomenon to create surreal effects—as when Vincent watches a coyote from the Hollywood hills crossing an empty, well-lit thoroughfare—or it exploits background scenery for expressionistic purposes. When Vin-cent tells Max about his tough childhood in Gary, Indiana, the cab moves alongside a series of oil refineries and highway lamps that suffuse the black sky with an orange glow; and when Vincent dies, we glimpse the first tinges of dark-blue daylight and the lonely silhouette of a passing tree through the train window beyond his head.

At an opposite extreme from *Collateral* are pictures that depend al-most entirely on computer animation. Partly because of the ubiquity and cost-saving utility of this sort of technology, and partly because most of today's Hollywood movies are aimed at adolescent audiences, the in-dustry as a whole increasingly tends toward the condition of animated film. Noirlike conventions have infiltrated the steady stream of comic-book movies, as one can see in Christopher Nolan's contribution to the *Batman* franchise, and in other cases digital animators have used the new technology to evoke the black-and-white, boldly graphic visual ef-fects associated with older films noirs. Christian Volckman's *Renaissance* (2006), which concerns a tough cop's search for a missing woman in a Paris of the future, was shot using actors in motion-capture suits; the result is a postmodern distillation of an older photographic style—an eerie world of faceless, deep-black "noirness." A more effective exper-iment, however, is Robert Rodriguez and Frank Miller's *Sin City* (2005), which involves a large cast of well-known Hollywood actors (Jessica Alba, Benicio Del Toro, Brittany Murphy, Clive Owen, Mickey Rourke, Bruce Willis, Elijah Wood) playing live-action scenes against animated backgrounds. In interviews for the DVD edition, Rodriguez explained that he wasn't attempting to turn Miller's "graphic novel" into a purely cinematic experience; instead, he tried to give a motion picture the attri-butes of a graphic novel, treating its action as a series of "snapshots" akin to the stylized panels in a comic book. To achieve this effect, the actors performed nearly all their scenes in front of green screens and during postproduction a small army of digital technicians—compositors, matte painters, 3-D and 2-D animators, rotoscope specialists, and so forth—created a surrounding world based on Miller's India-ink drawings.

The resulting film looks like a storyboard come to life. *Sin City* is shot in silky black and white with occasional bits of computer-generated color to highlight fetish points: the flash of a gun, the paint-job of a car, and above all the alluring attributes of beautiful women—their dresses, hair, flesh, eyes, and lips. As in Miller's series of graphic novels, the narrative creates a kind of mythical universe, similar in form to a video game or a Tolkien saga, in which multiple characters, each on their own deadly mission, intersect with one another in a fantastic space. The settings include the countryside lair of a villain and a series of iconic noir locales—penthouses, barrooms, prisons, back alleys, and low-rent hotels or apartments, all of them exaggerated in the manner of comic-strip fantasy. It's always night in Sin City, and it's usually raining or snowing. Wind caresses the women's long hair and billows the tails of the men's open trench coats, making them look like capes. The heroes are square-jawed, unshaved super-avengers who do battle with crooked cops, perverted priests, corrupt politicians, and a cannibal pedophile who knows kung fu. The women are uniformly voluptuous, garbed in spike heels, leather dominatrix outfits, cowboy chaps, fishnet stockings, and at one point simply a thong. Sexual activity is limited to a few kisses, but violence is everywhere, often characterized by zany, grotesquely amusing Grand Guignol. One of the bad guys keeps on speaking after having his head stuffed into an unflushed toilet, his hand chopped off, his forehead pierced, and his neck sliced into a virtual PEZ dispenser. One of the sympathetic antiheroes is killed only after he has been hit in the head with a sledge hammer, systematically beaten with baseball bats, shot with an AK-47, and given two massive jolts in the electric chair.

The film's language is sometimes evocative of classic noir. Every episode has a first-person, offscreen narrator who speaks sub-Chandleresque "poetry" and makes wisecracks in a whiskey-soaked voice. ("She shivers in the wind like the last leaf of a dying tree," one narrator muses; another remarks that contemporary automobiles "all look like electric shavers.") On the purely visual plane, however, *Sin City* is chiefly concerned with women. Each episode is filled with female eye candy for male viewers, but nearly all the interlocking stories involve tough-guy Galahads who try to protect innocent little girls or curvy beauties from

FIGURE 67. Graphic designs in *Sin City* (2005).

sadistic, almost supernatural, male predators. There are no femmes fatales (unless one counts a band of sympathetic female prostitutes who are armed to the teeth) but a fairly traditional misogynistic fantasy becomes apparent in two brief episodes that frame the central action. In both, a boyish hit man (Josh Hartnett) exterminates women, and his first job recalls a famous scene in *Double Indemnity:* he embraces his lovely target and shoots her as they kiss.

Like many other movies that rely on pop-culture pastiche, *Sin City* is ultimately made from a crazy-quilt of genres or sources. Sometimes it resembles a Mickey Spillane novel on steroids, at other times a particularly dark Chuck Jones cartoon. Perhaps because Quentin Tarantino served as "guest director" for one of the episodes, the action is infiltrated with touches from Hong Kong action movies and Japanese martial-arts adventures. Even so, the film as a whole has an imaginative unity that derives from Miller and probably can't be imitated successfully except by its original creators. Never less than visually fascinating, it often plays with a kind of iconographic discontinuity, reversing the values of black and white and allowing one of the "panels" in a sequence to become an almost abstract pen-and-ink design, as when two lovers in a wide shot become white silhouettes against a black background. Like Miller's comic, it also ventures into wildly expressionistic territory, allowing ceilings to become impossibly high, shadows to become impossibly elon-

FIGURE 68. Graphic designs in *Sin City* (2005).

gated, and realistic images to morph into dream symbols. The action often has a strangely suspended quality, less like slow motion than like a dynamic version of the old trick in which the actor stands still while the stage scenery moves. Thus when Mickey Rourke holds a villain outside a car window and drags him along the street, the car seems to remain in one spot while the world around it trundles past; and when Clive Owen jumps down an extremely long storm drain, his body hangs motionless at the exact center of the frame for the entire drop. Watching the film isn't at all like reading a comic book, but the addition of actors, sound, and movement seems to fulfill the potential of Miller's protocinematic drawings, creating a powerful synthesis of movies and motionless graphic compositions.

NOIR NEVER DIES

"Americans do not like dark," the chairman of CBS television announced in 2005. "I understand why creative people like dark," he went on, "but American audiences don't like dark. . . . They like strength, not weakness, a chance to work out any dilemma. This is a country built on optimism."[22] There may be truth in these maxims; mass entertainment in general has always been optimistic, and at the beginning of the twenty-first century CBS became the most-watched TV network in America on the strength of shows like *CSI* and *Survivor.* Relatively few Hollywood films described as either noir or neo-noir are truly bleak and depressing, but they've seldom produced mammoth profits. In 2006, NBC-TV cancelled a noirlike series entitled *Smith,* which concerned a career thief preparing for one last crime before his retirement, on the grounds that early episodes of the show attracted only about ten million viewers instead of fifteen or twenty. Mainstream television, like Hollywood movies, is no longer content with modest or reasonable success. Even so, there remains a substantial audience for cynical, sometimes darkly humorous entertainment leavened with a kind of glamour—as can be seen from *The Sopranos* on cable TV and Martin Scorsese's *The Departed* (2006) at the movies, neither of which can be classed as a niche production.

I've argued that noir has always been something of an in-between category, a form of popular entertainment that shades over into the art cinema and the darker forms of modernism or postmodernism. The implicit values supported by the discourse on noir are in many ways opposed to the values associated with the American heartland, and the classical or historical films noirs often had links to elite European culture and to the sort of writers who worked in opposition to genteel and slick-paper fiction. Noir tends to be about losers and has never been accused of promoting moral uplift or the American dream. It certainly isn't a proletarian art, but its protagonists are very often social outsiders or criminals. Now and then it deliberately seems to affront the hicks and the squares, as in the last scene of *Kiss Kiss, Bang Bang* (2006), in which Robert Downey Jr. turns to the camera and apologizes to the midwestern audience for his profanity. Yet noir is ubiquitous in contemporary culture. It influences such things as video games *(Max Shayne)* and Japanese anime *(Noir),* and it constitutes a major category of popular crime fiction, taking up whole walls of mass-market bookstores. Michael Connolly, one of the best-selling writers in the United States, is commonly described by reviewers as an author of noir fiction, and there is even a school of crime fiction in Scotland called "Tartan Noir," which includes such authors as Christopher Brookmyre, Val McDermid, Denise Mina, Ian Rankin, and Louise Welsh. In France the *serie noir* is alive and well, and two of France's darkest crime writers, Jean-Patrick Manchette and Thierry Jonquet, have recently been published in English translations by City Lights Books in San Francisco. A contemporary American series of pulp paperbacks labeled Hard Case Crime, edited by Charles Ardai, is virtually indistinguishable in style, format, and cover art from the pulp paperbacks of the 1950s and features both reprints and new novels. Sometimes the *roman noir* is capable of truly impressive literary achievement. Jonathan Lethem's *Motherless Brooklyn,* winner of the U.S. National Book Critics Circle Award for fiction in 1999, is a tour de force of first-person narration—funny, grim, and linguistically dazzling, involving a young man with Tourette's syndrome who tries to solve the murder of a low-level Brooklyn gangster. National Book Award winner Pete Dexter's *Train,* published in 2003, takes place in Los Angeles in 1953 (the year when Howard Hughes crashed his high-speed plane in Beverly Hills) and involves complex relations between poor black and rich white characters; its language is brutally yet poetically spare, and its plot, which deals with an odd combination of boxing and golf, is alternately suspenseful, poignant, and disturbing. Any history of the relation between the *roman noir* and "higher" fiction should also take note of the career of David Markson, who, in his youth, was a great admirer of such late modernists as Malcolm Lowry and William Gaddis. Markson wrote potboiler detective novels featuring Greenwich Village private eye Harry Fannin (*Epitaph for a Tramp* [1959] and *Epitaph for a Dead Boat* [1961] have recently been reissued), but eventually he morphed into the author of *The Last Novel* (2007), which might be described as an especially erudite form of postmodernism, or perhaps better, as a kind of post-postmodern meditation on *art maudit.*

Films noirs continue to be produced at a steady rate in the United States, even if they don't become blockbusters. Pastiches of classical noir take a variety of forms, as one can see from *Sin City; Kiss Kiss, Bang Bang;* and *Lucky Number Sleven* (2006). Among the more interesting pastiches, in this case played in straight-faced style, is *Brick* (2006), in which virtually the whole cast is made up of high school kids who speak like characters in a Dashiell Hammett story. *Brick* may not be the first "teen noir" (some would say *Rebel without a Cause* [1955] has that honor), but it proves that a nearly empty high school parking lot in broad daylight can become an effective noir setting. (In 1997 Quentin Tarantino's *Jackie Brown* proved a similar point by staging part of its action in a shopping mall.) Noir remakes occasionally appear—as with *The Deep End* (2001), a remake of *The Reckless Moment* (1949); and *Out of Time* (2003), the second remake of *The Big Clock*—and there has been no shortage of tough films noirs in contemporary style, including *Memento* (2001), *The Cooler* (2003), *Suspect Zero* (2004), *Hostage* (2005), *Derailed* (2006), and *Inside Man* (2006). As always, there are films on the margins of noir that might be placed on the list: Mary Harron's ingenious adaptation of Bret Easton Ellis's *American Psycho* (2000), Brad Anderson's Kafkaesque *The Machinist* (2004), Clint Eastwood's Acad-

emy Award boxing picture, *Million Dollar Baby* (2005), and David Cronenberg's hyperrealistic adaptation of John Wagner and Vince Locke's
graphic novel, *A History of Violence* (2006).

Many of these titles are worthy of discussion, but I want to devote the
remaining space to a couple of pictures I especially admire. First is British
director Mike Hodges and screenwriter Paul Meyersberg's *Croupier*
(1999), a relatively low-budget, British-French-German-Irish coproduction that marked Hodges's return to the tough crime genre after a long
hiatus (he directed the original version of *Get Carter* in 1970). *Croupier*
has the benefit of Clive Owen's charismatic but relatively deadpan performance in the title role and of an intelligent, cleverly constructed script
that makes good use of offscreen narration. Like Hodges's previous work,
the film creates a world of gaudy but vaguely seedy gangsters, gamblers,
and swindlers. Much of the action takes place in claustrophobic, wasteland settings: a small, rather tawdry, gambling casino with mirrored walls;
a Greek restaurant where casino workers hold after-hours parties in the
back room and have sex with prostitutes in the toilet; a tiny publisher's
office equipped with a functioning slot machine; a neat basement flat in
which the windows are barred; and a bedroom in an inexpensive hotel
called "Journey's End." Even when the story takes us to relatively posh
locations—a London shopping center, a country estate, a South African
resort—everything seems a bit sad and tawdry. The characters are either
cheerful cynics or guilt-ridden neurotics, and their lives assume what the
protagonist and narrator calls "an interesting pattern of betrayals" in
which he can never be sure if he is "the betrayer or the betrayed."

As in Wilder's *Sunset Boulevard,* the voluble offscreen narrator of
Croupier is a would-be writer who adopts an air of ironic, ghostly re-
move, turning his moral or ethical failings into an opportunity for a good
story. In the Wilder film the narrator is a dead man, and in *Croupier* he
belongs to the living dead; when we first meet him, however, he claims
to be in a position of complete power and calm, as if he were positioned
at what T. S. Elliot called "the still point of the turning universe." The
film opens with a shot of a motionless ivory ball atop the axis of a turning roulette wheel. Cut to the tuxedoed croupier (Owen), his jet-black
hair slicked back like a louche character in an old movie, calmly observing
the action as a Steadicam spins around him. "He had become the still
center of that spinning wheel of misfortune," his offscreen voice says.
"The world turned round him, leaving him miraculously untouched."
Throughout, he speaks in a remote, third-person style, attempting to
maintain godlike authorial power and a protective shield against the

"spinning wheel of misfortune" but also conveying a half-conscious self-contempt. His subjectivity soon becomes even more complicated; as the roulette ball drops into a slot, a flashback takes us to an earlier point in time, where we see him wearing casual clothes and a blond hairdo. "To begin with, he was Jack Manfred," the narrator says.

Now there are three characters in one—the narrator, the croupier, and Jack—the last of whom is an aspiring novelist who has moved from South Africa to London, far from the influence of his ne'er-do-well father (Nicholas Ball), a gambler and con man. Unemployed, Jack lives with his girlfriend Marion (Gina McKee) in her basement flat, where he sits all day wearing a black fedora, chain smoking, downing copious amounts of vodka, and pecking fruitlessly at the keyboard of a word processor. Marion, who works as a spy on shoplifters in a department store, is in love with Jack, in part because his artistic ambition suggests a kind of idealism; she encourages his writing, feeds him romantic dinners, and wears sexy black lingerie to bed. Jack, however, only half loves Marion. Guilty about his dependency, he attempts to conquer his writer's block by applying for hack work with a book editor who specializes in ghostwritten, high-concept projects by "personality authors." The editor advises Jack to write a proposal for a soccer novel: "Think about it. A couple of pages. Plenty of sex, of course." But Jack can't get past the novel's title page, which he keeps revising—first "On the Ball," then "In the Balls," and finally "Balls."

Circumstances change when Jack gets a long-distance telephone call from his father, Jack senior, who claims to have started a new company in South Africa (after the call we see the father returning to his job as a bartender). He urges "Jacko" to take advantage of an opportunity that has just opened at the Golden Lion gambling casino in London. Jack junior has worked as a dealer and croupier in South African casinos; he dislikes gambling and keeps insisting that he never practices it (to gamble would make him uncomfortably like his father), but when he applies for the job at the Golden Lion, we discover that he has considerable talent at the gaming table. He can deal blackjack and stack chips with lightning speed, and he counts better than the boss of the casino. "Welcome back, Jack," his narrating voice says, "to the house of addiction." (This is one of several instances when the narration shifts into inner monologue, speaking in ironic counterpoint with the dialogue.) Adapting to the new job with a kind of embittered relish, he dyes his hair black and assumes the zombielike, reified demeanor of an employee who knows that "speed is volume, volume is profit." Previously, his travels on the London Underground have made him fantasize about the day when the

FIGURE 69. Clive Owen in *Croupier* (1999).

other passengers will read his novels; now he wears a croupier's tuxedo, looking like a musician on his way to a concert. At the casino he remains dour, almost emotionless, but, as his narrating voice explains, his imagination is fired. He feels "up above the world, a writer looking down on his subject. . . . A wave of elation came over him. He was hooked again, watching people lose." He begins turning his experience into a semiautobiographical novel about the gambling world, which creates still another of his identities, a character named "Jake." When one of the players at the gaming table has a coughing fit and sprays germs all over the chips, the narrator remarks, "The croupier registered disgust. The writer made a note. Good scene for the book."

The narrator/croupier/novelist increasingly stands back from his life, dividing it into "chapters." His excitement at finding a literary subject, however, is always mingled with self-pity, class resentment, and barely suppressed anger. After work one evening, a customer he has caught cheating at the roulette table waylays him on a dark street, and in the ensuing fight Jack shows murderous rage, almost killing his attacker. At this point Jack's relationship with Marion starts to unravel; he spends an impulsive evening in bed with Bella (Kate Hardie), an ex-prostitute and drug addict who works at the casino, and his "chapters" begin to resemble a *roman noir*. One evening at the roulette table he encounters Yani (Alex Kingston), an attractive and mysterious lady from South Africa who gradually draws him into a scheme to rob the casino. Yani mixes sexual allure with appeals to trust and friendship; she claims that she's been forced into the robbery scheme by violent gangsters to whom she owes money, and she says that she's come to Jack for help because he's an "honest dealer" who won't be suspected of the crime. Jack has, in fact, been scrupulously honest at the casino's gambling table, but we've also seen plenty of evidence that he's a practiced liar and a man who knows how to stack a deck of cards. He recognizes that Yani is a potential femme fatale but is intrigued by her offer of twenty thousand pounds. "His father would have taken it like a shot," his narrating voice says, and then he suddenly realizes "it was Jake who was considering it." Jack can commit the crime in the interest of the novel, and instead of gambling he will be taking a "calculated risk" in which he will be paid in advance for a "service."

I won't describe all the twists and ironies of the film's concluding act, except to say that Jack's relationship with Marion comes to a violent end, leaving him crushed with guilt. Ultimately he writes a successful novel entitled *I, Croupier* (the first-person pronoun is one of several bitter jokes), which he signs "anonymous." Afterward, he rides the tube and watches the other passengers reading his work, but he realizes that he has become an "underground man" and learns an uncomfortable truth: "He was a one-book writer." To make matters worse, his ambivalence toward his father is intensified: "His father, eight thousand miles and twenty years away, was still dealing to Jack from the bottom of the deck." Despite this dark turn of events, the narrating voice explains that "Jake, the croupier, had a sense of humor." The film closes as it began, with the croupier standing at the roulette table, "watching you lose." He looks into the camera and smiles at you and me—a conclusion not unlike Norma Desmond embracing the audience at the end of *Sunset Boulevard*.

Although it relies on a good many noir conventions, *Croupier* is a realistic film without melodramatic effects. The plot offers only a couple of brief spasms of violence and is not at all concerned with the details of a heist or the mechanics of suspense; instead, we're given a psychological portrait of the romantic but flawed narrator and a sardonic yet morally acute sense of the various other characters' needs, weaknesses, and disloyalties to one another. The second film I want to discuss, David Lynch's *Mulholland Dr.* (2001), which requires a more detailed treatment, is something completely different—although, as its title suggests, it, too, can be related to *Sunset Boulevard*. In fact, in its first few minutes, a fantastically beautiful brunette who looks like a movie star is menaced by hired killers, suffers a late-night auto accident on Mulholland Drive, stumbles dazedly down the hillside, and crosses Sunset Boulevard in a little black dress and high heels. Meanwhile, back at the scene of the accident, a couple of LA cops in trench coats examine the smashed car and gaze out over the lights of the city. "Could be someone's missing, maybe," one of them says.

This archly allusive opening establishes the moodiness and iconography of many previous noirish pictures about Hollywood, but the film as a whole is unique, and one of the most harrowing and emotionally moving productions of Lynch's career. A superb example of "post" surrealism, *Mulholland Dr.* can be viewed as a companion piece to *Lost Highway,* this time from a female point of view. (It also looks forward to Lynch's *Inland Empire* [2006], another film about Hollywood, which also has a woman protagonist.) Both films are generic hodgepodges; both are set in Los Angeles; both make clever use of cameo appearances by minor celebrities; both employ touches of retro style; both involve themes of crime, murder, and sexual obsession; and both have a two-part structure, one part of which can be taken as "reality" and the other as "fantasy." Here let me note that in a long essay published after the first edition of *More Than Night,* Slavoj Žižek gently takes me to task for saying in chapter 7 that *Lost Highway* is "frozen in a kind of cinematheque" and is "just another movie about movies."[23] I've allowed my original statement to remain, but it now strikes me as a lapse of critical judgment. Žižek is entirely correct when he argues that Lynch deals with important issues and that his exaggerated use of movie clichés often has the effect of "the ridiculous sublime." *Mulholland Dr.* is an impressive instance of his technique and proof, if any were needed, that a movie saturated with references to other movies can transcend or reanimate its basic material, turning it into a powerful form of art.

In regard to *Lost Highway,* Žižek argues that "one should absolutely insist that we are dealing with a real story (of the impotent husband, etc.) that, at some point (that of the slaughter of Renee), shifts into psychotic hallucination in which the hero reconstructs the parameters of the Oedipal triangle that again make him potent. . . . [We] return to reality, precisely when . . . the impossibility of the hallucination reasserts itself" (15). I remain unconvinced that the narrative of *Lost Highway* is quite so realistic, but its second half is clearly designed to offer a compensatory fantasy. *Mulholland Dr.* has a roughly similar logic, though not exactly the same pattern. In the lengthy first part (one hour and fifty-six minutes), a wide-eyed, blond ingénue named Betty (Naomi Watts) arrives in Hollywood to seek a career as an actor and becomes caught up

FIGURE 70. Naomi Watts and Laura Elena Harring in *Mulholland Dr.* (2001).

in a mystery surrounding the raven-haired beauty we've seen running away from the accident on Mulholland Drive (Laura Elena Harring). The brunette sneaks into an apartment Betty has borrowed from an out-of-town aunt, and Betty discovers her standing naked in the bathroom shower. She has lost her memory, and when she sees an old movie poster for *Gilda* ("There never was a woman like Gilda," the poster proclaims), she decides to call herself "Rita," after Rita Hayworth. Her purse contains no identification but is filled with stacks of money and a strange blue key. Betty gives her shelter and helps her to recover bits of memory. Meanwhile, Betty has an audition at Paramount, where she makes a spectacular impression and attracts the interest of a young director, Adam (Justin Theroux), who is being forced by gangsters to cast a much less appealing blond named Camilla Rhodes in his latest picture. When Rita suddenly recalls the name "Diane Selwyn," she and Betty go to a bungalow apartment listed under that name, enter through a window, and discover the rotting corpse of a young woman on a bed, its face a gaping hole. That evening, the two traumatized women sleep together and recognize their mutual attraction. "I'm in love with you," Betty passionately and repeatedly whispers as she embraces the naked Rita.

For the moment I pass over a number of subsequent events and merely note that just as the mystery of Rita's identity seems to be approaching its solution, the film suddenly plunges into a black hole. Rita finds a blue metallic cube in her purse and opens it with the blue key; the camera swoops into the darkness of the open box and reemerges in a different world. Betty is now Diane Selwyn, who plays bit parts in movies, and Rita is Camilla Rhodes, a star who has been having an affair with Diane. Camilla breaks off the relationship, ostensibly because she is about to be married to her director, Adam, but actually because she has taken a new lover—the blond who, in the first part of the film, was the gangsters' choice to play in Adam's picture. (In part 1 Adam was repeatedly pushed around, but now he's confident and successful.) In response, Diane hires a thug to murder Camilla. The thug takes a stack of money from Diane and tells her that he will leave a blue key at her apartment when the job is done. When Diane finds the key in her room, she suffers a psychic breakdown; chased through her apartment by hallucinatory figures, she takes a gun from her bedside table, puts the barrel in her mouth, and commits suicide.

In several ways the film invites us to interpret its first part as Diane Selwyn's wish-fulfilling dream. Near the beginning we see an extreme close-up of a red bedsheet and a green blanket, and we hear the rhythmic breathing of someone asleep; when the second part begins, a ghostly, androgynous figure in a white, ten-gallon cowboy hat (similar in function to the Mystery Man in *Lost Highway*) enters Diane's bedroom and says, "Hey, pretty girl, time to wake up." Diane rises from the bed, and we glimpse the red sheet and green blanket from the earlier scene. Everything that follows in this short second part (twenty-five minutes) has the effect of a depressing, humiliating reality that systematically contrasts with Betty's adventures in part 1. Camilla lies nude on Diane's couch but rejects Diane's attempts to make love. Diane watches from the sidelines of a movie set as Adam coaches Camilla in a love scene. Alone in her apartment, Diane weeps and desperately masturbates. Camilla orders her chauffeured black limousine—the same car we saw in the film's opening— to bring Diane to Camilla's engagement party, where Diane suffers the indignity of watching Camilla acquire both a husband and a new lover. During the party we also learn that Diane once lost a part in a film to Camilla and that Camilla has "helped" her ever since.

Many details that seem unimportant on a first viewing become significant when we watch the film a second time. During Betty's audition at Paramount, for example, the actor who performs with her (Chad Everett) says that he wants to play the scene "nice and close, like we did with that other girl, the one with the black hair." And when Betty and Rita telephone Diane Selwyn, Betty remarks to Rita, "It's strange to be calling yourself." But Lynch keeps certain enigmas unresolved, making it difficult for us to construct a purely realist interpretation. Freud believed that our dreams are made from things we experience on the day we fall asleep, but if Diane is dreaming, then she dreams of several things—such as a ride in a limousine and her own death—that happen after she awakes. And what are we to make of the monstrous looking derelict, its face encrusted with fungus, who sits behind a dumpster at Winkie's Diner? This figure appears in a kind of dream within the dream and then in a brief scene after Diane Selwyn's death. "He's the one who's doing it," a character says at one point, and at the end of the film we see the derelict in possession of the blue metallic cube that provided a hinge between "dream" and "reality." Whatever his or her symbolic function might be (abject reality? the Lacanian "Real"? the Freudian id or "it"? the dirt and poverty we're afraid to recognize?), he or she exists both within and beyond the time-space inhabited by Betty and Diane, and he or she might well be dreaming everything.

The complex system of rhymes, reversals, and mirror-image relations between parts 1 and 2 of the film is remarkable when we consider that Lynch originally conceived *Mulholland Dr.* as an open-ended pilot for an ABC-TV series similar to *Twin Peaks*. The series, which would have involved various stories about the residents of the Havenhurst apartment complex where Betty stays, was cancelled by the network at the last moment. ABC planned to broadcast a drastically edited version of the pilot as a television movie. This would have made hash of Lynch's slow, dreamily paced style, but fortunately French producer Alain Sarde intervened and purchased the material for a theatrical version. Eighteen months later Lynch reassembled the original cast and crew, and in two and a half weeks of additional shooting he converted the project into a feature film. Signs of the transformation can be detected in a few places—for instance, Robert Forster is listed in the credits as one of the leading players but has only a single brief scene and one line of dialogue. The shift from television to cinema is perhaps more subtly apparent in the contrast between the narrative structures of parts 1 and 2. Part 1, in keeping with a TV series involving multiple characters, is structured by what Warren Buckland has described as a "paradigmatic logic," which shifts us inexplicably from story to story.[24] Rita sneaks into the Havenhurst apartments and falls asleep on a couch, and we cut directly to a daytime scene at Winkie's Diner, where two men have an eerie, vaguely homosexual conversation about a frightening dream. Next we witness a series of phone calls between a group of sinister characters, after which Betty arrives at

LAX, takes a cab to Havenhurst, and discovers Rita. Not long afterward
we cut to a self-contained, blackly comic episode involving an inept hit
man who shoots not only his target but also two innocent bystanders
and a vacuum cleaner. Another darkly comic scene shows a pair of mafia-
style gangsters forcing Adam to cast Camilla Rhodes in his next movie.
Eventually these fragments begin to cohere, but the narrative as a whole
is decentered, creating a feeling of surreal juxtaposition. Part 2 of the
film is more like a conventional movie; it plays disorienting tricks with
space and time, but as Buckland observes, it has a linear form—a "syn-
tagmatic" logic involving a single plotline centered on Diane.

Todd McGowan has interpreted the two contrasting parts of *Mulholland Dr.* as a Lacanian allegory and a "feminist version of *Lost Highway.*"[25] I'm skeptical that the film can be decoded as a feminist statement
or as a purely feminine sexual dream (torrid love scenes between beautiful females, such as the ones between Betty and Rita or Diane and
Camilla, are a staple of soft-core erotic movies designed for men); nevertheless, McGowan seems to me quite persuasive when he argues that
Mulholland Dr. is designed to reveal the disjuncture between fantasy and
desire. Diane dreams (or in my view the film dreams) that she is Betty, a
fantasmatic ego ideal who achieves blissful sexual love with Rita; afterward, Rita takes Betty to the beautifully tawdry, patently artificial Club
Silencio, a melancholic netherworld where fantasy begins to break down
and where, in McGowan's words, "we experience the loss of a relationship we have never had" (82). Unlike the male character in *Lost Highway,* Diane elaborates her fantasy to the point where Betty attains a moment of fulfillment, but this entirely imaginary experience is followed by
a scene of painful mourning, then by the black hole of the unrepre-
sentable, and then by an awakening into desire—a repetitive, excruciat-
ing longing for an object always out of reach, which can be ended only
in death.

The concluding section of the film is all the more painful because it
leaves us with a memory of Betty, who is an aspect of Diane and a completely lovable character. Naomi Watts contributes a great deal to this
effect because she is able to convey Betty's wide-eyed romance with Hollywood ("I just came here from Deep River, Ontario, and now I'm in this
dream place!"), her eager, Nancy Drew–like investigation of a mystery
("Come on! It'll be just like in the movies! We'll pretend to be somebody
else!"), and her good-hearted devotion to Rita without lapsing into cloy-
ing cuteness. The casting of Laura Elena Harring as Rita/Camilla seems
intended to throw even more sympathy toward Betty/Diane. Harring is

slightly wooden in both of her roles, and her crimson mouth and breast implants mark her as an alluring but depthless screen goddess. Watt's dual role, on the other hand, is a showcase for psychologically nuanced acting, and it contains a pair of amusing performances-within-perform-ance in which we glimpse the more experienced Diane beneath Betty's innocent exterior. When Betty rehearses for her audition at Paramount, she wears a housecoat and is photographed in a medium shot; her per-formance isn't bad, but she plays the scene with big emotional gestures, and at the end she bursts into laughter at the clichéd writing. When she goes to the studio, however, she plays in movie style. Wearing a tight skirt, she embraces her fellow actor (a smarmy older man named "Woody"), places his hand on her derriere, and brushes her lips teasingly against his. Throughout the scene, she whispers her lines in close-up, investing them with a steamy subtext. "Get out of here before I . . . ," she swoons; then she puts her arm around his neck, closes her hand into a fist, and kisses him hard. "Before I . . . kill you," she murmurs. Everyone in the room is stunned by her talent, and the dim witted director praises her interpretation as "very humanistic."

Like all of Lynch's films, *Mulholland Dr.* is affectively complex, os-cillating between *humor noir* and pathos, between horror and sweetness, between irony and sincerity. No director aside from Hitchcock has been able to invest subjective traveling shots with such uncanny and sus-penseful effects, as when Betty first moves through her apartment at Havenhurst or when she and Rita walk along a decaying courtyard to-ward Diane Selwyn's bungalow. By the same token, no director has been more inclined to insert grotesque or disgusting imagery into a Holly-woodish dream world, as when Betty enters the gates of colorful Haven-hurst (almost like Scotty moving through a tourist's version of San Fran-cisco in *Vertigo*) and notices a couple of dog turds on the clean pavement. Lynch also has an excellent sense of how music contributes to the film's varying moods. He composes incidental music of his own, but he is chiefly aided by Angelo Badalamenti, who wrote an eerie, sad, almost sublimely beautiful theme that appears at important junctures. (Badalamenti also makes a cameo appearance as an Italian gangster.) We hear this music when Betty arrives in Los Angeles and when Camilla leads Diane up a wooded hillside toward the engagement party; it sounds triumphant and joyful, but also slow and funereal, like a mysterious *Liebestod*.

Equally important is Lynch's use of pop tunes from the 1950s and 1960s—the Connie Stevens recording of "Sixteen Reasons," the Linda Scott recording of "I've Told Every Little Star," and above all Roy Orbison's lyrical masterpiece of passionate desire, "Crying," which, in the Club Silencio sequence, is sung in a Spanish version ("Llorando") by Rebekah Del Rio. During the club sequence Betty and Rita sit together in a darkened, half-empty auditorium, which looks rather like an old movie palace, and witness an evening of pantomime and lip-synch performances of prerecorded music (exactly the same technique we've seen in an earlier sequence, when a couple of women audition for Adam's movie). Rita wears a short blond wig that makes her look almost like Betty's sister. "No *hay banda,*" the master of ceremonies announces. "*Il n'y a pas d'orchestre!*" "It's all on tape!" When Del Rio sings, we see a close-up of her face, covered with stage makeup and decorated with an artificial tear at the corner of one of her eyes. The visible fakery, however, doesn't prevent the recorded voice and the song from being powerfully moving, any more than Lynch's manipulation of pop-cultural references prevents his film from generating strong emotions.

Betty and Rita weep as they hear "Llorando," and their tears foreshadow and amplify Diane's heartbreaking loss in the film's closing section, when she grieves beside her apartment sink. As she stands alone, framed in an off-center composition, she hears something and turns to look offscreen. "Camilla!" she sighs, her face haggard but smiling desperately. Cut to the perfectly beautiful Camilla, wearing a vivid red dress, like something Diane might be imagining. "You've come back!" Diane cries, her voice broken and her body trembling with desire. Like Diane, we in the audience are no longer experiencing an optimistic if occasionally disturbing Hollywood fantasy and are now in a more fully noirlike world. It is perhaps unimportant whether we give *Mulholland Dr.* a generic or stylistic label; but if we call it noir, and if film noir in its self-conscious, postmodern manifestations is occasionally capable of this kind of wrenching dramatic effect, then it remains capable of almost anything.

NOTES

INTRODUCTION

1. J. P. Telotte, *Voices in the Dark: The Narrative Patterns of Film Noir* (Urbana: University of Illinois Press, 1989), 3.

CHAPTER 1

1. Film noir is described as a genre in, among others, Robin Buss, *French Film Noir* (London: Marion Boyars, 1994); Charles Higham and Joel Greenberg, *Hollywood in the Forties* (New York: A. S. Barnes, 1968); Foster Hirsch, *The Dark Side of the Screen* (New York: A. S. Barnes, 1981); and Jon Tuska, *Dark Cinema: American Film Noir in Cultural Perspective* (Westport: Greenwood Press, 1984). It is a "series" in Raymond Borde and Étienne Chaumeton, *Panorama du film noir américain, 1941–1953* (Paris: Éditions de Minuit, 1955); a "movement," "period," "tone," and "mood" in Paul Schrader, "Notes on *Film Noir*," in *Film Noir Reader,* ed. Alain Silver and James Ursini (New York: Limelight Editions, 1996), 53–64; a "motif" and "tone" in Raymond Durgnat, "Paint It Black: The Family Tree of Film Noir," in Silver and Ursini, *Film Noir Reader,* 37–52; a "visual style" in Janey Place and Lowell Peterson, "Some Visual Motifs of *Film Noir,*" in Silver and Ursini, *Film Noir Reader,* 65–76; a set of "patterns of nonconformity" in David Bordwell, Janet Staiger, and Kristin Thompson, *The Classical Hollywood Cinema* (New York: Columbia, 1985), 74–77; a "canon" in J. P. Telotte, *Voices in the Dark: The Narrative Patterns of Film Noir* (Urbana: University of Illinois, 1989); a "phenomenon" in Frank Krutnik, *In a Lonely Street: Film Noir, Genre, Masculinity* (London: Routledge, 1991); and a "transgeneric phenomenon" in R. Barton Palmer, *Hollywood's Dark Cinema: The*

American Film Noir (New York: Twayne, 1994). For an argument similar to Palmer's, see John Belton, "Film Noir's Knights of the Road," *Bright Lights Film Journal* 12 (spring 1994): 5–15.

2. The dates 1941–1958 seem to have been first proposed by Schrader, who used *The Maltese Falcon* and *Touch of Evil* to mark the beginning and end of the noir period. Schrader's position is accepted by Place and Peterson, "Some Visual Motifs," and by a few writers in E. Ann Kaplan, ed., *Women in Film Noir* (London: BFI, 1980). Several other books on film noir implicitly endorse this periodization, even when they do not set fixed dates; see, for example, Telotte, *Voices in the Dark*, and Krutnik, *In a Lonely Street*. Most recent discussions treat film noir as a transgeneric form that begins somewhere in the late thirties or early forties and continues to the present day; see Palmer, *Hollywood's Dark Cinema*, and many of the essayists in Joan Copjec, ed., *Shades of Noir* (London: Verso, 1993). There are, however, skeptical voices. In the Copjec volume, for example, see Marc Vernet, "*Film Noir* on the Edge of Doom," 1–31, an essay that questions the usual historical and stylistic assumptions.

3. Alain Silver and Elizabeth Ward, eds., *Film Noir: An Encyclopedic Reference to the American Style* (Woodstock: Overlook Press, 1992), omit a number of titles that might be included—but as Marc Vernet has noted, one of the beauties of the category is that "there is always an unknown film to be added to the list" ("*Film Noir* on the Edge," 1). For a larger filmography, see Spencer Selby, *Dark City: The Film Noir* (Jefferson, N.C.: McFarland, 1984). See also Robin Buss, *French Film Noir*, who lists 101 examples of French film noir between 1942 and 1993, including *A Man Escaped* and *Weekend*. Patrick Brion's handsomely illustrated *Le film noir* (Paris: Éditions de La Martinière, 1992) discusses several movies that are not usually placed in the category—among them, Hitchcock's *North by Northwest*.

4. Michel Foucault, "What Is an Author?" in *Textual Strategies*, ed. Josué V. Harari (Ithaca: Cornell University Press, 1979), 153. Hereafter, this work is cited parenthetically in the text.

5. Vian used the pen name "Vernon Sullivan" on several occasions, and many of his readers believed that Vernon Sullivan was an African American. The name was inspired by two black jazz musicians from America—Paul Vernon and Joe Sullivan.

6. I am grateful to Peter Wollen for calling my attention to Boris Vian and his relevance to the postwar cultural climate in France. See Philippe Boggio, *Boris Vian* (Paris: Flammarion, 1993); also James Campbell, "Sullivan, the Invisible Man," *Times Literary Supplement* (28 January 1994): 7. In an earlier published essay that formed the basis of this chapter, I claimed that *J'irai cracher* was the basis for *I Spit on Your Grave* (1977), a low-budget American horror film directed by Emir Zarchi. I have subsequently discovered that Zarchi's film has no connection with Vian's novel. In 1997, Hawks and Sparrows Films, an independent company, optioned the rights to *J'irai cracher*. Production was scheduled to begin in 1998.

7. Academic feminism has shown that many of the films called noir are preoccupied with Freud's famous question, *Was will das Weib?* Laura Mulvey confirms this point in a recent interview: "It has been established very plausibly

through feminist film theory, *particularly around work on film noir,* that the woman in Hollywood cinema is not necessarily only the object of the gaze, but also the object of inquiry" (my emphasis). See Juan Suarez and Millicent Manglis, "Cinema, Gender, and the Topography of Enigmas: A Conversation with Laura Mulvey, *Cinefocus* 3 (1994): 3. Mulvey herself has emphasized the sadistic component of voyeurism, and her writings have been elaborated and debated in a large literature on psychoanalytic feminism. Among the best known examples are Kaplan, *Women in Film Noir,* and Mary Anne Doane, "Gilda: Epistemology as Striptease," *Camera Obscura,* no. 11 (1983): 7–27.

8. In France, today, *cinéma noir* refers to African-American cinema. Higham and Greenberg, *Hollywood in the Forties,* use "Black Cinema" as the title for their chapter on noir, but they employ the French term when they discuss films. For an interesting paper on films noirs directed by African Americans, see Manthia Diawara, "Noir by Noirs: Toward a New Realism in Black Cinema," in Copjec, *Shades of Noir,* 261–78.

9. Jacques Bourgeois, "La Tragédie policier," *Revue du cinema* 2 (1946): 70–72.

10. Palmer is almost the only writer on film noir who recognizes that movies have different meanings for different audiences. My survey of French criticism differs from his, but I recommend his discussion of writings on noir in *Hollywood's Dark Cinema,* 1–31. See also his anthology, *Perspectives on Film Noir* (New York: G. K. Hall, 1996), which contains useful translations of French writings.

11. For a discussion of the Americanization of French culture in general during this period, see Kristin Ross, *Fast Cars, Decolonization, and the Reordering of French Society* (Cambridge, Mass.: MIT Press, 1995).

12. For recent books on these films in English, see Edward Byron Turk, *Child of Paradise: Marcel Carné and the Golden Age of French Cinema* (Cambridge, Mass.: Harvard University Press, 1989); Alan Williams, *Republic of Images: A History of French Filmmaking* (Cambridge, Mass.: Harvard University Press, 1992); and Dudley Andrew, *Mists of Regret* (Princeton, N.J.: Princeton University Press, 1995). For an amusing discussion of "noir-like" aspects of French movies in the 1930s, see Manohla Dargis, "Cool Chats," *The Village Voice,* 6 July 1993: 50. The importance of noir in France both before and after the war has also been suggested in two essays by Ginette Vincendeau: "France 1945–1965 and Hollywood: The Policier as Inter-national Text," *Screen* 33, no. 1 (spring 1992): 50–80; and "Noir Is Also a French Word: The French Antecedents of Film Noir," in *The Book of Film Noir,* ed. Ian Cameron (New York: Continuum, 1993), 49–58.

13. Charles O'Brien, "Film Noir in France: Before the Liberation," *Iris* 21 (spring 1996): 7–20. Of course the term *noir* has an even older history; it describes the *roman noir,* or gothic novel, and in French literary criticism it suggests the decadent tendencies of late romanticism.

14. *The Philadelphia Inquirer* wrote that *The Maltese Falcon* was "worthy to stand with the English-made mysteries of Alfred Hitchcock" (25 October 1941), and *The New York Times* described John Huston as "a coming American match for Alfred Hitchcock" (12 October 1941). *Time* magazine compared *Falcon* with films by Hitchcock and Carol Reed (20 October 1941). Wilder's statement is quoted from *The Los Angeles Times* (6 August 1944).

15. The omission of Germany is not surprising, given the historical circumstances. The French "rediscovery" of German cinema began in the 1950s and was stimulated by the French publication of Lotte Eisner's work on expressionism. See Thomas Elsaesser, "A German Ancestry to Film Noir? Film History and Its Imaginary," *Iris* 21 (spring 1996): 129–43. In the mid 1940s, the French also failed to mention that the vogue for James M. Cain had started outside America: *The Postman Always Rings Twice* was adapted by the French themselves in 1939, and by the Italians in 1943. Among the British films that could have been discussed alongside the new Hollywood thrillers was *Hotel Reserve* (1944), which was based on an Eric Ambler novel. Directed by Lance Comfort, with James Mason and Herbert Lom in featured roles, this picture looks quite noirish in retrospect.

16. Nino Frank, "Un nouveau genre 'policier': L'aventure criminelle," *L'écran français* 61 (28 August 1946): 14; my translation. Hereafter, this work is cited parenthetically in the text. Frank mentions Hitchcock's *Suspicion* but only to note that he finds it an "absolute failure," unworthy of comparison with *Double Indemnity*.

17. Jean-Pierre Chartier, "Les Américains aussi font des films noirs," *Revue du cinéma* 2 (1946): 67; my translation. Hereafter, this work is cited parenthetically in the text.

18. One exception was Sigfried Kracauer, "Hollywood's Terror Films: Do They Reflect an American State of Mind?" *Commentary* (August 1946): 132–36. Kracauer had recently completed *From Caligari to Hitler*, and he used the same arguments to discuss American "terror films," including *Shadow of a Doubt*, *The Stranger*, *The Dark Corner*, *The Spiral Staircase*, and *The Lost Weekend*. His essay is discussed in Telotte, *Voices in the Dark*, 4–5, and in Edward Dimendberg, "Film Noir and Urban Space," Ph.D. diss., University of California Santa Cruz, 1992, 116–63.

19. André Bazin, "Six Characters in Search of *Auteurs*," in *Cahiers du Cinéma: The 1950s*, ed. Jim Hillier, trans. Liz Heron (Cambridge, Mass.: Harvard University Press, 1985), 37. Hereafter, Bazin's essay in Hillier's anthology is cited parenthetically in the text.

20. For information on Duhamel's involvement with surrealism, see Marcel Jean, ed., *The Autobiography of Surrealism* (New York: Viking Press, 1980). See also José Pierre, ed., *Investigating Sex: Surrealist Discussions, 1928–1932*, trans. Malcom Imrie (London: Verso, 1992).

21. Both the plots and the dialogue created confusion, and this confusion was not always to the liking of American reviewers. In *The New Republic* (24 August 1944), Manny Farber said that *Double Indemnity* was "the most incomprehensible film in years." He praised it for being "less repressed than usual," but he disliked the incessant talk: "I think you could get at the Underlying Thread of this film the same as you could in *The Maltese Falcon*—by being allowed to take the dialogue home with you to study at length."

22. Louis Aragon, "On Decor," in *The Shadow and Its Shadow: Surrealist Writings on Cinema*, ed. Paul Hammond (London: BFI, 1978), 29. I am indebted to Hammond's introduction to this volume, which provides an excellent commentary on surrealist film criticism.

23. Silver and Ward, *Film Noir*, 372. Among the other French writers who

might be mentioned in this context is Fereydoun Hoveyda, who published *Histoire du roman policier*, the first book on the *serie noire*, in 1956.

24. Marcel Duhamel, preface to Borde and Chaumeton, *Panorama du film noir américain*, vii; my translation. Hereafter, Borde and Chaumeton's work is cited parenthetically in the text. Duhamel alludes to several unnamed gangster films starring George O'Brien, and to William Wellman's *Chinatown Nights*. The Wellman film, however, was not released until 1929.

25. In the postscript to *Panorama du film noir américain*, Borde and Chaumeton also discuss the James Bond movies. Notice that the first James Bond film, *Dr. No*, makes the protagonist seem rather like a cold-blooded killer and borrows several ideas from Fritz Lang's *Mabuse* pictures of the 1920s and 1930s. The second film, *From Russia with Love*, is vaguely indebted to the Orient Express thrillers of Eric Ambler and Graham Greene, which are strongly associated with noir.

26. Untranslated, the text reads, *"onirique, insolite, érotique, ambivalent, et cruel."* I have translated *insolite* as "bizarre," but there is no good English equivalent. It connotes the gothic, somewhat like the Freudian *unheimlich*, but with a more shocking or horrific effect. Judging from its frequency, *insolite* is the most important adjective in the *Panorama*.

27. For a brilliant discussion of Julliette, see Angela Carter, *The Sadeian Woman* (New York: Pantheon, 1979). Carter points out that in contrast with Sade's Justine, who is derived from the virginal heroines of the sentimental novel, Julliette appropriates the values of patriarchy and uses them for her own ends. In one sense a radical, she is also a figment of the male imagination and a product of the system she exploits. Her most obvious representation in recent cinema is the antiheroine of John Dahl's *The Last Seduction* (1994), who uses all the men in her path and rides off victorious, in the back seat of a chauffeur-driven limousine.

28. Compare Sharon Stone's comments to a reporter about the role she played in *Basic Instinct* (1992): "I never thought the character really cared about sex at all. That's why it was so easy for her to use her sexuality—it had no value." *Parade Magazine* (30 January 1994): 10.

29. Rebecca West quoted in Roy Hoopes, *Cain: The Biography of James M. Cain* (New York: Holt, Rinehart and Winston, 1982), xiii. Hereafter, Hoopes's work is cited parenthetically in the text.

30. Hence the French treated Hollywood as if it were filled with primitives, unburdened by European sophistication. Godard, for example, argued that "the Americans, who are much more stupid when it comes to analysis, . . . have a gift for the kind of simplicity which brings depth. . . . The Americans are real and natural" (quoted in Hillier, *Cahiers du Cinema*, 8).

31. André Gide quoted by Diane Johnson, *Dashiell Hammett: A Life* (New York: Random House, 1983), 322 n. 7. See also Perry Miller, "Europe's Faith in American Fiction," *Atlantic Monthly* (December 1951): 50–56.

32. Jean-Paul Sartre, "The Situation of the Writer in 1947," in *What Is Literature?* trans. Bernard Frechtman (New York: Washington Square Press, 1966), 156. Hereafter, this work is cited parenthetically in the text.

33. Sartre quoted by Dana Polan, *Power and Paranoia: History, Narrative,*

and the American Cinema, 1940–1950 (New York: Columbia University Press, 1986), 252.

34. For a discussion of this tendency, see Robert Denoon Cummings's introduction to *The Philosophy of Jean-Paul Sartre* (New York: The Modern Library, 1966), 3–47.

35. Like all other French critics, Eric Rohmer believed that film noir had reached a dead end by the mid 1950s. He remarked that, for his generation, "the charm of these works lies in the delirious romanticism of their heroes and the modernism of their technique. Hollywood, shy of them for so long, suddenly noticed their existence, and a breath of the avant-garde made the studios tremble. What came of it? There is now enough distance for us to judge: the answer is very little, if anything." Rohmer, "Rediscovering America," in Hillier, *Cahiers du Cinema*, 91.

36. The political context in Paris is sometimes obscure, but in general the existentialist-inspired readings of film noir tend to be less activist or overtly left wing than the surrealist readings. Bazin himself was a liberal Catholic who appears to have been influenced by Emmanuel Mournier's "personalism." For a discussion of the politics of French intellectuals during the period, see Tony Judt, *Past Imperfect: French Intellectuals, 1944–1956* (Berkeley: University of California Press, 1992). On the avant-garde end of the political spectrum, a vaguely surrealist interest in film noir persisted throughout most of the 1950s, especially in the journal *Positif*. In 1957, activist Guy Debord, who was the leader of the French *Internationale situationiste*, published *The Naked City*, a collage map of Paris that took its title from the 1948 movie. For a discussion of Debord's appropriation of noir, see Thomas F. McDonough, "Situationist Space," *October* (winter 1994): 59–77. See also Jill Forbes, "The Série Noir," in *France and the Mass Media*, ed. Brian Rigby and Nicholas Hewett (London: Macmillan, 1993).

37. At about this time, France's leading academic phenomenologist, Maurice Merleau-Ponty, proclaimed in a lecture to the Collège de France that henceforth the work of cinema and the work of philosophy would be parallel. See Dudley Andrew, "*Breathless*: Old as New," in *Breathless*, ed. Dudley Andrew (New Brunswick: Rutgers University Press, 1987), 8.

38. Claude-Edmonde Magny, *The Age of the American Novel: The Film Aesthetic of Fiction between the Two Wars*, trans. Eleanor Hochman (New York: Ungar, 1972). This book, published in France in the 1950s, helped to transmit Sartre's ideas about the novel into French film theory.

39. François Truffaut, "A Wonderful Certainty," in Hillier, *Cahiers du Cinema*, 107; and Jacques Rivette, "On Imagination," in Hillier, *Cahiers du Cinema*, 105.

40. Claude Chabrol, "The Evolution of the Thriller," in Hillier, *Cahiers du Cinema*, 160, 163.

41. Dennis Hopper quoted by Leighton Grist, "Moving Targets and Black Widows: Film Noir in Modern Hollywood," in Cameron, *Book of Film Noir*, 267.

42. J. Hoberman and Jonathan Rosenbaum, *Midnight Movies* (New York: Harper and Row, 1983), 41. Hereafter, this work is cited parenthetically in the text.

43. The Harvard students were, of course, especially fond of *Casablanca,* which has never been called a film noir, even though it contains practically every-thing we associate with the form: a smoky nightclub, a fog-laden airport, a feel-ing of containment or *huis-clos,* Arthur Edeson's gothic photography, Bogart in a trenchcoat, Lorre and Greenstreet in supporting roles, and so on. Borde and Chaumeton excluded *Casablanca* from *Panorama du film noir américain,* argu-ing that it is nothing more than a wartime propaganda film with a romantic end-ing; and yet they describe Paramount's *This Gun for Hire,* which is equally pro-pagandistic and in some ways quite saccharine, as a definitive film noir. Perhaps the real reason for the absence of *Casablanca* from histories of noir has more to do with the specific content of its propaganda. The French may have been cool toward the film because of the way it depicts their role in the war.

44. Noel Burch, *Theory of Film Practice* (New York: Praeger, 1973), 123.

45. Durgnat, "Paint It Black: The Family Tree of Film Noir," *Film Comment* (6 November 1974): 6. Hereafter, all quotations are from this version of Durgnat's essay (condensed from an earlier, somewhat less playful article in the British journal *Cinema*).

46. Molly Haskell, *Love and Other Infectious Diseases* (New York: Mor-row, 1990), 101–2.

47. Schrader, "Notes on *Film Noir,*" in Silver and Ursini, *Film Noir Reader,* 53–61. Hereafter, this work is cited parenthetically in the text.

48. Schrader has a sophisticated literary education, and Martin Scorsese's early films are filled with fairly explicit allusions to James Joyce's *Portrait of the Artist as a Young Man.* According to Schrader's own account, he wrote the script of *Taxi Driver* when he was undergoing a spiritual and psychological crisis sim-ilar to the one T. S. Eliot describes in *The Waste Land.* I discuss the more gen-eral influence of literary modernism on Hollywood in chapter 2.

49. In much of the subsequent critical literature, *noir* is defined in such a way as to frustrate political or didactic reading. In Silver and Ward's *Film Noir,* for example, see Carl Macek's account of Cyril Endfield's left-wing, social-realist *Try and Get Me* (1950), which supposedly "functions better as a film noir than it does as a quasi-documentary exposing environment as the true producer of crime" (296). See also Dennis White's comments on *The Mask of Dimitrios* (1944): "It is possible that [Eric] Ambler's characters are not cynical enough for American noir or that his point of view is more radical than existential" (187).

50. An influential essay written at this time on contemporary Hollywood was Richard T. Jameson, "Son of Noir," *Film Comment* 10 (1974): 30–33. For evi-dence of how the term became popular within the industry, see Todd Erickson, "Kill Me Again: Movement Becomes Genre," in Silver and Ursini, *Film Noir Reader,* 307–29.

51. For an interesting commentary on this phenomenon, see Jonathan Rosen-baum, "Allusion Profusion," *Chicago Reader* (21 October 1994): 12, 25–26.

52. Fredric Jameson, *Postmodernism: Or, the Cultural Logic of Late Capi-talism* (Durham: Duke University Press, 1991). See also Marcia Landy and Lucy Fischer, "*Dead Again* or A-Live Again: Postmodern or Postmortem?" *Cinema Journal* 33, no. 4 (summer 1994): 3–22.

CHAPTER 2

1. George Orwell, "Raffles and Miss Blandish," in *A Collection of Essays by George Orwell* (New York: Doubleday Anchor, 1954), 154.

2. For the discourse on Americanism in Germany, see Anton Kaes, Martin Jay, and Edward Dimendberg, eds., *The Weimar Republic Sourcebook* (Berkeley: University of California Press, 1994). On Baudelaire and modernity, see Antoine Compagnon, *Five Paradoxes of Modernity*, trans. Franklin Phillip (New York: Columbia University Press, 1994).

3. Some modernist philosophers and artists were more critical of modernity than others. On the one hand were those who completely rejected Enlightenment rationalism and nineteenth-century liberalism: Martin Heidegger, Oswald Spengler, T. E. Hulme, T. S. Eliot, William Butler Yeats, and so on. On the other hand were those who criticized nineteenth-century ideas of progress and liberalism but who remained within a rationalist or humanist camp: Edmund Husserl, Thomas Mann, James Joyce, André Gide, and others.

4. Joseph Conrad's *Heart of Darkness* prefigures this theme, but I am of course alluding to Jim Thompson's *Killer inside Me* (1952), which is symptomatic of modernist themes in "cheap" fiction after World War II. Notice also the postwar novels of Cornell Woolrich, Fredric Brown, and—above all—Charles Willeford. Willeford's *High Priest of California* (1956) is the story of a sociopathic used-car salesman who enjoys reading Eliot, Joyce, and Franz Kafka in his spare time. For commentary on several hard-boiled novelists who worked in this vein, see Terry Curtis Fox, "City Nights," *Film Comment* 20, no. 5 (October 1984): 30–49. See also Patrick Raynal, "Écran blanc pour la série noire," *Cahiers du cinéma*, no. 490 (April 1995): 77–81.

5. David Lodge, "The Language of Modernist Fiction: Metaphor and Metonymy," in *Modernism: A Guide to European Literature, 1890–1930*, ed. Malcolm Bradbury and James McFarlane (Harmondsworth: Penguin, 1991), 481.

6. For a discussion of the effect of World War I on literary language, see Paul Fussell, *The Great War and Modern Memory* (New York: Oxford University Press, 1977), 21–24.

7. Over the next two decades, Eliot's Dark City was to become a touchstone for British and American modernism, influencing Scott Fitzgerald (*The Great Gatsby*), Evelyn Waugh (*A Handful of Dust*), and W. H. Auden (*The Age of Anxiety*).

8. As Mike Davis has shown in *City of Quartz: Excavating the Future in Los Angeles* (New York: Vintage Books, 1992), the "noir generation" of European exiles and hard-boiled writers in Hollywood was powerfully critical of the Southern California boosters and real-estate developers who had created the myth of a sunny, mission-style utopia. For filmmakers like Orson Welles, Billy Wilder, and Raymond Chandler, the American dream was at best a "bright, guilty world." (Hereafter, Davis's work is cited parenthetically in the text.)

9. Graham Greene quoted in Norman Sherry, *The Life of Graham Greene*, vol. 1 (New York: Viking, 1989), 597. Hereafter, this work and volume 2, published in 1994, are cited parenthetically in the text.

10. Joseph Conrad quoted in Tony Hilfer, *The Crime Novel: A Deviant Genre* (Austin: University of Texas Press, 1990), 98; my translation from the French.

11. Henry James, "The New York Preface," *The Turn of the Screw*, ed. Robert Kimbrough (New York: W. W. Norton, 1966), 120.

12. For example, Raymond Chandler's attack on Christie and Sayers in "The Simple Art of Murder" is strikingly similar to Ezra Pound's attacks on Amy Lowell and the British establishment in the period before World War I. Chandler's essays and letters are filled with savage comments on the women consumers of popular literature—as when he writes that pulp magazines "made most of the fiction of the time taste like a cup of luke-warm consomme at a spinsterish tearoom." Dashiell Hammett sometimes used the same metaphors. In one of his early book reviews, he remarked that S. S. Van Dine's upper-class detective, Philo Vance, had the conversational manner of "a high school girl who has been studying the foreign words and phrases in the back of her dictionary."

13. *Double Indemnity* was budgeted by Paramount for $980,000 and was one of the most critically admired films of the year. Although it was not among the box-office champions of the decade, it was widely regarded as a new and important kind of product. As *Boxoffice* magazine reported, *Indemnity* was a "precedent-setting, cycle-initiating hit" that elevated "the cops-and-robbers melodrama to a new stratum of exhibition importance" (2 February 1946).

14. Almost every Hollywood director who wanted to do something "deep" experimented with some variation of this style. Consider James Cruz (*Beggar on Horseback*, 1923), Josef von Sternberg (*Underworld*, 1927), King Vidor (*The Crowd*, 1928), Ben Hecht and Charles MacArthur (*Crime without Passion*, 1934), and John Ford (*The Informer*, 1935).

15. Eric Hobsbawm, *The Age of Extremes: A History of the World, 1914–1991* (New York: Pantheon, 1994), 182. Hereafter, this work is cited parenthetically in the text.

16. The institutionalization of modern art went hand in hand with a widespread dissemination of Freudian ideas. During the 1930s and 1940s in America, highbrow psychoanalysis had split into two terrains, described by Russell Jacoby as a "technical orthodoxy restricted to doctors" and a "looser revisionism that encouraged cultural and moral theorizing" (*The Repression of Psychoanalysis* [New York: Basic Books, 1983], 153). Meanwhile, the Frankfort School settled in New York and California, Theodor Adorno wrote psychoanalytic studies of the Hitlerian personality, and Freudian-inspired literary criticism began to appear everywhere. Among the most influential examples of such writing in the 1940s and 1950s are the translation of Marie Bonaparte's study of Edgar Allan Poe, Edmund Wilson's interpretation of "Turn of the Screw," and Lionel Trilling's essays on Freud and art. As many commentators have shown, Freudian ideas pervaded Hollywood in the 1940s, affecting all the genres and stars to some degree: compare John Wayne in *Stagecoach* (1939) with John Wayne in *Red River* (1948); or compare Ginger Rogers in *Top Hat* (1935) with Ginger Rogers in *Lady in the Dark* (1944). For a discussion of actual psychoanalysts who worked in Hollywood during this period, see Stephen Farber and Marc Green, *Hollywood on the Couch* (New York: William Morrow, 1993).

17. Fredric Jameson, "Reification and Utopia in Mass Culture," *Social Text* 1 (1979): 135.

18. Frederic Jameson, *The Political Unconscious* (Ithaca: Cornell University Press, 1981), 206.

19. I have discussed Hammett's career at greater length in an earlier essay, "Dashiell Hammett and the Poetics of Hard-Boiled Detection," in *Essays on Detective Fiction,* ed. Bernard Benstock (London: Macmillan, 1983), 49–72.

20. Lee Server, *Danger Is My Business: An Illustrated History of the Fabulous Pulp Magazines* (San Francisco: Chronicle Books, 1993), 9.

21. Joseph T. "Cap" Shaw quoted in Frank MacShane, *The Life of Raymond Chandler* (New York: E. P. Dutton, 1976), 46. Hereafter, this work is cited parenthetically in the text.

22. Dashiell Hammett, *Red Harvest* (London: Pan Books, 1975), 39; *The Maltese Falcon* (New York: Vintage, 1972), 227; *The Glass Key* (New York: Vintage, 1972), 169. Hereafter, these works are cited parenthetically in the text.

23. Blanche Knopf quoted in Diane Johnson, *Dashiell Hammett: A Life* (New York: Random House, 1983), 70. Hereafter, this work is cited parenthetically in the text.

24. David O. Selznick, *Memo from David O. Selznick*, ed. Rudy Behlmer (New York: Viking Press, 1972), 26.

25. Stephen Marcus, introduction to *The Continental Op,* by Dashiell Hammett (New York: Random House, 1974), xvii.

26. Dashiell Hammett, *The Thin Man* (New York: Vintage, 1972), 12. Hereafter, this work is cited parenthetically in the text.

27. Andrew Sarris quoted by Tom Milne in *Mamoulian* (Bloomington: Indiana University Press, 1970), 36.

28. James Agee quoted in Patricia King Hanson and Alan Gevinson, eds., *American Film Institute Catalog: Feature Films, 1931–1940* (Berkeley: University of California Press, 1993), 782.

29. I have discussed James Agee's comments and examined the "male myth" underlying the film in "John Huston and *The Maltese Falcon,*" reprinted in *The Maltese Falcon,* ed. William Luhr (New Brunswick: Rutgers University Press, 1995), 149–60. That volume contains a continuity script of the film and other useful material. For additional background on Huston, see Gaylyn Studlar and David Desser, *Reflections in a Male Eye: John Huston and the American Experience* (Washington, D.C.: Smithsonian Institution Press, 1993), where my essay on *Falcon* is also reprinted.

30. Jonathan Latimer's best novel, *Solomon's Vineyard,* is a synthesis of *The Maltese Falcon, Red Harvest,* and *The Dain Curse.* It was written in 1940 but was not published in the United States in an unexpurgated trade version until 1988. It deserves to be placed alongside Paul Cain's *Fast One* (1933) as one of the toughest, most sadomasochistic Hammett imitations of all time.

31. The myth that Hammett was a relatively simple stylist, together with the myth that he did not write about a world in which "gangsters can rule nations," seems to have been generated by Raymond Chandler in "The Simple Art of Murder." Critics have seldom noted that Hammett was also to some degree a typical southern writer (he was born in Maryland). He could render wild landscapes

with the accuracy of a man who has lived outdoors, and he must have loved dogs, because his books contain several beautifully observed descriptions of canine behavior. (The original Asta is as funny as MGM's but much less cute.)

32. Graham Greene, *The Ministry of Fear* (New York: Penguin, 1978), 65. Hereafter, this work is cited parenthetically in the text.

33. Graham Greene's religion and politics may seem contradictory, but they were consistent with his educational background. There was a strong tradition of Catholicism and high-church religion among British literary aesthetes, beginning with nineteenth-century figures like Cardinal Newman and Frederic Rolfe and culminating in "revolutionary classicists" T. E. Hulme and T. S. Eliot. However, many among Greene's generation at Oxford had also become interested in Karl Marx. Greene managed to keep the two impulses in balance, behaving like a high modernist in cultural matters but supporting socialist government.

34. Graham Greene, *Collected Essays* (Harmandsworth: Penguin, 1970), 167.

35. The quote is from Martin Seymour-Smith, *Who's Who in Twentieth-Century Literature* (New York: McGraw-Hill, 1976), 142.

36. Graham Greene, *A Gun for Sale* (New York: Penguin, 1974), 28. Hereafter, this work is cited parenthetically in the text.

37. During his early years in Paris, Eliot was attracted to the protofascist l'Action français. His style of anti Semitism in such poems as "Gerontion" and "Sweeny among the Nightingales" was fashionable among the intellectuals of his day, and it exerted a strong influence on the next generation. (See *The Great Gatsby*, which is filled with anti-Semitic references and wasteland imagery.) Interestingly, Eliot was also a great admirer of crime and detective fiction. He praised Charles Dickens and Wilkie Collins for their melodramatic effects, which he claimed were "perennial and must be satisfied," and he insisted that "literature" ought to give the same pleasure as "thrillers" (see Michael Shelden, *Graham Greene: The Man Within* [London: William Heinemann Ltd., 1994], 100–101; hereafter, this work is cited parenthetically in the text).

38. Graham Greene, *The Pleasure Dome: Collected Film Criticism, 1935–1940*, ed. John Russell Taylor (Oxford: Oxford University Press, 1980), 5. Hereafter, this work is cited parenthetically in the text.

39. For a discussion of *poetic realism* as a critical term, see Dudley Andrew, *Mists of Regret* (Princeton: Princeton University Press, 1995), especially 11–17. See also his discussion of Greene and the French cinema, 255–57.

40. *Red Harvest* inspired Akira Kurosawa's *Yojimbo* (1961) and Sergio Leone's *Fistful of Dollars* (1971). The Coen brothers used it as one of the sources for *Miller's Crossing* (1990), as did Walter Hill for *The Last Man Standing* (1996). In 1982, shortly after *Chinatown* had created a vogue for period movies about private detectives, Italian director Bernardo Bertolucci attempted to film *Red Harvest* in Hollywood. The picture was never produced, but Bertolucci's script, written with Marilyn Goldin, was impressive. The early scenes powerfully evoke the horrors of Personville, viewing them through the eyes of the Continental Op as he arrives in town. The hellish streets are enveloped in smoke, and a blade of fire spurs up an alley, running along the walls "in crazy patterns like a wild animal." Bill Quint, the Wobbly organizer, explains to the Op that the smoke and fire originate in one of the old mining tunnels nearby: "Fifteen years of discussion," he

says. "Who's going to put it out—the city or the state or the mining company or the Federal Government? Meanwhile, the fire's still going—burning houses, putting families in the street, poisoning people." At the end of the film, after the Op destroys a band of gangsters and discovers the identity of a murderer, the fire still burns, and even though occupied by the National Guard, the streets look as depressing as ever. On a train out of town, the Op finds himself sitting across from the brutal capitalist Elihu Willsson, who remarks, "I'm not going to let a man like you get away from me. . . . I want you to run for governor." (Unpublished screenplay by Bernardo Bertolucci and Marilyn Goldin, June 1982, Lilly Library manuscripts collection, Bloomington, Indiana.)

41. T. S. Eliot, *Selected Prose* (Harmondsworth: Penguin, 1953), 183. Hereafter, this work is cited parenthetically in the text.

42. George Orwell later wrote of Greene, "He appears to share the idea, which has been floating around ever since Baudelaire, that there is something rather *distingué* in being damned; Hell is a sort of high-class nightclub, entry to which is reserved for Catholics only" (quoted in Shelden, *Graham Greene*, 350). For a commentary on how *Brighton Rock* was appropriated by a later subculture, see Niel Nehring, "Revolt into Style: Graham Greene Meets the Sex Pistols," *PMLA* 106, no. 2 (March 1991): 222–37.

43. Graham Greene, *Brighton Rock* (New York: Viking Press, 1967), 58. Hereafter, this work is cited parenthetically in the text.

44. Norman Sherry has suggested that Ida Arnold was modeled on Mae West, whose films greatly amused Greene (Sherry, *Life of Graham Greene*, 1:635–36). But the name "Arnold" also points to Matthew Arnold, a liberal humanist whom T. S. Eliot described as an "undergraduate" in philosophy and a "philistine" in religion (Eliot, "Matthew Arnold," in *Selected Prose*, 165).

45. *A Gun for Sale* was published in America as *This Gun for Hire*. Throughout this chapter, I use the British title of the novel in order to distinguish it from the film adaptation.

46. Like the novel, the film gives a "psychoanalytic" and sociological interpretation of Raven, who has witnessed the hanging of his father, the suicide of his mother, and the horrors of an orphanage. Alan Ladd alludes to these experiences in a slightly mad speech to Veronica Lake as the two are hiding out from the police in an abandoned railway yard—a scene clearly influenced by radical scriptwriter Albert Maltz. His worst memory, however, seems to be of a cruel stepmother who broke his wrist with an iron.

47. *The Ministry of Fear* was directed by Fritz Lang, a great admirer of Greene's novel, who tried unsuccessfully to purchase the rights for himself. When Lang saw the studio's script (by Seton I. Miller, an alumnus of Warner Brothers in the 1930s), he tried to escape his contract (Peter Bogdanovich, *Fritz Lang in America* [New York: Praeger, 1969], 65). The completed picture is in fact significantly different from the novel. In Greene's version, the scruffy protagonist has just been released from prison for the mercy-killing of his wife; in the film, this character is a handsome fellow (Ray Milland) who is judged innocent of the killing. Paramount also fails to achieve anything like Greene's phantasmagoric descriptions of London during the blitz. The best moments are the scenes of violent action, which are staged and photographed in perversely witty fashion.

48. In Greene's novelized version of the story, Harry Lime is a surprisingly ordinary fellow (just as Kurtz is surprisingly small when Marlow discovers him in the jungle). By contrast, Welles is so compelling that he later became the star of a radio series in which Harry Lime was the hero.

49. "It won't do, boys. . . . It's sheer buggery," David Selznick told Carol Reed and Greene when he read the script of the movie. Greene later joked about Selznick's remark (Greene, *The Pleasure Dome*, 3). But in fact the relationship between Martins and Lime seems far more intense than schoolboy loyalty.

50. There are many differences between Greene's published novella and the film. In the novella, for example, the story is narrated by the British officer Callaway. The American and British versions of the film are also different: the American print contains a brief opening narration by Joseph Cotten, whereas the British print is narrated by Carol Reed. As Greene pointed out, Welles was responsible for Lime's famous speech about Italy and Switzerland; other uncredited writers for the film included Peter Smolka and Mabbie Poole. According to Joseph Cotten, Carol Reed improvised the ending to the film on the last day of shooting (see Joseph Cotten, *Vanity Will Get You Somewhere* [San Francisco: Mercury House, 1987], 97–98). In the British version, the closing shot runs much longer than in the American version, which was shortened by David Selznick in accordance with Hollywood practice.

51. In *The Ministry of Fear*, Greene describes the difference between childhood and adult reading:

> In childhood we live under the brightness of immortality—heaven is as near and actual as the seaside. Behind the complicated details of the world stand the simplicities: God is good, the grown-up man or woman knows the answer to every question, there is such a thing as truth, and justice is as measured and faultless as a clock. Our heroes are simple: they are brave, they tell the truth, they are good swordsmen and they are never in the long run really defeated. That is why no later books satisfy us like those which were read to us in childhood—for those promised a world of great simplicity of which we knew the rules, but the later books are complicated and contradictory with experience.

52. Ivan Moffat, "On the Fourth Floor of Paramount: Interview with Billy Wilder," in *The World of Raymond Chandler*, ed. Miriam Gross (New York: A and W Publishers, 1977), 49.

53. PCA report, December 1, 1943, Margaret Herrick Library of the Motion Picture Academy, Los Angeles.

54. Two of Cain's hard-boiled stories had been filmed in Hollywood prior to this time. *She Made Her Bed* (Paramount, 1934), starring Richard Arlen, was a loose adaptation of his famous satire of California road culture, "The Baby in the Icebox." *Money and the Woman* (Warner Brothers, 1940), starring Jeffrey Lynn, was a B-budget version of Cain's novella of the same title and might be described as a sentimental precursor of *Double Indemnity*.

55. Cain worked briefly for the *Baltimore Sun*, where H. L. Mencken became his mentor. His first short story, "Pastorale," a grotesquely comic tale of murder in the Appalachian backlands, was published in Mencken's *American Mercury* in 1928—the same year as Ernest Hemingway's *Men without Women*, and a year before Hammett's *Red Harvest*.

56. Edmund Wilson, "The Boys in the Back Room," in *Classics and Commercials* (New York: Farrar, Straus, 1950), 21.

57. Cain was seldom assigned film noir projects, but he received screen credit for *Algiers* (1937), a Hollywood remake of *Pépé le Moko*. He also worked on *The Shanghai Gesture* (1941), which Raymond Borde and Étienne Chaumeton regard as an important early instance of noir. Later, he performed uncredited and apparently insignificant labor on an adaptation of Daniel Mainwaring's *Build My Gallows High,* which eventually became *Out of the Past.*

58. H. L. Mencken, *Prejudices: A Selection,* ed. James T. Farrell (New York: Vintage, 1958), 247–48.

59. James M. Cain, *Double Indemnity* (New York: Vintage, 1978), 8. Hereafter, this work is cited parenthetically in the text.

60. Jacques Barzun, "The Illusion of the Real," in Gross, 162.

61. Raymond Chandler, *The Big Sleep,* in *Raymond Chandler: Stories and Early Novels* (New York: Library of America, 1995), 612.

62. As we have seen, Weimar intellectual life—including movies, cabaret, literature, and cultural criticism—was obsessed with industrial America, which seemed both seductive and frightening. (Consider the theory and criticism of figures like Sigfried Kracauer, Theodor Adorno, and Max Horkheimer.) Wilder is demonstrably preoccupied with this theme, but he also resembles such Americans as Mencken and Hecht, especially in his contempt for the populist masses. Interestingly, Horkheimer and Adorno's famous essay on the culture industry was written in California at almost the same time that *Double Indemnity* was made.

63. The *Double Indemnity* house is located at 6301 Quebec Street in Los Angeles, and today it costs considerably more than the "30 thousand bucks" estimated by Walter Neff.

64. Present-day viewers of *Double Indemnity* are seldom aware that the film is set in the recent past. When Walter Neff begins his Dictaphone message to Keyes, he announces the date as "July 16, 1938." This enables the filmmakers to show a market like Jerry's without wartime rationing. Throughout, the Los Angeles locales are free of any sign of military activity. Thomas Doherty has suggested that one reason for the night-for-night photography at the Glendale train station was the government's desire to keep information about such places secret.

65. In another famous film noir, *The File on Thelma Jordan* (1949), Wendell Corey discovers that Barbara Stanwyck has a dark past: he finds a photograph of her as a hard-boiled blond who looks just like Phyllis Dietrichson.

66. Richard Schickel, *Double Indemnity* (London: BFI, 1992), 64. Hereafter, this work is cited parenthetically in the text.

67. More than a decade passed before Hollywood attempted a similar scene again. In 1958, Robert Wise filmed a blow-by-blow account of a gas-chamber execution for *I Want to Live!,* which won Susan Hayward the Oscar. In 1961, Irvin Kershner and Don Murray devised a harrowing execution sequence for *Hoodlum Priest,* in which Keir Dullea plays the criminal.

CHAPTER 3

1. Cobbett Steinberg, *Reel Facts: The Movie Book of Records* (New York: Vintage Books, 1978), 464. Hereafter, this work is cited parenthetically in the text.

2. Will Hays quoted in Nancy Lynn Schwartz, *The Hollywood Writer's Wars* (New York: Alfred A. Knopf, 1982), 192. Hereafter, Schwartz's work is cited parenthetically in the text.

3. For more detailed discussions of figures such as Joseph Breen and Martin Quigley, see Leonard Leff and Jerrold L. Simmons, *The Dame in the Kimono: Hollywood Censorship and the Production Code from the 1920s to the 1960s* (New York: Anchor Books, 1990). Hereafter, this work is cited parenthetically in the text. See also Gregory D. Black, *Hollywood Censored: Morality Codes, Catholics, and the Movies* (New York: Cambridge University Press, 1996).

4. Unless otherwise noted, this form and all other Breen Office correspondence are quoted from the PCA files at the Margaret Herrick Library of the Motion Picture Academy in Los Angeles.

5. Christian Metz, *The Imaginary Signifier*, trans. Celia Britton, Annwyl Williams, Ben Brewster, and Alfred Guzzetti (Bloomington: Indiana University Press, 1982), 254.

6. Notice, however, that the Breen Office had been created partly in response to proto–films noirs such as *The Story of Temple Drake* (1933), Paramount's Bowdlerized adaptation of William Faulkner's *Sanctuary* (a novel that, as we have seen in chapter 1, was also an inspiration for Boris Vian's scandalous *roman noir* of 1946).

7. Marc Vernet, "*Film Noir* on the Edge of Doom," in *Shades of Noir*, ed. Joan Copjec (London: Verso, 1993), 24.

8. Even with these precautions, films were always subject to local censorship restrictions. In Ohio, censors cut the scene of Wilmer kicking Spade in *The Maltese Falcon*. They also cut the famous line about crime as a "left-handed form of endeavor" from *The Asphalt Jungle*. For additional information on such matters, see Matthew Bernstein's "A Tale of Three Cities: The Banning of *Scarlet Street*," *Cinema Journal* 35, no. 1 (1995): 27–52. Bernstein's research suggests that film noir in the 1940s was aimed primarily at "adult" and relatively cosmopolitan audiences and that it encountered resistance from review boards in the Midwest and South.

9. From 1947 to 1953, Mickey Spillane was the best-selling author in the United States, his success far exceeding anything ever achieved by Dashiell Hammett or Raymond Chandler. Even so, his sales came mainly from paperbacks, and Hollywood regarded him as a low-end vulgarian. Films based on his work tended to come from the fringes of the industry. For a discussion of his impact on American publishing, see Geoffrey O'Brien, *Hard-Boiled America* (New York: Van Nostrand Reinhold, 1981). See also Lee Server, *Over My Dead Body: The Sensational Age of the American Paperback: 1945–1955* (San Francisco: Chronicle Books, 1994).

10. James Agee, *Agee on Film*, vol. 1 (New York: McDowell, Obolensky, 1958), 217. Hereafter, this work is cited parenthetically in the text.

11. I take the term *Browderite* from Thom Andersen, "Red Hollywood," in *Literature and the Visual Arts in Contemporary Society*, ed. Suzanne Ferguson and Barbara Groseclose (Columbus: Ohio State University Press, 1985), 141–96. Hereafter, this work is cited parenthetically in the text. Andersen has elaborated his argument in a recent book, coauthored with Noel Burch: *Les Communistes*

de Hollywood: Autre choses que les martyrs (Paris: Presses universitaires de la Sorbonne Nouvelle, 1994). See also Brian Neve, *Film and Politics in America: A Social Tradition* (London: Routledge, 1992).

12. The history of this important cultural formation is described by Michael Denning in *The Cultural Front* (London: Verso, 1997). Denning observes that the American Left was interested in gangster narratives but was divided over the problem of whether serious writers could work in Hollywood. According to the naturalistic novelist James T. Farrell (author of *Studs Lonigan*), any writer who experimented with thrillers could not avoid capitulation to a "movietone realism" and "a melodramatically simplified conception of good girls and bad girls" (quoted in Denning, 257).

13. It should be emphasized that atmospheric crime movies of the 1940s and 1950s were always open to different political inflections. Robert Montgomery's *Ride the Pink Horse* (1947), scripted by Ben Hecht and Charles Lederer, has been described as "Republican noir." In most cases, however, Hollywood tried to avoid any clear-cut party allegiances.

14. To see how the prototypical film noir narrative could be made to suit conservative interests, consider the style and technique of Whittaker Chambers's famous memoir, *Witness*.

15. John Houseman quoted in Richard Maltby, "The Politics of the Maladjusted Text," in *The Book of Film Noir*, ed. Ian Cameron (New York: Continuum, 1993), 41. Maltby offers an especially intelligent commentary on the dubious, circular nature of zeitgeist criticism. He also notes that the tendency to relate film noir to a "postwar malaise" seems to derive from the mostly conservative sociological critics of the McCarthy years, who were worried about the political implications of certain movies. For another effective critique of historical generalizations about noir, see David Reid and Jayne L. Walker, "Strange Pursuit: Cornell Woolrich and the Abandoned City of the Forties," in Copjec, *Shades of Noir*, 57–96.

16. Chandler quoted in William Luhr, *Raymond Chandler and Film* (Tallahassee: Florida State University Press, 1991), 136.

17. John Houseman, *Front and Center* (New York: Simon and Schuster, 1979). Hereafter, this work is cited parenthetically in the text.

18. For other accounts that tell the same story of Chandler's work on *The Blue Dahlia*, see Frank MacShane, *The Life of Raymond Chandler* (New York: E. P. Dutton, 1976); Luhr, *Raymond Chandler and Film;* and Raymond Chandler, *The Blue Dahlia: A Screenplay*, ed. Matthew J. Bruccoli (Carbondale: Southern Illinois University Press, 1976). Hereafter, this last work is cited parenthetically in the text.

19. Raymond Chandler, "The Blue Dahlia: Treatment," manuscript collection, Margaret Herrick Library of the Motion Picture Academy, 87.

20. Unless otherwise noted, all quotations regarding the production background and scripts of *Crossfire* are taken from the files of the John Paxton collection at the Margaret Herrick Library in Los Angeles.

21. At about this time, Orson Welles, who had already suggested that Charles Foster Kane was anti-Semitic, was approaching the same theme from

another angle in *The Lady from Shanghai,* treating it more subtly and slightly in advance of either Darryl Zanuck or Dore Schary.

22. In the completed film, the date of Thomas Finlay's death has been changed to 1848. Keith Kelly and Clay Steinman suggest that this change enabled the filmmakers to allude to a crucial year in the prehistory of Marxism. See "*Crossfire:* A Dialectical Attack," *Film Reader* 3 (1978): 120. Hereafter, this work is cited parenthetically in the text.

23. Schary's copy of the script, together with other materials related to the production, is in the Special Collections department of the University of California, Los Angeles, library.

24. Kelly and Steinman interpret the "mystery man" as a self-conscious commentary on the unreliability of the film's narration ("*Crossfire,*" 117). In my own view, *Crossfire* is a realistic text, quite different from a radically ambiguous art movie such as Michelangelo Antonioni's *Blowup* (1966). Notice, however, that the Antonioni film contains a scene that operates according to exactly the same principle as the "mystery man" in *Crossfire*: during a conversation with Vanessa Redgrave, David Hemmings receives a telephone call from another woman; he gives Redgrave various explanations of his relationship to the caller and then systematically denies all of them.

25. See Louis E. Raths and Frank N. Trager, "Public Opinion and *Crossfire,*" *Journal of Educational Sociology* (February 1948): 345–69.

26. The literature on this topic is vast. Andersen, whose work I discuss later in more detail, offers an incisive review of the major writings. In addition to his "Red Hollywood," I recommend Schwartz, *Hollywood Writer's Wars;* and Larry Ceplair and Stephen Englund, *The Inquisition in Hollywood: Politics in the Film Community, 1930–1960* (Garden City, N.Y.: Garden City Press, 1980).

27. Charles Higham and Joel Greenberg, *Hollywood in the Forties* (New York: A. S. Barnes, 1968), 38. Hereafter, this work is cited parenthetically in the text.

28. For an eloquent defense of Andersen's position and a fine commentary on the politics of Nicholas Ray, John Berry, and Cyril Endfield, see Jonathan Rosenbaum, "Guilty by Omission," in *Placing Movies* (Berkeley: University of California Press, 1995). Hereafter, Rosenbaum's *Placing Movies* is cited parenthetically in the text.

29. *Big Jim McLain* was preceded by several examples of anticommunist noir, including *I Married a Communist* (1950, a.k.a. *The Woman on Pier 13*); *I Was a Communist for the F.B.I.* (1951, directed by "reformed" leftist Gordon Douglas); and *The Thief* (1952, a technical experiment, filmed entirely without dialogue). These films were neither artistically nor commercially successful, although *I Was a Communist for the F.B.I.* spun off into a widely syndicated television series entitled *I Led Three Lives.*

30. For more commentary and details on the production of this film, see Dana Polan, *In a Lonely Place* (London: BFI, 1994).

31. Quotations of *The Asphalt Jungle* scripts are taken from the John Huston collection at the Margaret Herrick Library.

32. One of the most interesting documents in *The Asphalt Jungle* file at the Herrick Library is a letter to Huston, addressed "Carissimo Gianni" and signed

Notes to pages 130–137

"Hugh," which offers sympathetic and intelligent criticism of the completed film. After praising Huston's work, the writer goes on to say,

> I am *not* impressed by Hardy's statement that the police send assistance calls for help, as if there were something magnificent about that. This is what they exist for and what they are paid to do. . . . Hardy's remark, "Suppose we had no police force," strikes me as very naive and irrelevant to the point under discussion. Nobody thinks in terms of "a police force or *no* police force." The whole problem is "a *good* police force or a *corrupt* police force."

33. I have discussed the FBI investigation of Welles in "The Trial: Orson Welles vs. The FBI," *Film Comment* (January–February 1991): 22–27.

34. Jules Dassin's and Joseph Losey's best European films are clearly in the noir tradition. Immediately after moving to France, Dassin made a commercially successful and influential "caper" movie, *Rififi* (1956). Losey's early credits in England included *The Sleeping Tiger* (1954, directed under the name "Joseph Walton"), *The Criminal* (1960), and *The Servant* (1963). For an interesting conversation with Dassin regarding his blacklist experience, see Patrick McGilligan, "'I'll Always be an American': Jules Dassin Interviewed," *Film Comment* (November–December 1996): 34–48.

35. The film version of *The Big Knife* belongs to a cycle of quasi-noirish movies about Hollywood that were released in the early 1950s. (Notice also that the Hollywood novel had long been a favored genre of the American modernists and the literary left.) The cycle was initiated by *Sunset Boulevard* (1950), and it included such films as *The Bad and the Beautiful* (1952), *A Star Is Born* (1954), and *The Barefoot Contessa* (1954). These pictures coincide not only with the blacklist, but also with the loss of studio-owned theater chains and the rise of television. They seem to reflect Hollywood's guilty conscience and its sense that an era was ending.

36. In this period, John Frankenheimer was responsible for two other highly effective movies that might be read as films noirs: *Seven Days in May* (1964), a tense, underrated thriller about a fascist coup in Washington, D.C.; and *Seconds* (1966), a darkly satiric "Twilight Zone" story about a middle-aged executive's desire to change himself into a younger man (played by Rock Hudson). The style of both films is indebted to Welles, but also to Frankenheimer's experience as a brilliant director of live television.

37. Michael Rogin, "Kiss Me Deadly: Communism, Motherhood, and Cold War Movies," *Representations* 6 (spring 1984): 6–7. Hereafter, this work is cited parenthetically in the text.

CHAPTER 4

1. See Jacques Rivette's comments on postwar French cinema in "Six Characters in Search of *Auteurs*," in *Cahiers du Cinema: The 1950s*, ed. Jim Hillier (Cambridge, Mass.: Harvard University Press, 1985), 4.

2. Elsewhere, I have discussed the French auteurists in the context of an emerging postmodernism. See "Authorship and the Cultural Politics of Film Criticism," *Film Quarterly* 44, no. 1 (fall 1990): 14–23. For an excellent account of how

auteurist criticism affected the career of Alfred Hitchcock and several other directors, see Robert E. Kapsis, *Hitchcock: The Making of a Reputation* (Chicago: University of Chicago Press, 1992).

3. Andrew Sarris, *The American Cinema* (New York: E. P. Dutton, 1968), 29. Hereafter, this work is cited parenthetically in the text.

4. Manny Farber, *Negative Space* (New York: Praeger, 1971), 16. Hereafter, this work is cited parenthetically in the text.

5. In the late 1950s, when Farber wrote about the "underground," the films he described were in fact playing in shabby, disreputable theaters. The film industry had become interested in spectacular, wide-screen productions, and many of the old action movies were being shown as re-releases in drive-ins or cheap urban settings.

6. The most wide-ranging attempt to explain the economic and industrial determinants for "B film noir" is Paul Kerr, "Out of What Past? Notes on the B Film Noir," in *The Hollywood Film Industry*, ed. Paul Kerr (London: Routledge and Kegan Paul, 1986), 220–44.

7. Among the top moneymaking films of 1941–1965, none of the classic films noirs were true industry leaders. If we construct the category loosely, its most profitable films would be *Casablanca, To Have and Have Not, Gilda, Leave Her to Heaven, The Lost Weekend, Mildred Pierce, Notorious, Spellbound, Possessed, Key Largo, A Place in the Sun, Detective Story, Dragnet, Pete Kelly's Blues, The Man with a Golden Arm, Anatomy of a Murder, Psycho, Portrait in Black, Midnight Lace,* and *Doctor Strangelove.* (This list is based on box-office statistics in Cobbett Steinberg, *Reel Facts: The Movie Book of Records* [New York: Vintage Books, 1978].) In 1994, *Entertainment Weekly* magazine published a list of "America's 100 All-Time Favorite Films," which was derived from an analysis of ticket sales and video rentals. The only classical-era film on the list that is even remotely connected with the noir category is *Casablanca*, although the contemporary films include *Fatal Attraction, Basic Instinct, Batman,* and *Batman Returns (Entertainment Weekly,* no. 220 [29 April 1994]: 22–40). Noir also scores weakly in terms of official recognition within the industry. Leaving aside *Citizen Kane,* noir nominees for Academy Awards in the Best Picture category between 1941 and 1965 were *The Maltese Falcon, Heaven Can Wait, Double Indemnity, Gaslight, The Lost Weekend, Spellbound, Mildred Pierce, Crossfire, Sunset Boulevard, Anatomy of a Murder,* and *The Hustler.* The most noirlike films to actually win the award were *Casablanca, The Lost Weekend, Hamlet, All the King's Men,* and *On the Waterfront.* Noirlike winners of "worst film" awards from *The Harvard Lampoon* in the same period included *Spellbound, Scarlet Street, Leave Her to Heaven, The Paradine Case, Sorry, Wrong Number, The Night Has a Thousand Eyes, Niagara,* and *I, the Jury.*

8. Charles P. Skouras quoted in Richard Maltby, "The Politics of the Maladjusted Text," in *The Book of Film Noir,* ed. Ian Cameron (New York: Continuum, 1993), 46. Hereafter, Cameron's work is cited parenthetically in the text.

9. Charles Korner is quoted by Anna Lewton in Joel E. Siegel, *Val Lewton: The Reality of Terror* (New York: The Viking Press, 1973), 40. Siegel's superb book contains a great deal of useful information about production conditions in the 1940s.

10. Unless otherwise noted, production data in this paragraph and in my subsequent discussion of the 1940s and 1950s comes from Todd McCarthy and Charles Flynn, eds., *Kings of the Bs: Working within the Hollywood System* (New York: E. P. Dutton, 1975).

11. In *The Avant-Garde Finds Andy Hardy* (Cambridge, Mass.: Harvard University Press, 1995), Robert B. Ray observes that one of the Hardy films, 1941's *Life Begins for Andy Hardy,* could be read as a film noir. "Inevitably, therefore, to advanced students only casually interested in the Hardy movies, this film seems the most 'serious' entry in the series" (159).

12. Lea Jacobs, "The B Film and the Problem of Cultural Distinction," *Screen* 33, no. 1 (spring 1992): 3.

13. For a more complete discussion of *T-Men* and an analysis of how Anthony Mann's career was affected by the change from B pictures to intermediates, see Cimberli Kearns, "Making Crime Matter: The Violent Style of the 'Formative' B-Film," *USC Spectator* (forthcoming 1998).

14. *My Name Is Julia Ross* even received a favorable review in *The New Yorker.* Joseph H. Lewis contributed to the notion that such films were true B movies. See Gerald Peary, "Portrait de en cinéaste l'artiste de serie 'B': Entretien avec Joseph H. Lewis," *Positif* (July–August 1975): 42–52. (This issue of *Positif* also has a special section on "*le film criminel,*" containing several interesting essays on American noir.)

15. For an intelligent discussion of *The Argyle Secrets*, see Jonathan Rosenbaum, *Movies as Politics* (Berkeley: University of California Press, 1997), 329–31.

16. Edgar G. Ulmer, quoted in Peter Bogdanovich, "Interview with Edgar G. Ulmer," McCarthy and Flynn, 396.

17. Perhaps because of his extremely tight schedule, Edgar G. Ulmer's cutting style is equally unorthodox. When Al places a long-distance call to Sue, we see an elaborate montage of long-distance operators and telephone lines, followed by a brief close-up of Sue holding a receiver in her hand; the entire conversation, however, is shown from Al's end of the line, and we never even hear Sue's voice. Several days later, when Al calls a second time, we see the *same* close-up of Sue; this time she says "hello," but Al hangs up.

18. Andrew Britton, "*Detour,*" in Cameron, *Book of Film Noir,* 174–83.

19. Dana Polan, *In a Lonely Place* (London: BFI, 1994), 268.

20. Alain Silver and Carl Macek, "Gun Crazy," in *Film Noir: An Encyclopedia of the American Style*, rev. ed., ed. Alain Silver and Elizabeth Ward (Woodstock: Overlook Press, 1992), 118. Hereafter, this work is cited parenthetically in the text.

21. A. I. Bezzerides, quoted in J. Hoberman, "The Great Whatzit," *The Village Voice* (15 March 1994): 43.

22. For a good discussion of Robert Aldrich's wavering attitude toward the film, see Edward Gallafent, "*Kiss Me, Deadly,*" in Cameron, *Book of Film Noir,* 240–46. My quote of Aldrich comes from page 240 of this essay.

23. For an interesting discussion of the film's potentially deconstructive, "apocalyptic discourse," see J. P. Telotte, *Voices in the Dark: The Narrative Patterns of Film Noir* (Urbana: University of Illinois Press, 1989), 198–215. For a

lively surrealistic reading in French, see Louis Seguin, "Kiss Me Mike," *Bizarre*, no. 2 (October 1955): 68–71.

24. Slightly before this film, Vince Edwards had been an effective costar with Cleo Moore in *Hit and Run* (1957), a sub–James M. Cain thriller produced by low-budget auteur Hugo Hass.

25. The Martin Scorsese film is an undeniably powerful remake. In my own view, however, it suffers from a kind of overstatement, both in technical and thematic terms. For a discussion of how it relates formally to its "precursor" texts, see Brian McFarlane, *Novel into Film* (London: Oxford University Press, 1996). For a dazzling analysis of how it grows out of Scorsese's cinephilia, and of how it exemplifies postmodern intertextuality in general, see Lesley Stern, *The Scorsese Connection* (London: BFI, 1995). Other elaborately produced noir remakes include *Against All Odds* (1984), which is based on *Out of the Past*, and *No Way Out* (1987), which is based on *The Big Clock*. Perhaps the most egregious instance of remake inflation is the 1988 version of *D.O.A.*, which is actually the *second* remake of a movie that was *already* a remake. The well known 1950 production, directed by Rudolph Mate, was loosely based on Robert Siodmak and Billy Wilder's 1931 German film, *Der Mann, Der Seinen Morder Sucht*. In 1969, Australian director Eddie Davis filmed *Color Me Dead*, an inexpensive and uninspired modernization of the same basic story. Then came Rocky Morton's expensive and loudly expressionistic retelling for the 1980s. The 1950 Mate film is a relatively straightforward thriller with a shocking plot twist (the star dies, after telling a couple of cops how he tracked down his own murderer), and much of its fascination derives from documentary-style shots of pudgy, sweating Edmond O'Brien as a small-time accountant running through San Francisco and Los Angeles. In contrast, the 1988 film casts trim, athletic Dennis Quaid in the role of a college English teacher, and it treats the action in the style of MTV art, using rapid cutting, lurid colors, tilted compositions, and every camera trick known to the industry.

26. Financial data and quotations from DTV producers are taken from Michele Willens, "Bypassing the Big Picture," *Los Angeles Times* "Calendar" section (Sunday, 28 November 1993): 25.

27. For information on the marketing of *Red Rock West*, see the "Arts and Entertainment" section of *The New York Times* (Sunday, 3 April 1994): 19.

28. Probably the award should have been given to Jaye Davidson, whose performance gave the film much of its shock value and popularity.

CHAPTER 5

1. Janey Place and Lowell Peterson, "Some Visual Motifs of *Film Noir*," in *Film Noir Reader*, ed. Alain Silver and James Ursini (New York: Limelight Editions, 1996), 69.

2. Geoffrey O'Brien, "The Return of Film Noir!" *New York Review of Books* (15 August 1991): 45.

3. In their "balance sheet" or summary argument about American film noir, Raymond Borde and Étienne Chaumeton make the following remarks on style:

"One notes the German influence and its taste for high-contrast lighting. The systematic investigation of depth of field is rare; it has best suited certain 'psychological' films where it is used to illustrate complex relationships among multiple characters who are arranged at different distances from the lens. . . . The subjective camera is used often, and, in the years 1945–47, an offscreen commentary that is nowadays reserved for the police procedural" (*Panorama du film noir américain, 1941–1953* [Paris: Éditions de Minuit, 1955], 179, my translation).

4. Edward Dimendberg, "Kiss the City Goodbye," *Lusitania* 7 (spring 1996): 56–57.

5. Dimendberg's argument is developed further in "City of Fear: Defensive Dispersal and the End of Film Noir," *Any*, no. 18 (1997): 14–18. His book on this issue, *Film Noir and the Spaces of Modernity*, is forthcoming from Harvard University Press. For a discussion of how technology affected style across the entire history of Hollywood, see Barry Salt, *Film Style and Technology: History and Analysis* (London: Starword, 1983).

6. Medical officer quoted in Thomas Doherty, *Projections of War: Hollywood, American Culture, and World War II* (New York: Columbia University Press, 1993), 264.

7. Tom Gunning's term, *the cinema of attraction*, is designed to indicate certain affinities between popular and avant-garde spectatorship in the earliest days of the movies. One of his most recent discussions of the idea may be found in "An Aesthetic of Astonishment," in *Viewing Positions: Ways of Seeing Film*, ed. Linda Williams (New Brunswick: Rutgers University Press, 1995), 114–33.

8. Three-strip Technicolor cameras of the 1930s cost as much as thirty thousand dollars to build. They were rented, not purchased, from the Technicolor organization, and the cost of making color release prints for distribution was significantly greater than the cost of black and white. *Variety* estimated that color added as much as 25 percent to the earning power of a film, but it could also increase the budget by as much as 30 percent. See Gorham A. Kinden, "Hollywood's Conversion to Color: The Technological, Economic, and Aesthetic Factors," *Journal of the University Film Association* 31, no. 2 (spring 1979): 29–36.

9. Guy Green quoted in Steve Neale, *Cinema and Technology: Image, Sound, Color* (Bloomington: Indiana University Press, 1985), 149.

10. This was also a period when a great many musical comedies were still being made in black and white. As only one example, consider *I'll See You In My Dreams* (1951), starring Doris Day and Danny Thomas.

11. Louise Nevelson quoted in Wodek, *Black in Sculptural Art* (Brussels: Atelier 340, 1993), 193. Hereafter, Wodek's work is cited parenthetically in the text.

12. David Anfam, *Franz Kline: Black and White, 1950–1961* (Houston: Houston Fine Art Press, 1994), 20–21. Hereafter, this work is cited parenthetically in the text.

13. Michael Leja, *Reframing Abstract Expressionism* (New Haven: Yale University Press, 1994), 110–11.

14. Leja points out that in 1949, *Life* magazine published a black-and-white photo of an unsmiling Jackson Pollock, standing next to one of his paintings and looking slightly off to the right; the near side of Pollock's face was illuminated by a hard light, and the far side was hidden by the long shadow he cast against

the canvas. The caption beneath the image asked whether he might be "the greatest living painter in the United States." Leja remarks that this "*noir*-ish presentation was often more influential in the culture's absorption of the New School artists than was their work" (*Reframing Abstract Expressionism,* 113).

15. For a discussion of the cultural politics of postwar modernism, see Serge Guilbaut, *How New York Stole the Idea of Modern Art,* trans. Arthur Goldhammer (Chicago: University of Chicago Press, 1983).

16. John Alton, *Painting with Light* (Berkeley: University of California Press, 1995), 45. Hereafter, this work is cited parenthetically in the text.

17. Conversation with the author, Hollywood, California, May 1996.

18. In his useful introduction to the 1955 edition of Alton's *Painting with Light,* Todd McCarthy observes that "Alton habitually wears a beret and has the air of a Continental bohemian of the 1920s" (xvi). At MGM, Alton became one of Vincente Minnelli's favorite cameramen and was given an Academy Award for the Technicolor dream sequence in *An American in Paris.* Besides that film, his color work with Minnelli includes *Designing Woman,* which occasionally parodies the hard-boiled style. He also photographed the noirlike nightmare in *Father of the Bride.*

19. Notice also that *Out of the Past* contains several brief but eloquent camera movements—as in the scene in which the camera pans slowly from Jeff Bailey, who is seated at a bar, to Kathie Moffat, who enters the room. Midway through the pan, the image dissolves, signifying the passage of time. This photographic lyricism, which is evident in both low-key and high-key scenes, can also be found in Tourneur's other great film noir, *Nightfall* (1957), photographed by Burnett Guffey.

20. Whether we are speaking of black and white or color, it is much more difficult for a photographer to make films look interesting in daylight than in darkness. On sunny days, it helps a great deal to have the spectacular mountain scenery and expansive sky of westerns, as in *Out of the Past.* The most difficult scenes in daytime are the ones shot on city streets. "If you have a totally dark room and you have a night scene," photographer Michael Chapman observes, "you do it all. . . . But if you have a day exterior, there's just plain less you can do on it. . . . I think a lot of [the problem] is simply the enormous recalcitrance of daytime. It's simply unavoidable" (Dennis Schaefer and Larry Salvato, *Masters of Light: Conversations with Contemporary Cinematographers* [Berkeley: University of California Press, 1984], 106).

21. Most of the statistics in this paragraph are derived from Kinden, "Hollywood's Conversion to Color." An extensive discussion of color technology and its ideological implications may be found in Neale, *Cinema and Technology.*

22. François Truffaut, *Hitchcock/Truffaut* (New York: Simon and Schuster, 1967), 131–32. Hereafter, this work is cited parenthetically in the text.

23. A similar lighting style was used in *The Dark Corner* (1946), an impressive black-and-white thriller on which Henry Hathaway and Joe MacDonald also collaborated.

24. To get a sense of how foreign pictures were perceived in America at the time, see J. Lee Thompson's comedy, *What a Way to Go!* (1964), which parodies a wide range of contemporary styles, including a Ross Hunter melodrama in wide screen, and a European art movie in black and white.

25. *Raging Bull* also mixes color with black and white, but it reserves the color for a brief montage of grainy home movies. Martin Scorsese used the release of the film as an occasion to argue publicly for the preservation of old Technicolor prints and to call attention to the inferiority of contemporary color stocks. It should also be noted that most of the filmmakers I have mentioned were quick to protest television mogul Ted Turner's attempt to computer-colorize the classic black-and-white movies.

26. There are practical as well as cultural reasons for New York cinema's affinity with darkness. Hollywood cameraman Bill Butler, who began his career in Chicago and who later photographed such noirlike pictures as *The Conversation* (1974), remarks that "the people who shoot the best at night come out of New York. They've shot on the streets of New York so much, they don't use anything hardly in the way of light. But they've got street lights and store windows to do it there" (Schaefer and Salvato, *Masters of Light*, 86).

27. Gordon Willis says that the technique of amber light "broke out like a plague" after he completed *The Godfather*. "And today, people still apply it. It's applied indiscriminately, I might add. Because doing that does not automatically make it a period movie" (Schaefer and Salvato, *Masters of Light*, 288). Another fashion—now happily passing away—was the use of fog machines to give a smoky *Stimmung* to interiors. Along similar lines, the better photographers of the period began to shoot outdoor scenes at the "magic hour" of dusk—a technique that gave the actors a natural rimlight, and the world around them a kind of glow. This style was used effectively by Jordan Cronenweter in one of the most unusual and neglected films noirs of recent decades: Ivan Passer's *Cutter's Way* (1981).

28. Schaefer and Salvato, *Masters of Light*, 111.

29. Throughout this discussion, I omit camera movements, but it should be noted that most of the best-known "neo-noirs" contain spectacular tracking shots made possible by Steadicams or other new technologies. Portable cameras and "optical tracking" movements made possible by zoom lenses are in fact the chief markers of post-1970s cinematography. Scorsese's work, not only in *Taxi Driver,* but also in *Raging Bull, Goodfellas,* and *Casino,* is particularly dependent on these shots. Brian DePalma and other directors often use 360-degree tracking movements in place of shot–reverse shot combinations. The opening sequence of Kathryn Bigelow's *Strange Days* (1995) is a subjective POV shot that covers a violent robbery from beginning to end, starting in the back seat of an automobile and running up and down several floors of a building.

30. Peter Wollen, "MTV, and Postmodernism, Too," in *Futures for English,* ed. Colin MacCabe (New York: St. Martin's Press, 1989), 168.

31. Frederic Jameson argues that parody is always critical and mocking and is typical of a society that has a normative conception of language. He therefore sharply distinguishes parody from pastiche, which he defines as a "neutral" or "blank" imitation of dead styles—a mimicry "without a satirical impulse, without laughter, without that still latent feeling that there exists something *normal* compared to which what is being imitated is rather comic" ("Postmodernism and Consumer Society," in *The Anti-Aesthetic*, ed. Hal Foster [Port Townsend, Wash.: Bay Press, 1983], 114). My own use of the term is closer to the one in

Linda Hutcheon's useful book, *A Theory of Parody*. Hutcheon argues that parody need not be comic; its general purpose is to establish a "difference and distance from the original text or set of conventions," and it has a variety of uses in contemporary art. Its modern forms usually presuppose "both a law and its transgression, or both repetition and difference." As a result, depending on its specific context, parody can be "both conservative and transformative, both 'mystificatory' . . . and critical" (*Theory of Parody* [New York: Methuen, 1985], 101).

32. Raymond Chandler's eye for fashion is discussed by Dana Thomas in "Pulp Fashion," *The New York Times Magazine* (4 December 1994): 104–5.

33. At the height of the craze for James M. Cain in the late 1930s, there was a popular song entitled "The Postman Always Rings Twice, the Iceman Walks Right In." There were also countless parodies of Cain, including James Thurber's "Hell Only Breaks Loose Once." Where movie musicals are concerned, see George Cukor's *Les Girls* (1957), which contains an elaborate parody of Brando in *The Wild One* (1954), performed by Gene Kelly.

34. "I am constantly tempted to burlesque the whole thing," Chandler remarked after completing *The Big Sleep*. "I find myself kidding myself. . . . Why is it that Americans—of all people the quickest to reverse their moods—do not see the strong element of burlesque in my writing?" (quoted in Frank MacShane, *The Life of Raymond Chandler* [New York: E. P. Dutton, 1976], 93). He also claimed that two of his early stories, "Blackmailers Don't Shoot" and "Smart-Aleck Kill," were "pure pastiche" (Frank MacShane, ed., *Selected Letters of Raymond Chandler* [New York: Columbia University Press, 1981], 187). In the 1940s, S. J. Perelman wrote a parody of Chandler for *The New Yorker* ("Farewell, My Lovely Appetizer"). Chandler loved it, and he and Perelman became good friends.

35. Even though the Germans had a crucially important influence on historical film noir, Wim Wenders claimed that he was unable to make "any connections between the films Fritz Lang made in America and the ones he made in Germany." For him, noir was a Hollywood invention, associated with the flood of American pop culture that spread throughout Germany at the end of the war. Because of his ambivalence about this culture, Wenders paid oblique, ironic tribute to American sources of the 1940s and 1950s, casting pop icon Dennis Hopper as an American crook who wants to "bring the Beatles back to Hamburg," Samuel Fuller as a Mafia dealer in international pornography, and Nicholas Ray as an artist who lives by forgery.

36. According to Leigh Brackett, the script was designed to make Chandler's novel more straightforward, less morally ambiguous and inconclusive: "Our only achievements were two: Terry Lennox has become a clear-cut villain, and it seemed that the only satisfactory ending was for the cruelly-diddled Marlowe to blow Terry's guts out." (Leigh Brackett, "From *The Big Sleep* to *The Long Goodbye*, and More or Less How We Got There," *Take One* 1, no. 1 [1974]: 27–28.) For his own part, Altman wanted to create an anti-Bogart movie: "I think Marlowe's dead. I think *that* was 'the long goodbye.' I think it's a goodbye to that genre—a genre that I don't think is going to be acceptable any more." (Jan Dawson, "Robert Altman Speaking," *Film Comment* [March–April 1974]: 41.)

37. Photographer John Alonzo recalls that Polanski "liked putting the cam-

era very close to the performers, right on top of them. Now that's an intimidating thing to any actress who is so beautiful [as Faye Dunaway]. Well, it added to her performance. I really believe, it made her nervous" (Schaefer and Salvato, *Masters of Light*, 32).

38. John G. Cawelti, "*Chinatown* and Generic Transformation in Recent American Films," in *Film Theory and Criticism,* 2d ed., ed. Gerald Mast and Marshall Cohen (New York: Oxford University Press, 1979), 200. Hereafter, this work is cited parenthetically in the text.

39. Barbara Creed, "From Here to Modernity: Feminism and Postmodernism," in *A Postmodern Reader,* ed. Joseph Natoli and Linda Hutcheon (Albany: State University of New York Press, 1993), 407

40. For a discussion of consumerism and postmodern spectatorship, see Anne Friedberg, *Window Shopping: Cinema and the Post-Modern Condition* (Berkeley: University of California Press, 1993).

41. Quentin Tarantino quoted in Paul A. Woods, *King Pulp: The Wild World of Quentin Tarantino* (New York: Thunder's Mouth Press, 1996), 103. Hereafter, Woods's work is cited parenthetically in the text.

42. Peter Bogdanovich and Jonathan Rosenbaum, *This Is Orson Welles* (New York: HarperCollins, 1993), 168.

CHAPTER 6

1. E. Ann Kaplan, ed., *Women in Film Noir* (London: BFI, 1980), 4. Hereafter, this work will be cited parenthetically in the text.

2. See especially the essays by Sylvia Harvey and Janey Place in Kaplan, *Women in Film Noir.* It should also be noted that the sexual politics of film noir are complicated by a strong current of masochistic eroticism. For a particularly cogent discussion of such matters, see Gaylyn Studlar, *In the Realm of Pleasure: Von Sternberg, Dietrich, and the Masochistic Aesthetic* (Urbana: University of Illinois Press, 1988).

3. Frank Krutnick, *In a Lonely Street: Film Noir, Genre, Masculinity* (London: Routledge, 1991), 91. For an analysis of the "masculinity in crisis" argument in recent film study, see Tania Modleski, *Feminism without Women* (New York: Routledge, 1991).

4. R. Barton Palmer, *Hollywood's Dark Cinema: The American Film Noir* (New York: Twayne, 1994), 171.

5. See the commentary on *Blue Steel* and *Love Crimes* in Alain Silver and Elizabeth Ward, eds., *Film Noir: An Encyclopedia of the American Style,* rev. ed. (Woodstock: Overlook Press, 1992), 418–19.

6. Manthia Diawara, "Noirs by Noirs: Towards a New Realism in Black Cinema," in Joan Copjec, ed. *Shades of Noir* (London: Verso, 1993), 262.

7. A wide-ranging discussion of Orientalist motifs in other kinds of movies may be found in Matthew Bernstein and Gaylyn Studlar, eds., *Visions of the East: Orientalism in Film* (New York: Columbia University Press, 1997).

8. Dashiell Hammett, "Dead Yellow Women," in *The Big Knockover,* ed. Lillian Hellman (New York: Vintage, 1972), 246.

9. For discussion of this and other kinds of Hollywood films involving romantic relations between Asians and Anglos, see Gina Marchetti, *Romance and the "Yellow Peril": Race, Sex, and Discursive Strategies in Hollywood Fiction* (Berkeley: University of California Press, 1993).

10. A particularly informative interview with Wayne Wang about these and other matters may be found in Owen Shapiro and Chen-Tsung Yau, "Film-Making and Ethnic Boundaries: A Conversation with Wayne Wang," *Point of Contact* (winter/spring 1997): 71–87. Wang says that he would like to make films "with a Chinese content, but which also have something in the structure that is Chinese." At the same time, he notes, "it becomes a tricky question as to what is the Chinese aesthetic in film" and "even more complicated when asked about Chinese-American aesthetics." His own practice is strongly influenced by the Frenchman Jean-Luc Godard and the Japanese Yasujiro Ozu. Although he never mentions noir, his interview is filled with references to motifs we can associate with the form: multiple perspectives, offscreen narration, mirror shots, imagery of water, and so on.

11. Wayne Wang quoted in Peter Feng, "Being Chinese American, Becoming Asian American: *Chan Is Missing*," *Cinema Journal* 35, no. 4 (summer 1996): 99.

12. Julian Stringer, "'Your tender smiles give me strength': Paradigms of Masculinity in John Woo's *A Better Tomorrow* and *The Killer*," *Screen* 38, no. 1 (spring 1997): 25–41.

13. See Rolando J. Romero, "The Postmodern Hybrid: Do Aliens Dream of Alien Sheep?" *Post Script* 16, no. 1 (fall 1996): 41–52. The Chicano character does not exist in the Philip K. Dick novel that was the source of *Blade Runner*, but the William Burroughs story that gave the film its title involves a dystopian influx of Puerto Ricans and African Americans into Manhattan. Romero notes that the original script for the film was written by Hampton Fancher, who was himself partly Chicano. Both versions of the completed picture, he argues, reflect "postmodernism's ambivalence toward hybridity," together with a certain "indeterminacy towards the representation of the most visible population in the California landscape" (43).

14. Notice also that both adaptations of *Farewell, My Lovely* are more misogynistic than Raymond Chandler had been. In the novel, Velma Valento–Helen Grayle sacrifices her life to avoid causing trouble for the rich man she has married; indeed Marlowe's attitude in telling the story (as the title of the book suggests) is elegiac. The Dick Richards movie is especially out of keeping with this effect. It not only portrays Velma-Helen as a conventional femme fatale, but also has Marlowe kill her off at the end.

15. For a discussion of "existential" motifs in American film noir, see Robert Porfirio, "No Way Out: Existential Motifs in the Film Noir," in *The Film Noir Reader*, ed. Alain Silver and James Ursini (New York: Limelight Editions, 1996). For the quote, see Roger Rosenblatt, *Black Fiction* (Cambridge, Mass.: Harvard University Press, 1974), 162.

16. For additional discussion of African-American writers in Paris during the 1940s and 1950s, see Christopher Sawyer-Lauçanno, *The Continental Pilgrimage: American Writers in Paris, 1944–1960* (New York: Grove Press, 1992).

17. Richard Wright himself directed and starred in a disappointing film adaptation of *Native Son* in the late 1950s. For a discussion of this film, see Peter Brunette,

"Two Wrights, One Wrong," in Gerald Peary and Roger Shatzkin, eds., *The Modern American Novel and the Movies* (New York: Ungar, 1978), pp. 131–42.

18. An excellent discussion of this production may be found in Robert Stam, "Orson Welles, Brazil, and the Power of Blackness," *Persistence of Vision*, no. 7 (1989): 93–112.

19. All quotations from Welles's *Heart of Darkness* are from the script dated November 30, 1939, in the Orson Welles archive at the Lilly Library in Bloomington, Indiana. This and other materials on the film are located in box 14, folders 15–19.

20. George Schaefer quoted in Frank Brady, *Citizen Welles* (New York: Anchor Books, 1989), 215.

21. For an extended discussion of the introduction and its relationship to the film as a whole, see Guerric DeBona, "Into Africa: Orson Welles and *Heart of Darkness*," *Cinema Journal*, 33, no. 3 (1994): 16–34.

22. Patrick Brantlinger, "*Heart of Darkness*: Anti-Imperialism, Racism, or Impressionism?" in *Heart of Darkness*, ed. Ross C. Murfin (New York: St. Martin's Press), 364–65.

23. For a more complete history of African Americans in these and other Hollywood films, see Donald Bogle, *Toms, Coons, Mulattoes, Mammies, and Bucks: An Interpretive History of Blacks in American Films* (New York: Continuum, 1991); Thomas Cripps, *Black Film as Genre* (Bloomington: Indiana University Press, 1979); and Mark Reid, *Redefining Black Film* (Berkeley: University of California Press, 1993).

24. Bogle, *Toms, Coons, Mulattoes, Mammies, and Bucks*, 140. Hereafter, this work is cited parenthetically in the text.

25. Robyn Wiegman, "Black Bodies/American Commodities: Gender, Race, and the Bourgeois Ideal in Contemporary Film," in *Unspeakable Images: Ethnicity and the American Cinema*, ed. Lester D. Friedman (Urbana: University of Illinois Press, 1991), 323.

26. Diawara, "Noirs by Noirs," in Copjec, *Shades of Noir*, 273.

27. Charles Burnett, "Inner City Blues," in *Questions of Third Cinema*, ed. Jim Pines and Paul Willemen (London: BFI, 1989), 224. An even more direct critique of the black "gangsta" movies (also written from a black perspective) may be found in Jacquie Jones, "The New Ghetto Aesthetic," *Wide Angle* 13, nos. 3–4 (July–October 1991): 32–43.

28. Paul Arthur, "Los Angeles as Scene of the Crime," *Film Comment* (July–August 1996): 26.

29. For commentary on this strategy in another film about passing, see Lauren Berlant, "National Brands/National Body: *Imitation of Life*," in *Phantom Public Sphere*, ed. Bruce Robbins (Minneapolis: University of Minnesota Press, 1993), 173–208.

CHAPTER 7

1. Arjun Appadurai, "Disjuncture and Difference in the Global Cultural Economy," *Public Culture* 2, no. 2 (spring 1990): 2.

2. Intriguingly, Fredric Wertham's writings had been read by Joseph Losey, as background for the character of the child-murderer in the remake of *M* (1951).

3. For good discussions of *The Fugitive* and *Miami Vice*, see James Ursini, "Angst at Sixty Fields per Second," and Jeremy G. Butler, "*Miami Vice:* The Legacy of *Film Noir*," in Alain Silver and James Ursini, eds., *The Film Noir Reader* (New York: Limelight Editions, 1996).

4. Alain Silver and Elizabeth Ward, eds., *Film Noir: An Encyclopedic Reference to the American Style* (Woodstock: Overlook Press, 1992), 1.

5. Barbara Klinger, *Melodrama and Meaning: History, Culture, and the Films of Douglas Sirk* (Bloomington: Indiana University Press, 1994), 140.

6. This picture has in fact influenced the way contemporary audiences view the past. The current laser-disk edition of *Possessed* (1947) carries a blurb describing the film as a "*Fatal-Attraction* thriller."

7. R. Barton Palmer, *Hollywood's Dark Cinema: The American Film Noir* (New York: Twayne, 1994), 184.

8. Thomas Pynchon, *Vineland* (New York: Penguin, 1991), 326.

9. For an intelligent and more sympathetic account of the postmodern marketplace, see Timothy Corrigan, *A Cinema without Walls* (New Brunswick: Rutgers University Press, 1991). Corrigan offers a wide-ranging discussion of the ways in which contemporary movies affect spectatorship, genres, and auteurs.

10. In 1991, Stephen Soderbergh filmed *Kafka,* which is perhaps his most unalloyed art movie.

11. A more deconstructive use of similar materials in literature may be found in Robert Coover's short story "Gilda's Dream," in *Night at the Movies: Or, You Must Remember This* (Normal, Ill.: Dalkey Archive Press, 1997).

CHAPTER 8

1. On the other hand, it seems odd to describe Joseph von Sternberg as a naturalist and to treat *The Blue Angel* as a pure product of the German imagination. Sternberg, a flamboyant stylist of erotic and oneiric films, was of course an American, and *The Blue Angel,* which was shot in Germany with German actors, was chiefly produced by Paramount Pictures under the terms of the Parufamet agreement.

2. In 2001, Broadway staged a musical adaptation of *Therese Raquin,* entitled *Thou Shalt Not,* with book by David Thomson and music by Harry Connick Jr. The show was set in New Orleans during the years just after World War II, which is the period of both Tennessee Williams's *Streetcar Named Desire* and the glory days of U.S. film noir. It failed, but in 2005 it was revived for a short run at the Circle Theatre in Chicago. The *Chicago Tribune* described it in almost the same way one could describe the original Zola novel, as " 'Desperate Housewives' meets film noir" (June 3, 2005).

3. Thomas Elsaesser, "A German Ancestry to Film Noir? Film History and Its Imaginary," *Iris,* no. 21 (spring 1996): 129–43.

4. William Hannigan, *New York Noir: Crime Photos from the* Daily News *Archive,* introduction by Luc Sante (New York: Rizzoli, 1999).

5. For a discussion of Weegee and the movies, see Alain Bergala, "Weegee and Film Noir," in *Weegee's World,* ed. Miles Barth (Boston: Bulfinch Press, 1997), 69.

6. See Michel Foucault, *The Order of Things: An Archaeology of the Human Sciences* (New York: Vintage Books, 1970), xv. Hereafter, this work is cited parenthetically in the text.

7. Raymond Borde and Etienne Chaumeton, *A Panorama of American Film Noir, 1941–1953,* trans. Paul Hammond (San Francisco: City Lights Books, 2002), 161–63. Hereafter, all references are to this text, and page numbers are indicated parenthetically.

8. The Wikipedia list is available at http://en.wikipedia.org/wiki/Film_noir (accessed January 20, 2007).

9. For an interesting discussion of this film, see Ginette Vincendeau, " 'Avez-vous lu Freud?': Maurice Chevalier dans *Pièges* de Robert Siodmak," *Iris,* no. 21 (spring 1996): 89–98.

10. Adun Englelstad, *Losing Streak Stories: Mapping Norwegian Film Noir* (Oslo: Faculty of Humanities, University of Oslo, 2006).

11. Rick Altman, *Film/Genre* (London: British Film Institute, 1999); Steve Neale, *Genre and Hollywood* (London: Routledge, 2000).

12. Mark T. Conrad, ed., *The Philosophy of Film Noir* (Lexington: University Press of Kentucky, 2005); Alain Silver and James Ursini, eds., *Film Noir Reader 2* (New York: Limelight Editions, 2000); Alain Silver, James Ursini, and Robert Porfirio, *Film Noir Reader 3* (New York: Limelight Editions, 2004); Alain Silver and James Ursini, eds., *Film Noir Reader 4* (New York: Limelight Editions, 2004); Jans B. Wager, *Dames in the Driver's Seat: Rereading Film Noir* (Austin: University of Texas Press, 2005); Sheri Chinen Biesen, *Blackout: World War II and the Origins of Film Noir* (Baltimore: Johns Hopkins University Press, 2005); John T. Irwin, *Unless the Threat of Death Is Behind Them: Hard-Boiled Fiction and Film Noir* (Baltimore: Johns Hopkins University Press, 2006); Paula Rabinowitz, *Black and White and Noir: America's Pulp Modernism* (New York: Columbia University Press, 2002); Alexander Nemerov, *Icons of Grief: Val Lewton's Home Front Pictures* (Berkeley: University of California Press, 2006).

13. David Andrews, "Sex Is Dangerous, so Satisfy Your Wife: The Softcore Thriller in Its Contexts," *Cinema Journal* 45, no. 3 (2006): 59–89; see also Linda Williams, *The Erotic Thriller in Contemporary Cinema* (Edinburgh: Edinburgh University Press, 2005).

14. As I write this chapter, Vivian Sobchack's essay is due to be published soon in the *Journal of Visual Culture.*

15. Erik Dussere, "Out of the Past, Into the Supermarket: Consuming Film Noir," *Film Quarterly* 60, no. 1 (fall 2006): 16–27.

16. Edward Dimendberg, *Film Noir and the Spaces of Modernity* (Cambridge, Mass.: Harvard University Press, 2004).

17. John Boorman, quoted in Robert Carringer, "Hollywood's Los Angeles: Two Paradigms," in *Looking for Los Angeles: Architecture, Film, Photography, and the Urban Landscape,* ed. Charles G. Salas and Michael S. Roth (Los Angeles: Getty Research Institute Publications, 2001). Hereafter, this work is cited parenthetically in the text.

18. See James Naremore, "Love and Death in *A.I. Artificial Intelligence,*" *Michigan Quarterly Review* (spring 2005): 256–84. A slightly different version of this essay can also be found in the last chapter of my book *On Kubrick* (London: British Film Institute, 2007).

19. David Bordwell, *Figures Traced in Light: On Cinematic Staging* (Berkeley: University of California Press, 2005), 27.

20. Steven Soderbergh's *The Good German* (2006), which is set in 1946, is photographed in black and white and employs techniques associated with a studio like Warner Brothers in the 1940s. Soderbergh used wide-angle lenses, eschewed "coverage," and shot the film so that it gave little opportunity for alternative editing. See Dave Kehr, "You Can Make a Movie Just the Way They Used To," *New York Times,* "Arts and Entertainment" sec. (November 12, 2006), 1, 15.

21. Thom Andersen, "Collateral Damage," *Cinema Scope,* no. 20 (2004): www.cinema-scope.com/cs20/ar_andersen_collat.htm (accessed January 21, 2007).

22. Leslie Moonves, chairman of CBS, quoted in Lynn Hirschberg, "Giving Them What They Want," *New York Times Magazine,* September 4, 2005, 30.

23. Slavoj Žižek, "The Art of the Ridiculous Sublime: On David Lynch's *Lost Highway,*" Walter Chapin Simpson Center for the Humanities, Occasional Papers no. 1 (Seattle: University of Washington, 2000). Hereafter, references are to this edition, and page numbers are indicated in the text.

24. Warren Buckland, " 'A Sad, Bad Traffic Accident': The Televisual Prehistory of David Lynch's Film *Mulholland Dr.,*" *New Review of Film and Television Studies* 1, no. 1 (November 2003): 131–47.

25. Todd McGowan, "Lost on Mulholland Drive: Navigating David Lynch's Panegyric to Hollywood," *Cinema Journal* 43, no. 2 (2004): 68.

BIBLIOGRAPHY

Adorno, Theodor W., and Max Horkheimer. *Dialectic of Enlightenment*. 1944. New York: Seabury, 1972.

Agee, James. *Agee on Film*. Vol. 1. New York: McDowell, Obolensky, 1958.

Alton, John. *Painting with Light*. Berkeley: University of California Press, 1995.

Andersen, Thom. "Red Hollywood." In *Literature and the Visual Arts in Contemporary Society,* ed. Suzanne Ferguson and Barbara Groseclose, 141–96. Columbus: Ohio State University Press, 1985.

Andersen, Thom, and Noel Burch. *Les Communistes de Hollywood: Autre choses que les martyrs*. Paris: Presses universitaires de la Sorbonne Nouvelle, 1994.

Andrew, Dudley. *Mists of Regret*. Princeton: Princeton University Press, 1995.

———, ed. *Breathless*. New Brunswick: Rutgers University Press, 1987.

Anfam, David. *Franz Kline: Black and White, 1950–1961*. Houston: Houston Fine Art Press, 1994.

Appadurai, Arjun. "Disjuncture and Difference in the Global Cultural Economy." *Public Culture* 2, no. 2 (spring 1990): 1–24.

Arthur, Paul. "Los Angeles as Scene of the Crime." *Film Comment* (July–August 1996): 20–26.

Belton, John. "Film Noir's Knights of the Road." *Bright Lights Film Journal* 12 (spring 1994): 5–15.

Berlant, Lauren. "National Brands/National Body: *Imitation of Life*." In *Phantom Public Sphere,* ed. Bruce Robbins, 173–208. Minneapolis: University of Minnesota Press, 1993.

Bernstein, Matthew. "A Tale of Three Cities: The Banning of *Scarlet Street*." *Cinema Journal* 35, no. 1 (1995): 27–52.

Bernstein, Matthew, and Gaylyn Studlar, eds. *Visions of the East: Orientalism in Film*. New York: Columbia University Press, 1997.

Black, Gregory D. *Hollywood Censored: Morality Codes, Catholics, and the Movies*. New York: Cambridge University Press, 1996.

Bogdanovich, Peter. *Fritz Lang in America*. New York: Praeger, 1969.

Bogdanovich, Peter, and Jonathan Rosenbaum. *This Is Orson Welles*. New York: HarperCollins, 1993.

Bogle, Donald. *Toms, Coons, Mulattoes, Mammies, and Bucks: An Interpretive History of Blacks in American Films*. New York: Continuum, 1991.

Borde, Raymond, and Étienne Chaumeton. *Panorama du film noir américain, 1941–1953*. Paris: Éditions de Minuit, 1955.

Bordwell, David, Janet Staiger, and Kristin Thompson. *The Classical Hollywood Cinema*. New York: Columbia, 1985.

Bourgeois, Jacques. "La Tragédie policier." *Revue du cinéma* 2 (1946): 70–76.

Brackett, Leigh. "From *The Big Sleep* to *The Long Goodbye*, and More or Less How We Got There." *Take One* 1, no. 1 (1974): 26–28.

Brady, Frank. *Citizen Welles*. New York: Anchor Books, 1989.

Brantlinger, Patrick. "*Heart of Darkness*: Anti-Imperialism, Racism, or Impressionism?" In *Heart of Darkness*, ed. Ross C. Murfin, 277–98. New York: St. Martin's Press.

Brion, Patrick. *Le film noir*. Paris: Éditions de la martinière, 1992.

Brunette, Peter. "Two Wrights, One Wrong." In *The Modern American Novel and the Movies*, ed. Gerald Peary and Roger Shatzkin, 131–42. New York: Ungar, 1978.

Burch, Noel. *Theory of Film Practice*. New York: Praeger, 1973.

Burnett, Charles. "Inner City Blues." In *Questions of Third Cinema*, ed. Jim Pines and Paul Willemen, 223–26. London: BFI, 1989.

Buss, Robin. *French Film Noir*. London: Marion Boyars, 1994.

Cain, James M. *Double Indemnity*. New York: Vintage, 1978.

Cameron, Ian, ed. *The Book of Film Noir*. New York: Continuum, 1993.

Carter, Angela. *The Sadeian Woman*. New York: Pantheon, 1979.

Cawelti, John G. "*Chinatown* and Generic Transformation in Recent American Films." In *Film Theory and Criticism*, 2d ed., ed. Gerald Mast and Marshall Cohen, 559–79. New York: Oxford University Press, 1979.

Ceplair, Larry, and Stephen Englund. *The Inquisition in Hollywood: Politics in the Film Community, 1930–1960*. Garden City, N.Y.: Garden City Press, 1980.

Chandler, Raymond. *The Blue Dahlia: A Screenplay*, ed. Matthew J. Bruccoli. Carbondale: Southern Illinois University Press, 1976.

———. *Raymond Chandler: Later Novels and Other Writings*. New York: Library of America, 1995.

———. *Raymond Chandler: Stories and Early Novels*. New York: Library of America, 1995.

Chartier, Jean-Pierre. "Les Américains aussi font des films 'noirs.'" *Revue du cinéma* 2 (1946): 67–70.

Christopher, Nicholas. *Somewhere in the Night: Film Noir and the American City*. New York: Free Press, 1997.

Compagnon, Antoine. *Five Paradoxes of Modernity*. Trans. Franklin Phillip. New York: Columbia University Press, 1994.

Coover, Robert. *Night at the Movies: Or, You Must Remember This*. Normal, Ill.: Dalkey Archive Press, 1997.

Copjec, Joan, ed. *Shades of Noir*. London: Verso, 1993.

Corrigan, Timothy. *A Cinema without Walls*. New Brunswick: Rutgers University Press, 1991.

Cotten, Joseph. *Vanity Will Get You Somewhere*. San Francisco: Mercury House, 1987.

Creed, Barbara. "From Here to Modernity: Feminism and Postmodernism." In *A Postmodern Reader*, ed. Joseph Natoli and Linda Hutcheon, 398–418. Albany: State University of New York Press, 1993.

Cripps, Thomas. *Black Film as Genre*. Bloomington: Indiana University Press, 1979.

Davis, Mike. *City of Quartz: Excavating the Future in Los Angeles*. New York: Vintage Books, 1992.

Dawson, Jan. "Robert Altman Speaking." *Film Comment* (March–April 1974): 40–41.

DeBona, Guerric. "Into Africa: Orson Welles and *Heart of Darkness*." *Cinema Journal* 33, no. 3 (1994): 16–34.

Denning, Michael. *The Cultural Front*. London: Verso, 1997.

Diawara, Manthia, ed. *Black American Cinema*. New York: Routledge, 1993.

Dimendberg, Edward. "City of Fear: Defensive Dispersal and the End of Film Noir." *Any*, no. 18 (1997): 14–18.

———. *Film Noir and the Spaces of Modernity*. Forthcoming, Harvard University Press.

———. "Kiss the City Goodbye." *Lusitania* 7 (spring 1996): 56–66.

Doane, Mary Anne. "*Gilda*: Epistemology as Striptease." *Camera Obscura*, no. 11 (1983): 7–27.

Doherty, Thomas. *Projections of War: Hollywood, American Culture, and World War II*. New York: Columbia University Press, 1993.

Durgnat, Raymond. "Paint It Black: The Family Tree of Film Noir." *Film Comment* (6 November 1974): 6–7. (Longer version in *Cinema*, nos. 6–7 [1970]: 49–56; reprinted in *Film Noir Reader*, ed. Alain Silver and James Ursini, 37–51. New York: Limelight Editions, 1996.)

Eliot, T. S. *Selected Prose*. Harmondsworth: Penguin, 1953.

Elsaesser, Thomas. "A German Ancestry to Film Noir? Film History and Its Imaginary." *Iris* 21 (spring 1996): 129–43.

Farber, Manny. *Negative Space*. New York: Praeger, 1971.

Farber, Stephen, and Marc Green. *Hollywood on the Couch*. New York: William Morrow, 1993.

Feng, Peter. "Being Chinese American, Becoming Asian American: *Chan Is Missing*." *Cinema Journal* 35, no. 4 (summer 1996): 88–118.

Fiedler, Leslie. *Love and Death in the American Novel*. New York: Stein and Day, 1966.

Forbes, Jill. "The Série Noir." In *France and the Mass Media*, ed. Brian Rigby and Nicholas Hewett, 85–97. London: Macmillan, 1993.

Foucault, Michel. "What Is an Author?" In *Textual Strategies*, ed. Josué V. Harari, 141–60. Ithaca: Cornell University Press, 1979.

Fox, Terry Curtis. "City Knights." *Film Comment* 20, no. 5 (October 1984): 30–49. (Contains an appendix of supplementary material by Meredith Brody, Marcia Froelke Coburn, David Chute, Richard Gehr, and Jonathan Rosenbaum.)

Frank, Nino. "Un nouveau genre 'policier': L'aventure criminelle." *L'Écran français* 61 (28 August 1946): 14–16.

Friedberg, Anne. *Window Shopping: Cinema and the Post-Modern Condition.* Berkeley: University of California Press, 1993.

Fussell, Paul. *The Great War and Modern Memory.* New York: Oxford University Press, 1977.

Genette, Gérard. *Narrative Discourse: An Essay in Method.* Trans. Jane E. Lewin. Ithaca: Cornell University Press, 1980.

Gifford, Barry. *The Devil Thumbs a Ride, and Other Unforgettable Films.* New York: Grove Press, 1988.

Greene, Graham. *Brighton Rock.* New York: Viking Press, 1967.

———. *A Gun for Sale.* New York: Penguin, 1974.

———. "The Last Buchan." In *Collected Essays.* Harmondsworth: Penguin, 1970.

———. *The Ministry of Fear.* New York: Penguin, 1978.

———. *The Pleasure Dome: Collected Film Criticism, 1935–1940.* Ed. John Russell Taylor. New York: Oxford University Press, 1980.

Gross, Miriam, ed. *The World of Raymond Chandler.* New York: A and W Publishers, 1977.

Guilbaut, Serge. *How New York Stole the Idea of Modern Art.* Trans. Arthur Goldhammer. Chicago: University of Chicago Press, 1983.

Gunning, Tom. "An Aesthetic of Astonishment." In *Viewing Positions: Ways of Seeing Films,* ed. Linda Williams, 114–33. New Brunswick: Rutgers University Press, 1995.

Hammett, Dashiell. *The Big Knockover.* Ed. Lillian Hellman. New York: Vintage, 1972.

———. *The Continental Op.* Ed. Stephen Marcus. New York: Random House, 1974.

———. *The Glass Key.* New York: Vintage, 1972.

———. *The Maltese Falcon.* New York: Vintage, 1972.

———. *Red Harvest.* London: Pan Books, 1975.

———. *The Thin Man.* New York: Vintage, 1972.

Hammond, Paul, ed. *The Shadow and Its Shadow: Surrealist Writings on the Cinema.* London: BFI, 1978.

Hanson, Patricia King, and Alan Gevinson, eds. *American Film Institute Catalog: Feature Films, 1931–1940.* Berkeley: University of California Press, 1993.

Haskell, Molly. *Love and Other Infectious Diseases.* New York: Morrow, 1990.

Higham, Charles, and Joel Greenberg. *Hollywood in the Forties.* New York: A. S. Barnes, 1968.

Hilfer, Tony. *The Crime Novel: A Deviant Genre.* Austin: University of Texas Press, 1990.

Hillier, Jim, ed. *Cahiers du Cinema: The 1950s.* Cambridge, Mass.: Harvard University Press, 1985.

Hirsch, Foster. *The Dark Side of the Screen.* New York: A. S. Barnes, 1981.

Hoberman, J. "The Great Whatzit." *The Village Voice* (15 March 1994): 43.

Hoberman, J., and Jonathan Rosenbaum. *Midnight Movies*. New York: Harper and Row, 1983.

Hobsbawm, Eric. *The Age of Extremes: A History of the World, 1914–1991*. New York: Pantheon, 1994.

Hoopes, Roy. *Cain: The Biography of James M. Cain*. New York: Holt, Rinehart and Winston, 1982.

Houseman, John. *Front and Center*. New York: Simon and Schuster, 1979.

Hutcheon, Linda. *A Theory of Parody*. New York: Methuen, 1985.

Huyssen, Andreas. *After the Great Divide*. Bloomington: Indiana University Press, 1986.

Jacobs, Lea. "The B Film and the Problem of Cultural Distinction." *Screen* 33, no. 1 (spring 1992): 1–13.

Jacoby, Russell. *The Repression of Psychoanalysis*. New York: Basic Books, 1983.

Jameson, Fredric. "On Raymond Chandler." *The Southern Review* 6 (1970): 624–50.

———. *The Political Unconscious*. Ithaca: Cornell University Press, 1981.

———. "Postmodernism and Consumer Society." In *The Anti-Aesthetic*, ed. Hal Foster, 111–25. Port Townsend, Wash.: Bay Press, 1983.

———. *Postmodernism: Or, the Cultural Logic of Late Capitalism*. Durham: Duke University Press, 1991.

———. "Reification and Utopia in Mass Culture." *Social Text* 1 (1979): 130–49.

Jameson, Richard T. "Son of Noir." *Film Comment* 10 (1974): 30–33.

Jean, Marcel, ed. *The Autobiography of Surrealism*. New York: Viking Press, 1980.

Johnson, Diane. *Dashiell Hammett: A Life*. New York: Random House, 1983.

Jones, Jacquie. "The New Ghetto Aesthetic." *Wide Angle* 13, nos. 3–4 (July–October 1991): 32–43.

Judt, Tony. *Past Imperfect: French Intellectuals, 1944–1956*. Berkeley: University of California Press, 1992.

Kaes, Anton, Martin Jay, and Edward Dimendberg, eds. *The Weimar Republic Sourcebook*. Berkeley: University of California Press, 1994.

Kaplan, E. Ann, ed. *Women in Film Noir*. London: BFI, 1980.

Kapsis, Robert E. *Hitchcock: The Making of a Reputation*. Chicago: University of Chicago Press, 1992.

Kearns, Cimberli. "Making Crime Matter: The Violent Style of the 'Formative' B-Film." *USC Spectator* (1998), forthcoming.

Kelly, Keith, and Clay Steinman. "*Crossfire*: A Dialectical Attack." *Film Reader* 3 (1978): 106–27.

Kerr, Paul. "Out of What Past? Notes on the B Film Noir." In *The Hollywood Film Industry*, ed. Paul Kerr, 220–44. London: Routledge and Kegan Paul, 1986.

Kinden, Gorham A. "Hollywood's Conversion to Color: The Technological, Economic, and Aesthetic Factors." *Journal of the University Film Association* 31, no. 2 (spring 1979): 29–36.

Klinger, Barbara. *Melodrama and Meaning: History, Culture, and the Films of Douglas Sirk*. Bloomington: Indiana University Press, 1994.

Kracauer, Sigfried. "Hollywood's Terror Films: Do They Reflect an American State of Mind?" *Commentary* (August 1946): 132–36.

Krutnick, Frank. *In a Lonely Street: Film Noir, Genre, Masculinity.* London: Routledge, 1991.

———. "Something More Than Night: Tales of the Noir City." In *The Cinematic City*, ed. David B. Clarke, 83–109. New York: Routledge, 1997.

Lakoff, George. *Women, Fire, and Dangerous Things: What Categories Reveal about the Mind.* Chicago: University of Chicago Press, 1987.

Landy, Marcia, and Lucy Fischer. "*Dead Again* or A-Live Again: Postmodern or Postmortem?" *Cinema Journal* 33, no. 4 (summer 1994): 3–22.

Leff, Leonard, and Jerrold L. Simmons. *The Dame in the Kimono: Hollywood Censorship and the Production Code from the 1920s to the 1960s.* New York: Anchor Books, 1990.

Leja, Michael. *Reframing Abstract Expressionism.* New Haven: Yale University Press, 1994.

Lodge, David. "The Language of Modernist Fiction: Metaphor and Metonymy." In *Modernism: A Guide to European Literature, 1890–1930*, ed. Malcom Bradbury and James McFarlane, 481–96. Harmondsworth: Penguin, 1991.

Luhr, William. *Raymond Chandler and Film.* Tallahassee: Florida State University Press, 1991.

———, ed. *The Maltese Falcon.* New Brunswick: Rutgers University Press, 1995.

MacShane, Frank. *The Life of Raymond Chandler.* New York: E. P. Dutton, 1976.

———, ed. *Selected Letters of Raymond Chandler.* New York: Columbia University Press, 1981.

Magny, Claude-Edmonde. *The Age of the American Novel: The Film Aesthetic of Fiction between the Two Wars.* Trans. Eleanor Hochman. New York: Ungar, 1972.

Marchetti, Gina. *Romance and the "Yellow Peril": Race, Sex, and Discursive Strategies in Hollywood Fiction.* Berkeley: University of California Press, 1993.

Marcus, Stephen. Introduction to *The Continental Op*, by Dashiell Hammett, ix–xxix. New York: Random House, 1974.

McArthur, Colin. *The Big Heat.* London: British Film Institute, 1992.

McCarthy, Todd, and Charles Flynn, eds. *Kings of the Bs: Working within the Hollywood System.* New York: E. P. Dutton, 1975.

McDonough, Thomas F. "Situationist Space." *October* (winter 1994): 59–77.

McFarlane, Brian. *Novel into Film.* London: Oxford University Press, 1996.

McGilligan, Patrick. "'I'll Always Be an American': Jules Dassin Interviewed." *Film Comment* (November–December 1996): 34–48.

Mencken, H. L. *Prejudices: A Selection.* Ed. James T. Farrell. New York: Vintage, 1958.

Metz, Christian. *The Imaginary Signifier.* Trans. Celia Britton, Annwyl Williams, Ben Brewster, and Alfred Guzzetti. Bloomington: Indiana University Press, 1982.

Milne, Tom. *Mamoulian.* Bloomington: Indiana University Press, 1970.

Modleski, Tania. *Feminism without Women.* New York: Routledge, 1991.

Morgan, Janice, and Dudley Andrew, eds. *Iris: A Journal of Theory on Image and Sound* 21 (spring 1996). Special issue on "European Precursors of Film Noir."

Naremore, James. "Authorship and the Cultural Politics of Film Criticism." *Film Quarterly* 44, no. 1 (fall 1990): 14–23.

———. "Dashiell Hammett and the Poetics of Hard-Boiled Detection." In *Essays on Detective Fiction,* ed. Bernard Benstock, 49–72. London: Macmillan, 1983.

———. "John Huston and *The Maltese Falcon.*" In *Reflections in a Male Eye,* ed. Gaylyn Studlar and David Desser, 119–35. Washington, D.C.: Smithsonian Institution Press, 1991. Also in *The Maltese Falcon,* ed. William Luhr. New Brunswick: Rutgers University Press, 1995.

———. *The Magic World of Orson Welles.* Rev. ed. Dallas: Southern Methodist University Press, 1988.

———. "The Trial: Orson Welles vs. the FBI." *Film Comment* (January–February 1991): 22–27.

Neale, Steve. *Cinema and Technology: Image, Sound, Color.* Bloomington: Indiana University Press, 1985.

Nehring, Niel. "Revolt into Style: Graham Greene Meets the Sex Pistols." *PMLA* 106, no. 2 (March 1991): 222–37.

Neve, Brian. *Film and Politics in America: A Social Tradition.* London: Routledge, 1992.

O'Brien, Charles. "Film Noir in France: Before the Liberation." *Iris* 21 (spring 1996): 7–20.

O'Brien, Geoffrey. *Hard-Boiled America.* New York: Van Nostrand Reinhold, 1981.

———. "The Return of Film Noir!" *New York Review of Books* (15 August 1991): 45–48.

Orwell, George. "Raffles and Miss Blandish." In *A Collection of Essays by George Orwell,* 139–54. New York: Doubleday Anchor, 1954.

Palmer, R. Barton. *Hollywood's Dark Cinema: The American Film Noir.* New York: Twayne, 1994.

———, ed. *Perspectives on Film Noir.* New York: G. K. Hall, 1996.

Peary, Gerald. "Portrait de en cinéaste l'artiste de série 'B': Entretien avec Joseph H. Lewis." *Positif* (July–August 1975): 42–52.

Pierre, José, ed. *Investigating Sex: Surrealist Discussions, 1928–1932.* Trans. Malcom Imrie. London: Verso, 1992.

Place, Janey, and Lowell Peterson. "Some Visual Motifs of *Film Noir.*" In *Film Noir Reader,* ed. Alain Silver and James Ursini, 65–76. New York: Limelight Editions, 1996.

Polan, Dana. *In a Lonely Place.* London: BFI, 1994.

———. *Power and Paranoia: History, Narrative, and the American Cinema, 1940–1950.* New York: Columbia University Press, 1986.

Pynchon, Thomas. *Vineland.* New York: Penguin, 1991.

Raths, Louis E., and Frank N. Trager. "Public Opinion and *Crossfire.*" *Journal of Educational Sociology* (February 1948): 345–69.

Ray, Robert B. *The Avant-Garde Finds Andy Hardy.* Cambridge, Mass.: Harvard University Press, 1995.

———. *A Certain Tendency of the Hollywood Cinema: 1930–1980*. Princeton: Princeton University Press, 1985.

Raynal, Patrick. "Écran blanc pour la série noire." *Cahiers du cinéma*, no. 490 (April 1995): 77–81.

Reid, Mark. *Redefining Black Film*. Berkeley: University of California Press, 1993.

Rogin, Michael. "Kiss Me Deadly: Communism, Motherhood, and Cold War Movies." *Representations* 6 (spring 1984): 1–36.

Romero, Rolando J. "The Postmodern Hybrid: Do Aliens Dream of Alien Sheep?" *Post Script* 16, no. 1 (fall 1996): 41–52.

Rosenbaum, Jonathan. "Allusion Profusion." *Chicago Reader* (21 October 1994): 12, 25–26.

———. *Movies as Politics*. Berkeley: University of California Press, 1997.

———. *Placing Movies*. Berkeley: University of California Press, 1995.

Rosenblatt, Roger. *Black Fiction*. Cambridge, Mass.: Harvard University Press, 1974.

Ross, Kristin. *Fast Cars, Decolonization, and the Reordering of French Society*. Cambridge, Mass.: MIT Press, 1995.

Salt, Barry. *Film Style and Technology: History and Analysis*. London: Starword, 1983.

Sarris, Andrew. *The American Cinema*. New York: E. P. Dutton, 1968.

Sartre, Jean-Paul. *The Philosophy of Jean-Paul Sartre*. Ed. Robert Denoon Cummings. New York: The Modern Library, 1966.

———*What Is Literature?* Trans. Bernard Frechtman. New York: Washington Square Press, 1966.

Sawyer-Lauçanno, Christopher. *The Continental Pilgrimage: American Writers in Paris, 1944–1960*. New York: Grove Press, 1992.

Schaefer, Dennis, and Larry Salvato. *Masters of Light: Conversations with Contemporary Cinematographers*. Berkeley: University of California Press, 1984.

Schickel, Richard. *Double Indemnity*. London: BFI, 1992.

Schrader, Paul. "Notes on *Film Noir*." In *Film Noir Reader*, ed. Alain Silver and James Ursini, 53–64. New York: Limelight Editions, 1996.

Schwartz, Nancy Lynn. *The Hollywood Writer's Wars*. New York: Alfred A. Knopf, 1982.

Seguin, Louis. "Kiss Me Mike." *Bizarre*, no. 2 (October 1955): 68–71.

Selby, Spencer. *Dark City: The Film Noir*. Jefferson, N.C.: McFarland, 1984.

Selznick, David O. *Memo from David O. Selznick*. Ed. Rudy Behlmer. New York: Viking Press, 1972.

Server, Lee. *Danger Is My Business: An Illustrated History of the Fabulous Pulp Magazines*. San Francisco: Chronicle Books, 1993.

———. *Over My Dead Body: The Sensational Age of the American Paperback, 1945–1955*. San Francisco: Chronicle Books, 1994.

Seymour-Smith, Martin. *Who's Who in Twentieth-Century Literature*. New York: McGraw-Hill, 1976.

Shapiro, Owen, and Chen-Tsung Yau. "Film-Making and Ethnic Boundaries: A Conversation with Wayne Wang." *Point of Contact* (winter/spring 1997): 71–87.

Shelden, Michael. *Graham Greene: The Man Within.* London: William Heine-
mann Ltd., 1994.
Sherry, Norman. *The Life of Graham Greene.* Vol. 1. New York: Viking, 1989.
————. *The Life of Graham Greene.* Vol. 2. New York: Viking, 1994.
Siegel, Joel E. *Val Lewton: The Reality of Terror.* New York: Viking, 1973.
Silver, Alain, and James Ursini, eds. *Film Noir Reader.* New York: Limelight Edi-
tions, 1996.
Silver, Alain, and Elizabeth Ward, eds. *Film Noir: An Encyclopedic Reference to
the American Style.* Rev. ed. Woodstock: Overlook Press, 1992.
Sklar, Robert. *City Boys: Cagney, Bogart, Garfield.* Princeton: Princeton Uni-
versity Press, 1992.
Sontag, Susan. *Against Interpretation.* New York: Dell, 1966.
Stam, Robert. "Orson Welles, Brazil, and the Power of Blackness." *Persistence
of Vision,* no. 7 (1989): 93–112.
Steinberg, Cobbett. *Reel Facts: The Movie Book of Records.* New York: Vintage
Books, 1978.
Stern, Lesley. *The Scorsese Connection.* London: BFI, 1995.
Stringer, Julian. "'Your tender smile gives me strength': Paradigms of Masculin-
ity in John Woo's *A Better Tomorrow* and *The Killer.*" *Screen* 38, no. 1 (spring
1997): 25–41.
Studlar, Gaylyn. *In the Realm of Pleasure: Von Sternberg, Dietrich, and the
Masochistic Aesthetic.* Urbana: University of Illinois Press, 1988.
Studlar, Gaylyn, and David Desser. *Reflections in a Male Eye.* Washington, D.C.:
Smithsonian Institution Press, 1993.
Suarez, Juan, and Millicent Manglis. "Cinema, Gender, and the Topography of
Enigmas: A Conversation with Laura Mulvey." *Cinefocus* 3 (1994): 2–10.
Telotte, J. P. *Voices in the Dark: The Narrative Patterns of Film Noir.* Urbana:
University of Illinois Press, 1989.
Thompson, Jon. *Fiction, Crime, and Empire.* Urbana: University of Illinois Press,
1993.
Truffaut, François. *Hitchcock/Truffaut.* New York: Simon and Schuster, 1967.
Turk, Edward Byron. *Child of Paradise: Marcel Carné and the Golden Age of
French Cinema.* Cambridge, Mass.: Harvard University Press, 1989.
Tuska, Jon. *Dark Cinema: American Film Noir in Cultural Perspective.* West-
port: Greenwood Press, 1984.
Vernet, Marc. "*Film Noir* on the Edge of Doom." In *Shades of Noir,* ed. Joan
Copjec, 1–31. London: Verso, 1993.
Vincendeau, Ginette. "France 1945–1965 and Hollywood: The Policier as Inter-
national Text." *Screen* 33, no. 1 (spring 1992): 50–80.
Wiegman, Robyn. "Black Bodies/American Commodities: Gender, Race, and the
Bourgeois Ideal in Contemporary Film." In *Unspeakable Images: Ethnicity
and the American Cinema,* ed. Lester D. Friedman, 308–28. Urbana: Uni-
versity of Illinois Press, 1991.
Williams, Alan. *Republic of Images: A History of French Filmmaking.* Cambridge,
Mass.: Harvard University Press, 1992.
Williams, Linda. *Hard Core: Power, Pleasure, and "The Frenzy of the Visible."*
Berkeley: University of California Press, 1989.

Wilson, Edmund. "The Boys in the Back Room." In *Classics and Commercials*. New York: Farrar, Straus, 1950.

Wodek, ed. *Black in Sculptural Art*. Brussels: Atelier 340, 1993.

Wollen, Peter. "MTV, and Postmodernism, Too." In *Futures for English*, ed. Colin MacCabe, 214–20. New York: St. Martin's Press, 1989.

Wood, Robin. *Hollywood from Vietnam to Reagan*. New York: Columbia University Press, 1985.

Woods, Paul A. *King Pulp: The Wild World of Quentin Tarantino*. New York: Thunder's Mouth Press, 1996.

Zolotow, Maurice. *Billy Wilder in Hollywood*. New York: Limelight Editions, 1987.

SUPPLEMENTAL BIBLIOGRAPHY FOR THE 2008 EDITION

Altman, Rick. *Film/Genre*. London: British Film Institute, 1999.

Andersen, Thom. "Collateral Damage." *Cinema Scope*, no. 20 (2004): www.cinema-scope.com/cs20/ar_andersen_collat.htm.

Andrews, David. "Sex Is Dangerous, so Satisfy Your Wife: The Softcore Thriller in Its Contexts." *Cinema Journal* 45, no. 3 (2006): 59–89.

Bergala, Alain. "Weegee and Film Noir." In *Weegee's World*, ed. Miles Barth, 69–77. Boston: Bulfinch Press, 1997.

Biesen, Sheri Chinen. *Blackout: World War II and the Origins of Film Noir*. Baltimore: Johns Hopkins University Press, 2005.

Borde, Raymond, and Etienne Chaumeton. *A Panorama of American Film Noir, 1941–1953*. Trans. Paul Hammond. San Francisco: City Lights Books, 2002.

Bordwell, David. *Figures Traced in Light: On Cinematic Staging*. Berkeley: University of California Press, 2005.

Buckland, Warren. " 'A Sad, Bad Traffic Accident': The Televisual Prehistory of David Lynch's Film *Mulholland Dr.*" *New Review of Film and Television Studies* 1, no. 1 (November 2003): 131–47.

Carringer, Robert. "Hollywood's Los Angeles: Two Paradigms." In *Looking for Los Angeles: Architecture, Film, Photography, and the Urban Landscape*, ed. Charles G. Salas and Michael S. Roth, 250–68. Los Angeles: Getty Research Institute Publications, 2001.

Conrad, Mark T., ed. *The Philosophy of Film Noir*. Lexington: University Press of Kentucky, 2006.

Dimendberg, Edward. *Film Noir and the Spaces of Modernity*. Cambridge, Mass.: Harvard University Press, 2004.

Dussere, Erik. "Out of the Past, Into the Supermarket: Consuming Film Noir." *Film Quarterly* 60, no. 1 (fall 2006): 16–27.

Elsaesser, Thomas. "A German Ancestry to Film Noir? Film History and Its Imaginary." *Iris*, no. 20 (spring 1996): 129–43.

Englelstad, Adun. *Losing Streak Stories: Mapping Norwegian Film Noir*. Oslo: Faculty of Humanities, University of Oslo, 2006.

Foucault, Michel. *The Order of Things: An Archaeology of the Human Sciences.* New York: Vintage Books, 1970.

Hannigan, William, ed. *New York Noir: Crime Photos from the* Daily News *Archive.* New York: Rizzoli, 1999.

Hirsch, Joshua. "Film Gris Reconsidered." *The Journal of Popular Film and Television* 34.2 (2006): 82-93.

Hirschberg, Lynn. "Giving Them What They Want." *New York Times Magazine,* September 4, 2005.

Irwin, John T. *Unless the Threat of Death Is Behind Them: Hard-Boiled Fiction and Film Noir.* Baltimore: Johns Hopkins University Press, 2006.

McGowan, Todd. "Lost on Mulholland Drive: Navigating David Lynch's Panegyric to Hollywood." *Cinema Journal* 43, no. 2 (2004): 67-89.

Naremore, James. "Love and Death in *A.I. Artificial Intelligence.*" *Michigan Quarterly Review* (spring 2005): 256-84.

———. *On Kubrick.* London: British Film Institute, 2007.

Neale, Steve. *Genre and Hollywood.* London: Routledge, 2000.

Nemerov, Alexander. *Icons of Grief: Val Lewton's Home Front Pictures.* Berkeley: University of California Press, 2006.

Nieland, Justus J. "Race-ing *Noir* and Re-Placing History: The Mulatta and Memory in *One False Move* and *Devil in a Blue Dress.*" *The Velvet Light Trap* 43 (spring 1999): 61-77.

Rabinowitz, Paula *Black and White and Noir: America's Pulp Modernism.* New York: Columbia University Press, 2002.

Silver, Alain, and James Ursini, eds. *Film Noir Reader 2.* New York: Limelight Editions, 2000.

———. *Film Noir Reader 4.* New York: Limelight Editions, 2004.

Silver, Alain, James Ursini, and Robert Porfirio, eds. *Film Noir Reader 3.* New York: Limelight Editions, 2004.

Sobchack, Vivian. "Chasing the Maltese Falcon: On the Fabrications of a Film Prop." *Journal of Visual Culture* (scheduled for publication in 2007).

Vincendeau, Ginette. " 'Avez-vous lu Freud?': Maurice Chevalier dans *Pièges* de Robert Siodmak." *Iris,* no. 20 (spring 1996): 89-98.

Wager, Jans B. *Dames in the Driver's Seat: Rereading Film Noir.* Austin: University of Texas Press, 2005.

Williams, Linda. *The Erotic Thriller in Contemporary Cinema.* Edinburgh: Edinburgh University Press, 2005.

Žižek, Slavoj. "The Art of the Ridiculous Sublime: On David Lynch's *Lost Highway.*" Walter Chapin Simpson Center for the Humanities, Occasional Papers no. 1. Seattle: University of Washington, 2000.

GENERAL INDEX

Film and Broadcast Index